Uyghur Nation

Uyghur Nation

*Reform and Revolution
on the Russia-China Frontier*

David Brophy

Harvard University Press

Cambridge, Massachusetts

London, England

2016

Library of Congress Cataloging-in-Publication Data

Brophy, David John, author.

   Uyghur nation : reform and revolution on the Russia-China frontier / David Brophy.
      pages cm

   Includes bibliographical references and index.

   ISBN 978-0-674-66037-3 (alk. paper)

   1. Uighur (Turkic people)—History.   2. Uighur (Turkic people)—Ethnic identity.
3. Uighur (Turkic people)—Politics and government.   4. Xinjiang Uygur Zizhiqu
(China)—Ethnic relations—History.   5. China—Boundaries—Russia (Federation)
6. Russia (Federation)—Boundaries—China.   I. Title.

DS731.U4B76 2016

951'.5—dc23   2015033377

To my parents

Contents

Maps and Illustrations

Maps

Illustrations

Note on Transliteration

In this book, which moves frequently between China and Russia and spans the 1917 divide, there is considerable variation in the way names and places are spelt in my sources. Where possible, I have sought to adopt the most commonly recognized spelling of toponyms (e.g., Kashgar, Moscow). One slight exception to this is my preference for "Turkistan" in place of "Turkestan" (except when transcribing from Russian). Otherwise, Chinese and Russian names and places are transcribed according to the standard pinyin and Library of Congress systems respectively, though I have removed Russian soft signs in the body of the text. Lest the juxtaposition of Chinese and Russian terminology lead to confusion, I have translated administrative terms into English as far as possible (e.g., "circuit" instead of Chinese *dao*, "province" for Russian *oblast'*, etc.). In dealing with Muslim names I have opted for a simplified, diacritic-free transcription based on Arabic-script spellings (e.g., Rozibaqiev, not Rozybakiev). For technical terms and citations I have based my approach on the principles outlined in the *International Journal of Middle East Studies*, while seeking to give some expression to the idiosyncrasies of a period in which Arabic-script orthography was in constant flux. Depending on the place of publication, I have vocalized the titles of Turkic works according to either Tatar/Chaghatay (for Turkistani/Uzbek publications) or Uyghur transcriptions (for "Soviet" Uyghur and pre-1949 publications in Xinjiang). In transcribing Uyghur, I prefer the a/ä/e system to the a/e/é of the new Uyghur Internet orthography.

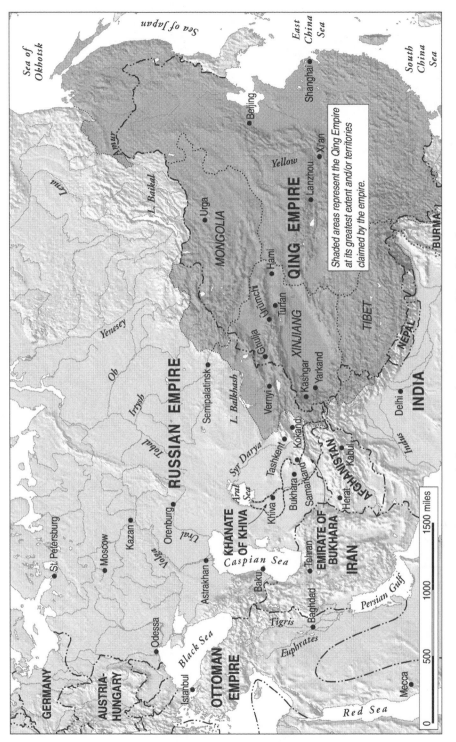

Eurasia in the late nineteenth century. © 2016 David Brophy.

Shaded areas represent the Qing Empire at its greatest extent and/or territories claimed by the empire.

Introduction

This book is a study of the modern history of the Turkic-speaking Muslims of Xinjiang, the Uyghurs. It is a history of creative responses from below to imperial, national, and revolutionary state policies, told from the point of view of people whose life stories not only span the boundary between China and Russia but intersect with the history of the Ottoman Empire as well. At the meeting point of these empires a political space emerged that was structured by the interplay of imperial and spiritual loyalties, institutions of autonomy and extraterritoriality, and negotiations between rulers and ruled. My book details the place of Xinjiang in the wider history of imperial and Islamic reform in the early twentieth century and tells the story of efforts to mobilize a diverse diaspora of Xinjiang Muslims in the wake of the Russian Revolution to intervene in the revolutionary process. In doing so I trace the emergence of a new rhetoric of Uyghur nationhood in the Soviet 1920s and follow its transmission back to Xinjiang.

The idea of a Uyghur nation connects today's Uyghurs to a Uyghur people who featured prominently in the pre-Islamic history of Central Asia, before fading from the historical record in the sixteenth and seventeenth centuries. Talk of a Uyghur nation was an innovation in the early 1920s, and its meaning was often questioned, but by the mid-1930s the Uyghurs had been accorded official recognition as a nation in both the Soviet Union and the Chinese province of Xinjiang. While it is customary to view the creation of the Uyghur nation from within the study of Soviet nationalities policy, it deserves to be situated in a wider frame of reference, as one of a number of radical national reinventions that occurred around the world in the first half of the twentieth century. From this point of view, it was a highly successful undertaking. Yet when judged in terms of the aspirations that drove this reinvention—that by

1

becoming national the Muslims of Xinjiang would resolve the political and social difficulties that they faced in China—the results have been mixed at best. For all the issues confronting the republics of Central Asia, independent nations such as the Uzbeks and Kazakhs at least have something to show for the experience of early Soviet nation building. The outcome of the Uyghur national project has been much more ambiguous.

Thanks in large part to the ongoing conflict in Xinjiang, the Uyghurs today are much better known than when I first commenced research for this book. Numbering some ten million, they comprise one of the largest of China's *minzu*—a term once rendered as "nationality" but more frequently glossed as "ethnic group" in China today. Their historical claims to Xinjiang have been given limited recognition in the form of the Xinjiang Uyghur Autonomous Region. Less well known is the fact that a substantial community of Uyghurs resides across the border to China's west, in what was the Russian Empire, became the Soviet Union, and now consists of the independent republics of Kazakhstan, Kirghizstan, and Uzbekistan. Numbering around a hundred thousand at the time of the Russian Revolution, in terms of size this émigré community has always been insignificant in comparison to the Uyghurs of Xinjiang. Within Central Asia, too, they have rarely registered in the region's history and remain a marginal community today. In acting as a bridge between Xinjiang and the Islamic and Soviet worlds, though, they are of immense importance for the story to be told in this book.

Residing along the fault line dividing Central Asia into two halves (referred to in this book as Chinese and Russian Turkistan), the history of the Uyghurs has been similarly divided in two. Among the small community of scholars of Xinjiang it is common to refer to distinct groups of "Soviet Uyghurs" and "Xinjiang Uyghurs." This division reflects the pressure that Uyghurs have faced to inscribe their own history within the political boundaries that others have drawn around them.[1] There have been points in the twentieth century when political conditions permitted the "Soviet Uyghurs" to express solidarity with their ethnic brethren in Xinjiang, but this was always secondary to celebrating the "flowering of Uyghur culture" in the more favorable conditions of the Soviet Union.[2] Similarly in the People's Republic of China, each *minzu* is thought of as a self-contained member of a Chinese family of nations, with little avenue for exploration of international ties.[3]

In confronting this situation, my book seeks to weave a story spanning both sides of this frontier into a single narrative. This is not simply of value to Uyghur history, I believe, but to Central Asian history more generally. Few studies in any discipline devote equal space to either side of the Russia-China divide, as this book does. Historians of Central Asia, particularly in the West, tend to approach the region as either a Russian or a Chinese frontier and only occasionally peer across the fence into the neighboring backyard. Despite the current emphasis on transnational and comparative history, the task of integrating the history of the two Turkistans is rarely attempted. To the extent that these two neighboring regions are connected in scholarship, it is primarily in the history of Sino-Russian trade, and Russian/Soviet foreign policy toward Xinjiang. My book intersects with this body of work in a number of ways, but does so from a local perspective, connecting the impersonal historiography of economic ties and interstate relations with the social dynamics and political aspirations among the majority Turkic-speaking population.

My aim here is not simply to add the history of the "Soviet Uyghurs" to that of the "Xinjiang Uyghurs," but by combining the two to reveal what these categories conceal. Most important in this respect is to bring to light the history of those who move between these two groups, people who were active in the Soviet Union while remaining Chinese citizens with connections to Xinjiang. In the early-twentieth-century history of Xinjiang, there is hardly a prominent individual whose life story does not intersect with the Soviet Union in some way, but such ties remain the stuff of legend, not scholarship. On the Soviet side, the history of the construction of the Uyghur nation within the Soviet Union also leaves little room for these natives of Xinjiang, focusing almost exclusively on those who were born on Russian or Soviet soil and on the emergence of the Uyghurs as a Soviet nation conforming to the template set by Stalin's theory of the nation. By recovering the story of the sojourning Chinese citizens, my book seeks to complicate this familiar narrative of a nation-in-formation.

For many scholars, the primary frame of reference for Soviet nations is the state, with its classificatory schemes and nationalities policy. I argue in this book that an account of the emergence of the Uyghur nation must begin elsewhere. I describe it as the convergence of two distinct stories, a convergence that was by no means inevitable, and in some respects highly unlikely. One of these stories is that of the rediscovery of the Turkic past among intellectuals connected to the Russian Muslim and Ottoman world of letters. This was the work of self-styled modernizers, who identified with the prerevolutionary cause of educational reform and the "Jadidist" tradition. The second is the history of efforts to capitalize on the breach created by the Russian Revolution to effect political change in Xinjiang. The historical legacy of the Uyghurs, I will show, served as a rallying point for this intervention, and its political significance often outweighed the ethnic or national connotations that the term held. This was a complicated process, much of which occurred beyond the bounds of Soviet policy making, and many misconceptions still remain as to the motivations for, and import of, early invocations of Uyghur nationhood.

Some of the activism described in this book fits within a classic definition of nationalism, proposing the existence of a Uyghur nation with rights to a Uyghur state in Xinjiang. Much of it, though, does not. As a historical symbol, the Uyghur legacy fit within a variety of evolving communal narratives in the early twentieth century, which were at times complementary and at times competing. The romantic rediscovery of Uyghur civilization gave rise to a bifurcated discourse between narratives that identified the Uyghurs with a golden age that was the common inheritance of the world's Turkic-speaking peoples and those that accorded certain peoples and places privileged claims to the Uyghur past. As an element of communal genealogy, "Uyghur" had both pan-Turkic and ethnonational applications, and the two remained in dialogue throughout the early twentieth century. Instead of squeezing these diverse appropriations of the Uyghur past into a narrow notion of Uyghur nationalism, I refer in this book to forms of "Uyghurist" politics. Even with the consolidation of authorized versions of Uyghur identity in Soviet and Chinese administrative regimes, the dialectic of pan-Turkic and particularist narratives can be seen in efforts to flesh out a national history for the Uyghurs.

Given its multivalence, it is not surprising that the Uyghur symbol was popularized as a political rallying point before it was widely thought of as a form of national identity. For such a radical revision of communal identity to be carried out successfully, I suggest, a political enterprise was essential. While existing accounts of the Uyghurs make reference to the rapid emergence of discourse on a Uyghur nation in the Soviet 1920s, few acknowledge the fact that redefining the community is a radical, indeed revolutionary, act, as likely to divide its putative members as to unite them. A common sense of belonging to a community of Xinjiang Muslims was not sufficient to persuade someone to identify as Uyghur in the 1920s. Nor did the Soviet Union have the intention, or the ability, to simply impose national identities on its population. The Soviet political and ethnographic mission was to identify and rationalize national classifications, not to invent them from whole cloth. In the case of the other nations of Central Asia—for example the Kazakhs—there was precedent for identifying people in these terms, even if these categories were contested or were not necessarily a primary focus of communal identification. Sponsoring the revival of long-lost ethnonyms such as "Uyghur" was never an objective of Soviet policy.

A landmark-naming event in the history of the Qing dynasty offers a point of comparison. When the khan Hong Taiji decreed in 1635 that henceforth his people were to be known as "Manchus," the unfamiliar ethnonym served as a rallying point for the Manchu invasion of China. Qing historians continue to debate the extent to which this redefinition had, or eventually took on, ethnic and national significance in the course of the Qing dynasty.[4] All would agree, though, that without the "great enterprise" of the Qing conquest, Hong Taiji's proclamation of a new Manchu identity would have been meaningless. My approach to the Uyghurs is similar. The Russian Revolution created a space in which stable social categories fractured and were redefined. As Peter Holquist's study of the Don Cossacks has shown, the revolution and civil war was a period in which the line between estate divisions, political organizations, and nationality became blurred, and "political allegiance could determine 'social' identity."[5] It was in this space, well before the crystallization of official Soviet nationalities policy in the mid-1920s, that activists cultivated the new Uyghurist view of the Muslims of Chinese Turkistan.[6]

Here I should distinguish my approach from the historical study of what we now refer to as Uyghur identity, or Uyghur ethnicity. Much scholarly work on the Uyghurs invokes these categories, inquiring into historical trends that gave rise to expressions of identity and difference among the Tarim Basin Muslims, how Uyghur identity has been constructed and maintained socially, or the ability of Uyghur identity to inspire resistance to Chinese policies.[7] It may be the case that protonational forms of ethnic identification that conform to the contours of today's Uyghur nation can be found in the historical record in Xinjiang. Certainly, communal narratives that predate the twentieth century play a part in the construction of Uyghur national identity today.[8] My research has led me to conclude, however, that the emerging Uyghurist discourse was not initially grounded in these symbols of ethnic identity. The constituency imagined by this genealogical thinking was defined by religion and subjecthood, as the Muslims of China. As such, its earliest formulations included people who were not part of the protonational "we" of Chinese Turkistan, most significantly the Chinese-speaking Muslims, known as Hui or Dungan. The association of the Uyghur category with ethnic symbols—its ethnicization—was a secondary step, and is difficult to trace with any accuracy in the sources we have at hand. My book therefore maintains a focus on the political applications that various actors have found for this category, and the way it has been substantiated through networks, organizations, and state institutions on either side of the Russia-China boundary.

Intersecting Empires and the Xinjiang Treaty Ports

As in any national history, there is an intellectual story to be told about why the connotations of the Uyghur national symbol held the emotive attractions that it did. Chapter 1 provides that background by tracing the history of the original Uyghurs and the meaning imparted to that history by scholars, administrators, and eventually reformers of a variety of backgrounds in the early twentieth century. From that point on my interest will be in the way that politics was constituted along the Xinjiang-Russia border, the shape of the diaspora communities that developed along it, and the experience of various sections of the Xinjiang Muslim community in Russian Turkistan during the revolution and its aftermath. Through periods of modernizing reform and revolution these structures and practices evolved, but nevertheless they constitute a core around which a history such as this can be told.

It seemed to many in the nineteenth century that Qing dominion in Xinjiang would not last long. In the 1820s, the Russian Orthodox monk and sinologist Nikolai Bichurin mischievously insisted that "Chinese Turkistan" was a misnomer for the region, "since East Turkistan cannot remain forever under the rule of China."[9] As imperial competition in Asia intensified, the Qing Empire was stretched to breaking point by internal rebellions. No sooner had the court pacified the Taiping Heavenly Kingdom (1854–1864) than the great Muslim uprising of the northwest broke out. In the 1860s, as the violence spread to Xinjiang, the province was partitioned by a string of rebel regimes. The emirate of Yaqub Beg (d. 1877) in Kashgar was the longest lasting and ultimately looked to the Ottoman Empire for confirmation and support. To its north an independent sultan was installed in the Ili Valley, but he was soon to be dethroned and exiled by the Russians, who occupied Ili from 1871 to 1882. Meanwhile in Ürümchi, today the capital of the Xinjiang Uyghur Autonomous Region, a Chinese-speaking Muslim (Hui) king emerged, linked by his Sufi affiliations to the Muslims of Gansu. In this three-way division of the province we see a set of alternatives to Beijing-centered rule in Xinjiang, which in many ways defined the limits of possibility for the years to follow: Xinjiang as a Kashgar-centered, Istanbul-aligned Islamic state; as the next stage in Russia's colonial advance across the steppe; or as a sanctuary for Chinese-speaking Muslim rebels fighting for autonomy in regions further east.

The outcome in the 1870s was none of these, as Zuo Zongtang's Hunanese army succeeded in reconquering Xinjiang for the Qing: Chinese Turkistan, for the time being, remained Chinese. The revolt and the Russian occupation left a significant mark, though, as the evacuating Russians took with them the majority of the Ili Valley's Muslim population. This migration laid the foundation for the most compact population of Xinjiang Muslims in Russian territory—the Taranchis and Dungans of Semireche province. The second consequence of Russian withdrawal from occupied Ili was the Treaty of Saint Petersburg of 1881, which created the preconditions for a new influx of Russian commerce into China's northwest and extended the tsar's protection across the already significant mercantile networks of Central Asian Muslims in Xinjiang.

While previous Qing administrations had felt little need to delimit a clear boundary to Xinjiang's west, preferring to view it as a zone of remote tributaries, the late Qing was in no position to maintain this fiction. As Russian Turkistan became Russian, and all of India became British, each of these neighbors drew Xinjiang into a colonial periphery of its own. The Qing court's ability to maintain its authority in Xinjiang depended on the disposition of these two Great Game rivals, who eyed each other across a space they treated not so much as inalienable Qing territory as a buffer zone of ambiguous sovereignty. While retaining its ethnic distinctiveness, provincial Xinjiang increasingly resembled the spheres of influence spreading throughout coastal China and Manchuria, dotted by treaty ports where foreigners enjoyed special privileges. In an effort to strengthen Xinjiang's bonds to the center, Zuo Zongtang's reconquest led to the restructuring of Xinjiang as a fully fledged Chinese province, but it did not take long for officials to abandon the ambitious thinking that lay behind provincialization. Muhammad Imin Bughra, a leader in Republican-era politics in Xinjiang, refers to this period as that of the "two-and-a-half governments"—Russia and Britain counting for one each, and the Qing only half—a pithy description of what scholars refer to as semicolonialism.[10]

In commencing my narrative at this point, I pick up where recent English-language scholarship on Xinjiang leaves off, much of it categorized as part of the so-called New Qing History.[11] Motivated by a desire for a less sinocentric view of Qing history, scholars have come to depict the Qing as an empire among empires, with a focus on the institution and manipulation of "difference" as a key to elucidating the empire's inner workings. With an emphasis on Manchu empire building, this work breaks with earlier efforts to construct a "China-centered" social history that dealt with China's core economic regions, calling instead for a "Qing-centered" history of the Qing. This has given impetus to the study of the Qing as an expansive Inner Asian polity, adapting techniques of Eurasian state building in ways comparable to contemporary land-based empires such as Russia, and to the study of its colonial possessions such as Xinjiang. For its eighteenth- and early-nineteenth-century history, such an approach to Xinjiang has much to recommend it, but for provincial Xinjiang a "Qing-centered" focus on Manchu and Mongol military actors, colonial administrators, and Chinese settlers is not enough. From the point of view of the Qing court, provincial Xinjiang was still its "new frontier," but it cannot be studied from this single center/periphery perspective alone. In this respect, a "Qing-centered" history remains all too China-centered to be applied to late-Qing Xinjiang. To think of Xinjiang as a Chinese province abutting neighboring colonial empires requires us to explore the way in which projections of sovereignty and authority from multiple directions interacted in this new environment.

Although it has done much to legitimate the study of non-Chinese regions, the popularity of frontier history has tended to isolate the region as something different from the society of the Chinese heartland, requiring tools of analysis particular to frontier specialists. This has, paradoxically, limited our ability to incorporate the frontier into Chinese history, since it asks different questions of it. If, as I suggest, Xinjiang from the late nineteenth century onward may be productively compared to China's cosmopolitan modernizing coastal centers and their hinterlands, then we need a different way of thinking about Xinjiang as part of China. The challenge in applying such a perspective to Xinjiang is that we must bring the majority Muslim population into our analysis. This is not always easy on the basis of Chinese sources, but becomes possible by synthesizing the multiple colonial archives produced in provincial Xinjiang and incorporating local Islamic sources into our work.

Adopting this treaty port perspective brings us back to some familiar themes in late-nineteenth-century Qing history. Studies of the consequences of extra-territoriality, the manipulation of categories of subjecthood, or the cultural impact of the treaty ports, all offer points of comparison for the study of provincial Xinjiang.[12] Beyond this, we should also consider the lessons of the social history of the post-Taiping Yangtze delta, which has highlighted the intrusion of the local gentry into spheres of activity previously occupied by official actors.[13] In Xinjiang, as much as in the empire's heartland of the Yangtze delta, state-sponsored enterprise and initiatives toward local autonomy saw a new stratum of rich merchants emerge as conspicuous collaborators with the late-Qing bureaucracy. Yet these *bays* (an epithet meaning "wealthy"), as they were known, can be only hazily perceived in the records of Xinjiang's Chinese bureaucracy, and their relations with Chinese officialdom must be studied on the basis of non-Chinese sources. Such an approach offers, I think, a better prospect of an integrative history of the late Qing, one that is capable of making meaningful comparisons between regions often studied in isolation.

This approach may lead us to rethink some of our familiar categories in Chinese history. To take one example, in contrast to earlier periods of tight border controls, provincial Xinjiang witnessed an ever-increasing flow of people and goods across its borders. Some of these migrants were political exiles leaving Chinese territory for good, but others formed part of the empire-wide exodus of traders and laborers—a flow that is often subsumed within a notion of the "Chinese diaspora" (*huaqiao*). Bringing treaty-port Xinjiang into this story requires us to modify our terminology and think instead in terms of a history of the experience of Qing subjects abroad. As elsewhere in the empire, motivations for travel were many and varied. In this book I discuss the flight from failed nineteenth-century rebellions that took thousands of Qing subjects into Russian Turkistan; the equally politicized but controlled migration of Xinjiang Muslims in the 1880s, sanctioned by the Treaty of Saint Petersburg; organic flows of merchants, creating a Kashgari commercial network in Russia; and a growing exodus of migrant labor that peaked during World War I. Like the Qing diaspora elsewhere, these movements were prompted both by policies and by individual choices, and created an internally differentiated diaspora community.

There were of course differences between China's continental and coastal treaty ports. Xinjiang was one of several Qing borderlands where the "big imperialism" of foreign powers intruded on the "little imperialism" of the Qing (to borrow Stevan Harrell's terms). In Xinjiang, Qing officials and Russian consuls presided over Muslims who had much more in common with each other than they did with those ruling them. Imperial subjecthood, rather than religion or ethnicity, was the key dividing line between foreigner and native, and one that was easy for locals to cross.[14] The confusion of subjecthood categories, or the "subjecthood question" as it was known, was a constant challenge for officials in Qing and Republican Xinjiang, and elements of it persisted well into the second half of the twentieth century.

A second distinctive feature of this environment was the way in which colonial relationships were replicated within diaspora communities. Muslim subjects of the tsar benefited from the terms of Russia's treaties with the Qing and enjoyed the same privileges of extraterritoriality as did ethnic Russians. Yet these Muslims still stood in a colonial relationship to the Russian consular officials appointed among them. As a result, the Russian presence in Xinjiang re-created forms of native autonomy that had been instituted in Russian Turkistan itself. Chief among these was the position of trading headman, or *aqsaqal*, who mediated the three-way relationship of Russia, Qing China, and the trading network itself. While never mentioned in any treaty between Russia and the Qing, the *aqsaqal* not only thrived in provincial Xinjiang but came to be viewed as a valid alternative to formal means of supervising trading communities abroad and was eventually incorporated into Chinese policy.

The history of institutions such as the *aqsaqal* is important, I believe, in helping us to identify the distinct forms of political authority created in this frontier environment, in the way that historians have done for the Chinese diaspora of Southeast Asia.[15] It also helps us to avoid two historiographical pitfalls: one, reducing these communities to pawns in a Russia-China conflict; the other, situating these Muslims outside that conflict entirely, as a mobile and evasive network that sought to conceal its activities from the state. In the case of Xinjiang, such an approach has been fostered by work relying on Chinese sources that give little sense of the close involvement of Kashgari *bays* with local officials. In correcting this bias, provincial Xinjiang and its bazaars start to look comparable in important ways to the treaty port societies of coastal China, witness to increasing collaboration between the bureaucracy and local elite, as well as to the dynamics of colonial extraterritoriality. This book will trace the ways in which these trading networks became conduits for border-crossing political projects and the activities of the Kashgari merchantry as cultural patrons. Throughout this story the *aqsaqal*, as both a commercial and communal representative, will play a prominent part.

Jadidism and the Nation in Russia and China

I have highlighted here the economic and diplomatic imbalance between Russia and the Qing, but even at its height the Manchu emperors never viewed their Muslim subjects in the same way as did the tsars. Russia was a confessional state sharing a border with the Ottoman Empire and frequently clashed with it in the Caucasus, Black Sea, and the Balkans. In its diplomacy with the Ottomans, Russia positioned itself as a defender of Orthodoxy and champion of Slavic interests and saw its Muslim population as part of an Islamic world in which its loyalties were potentially divided. The Qing had a different view of Islam, not influenced by geopolitical strategy or Orientalist discourse on the fanaticism or stagnation of Muslim society. For the Qing, if the empire's Muslims presented a threat, it was because of heterodox customs such as the blind following of charismatic Sufi shaykhs, not any connection to the Ottoman sultan or trans-imperial hajj networks. In this environment, though Qing officials policed Sufi brotherhoods among the Chinese-speaking Hui (Dungans) closely, expressing loyalty in a spiritual sense to the Ottoman sultan as the caliph of all Muslims, even praying for him during the communal worship on Fridays, was not treated as a threat.

From the 1880s onward, Manchu rulers and Chinese scholar-officials adopted stop-start measures toward "nationalizing" the empire and inculcating elements of Chinese culture among its Muslims. The conversion of Xinjiang to a province and the introduction of Chinese primary schooling (the *xuetang*) were aspects of this sinicizing revival. Yet by 1911 these efforts were widely seen to have failed. When Chinese revolutionaries drew stars on their flag to represent the nation's provinces, they drew only the eighteen of what we might call "China proper." Xinjiang, the empire's nineteenth province, remained a colonial dependency in the new nation's self-imagination, and one that some were willing to jettison. In practice, too, Chinese republicanism in Xinjiang enjoyed only a brief moment in the sun. The province's first republican governor, Yang Zengxin (1864–1928), practiced a conservative style of post-Qing politics, carefully balancing the interests of non-Chinese elites and resisting calls from rival warlords and nationalists to colonize and develop the nation's periphery.[16]

The weakness of the Qing and its laissez-faire approach to Islam in Xinjiang offered easy entrée for intellectual trends from the outside world to Xinjiang. There were many conduits for such trends—long-standing religious and scholarly networks linking China to the rest of the Islamic world, now reinforced by the circulation of print journalism, and the presence of many Russian Muslims, along with a few Ottoman Muslims, living and working in Xinjiang. The conditions that permitted such ties to flourish gave foreign Muslims a positive impression of communal freedom in China, which contrasted favorably with restrictions on Muslim autonomy in Russia. Yet the light hand of the Qing also meant that foreign notions of a crisis in the Islamic world, and exhortations to modernize, often fell on deaf ears in Xinjiang. It was primarily Xinjiang Muslims who found themselves in new political contexts in Russia and the Ottoman Empire, who inserted Xinjiang and its Muslims into these new discourses.

The most significant response among Muslims in Russia to the pressure of the confessional empire was a derivative discourse of modernization known as Jadidism. Initially focusing on the implementation of the New Method (*uṣūl-i jadīd*) of primary schooling, the Jadidist critique spilled into many spheres of sociability. Jadidism was but one expression of a widely felt aspiration in the colonial world: that appropriating standards of enlightenment and civilization propounded by the colonial empires was the best way to ward off these threats. As Adeeb Khalid has discussed, the Jadidists eschewed questions of sovereignty, instead urging Muslims to first advance along the path to modernity through educational reform.[17] Xinjiang was the one place in the world where the prescriptions of Jadidist schooling and cultural innovation were applied outside Russia, and this book extends the historiography of Jadidism by tracing this transmission. While the Ili Valley, linking the Russian province of Semireche and Xinjiang, served as a conduit for Tatar Jadidism, pedagogical experiments elsewhere in the province drew on Bukharan and Ottoman trends.

Xinjiang's links to the Ottoman Empire figure prominently in politicized narratives of Xinjiang's history. Chinese scholars and analysts often trace the threat to stability in Xinjiang today to the "two pan's" (*shuangfan zhuyi*)—pan-Islamism and pan-Turkism—which they depict as striking the province like a spreading infection in the late nineteenth century. At the turn of the century both Britain and Russia kept tabs on what they regarded as a pan-Islamist and Ottoman threats to their colonies in Asia, threats that occasionally seemed to implicate the oasis dwellers of Chinese Turkistan. Yet there is good reason to be skeptical of these alarmist narratives. While not entirely dismissive of the emotive bonds represented by notions of transnational Muslim or Turkic identity, recent studies have found little evidence of any proactive pan-Islamic or pan-Turkist Ottoman policy. As Michael Reynolds's study of the

Ottoman approach toward the Muslims of Russia has shown, Istanbul statesmen occasionally drew on transnational visions of community as legitimating devices, but remained focused at all times on the empire's survival. Similarly, James Meyer depicts the work of early pan-Turkists such as Yusuf Akçura as a pragmatic response to the crisis facing the Ottomans and not a political program for the world's Turks.[18]

In the case of China, the demonization of pan-Islamism and pan-Turkism is doubly misplaced. Whether in Istanbul or Kazan, Muslims looking on at the Qing did not see there an oppressive empire that could be compared to the threat that Russia or Britain posed to the Islamic world. At first, modernist intellectuals articulated a view of China that had much in common with prevailing (and highly negative) Orientalist views, treating it as a civilizational unity distinct from the Muslim world.[19] This was gradually tempered by an emerging discourse that tended to exaggerate the size and political significance of China's Muslim population, inspiring hope of an Islamic revival in the East. For some, the Russo-Japanese war of 1904–1905 consolidated this growing identification with Asia, and with it a view of China as a victim of colonialism, and which Chinese Muslims should therefore defend. The radicalizing climate of World War I brought about a turn to more racialized Turkist political visions, which further consolidated a sense of Asian identity and a bond of solidarity with China among these Muslims. To the extent that we consider these various ideological currents, therefore, we should not limit ourselves to the "two pan's," but take into consideration a third: pan-Asianism. When Russian Muslim and Ottomans enjoined Xinjiang Muslims, as Muslims, to tread the path toward enlightenment, they envisaged this as a collaborative project between Muslims and Chinese to defend the Chinese nation from European imperialism.

From the late nineteenth century onward, intellectual shifts in the Ottoman Empire found a reflection among a small group of Xinjiang Muslims who were either living in Ottoman domains or following the empire's tribulations from afar. The Ottoman turn to pan-Islamic discourse during the reign of Sultan Abdulhamid (r. 1876–1909), as Cemal Aydin has discussed, was prompted by disillusionment with efforts to fend off imperial aggression by matching the civilizational standards of the West. This in turn gave way to efforts among intellectuals, particularly those who were critical of Sultan Abdulhamid's authoritarianism, to stake out a specifically Turkic civilizational narrative for themselves. This was fueled in part by Arab-Turk conflict in the Ottoman provinces, but also by the scholarly rediscovery of the ancient Turkic past that was then occurring on Orientalist expeditions to Mongolia and China. Such a revision raised the status of Turkistan as the native land of the Turks, and the Uyghurs as pioneers of Turkic civilization.

Turn-of-the-century Turkism found a degree of support in Russia, for example in Ismail Gasprinskii's call for readers of his Russo-Turkic daily *The Interpreter* (*Tärjeman*) to adopt a pan-Turkic literary standard. Gasprinskii's Turkism was an intervention into a debate among Russian Muslims that had previously centered on the applicability of notions of "Bolghar" or "Tatar" identity in the history of the Russian Muslims. Cultural pan-Turkism, in turn, fell from favor among a rising generation of Russian Muslim intellectuals in first decade of the twentieth century, who swung behind a territorialized vision of a Kazan-centered Tatar nation. Scholars attribute the growth of the Tatarist camp to a variety of factors: the influence of missionary pedagogies tailored to the ethnic particularities of the peoples of the Volga; the political discrediting of pan-Islamic and pan-Turkic rhetoric; and the attraction of social Darwinist theories.[20] Michael Friedrich highlights the fact that in Russia's conservative Third Duma period (1907–1912), the notion of an "established national literature" was invoked to discriminate in education policy between "Western" nationalities such as the Finns and backward "Eastern" nationalities such as the "Muslims."[21] For a minority of Russian Muslims, the environment necessitated a sharp turn toward constructing an explicitly Tatar literature and culture, fashioned out of the language of the village and not of the madrasa. In the process, the Tatarist avant-garde created a template for other non-Russian nationalities of the empire to follow in constructing a national history.

To simplify what in reality was an interconnected process, the turns toward "Turkification" in Anatolia and "Tatarization" in Russia presented a choice to those Muslims from Xinjiang who felt a similar need to revise their communal narratives in national terms. Those living within the Russian Empire were more likely to be drawn to the particularistic Tatar approach to national culture and identity, while those in Istanbul (and Xinjiang) found it easy to simply shift the emphasis from Muslim to Turk. Some of these were committed Jadidists, while others were already disillusioned with the transformative capacity of Jadidist cultural politics. What they had in common was a marginal position in local society. It was not the strength of their ideas that propelled some of these men to positions of leadership in the community. It was the rupture, and the political vacuum, created by the Russian Revolution.

Caravans and Communists

The transition from reform to revolution is a well-worn historiographical path. Yet not everyone who rose to prominence in Soviet Central Asia had a Jadidist background, and it would be wrong to think of the history of revolutionary Turkistan simply as the working out of the unfinished business of prerevolutionary Jadidism. As historians of the Russian Revolution know, it is easy enough to study the publicists and theorists among Russian radicals through their speeches and publications. It is harder to trace the lives of less visible revolutionaries who built up networks of contacts through hazardous, and unglamorous, careers in the revolutionary underground. In Central Asia, the ex-Jadidists have left a legacy of literate advocacy for national interests. To balance the picture in this book, I set them alongside a different group, the border-crossing Kashgaris, who emerged from a largely invisible world of the Kashgari diaspora to rival the Jadidists for leadership of the Xinjiang Muslims in the 1920s.

As much as the revolution thrust these groups of intellectuals and petty entrepreneurs into collaboration, it also highlighted the great social gulf between them. Russian-born Jadidists cast themselves as the sophisticated spokespeople of a predominantly peasant community, whose livelihood depended above all on securing a positive outcome from the Soviet land reform process. The Kashgaris, by contrast, were sojourning traders and laborers, who had quite different concerns. Both groups, backed occasionally by sympathetic Soviet officials, invoked what Terry Martin has called the "piedmont principle."[22] That is, in theory it was far better to be the potential vanguard of a new revolutionary push into China than remain a small and insignificant minority within someone else's national republic. Yet they invoked this principle in different ways. Those who were Soviet citizens, lacking a direct connection to politics in China, placed the emphasis on an imagined national unity with the Muslims of Xinjiang—as Uyghurs. These Jadidists were already the section of the émigré community most invested in the politics of national identity, and their isolation from events in Xinjiang increased this. For the Kashgari traders, by contrast, no new national imaginary was required to point out their connection to a potential revolution in Xinjiang: Kashgar was their home, they knew it and its politics intimately. Thus the Uyghur question became a battleground between a Jadidist group for whom the new conception of the nation was critically important and Kashgaris who remained indifferent to cultural explorations of national identity.

On this basis two strategic orientations developed, each with accompanying rhetoric, existing side by side in the emerging Uyghurist politics. The first was to carve out a place for the Uyghurs within the family of Soviet nations; the second focused on directing the energy of the Soviet revolution to effect political transformation in Xinjiang. Party members in good standing, the Jadidists-cum-Communists were sensitive to the evolving demands of Soviet orthodoxy in domestic and foreign policy. Yet the more this group insisted on the revolutionary potential of the Turkic-speaking Muslims of China, the more they ceded leadership of the Uyghurs-in-formation to a different revolutionary subject—the sojourning Kashgaris who moved back and forth between Soviet territory and Xinjiang, and had a different strategy. They were interested in fast results and had little time for the subtleties of Leninist theory. Many were drawn to the Soviet Union, not out of any knowledge of Bolshevik policy, but due to the Soviet Union's friendship with modernizing states in the Islamic world, particularly Ottoman Turkey. Although the history of Istanbul-aligned Turkic nationalism among the Muslims of Xinjiang is often written so as to bypass the Soviet Union, in fact it ran straight through it.

Unlike other nations to emerge from within the Soviet Union, therefore, the Uyghurs must be looked at from two perspectives: not only that of national construction but also of revolutionary internationalism. The first is the story of the creation of the nation, tailored to fit the Stalinist criteria of a "common language, territory, economic life, and psychological make-up manifested in a common culture."[23] The second is the story of the Muslims of Xinjiang as part of the spread of Bolshevik revolution to the colonial world. For both of these perspectives we do not lack existing scholarship and case studies to draw on. What renders the Uyghur case distinctive is the way in which these two narratives must be examined in a constant dialogue, as parallel projects that were at times complementary, at times contradictory.

A conference that took place in Tashkent in 1921 is where these two stories first intersect. The Congress of Kashgari and Jungharian Workers is frequently described as the point at which Turkic-speaking Muslims from Xinjiang adopted the new "Uyghur" name for themselves.[24] This, I argue, is a misconception. The Tashkent Congress in 1921 was not the place for an intellectual debate on the correct ethnic designation for the Muslims of Xinjiang. Officially, it was not a national forum at all, but an event for representatives of all Chinese subjects residing in Soviet Turkistan. They met to determine the implications of the revolutionary process for this community and those to whom they were connected in China. Only a few months earlier, in the oil town of Baku, the Comintern had called on its allies among the "Peoples of the East" to rise up against colonialism wherever it reared its head. In Bukhara and Khiva, revolutionary councils now ruled in place of tsarist Russia's client monarchs. In Mongolia, Soviet cavalry and Mongolian partisans were battling the Whites for control of Urga, and the Red Army was preparing for a similar incursion into Xinjiang, to root out its civil war enemies. Further east, preparations were in train for the founding congress of the Chinese Communist Party, held in secret in Shanghai that July. Within this revolutionary context, the chief concern for all actors was to assemble the most effective alliance that they could, either to bid for Soviet sponsorship, or simply to take advantage of the destabilizing rupture that the Russian Revolution had created.

In the 1920s, revolutionary strategizing implicated the Muslims of Xinjiang in three possible ways. The first was as part of the Islamic world, both as an extension of the Bolshevik alliance with Turkey and as a bridge to India. The second was as a nationally distinct part of the Chinese periphery, which like Mongolia might be deserving of liberation from Chinese colonialism. The third was the Chinese revolution itself, as a Soviet-backed alliance of the Chinese Communist Party and the Guomindang sought to unite the nation in the mid-1920s. Yet none of these revolutionary scripts cast the Muslims of Xinjiang in the leading role. At best they created organizational possibilities and registers of political speech within which those Muslims might try to situate themselves most advantageously.

Although it was not the intention, the fledgling organization of Xinjiang émigrés founded in Tashkent in 1921 did provide a forum into which a small group of Jadidists could introduce the Uyghurist discourse that they had cultivated in cultural circles in urban Semireche, far from the social world of the bazaars and cotton fields where the Kashgaris could be found. Through the twists and turns of the early 1920s, a shifting constituency continued to find use for this language to carve out a niche for themselves in Soviet politics. This early period was crucial in establishing a precedent for talk of a Uyghur nation, robust enough to withstand scrutiny during the national delimitation of Soviet Turkistan, a policy that was introduced in 1924. The division of Soviet Turkistan into new national republics is often described as the high point of Soviet national building in Central Asia, leading to the consolidation of new forms of territorial nationhood. It was at this time that Muslims from Xinjiang started to speak in terms of an actually existing Uyghur nation, with all the traits that the emerging Stalinist orthodoxy demanded of it. Yet as much as the national delimitation created an incentive to speak in terms of a Uyghur nation, it also threatened the fragile alliance that had emerged around this idea, as Central Asia's new political boundaries widened divisions among Muslims from Xinjiang.

There is no denying the role of Soviet policy in establishing orthodox forms for interaction with the state and fostering an increasingly nationalized political environment. To this limited extent we can say that the Soviets created the conditions for the emergence of the Uyghur nation, but there is no evidence that they were invested in the project themselves. Soviet officials were mostly oblivious to the goings-on among Muslims from Xinjiang and made no comment on the desirability of recognizing a Uyghur nation. Nor is there any evidence that Orientalists and ethnographers, a second group often mentioned as participants in the nation-building project, were involved. Had he been consulted, the Orientalist V. V. Bartold would have likely ridiculed the idea of a Uyghur nation. As he saw it in 1925, the very idea proved that "even among the most educated natives, their view of their region's past is extremely hazy."[25] When Soviet Turkologists were finally called upon to comment on questions of Uyghur language or culture in 1930, they were presented with a fait accompli. The real interlocutors and collaborators in the Uyghurist enterprise were fellow Muslims, particularly from the Volga region, who shared an enthusiasm for the anticipated Uyghur national revival. While acknowledging the contribution of scholarship that treats Soviet nationalities in terms of union-wide policies or intellectual traditions, the case of the Uyghurs cautions us against assuming that Soviet nationalities all followed the same path to nationhood.[26]

Xinjiang in a Revolutionary World

The fact that Soviet officials cultivated a link to Xinjiang was only ever partly out of its revolutionary interest in China's northwest. All along, Soviet policy toward Xinjiang was equally driven by economic objectives: at first, the need to access the province's resources to relieve famine in Semireche; through the mid-1920s, to catch up with foreign competitors by flooding the province with Soviet exports; and by the end of the decade, to secure a base of resources with which to combat an anticipated imperialist war against the Soviet Union. Along the Soviet Union's border with Xinjiang, activists keenly felt the widening contradiction between the imperative to consolidate the Soviet Union within its existing boundaries by seeking diplomatic allies and trading partners, and the new revolutionary conquests promised by the Comintern. This process placed increasingly stringent demands on activists to subordinate their activity to the twists and turns of party directives. Some complied, but others turned toward independent and illegal revolutionary activity.

Xinjiang was one of several Soviet borderlands in the 1920s and 1930s whose inhabitants looked on as the Bolshevik transformation played out, and weighed up the pros and cons of aligning themselves with it.[27] Claims about identity were laid over these deeper political questions, which were not fully resolved until 1949 and the incorporation of Xinjiang into the People's Republic of China. For locals in Xinjiang who had invested in connections to Russia in the prerevolutionary period, there was little choice but to seek an accommodation with the Soviets. Those involved in long-distance trade with Russia were prominent among pro-Soviet elements in Xinjiang. Traveling through Turfan in the 1920s, the American explorer Owen Lattimore met with cotton entrepreneurs in the oasis, and he found one Russian-speaking young man to be an enthusiastic claimant to the Uyghur legacy. The budding Uyghurist had twice visited the Nizhnii-Novgorod trading fair in Russia, "whence he had brought back shiny yellow boots and the theory of evolution."[28] Yet such self-styled progressives were a tiny minority in Xinjiang. For most people in the province, who had little to no contact with the politics of Soviet nation building, if "Uyghur" meant anything at all in the 1920s, it meant Communist.

For those who wished to avoid the Sovietization of Xinjiang, the alternative was to engage in Chinese politics. China's incomplete transition from empire to nation meant that in the 1920s institutional relics of Qing authority could still be seen as bastions of Muslim autonomy. Although considerably weaker than when they were first created in the eighteenth century, the province's aristocratic *wangs* belonged to elite Muslim networks connected to the capital, where constitutional discussions dwelt on the status of the "Muslims" as one of China's five racial constituencies. Here the key question was the possibility of collaboration between Xinjiang's Turkic-speaking Muslims and the Chinese-speaking Muslims. To some this seemed a viable strategy, but others sought direct contact with the Nationalists of the interior, resurrecting the Jadidist goal of collaboration with Chinese Republicanism. In these circles there developed a counterdiscourse to the Soviet Uyghurist position, which married a pan-Turkic insistence on the unity of the Turkic-speaking peoples to Sun Yat-sen's view of the Muslims of China as the "Turks who profess Islam" (*Huijiao zhi Tujue*).

Besides these local aspirations, Xinjiang also served as a place of refuge for Central Asian Muslims escaping Soviet repression, who were connected to a politicized Turkistani diaspora in Europe and the Middle East. In this expatriate scene, there was a growing sense that the Soviet model of nation building was a trap that the Muslims of Turkistan had stumbled into. This critique featured prominently in the propaganda of Guomindang-allied Muslims in the 1940s.

The questions for Xinjiang raised by the Russian Revolution came to the fore in the Muslim rebellion of the 1930s, which I treat in the final chapter of this book. The rebellion, which broke out in the east of the province, drew interventions first from Chinese-speaking Muslims of Gansu, then from the Mongolian People's Republic, and finally from the Soviet Union. Viewed from one angle, it was a restorative uprising, aimed at preserving patrimonial privileges from the Qing. Others preferred to see it as the start of a progressive struggle for national liberation. Its most eye-catching result, the short-lived East Turkistan Republic, embodied a modernizing Islamic vision for Xinjiang that fit neither Chinese Republican nor Soviet paradigms. Our view of the events on the ground is still hindered by a lack of local sources that would allow us to deepen the narratives that circulate among Uyghurs in exile or in memoir accounts in Xinjiang.[29] Nevertheless, the opening of the Soviet archives has given us a number of new perspectives on the events of 1931–1934, particularly on political deliberations in the Politburo and the Comintern, and also in Soviet military circles. While mine is not the first work to utilize this material, I do so in light of the history of Uyghur politics in the Soviet Union and seek to connect the questions of Soviet policy to the activities of both dissident Uyghur Communists, as well as those Soviet-trained Uyghurs who served in the provincial administration of Sheng Shicai.[30] I also incorporate new research from Mongolia, which sheds much light on the uprising's early contacts with the neighboring Mongolian People's Republic.

The creation of a Soviet-aligned Chinese regime in Ürümchi, and the recognition of the Uyghurs as an official nationality of Xinjiang in 1934, is where this book ends. In granting cultural autonomy to a Uyghur nation in Xinjiang, the warlord Sheng Shicai sought to co-opt a cohort of native intellectuals while curtailing the threat of Muslim opposition. This was the first of a series of such efforts in Xinjiang. Then, as now, the initiative was fraught with contradictions. The Uyghur national project was not a product of Soviet or Chinese policy, nor could it be entirely controlled by them. Given the turbulence in Soviet Central Asia in the early 1930s, "Soviet" notions of nationality were introduced to

Xinjiang as much by dissident Uyghurs, runaways from the Soviet Union, as they were through official contacts. This tension meant that Soviet categories of ethnicity were formally implemented in Xinjiang through a highly repressive process, laying the ground for further rounds of violence, and for renegotiations of the relationship between categories of nationality and political authority in Xinjiang. Neither a classic case of state-sanctioned national construction nor of a national liberation struggle in the colonial world, the Uyghurs have had a rocky relationship with both dimensions of the Communist vision for Asia.

CHAPTER ONE

People and Place in Chinese Turkistan

Twentieth-century invocations of the Uyghurs constructed a narrative of perennial nationhood—of nationhood lost and found. This discourse of Uyghur nationhood tapped into a rich historical and philological legacy, harking back to a golden age of Uyghur civilization and by extension pointing to the decline that had since reduced the community to a fractured and colonized condition. It was, no doubt, an ambitious act of redefinition. Yet those who pioneered this discourse must have felt sufficiently confident that its historical claims were justified, and that a vision of common Uyghur origins corresponded in some way to an existing reality. For this reason it is necessary to begin this study with a review not only of the history of the first Uyghurs but of the various communal narratives that existed among the Muslims of Chinese Turkistan at the start of the twentieth century. These registers of identification were created both from above and from below, in the interaction of rulers and ruled, and of the Muslims of Chinese Turkistan with the outside world. The rhetoric of Uyghur nationhood drew heavily on Xinjiang's local Islamic traditions, though it resituated these symbols in a new narrative of Turkic civilization. To account for this transformation, we must also move beyond Xinjiang and look at the revision of Turkic history that that late-nineteenth-century Orientalist and Turkological scholarship carried out.

The ability of states to relocate and reclassify their subjects, the cultural shifts that follow in the wake of religious conversion, and the prestige of scholarly traditions have all contributed to defining the peoples and places that we meet in historical sources on Chinese Turkistan. With a steppe zone running through its north (Jungharia), and a society of settled oasis dwellers in its south (the Tarim Basin), the region now known as Xinjiang has always been a meeting point of nomadic and sedentary communities. The rise and fall of states in the

22

steppe has left its mark on the region's history on many occasions, but three key moments stand out in this respect: the dissolution of the original Uyghur state in Mongolia and the flight of the Uyghurs south; the incorporation of the region into Chinggis Khan's world empire; and the hegemony of the Junghar Mongols in the seventeenth and eighteenth centuries. The sediment of administrative schemes and communal narratives left by these regimes shaped the eastern half of Central Asia in the form that it took on the eve of the Qing conquest in the 1750s.

From the Steppe to the Sown:
The Uyghurs and Uyghuristan

A nomadic people called the Uyghurs enter the historical record in the sixth century, as one of a number of groups occupying the middle ground between the Tang dynasty and the empire of the Turks, with whom they had much in common linguistically and culturally. When the Turk empire collapsed in the eighth century, the Uyghurs filled the void, establishing their rule in what is now Mongolia. Chinese chronicles describe the Uyghur empire as composed of an elite of "inner" tribes surrounded by a series of affiliated "outer" tribes. The confederation held for almost a century, until the Uyghurs were driven from the steppe by an invasion from the north. Fleeing south, some threw themselves on the mercy of the Tang emperors. Others settled in the no-man's-land between China and Central Asia, in the oases of Ganzhou, Hami, and Turfan. These Uyghur principalities adopted Buddhism from their Iranian and Chinese neighbors, and patronized the flowering of a new Turkic Buddhist civilization. Uyghuristan—the land of the Uyghurs—was the name that Muslim geographers gave to this region.[1]

At its height, Uyghur control extended as far west as Kucha and Lake Issiq Köl. Chinese sources attest that Uyghurs migrated as far as the Pamir region, as did former members of the Uyghur confederation such as the Qarluq. It was from this tribal mix that the Qarakhanid dynasty emerged in the tenth century, a polity of equal significance to Uyghuristan in the twentieth-century construction of a Muslim Uyghur history. The Qarakhanids were the first Turkic-speaking nomads to maintain both a royal Turkic tradition and to adopt Islam. From twin capitals in Kashgar and Balasaghun (now in Kirghizstan), the Qarakhanids raided along the edges of the Taklamakan Desert, carrying out the first wave of Islamization of the Tarim Basin. By the early eleventh century they had succeeded in overthrowing the Buddhist kingdom of Khotan, but further inroads into Uyghuristan were checked by the arrival of the Western Liao dynasty, and following them, Chinggis Khan's Mongols. Wars with the Buddhists of Khotan and Uyghuristan resulted in a series of localized saintly traditions in the Tarim Basin, linked to the graves of holy warriors and martyred imams. The cult of the Qarakhanid monarch Satuq Bughra Khan (fl. 930–950), whose tomb lies on the outskirts of Artush, only grew in popularity as the centuries passed.

The trappings of sedentary civilization proved to be a mixed blessing for the inhabitants of Uyghuristan. In the early thirteenth century, the Mongols were so impressed by Uyghur literacy that they employed Uyghur scribes throughout their chancelleries and armies, scattering them to the ends of the Eurasian continent. The best-known of these Uyghurs ended up in China as scholar-officials of the Yuan dynasty (1271–1368), one of several successor states to Chinggis Khan's vast empire. When the Yuan fell, a few of these elite families returned to Uyghuristan, while others migrated to Korea.[2] Some who served the Mongols ended up in south China, where they eventually adopted Islam and blended into the emerging community of Chinese-speaking Muslims (Hui).[3] Others marched west with the armies of Chinggis Khan's first son Jochi to the Russian steppe, returning to Turkistan centuries later as part of the tribal confederacy known as the Uzbeks.[4] Still others found service in Mongol successor states elsewhere: in Ilkhanid Iran, or with the Seljük rulers of Anatolia. In the middle of the fourteenth century, in the turbulent aftermath of Mongol rule in the Muslim world, one such family rose to prominence as one of Anatolia's independent princely dynasties—the Sons of Eretna (Eretna oğulları).[5]

It is hard to gauge the extent to which these widely dispersed Uyghurs felt themselves part of a single ethnic group or members of a diaspora. During the Yuan dynasty, elite Uyghurs in China maintained social ties to Uyghuristan and continued to give their children Uyghur names while adapting to Chinese literati society. It makes sense to suppose that such "diasporic" qualities of the community weakened as Uyghuristan itself lost its distinct political and religious identity. During the break-up of the Mongol empire, Uyghuristan was situated between the Yuan dynasty and the eastern half of the *ulus* of Chaghatay, Chinggis Khan's second son. When the Ming dynasty sent its emissaries to Amir Timur's court in Samarkand, there were already many Muslims living among the Buddhist Uyghurs of Hami and Turfan. According to the envoy Chen Cheng (1365–1457), the Buddhists and Muslims spoke a common Turkic language but were distinguished from one another by religious and cultural markers. For example, Uyghur men grew their hair long, while the Muslims shaved their heads; Uyghur women donned black veils, while Muslim women dressed in white.[6]

The Ming court took these distinctions into account as it extended its network of military garrisons into Uyghuristan in the early fifteenth century. In 1406 the Ming emperor enfeoffed a Buddhist aristocrat of Chaghatayid origins as the Loyal and Submissive King (*Zhongshun wang*), who presided over three military governors in Hami—one each for the Muslims, the Uyghurs, and the Ha-la-hui (most likely a Mongol group).[7] Although cultural boundaries between the three groups were gradually eroding, these institutional boundaries preserved the Uyghurs as a distinct community, at least from the viewpoint of Chinese sources.

In the early sixteenth century, as Ming authority in Central Asia declined, Uyghuristan fell under the sway of the Muslim Chaghatayids. In the course of this conflict, Muslim raids and Ming reprisals sent a number of Uyghurs fleeing east into the Gansu corridor, where they settled around the frontier towns of Suzhou and Ganzhou. Following in the footsteps of the Chaghatayid holy warriors, Sufi missionaries traveled to Uyghuristan, seeking converts among its remaining infidels. The last reference to non-Muslim Uyghurs in an Islamic source comes from the hagiography of a Sufi saint of the late sixteenth century, the Naqshbandi Sufi Ishaq Vali of Samarkand. Here it is told how one of the saint's disciples led a trading mission from Yarkand to Suzhou, where he lodged with a local qadi (Islamic judge), Khoja Abdusattar, whose daughter was gravely ill. Through his disciple's entreaties, Ishaq Vali manifested himself from many miles away in Yarkand and miraculously cured the qadi's daughter. "At that time," we read, "close to three thousand Uyghur infidels had gathered around Khoja [Abdusattar]. They all became Muslims, and secretly they became devotees of His Holiness [Ishaq Vali]."[8]

Conversion to Islam resituated the Uyghurs on the eastern fringe of a Turkic-speaking Muslim world whose political center was the Chaghatayid court of Yarkand to the south but drew on cultural models from the Timurid courts of Samarkand and Bukhara. The new faith brought with it a new Turkic literary language known as Chaghatay and a new canon of Sufi poetry and hagiography. In this process local Uyghur dialects were assimilated to a Tarim Basin standard, and the Sogdian-Uyghur script gave way to Arabic. By the late sixteenth century, Ming court translators who had studied the vertical Uyghur script in order to handle correspondence with Turfan and Hami found their training to be obsolete. Since "tributary" missions from these parts were now carrying letters in Arabic script, they were assigned to the Muslim Bureau, which had previously dealt with states and peoples from farther west.[9] The linguistic handbooks that these translation bureaus published give some indication of the transformation that was taking place. In a vocabulary list that was used in the Muslim Bureau, the Chinese name for Turfan and its peoples—Gaochang—was glossed simply as *Turki*, the name by which the language of the sedentary oasis-dwelling communities of Turkistan was now known.[10]

The Turko-Mongol Legacy

As a political entity, Uyghuristan faded from view as the Chaghatayids subsumed it into a realm that they called Moghulistan, reflecting the ruling elite's own sense of Moghul (i.e. Mongol) identity. During the early history of the Chaghatayid *ulus*, while it was centered to the north of the Tianshan, Moghulistan referred to these mountains and to Jungharia. This was the steppe zone that the traditionalist Moghuls preferred, in contrast to their Timurid cousins, who were now ruling from the cities of Transoxiana. Those among the Moghuls who migrated south to the Tarim Basin initially felt that they had left Moghulistan behind. In the early sixteenth century, however, when the Chaghatayids established a new court in Yarkand, it engendered a sense of Moghulistan as encompassing the Tarim Basin.[11] Although the nomadic Moghuls soon blended into the local Muslim community and lost their distinct corporate identity, the concept of Moghulistan survived, particularly in the local literary imagination.[12]

The Chaghatayids directed a second wave of Islamization in the Tarim Basin, both by military means and by patronizing the activities of Sufi shaykhs (known by the title *khoja*). Some of these *khoja*s belonged to local saintly families, but many were affiliated with brotherhoods originating to the west, most notably the Naqshbandiyya from Bukhara. As Devin DeWeese has argued, conversion narratives provided important grounds for communal identity in Central Asia.[13] Islamic rulers and prominent shaykhs had an interest in reconciling the Tarim Basin's two royal traditions—the Qarakhanid and the Chaghatayid—and presenting themselves as heirs to an unbroken legacy of Islamic sovereignty. In this process the activities of a sixteenth-century Sufi shaykh named Khoja Muhammad Sharif occupied an important position. By touring the Tarim Basin and miraculously "rediscovering" the shrines of such legendary Qarakhanid Islamizers as Satuq Bughra Khan, Muhammad Sharif linked his Chaghatayid patrons at the Yarkand court to earlier royal traditions.[14] Intermarriage, as well as corrupted genealogies, also facilitated the merging of sources of authority, allowing the tripartite ruling class of khan, amir (or *beg*), and shaykh to present themselves as an interconnected unity. By the eighteenth century, Xinjiang's Naqshbandiyya *khoja*s could claim illustrious Chaghatayid or Qarakhanid genealogy, with some assuming the title of "khan khoja."

Conversion played an important role in assimilating the Uyghurs to surrounding communities, but it did not erase all memory of them. Irrespective of its infidel associations, Uyghur culture retained a certain prestige in parts of the Islamic world, particularly where Turkic ruling elites confronted Iranian claims to cultural superiority. In the Timurid center of Samarkand, for example, the Uyghur script enjoyed something of a revival in the fifteenth century. Although linguists today distinguish the Buddhist Uyghur written language from the Chaghatay that succeeded it, not all saw this as such a sharp break. The fifteenth-century author Qidirkhan Yarkandi, for example, praised in the introduction to his *divan* the Chaghatay poets Lutfi and Sakkaki, who were, as he put it, "fluent in the Uyghur parlance and eloquent in the Turki tongue."[15] Cultural reference points such as these helped to preserve a geographic notion of Uyghuristan in the wake of its political downfall. Writing in the middle of the seventeenth century, the Balkh historian Mahmud b. Vali adopted the term "Uyghuristan" for the entire khanate of the Yarkand Chaghatayids.[16] A century and a half later, a native of Kashgar living in exile in Samarkand made the same expansive use of "Uyghuristan."[17] Some outsiders held similar conceptions; Riza Quli Khan, an Iranian envoy to Khiva in the early nineteenth century, for example, wrote in his travelogue that "Kashgar is a well-known city of the sixth clime, in the country of the Uyghurs of Turkistan, and is the capital of that region."[18]

Popular accounts of communal origins in Islamic Turkistan synthesized Islamic genesis stories, Turkic and Mongolian tribal genealogies, and the Iranian epic tradition. These stories provided a potted history of the world's peoples, which personified tribes, states, and dynasties as individuals linked by genealogy, with migration, war, and religious conversion described in the terms of familial conflict. The Ilkhanid vizier and historian Rashiduddin's early-fourteenth-century *Compendium of Chronicles* is a storehouse of such accounts. Of particular importance in this mythic cycle was the figure of Oghuz

Khan, identified as the first khan of the Turks to adopt Islam. Rashiduddin described the Uyghurs as a group who had united with Oghuz Khan when he defied his father Qara Khan and embraced the new religion, and the ethnonym Uyghur, by folk etymology, was interpreted to mean "those who unite."[19] Later works such as Abu'l-Ghazi Bahadur Khan's seventeenth-century *Genealogy of the Turks* provided a comprehensive narrative of Turkic ethnogenesis stretching back to Turk, son of Yafis (Japheth), son of Nuh (Noah). From Turk issued the "Sons of Yafis," which in turn led to two mighty brothers: Tatar Khan and Moghul Khan. The narration of these personified tribes and clans led to the lineage of Chinggis Khan, and could be continued, as it was in one version from Kashgar, down to the Chaghatayid khans of Yarkand and the Moghul clans who supported them.[20]

On the one hand, the genealogical motif created a nested set of identities that could permit very broad senses of community. In his travelogue of Xinjiang, for example, the British tea planter Robert Shaw expressed his delight at discovering that, like him, the natives of Kashgar considered themselves descendants of Japheth.[21] Following in Shaw's footsteps, in the early 1880s the British envoy Walter Bellew met the local Muslim governor of Artush, who had switched camps from the emirate of Yaqub Beg to the incoming Qing. In justifying his collaboration with the Manchus, he told Bellew that whether Turk, Moghul, Manchu or Khitay, "we are all Tatars."[22]

On the other hand, these same origin myths could lend strength to specific local narratives that divided the Muslims of Xinjiang. The oasis of Khotan offers a compelling example of this. Owing to its resistance to the Islamizing Qarakhanids in the eleventh century, Buddhist Khotan came to be identified not with the mainstream tradition of Qara Khan and his son Oghuz Khan, but with the lineage of Machin, son of Chin, son of Turk. Chin and Machin were originally geographic concepts deriving from Islamic accounts of China, in which the land of Machin referred to "Greater China" (from the Sanskrit *maha-chin*). As time went by, these terms came to be transplanted to the Tarim Basin and adopted by the locals. Khotanese legends tell how Machin son of Chin instructed the people of Khotan to spin wool and weave silk—possibly an echo of the legend of how silk weaving traveled to Khotan from China.[23] Muslims from Khotan came to be known as the people of Machin and adopted it as their *nisba* (a suffix identifying one's place of origin). An eighteenth-century Iranian chronicle calls the Khotanese the "people of Machin" (*ṭāʾifa-i Māchīnī*), and mentions individuals such as Latif Khan Machini.[24]

A distinctive Khotanese tradition survived at least until the end of the nineteenth century. When the Russian explorer Nikolai Przhevalskii traveled from Lop Nur to Khotan at the end of the nineteenth century, he found locals along the way identifying themselves as the people of Machin (*Machintsy* in Russian), though he noted that the term's popularity was declining.[25] Having been cast in the role of the infidel nation of the east, the Muslims of Machin had assimilated Islamic narratives to their own worldview, shrinking them down to fit the scale of the Tarim Basin. In legends deriving from the Iranian epic *Shahnama*, Khotan was known as the seat of Afrasiab, the king of Turan, the land of the Turks. With this translocation, the Machintsy came to identify the rest of the Tarim Basin in terms derived from Iranian geography. Przhevalskii records that for the people of Machin, the Aqsu and Kashgar region was known as Ardabil, and to the north the oasis of Turfan was identified as Khurasan.[26]

The Junghar Estate System

From the middle of the seventeenth century, the Junghars, a confederacy of Oirat Mongols based to the north of the Tianshan Mountains, displaced the Chaghatayid khans of Moghulistan and competed with the rising Qing dynasty for control of Mongolia and Tibet. The Junghars were content to administer the Tarim Basin through loyal intermediaries, extracting tribute payments in textiles and cash that were enforced by only small garrisons. Yet while ruling the south with a light hand, the Junghars also drew various populations from Turkistan to their fortified encampments in the Altay, and subsequently in Ili. The practice of hostage taking brought to the Ili Valley Muslim nobility from various ruling families of Central Asia, including Chaghatayids from Yarkand, eminent Sufi shaykhs from Kashgar, and even a prince of Bukhara. In the words of a Muslim historian writing around 1800, the court of Tsewang Rabdan (r. 1697–1727) was "the meeting place for the khans of Piskent, the nobles of Tashkent, and the kings of Badakhshan."[27] In 1720 a Russian envoy to the Junghars, Petr Unkovskii, encountered these aristocrats in Tsewang Rabdan's entourage.[28] "To this day," he reported, "Erke Khan, and many begs and the best Bukharans, roam with him in captivity." (Russians referred to all Muslims who served the Junghars as Bukharans, and to the Tarim Basin as "Little Bukhara.")

Besides removing prominent individuals, the Junghars also displaced entire communities, which had a disruptive impact on oasis society. In the 1720s the Turfan oasis emerged as a sensitive frontier zone, contested between the

Junghars and the Qing. When the Junghars ceded Turfan to their rivals, they took part of its population south to the town of Uch. From this point on, Uch became known as Uchturfan, while new settlements around it took the names of other towns in the Turfan oasis, such as Lükchün and Pichan. Large-scale deportation was also employed as a punitive measure. Shortly after the depopulation of Turfan, the Tarim Basin rose in revolt against the Junghars and appealed to the Yongzheng emperor for support against Tsewang Rabdan. To punish these rebellious locals, the Junghars burnt Uch to the ground and exiled a hundred households of its surviving inhabitants to the Ili Valley.[29]

The Junghars headed an alliance of Mongolian-speaking ethnic groups known as "bones" (*yasu*), a formation that was widely known as the "Four Oirat" but that actually consisted of many more than four divisions. These bones, which included the Torghud, Khoshud, and Choros, were divided further into *otog*s, which Christopher Atwood refers to as "sub-ethnies."[30] Many of these *otog*s conformed to classic notions of nomadic tribal identity, deriving their name from a prominent eponymous founder—whether mythical or real. Yet other *otog*s fell outside this inner core of bones, and were identified instead by occupation, suggesting a more recent incorporation into the Junghar confederacy. These we might think of as estates rather than ethnic groups, including the "Craftsmen" (*Urad*), the "Goldsmiths" (*Altachin*), and the "Border Guards" (*Zakhachin*).

When Muslims from the oases of Xinjiang and elsewhere in Central Asia entered Junghar service, a similar system was applied. Some Muslims were enrolled in the Junghar army as artillerymen, known as the "Gunners" (*fuchin*). Others served the Junghars by leading long-distance trading caravans, and in the process doubled as diplomatic envoys on missions to Moscow or Beijing. Within the Junghar estate classification, these were known variously as the "Merchants" (*Bāzārgān*) or the "Caravaneers" (*Kārvāniyya*).[31] Like other *otog*s, these estates developed a corporate identity and social hierarchies of their own. Muhammad Amin Kashgari, author of a work dealing with the Junghar conquest of the Tarim Basin, described the Caravaneers in Islamic terms as a distinct social group (*tā'ifa*), headed by an elite of wealthy amirs and mirzas.[32]

The largest, and most historically significant, of these new *otog*s were the "Peasants" (*Taranchi*), Muslim captives who were transported north to boost the agricultural output of the Junghar heartlands. The foothills of the Altay were one of the first destinations for these Taranchis. As early as 1639 a Russian explorer along the Irtysh River found "Bukharans working in agriculture," and in 1654 the tsar's emissary, Baikov, noted the presence of many "farming Bukharans" along the same route to Beijing.[33] This policy may also account for the origins of the Khotongs of Western Mongolia, a Muslim community in the service of local Mongol aristocrats since the eighteenth century.[34] In the early eighteenth century the center of Junghar authority shifted southward, making the Ili Valley the focus of Taranchi resettlement. In the 1720s the Russian Unkovskii saw there that "Bukharans in the Kontaishi's domains have established fields of wheat and various fruits."[35] The Junghar aristocracy drew most of these agricultural slaves from the Tarim Basin, but also conducted raids on rural populations farther west. To this day a small group of Turkic-speakers in the Ili Valley preserve the memory of an eighteenth-century migration from the Ferghana Valley.[36]

At a number of points in Central Asian history such occupational classifications have evolved into ethnic categories. The word "Sart" is a classic case of this: derived from a Sanskrit word meaning "merchant," it came to refer widely to sedentary Turkistani Muslims. It is difficult to determine if or when these Junghar estate categories developed into something more robust, into a sense of Bazargan or Taranchi community defined in historical or cultural terms. Although the Taranchis were internally divided by the community's diverse points of origin, it seems likely that the common experience of exile would have fostered new bonds among them. For some elite captives and their followings, adaptation to the Mongolian language and Buddhist culture of Junghar-held Ili also created a new divide between them and the Muslims of the south.

Accounts of the Qing invasion of Junghar-held Ili also created among the Ili Muslims. When Qing armies first reached the Junghar stronghold in the 1750s they freed two Naqshbandi shaykhs, Burhanuddin and Khoja Jahan, and sent them south to act as deputies in the Tarim Basin. The *khoja*s mobilized a following of loyal Ili Valley Muslims and seized control of Kashgar and Yarkand. In a striking passage in the *Tazkira-i Azizan* (ca. 1780), Muhammad Sadiq Kashgari described the coming of these Ili Valley Muslims as a shock for the locals. When the chiefs of the Tarim Basin went out to meet the two *khoja*s, he wrote, "they saw that their deportment was different, their speech was different, and their mannerisms were entirely different. They interacted among themselves differently, they looked different, the relationship between shaykh and disciple was different, their symbols of royal and religious authority were different, . . . the way they greeted each other was different, as was the way they said farewell."[37] This suggests that, to some at least, by the time of the Qing conquest the north/south divide among Xinjiang's Muslims looked stark, and the short-lived regime that the two *khoja*s instituted no doubt heightened this division. As one Kashgari informant recounted to Qing officials, "Khoja Jahan held a grudge against the old elites in Yarkand and Kashgar and killed them all, and depended entirely on the Oirat, Taranchis, and Bazargan."[38] Before long, the two *khoja*s broke ties with the Qing and rebelled, prompting the Qianlong emperor to dispatch an invasion of the south and annex it to his domains.

Who Were the Turban-Wearing Muslims?

Up until this point, Qing officials had had little experience in dealing with Turkic-speaking Muslims, and as they encroached on Junghar territory there was a tendency to treat them as a type of Mongol. They knew that the Muslim rulers of the Tarim Basin were descended from Chinggis Khan's second son, Chaghatay, and they had also encountered Muslims in the service of the Junghars, either as emissaries or official caravan leaders, who were familiar with Mongolian speech and customs. At the time of the Qing invasion of Xinjiang, there seems to have been a high degree of Mongol-Turkic bilingualism among its Muslim elite, particularly in the north. The Jesuit missionary Jean-François Gerbillon, a confidant of the Kangxi emperor, wrote regarding the "Tartars" of Hami and Turfan that "the language of these Tartars, which is apparently the same with that of the Yusbeks [i.e., the Uzbeks], is different from the Mongol tongue, but this last is commonly understood by reason of the great Commerce between the two Nations."[39] On this basis, the Kangxi emperor pronounced that "the Muslims do not differ in their customs from the Mongols," and the first Muslims of Hami and Turfan to submit to the Qing were treated in the same way as Mongolian aristocrats.[40]

The steppe route via Mongolia was the Qing court's main communication link with Xinjiang, so it was natural that it would tend to view these Muslims through a Mongol lens. Those who were observing the collapse of the Junghars from Gansu, by contrast, had a different perspective on the region. At the far end of the Gansu corridor, Qing officials encountered communities of Uyghurs who had been living in the outposts of Suzhou and Ganzhou since taking refuge there in the fifteenth century, and there is evidence that officials here viewed the Muslims of Xinjiang similarly as Uyghurs. The 1779 Qing gazetteer of Ganzhou, for example, in describing the conquest of Xinjiang, refers to the anti-

Qing rebels of the 1750s, Burhanuddin and Khoja Jahan, as the "Uyghur leaders" (*Huihu shouzhang*).[41]

In the wake of its conquest the Qing court was content to treat its new subjects simply as Muslims (Huizi), though this was not simply a recognition of the community's confessional status. While Qing officials knew that Muslims were followers of Islam and its Prophet Muhammad, they did not treat the empire's Muslims as a single religious community. For the Qing bureaucracy, the sedentary Muslims of the Tarim Basin were clearly distinct from their Kazakh or Kirghiz neighbors, whom they often excluded from the category of Muslim entirely. To distinguish them from the Chinese-speaking Muslims, officials referred to the Muslims of Xinjiang as "Turban-Wearing Muslims" (Chantou Huizi). In the empire's political geography, this sense of the Xinjiang Muslims as a territorially bounded community corresponded to the notion of the Tarim Basin as the "Muslim territory," Xinjiang's Huibu.

While this terminology suited the Qing interest in "fixing frontier peoples in distinct places, with distinct identities," as Peter Perdue puts it, it equally corresponded to a territorialized sense of Muslim identity prevailing among Xinjiang Muslims.[42] Although Islam linked these Muslims to a religious community beyond the bounds of the Qing, it would be wrong to assume that they thought of themselves as part of anything like an "Islamic world." Among Chinese-speaking Muslims in the interior, narratives of communal identity emphasized a migration from the lands of Islam's founding, but for the Muslims of Xinjiang, there was no such legend of exodus from the Holy Land. Islam had come to Xinjiang and constructed a new spiritual landscape out of sites that already held meaning for local communities. This sense of Muslim community is reflected in sources such as Muhammad Sadiq Kashgari's *Tazkira-i Azizan*, which details the history of a Tarim basin society defined by its devotion to local saintly dynasties, and threatened as much by its Kirghiz or Kazakh neighbors as by the pagan Junghar Mongols.[43] Similarly, local authors often drew a distinction between Turkic-speaking Muslims as "the Muslims" and Xinjiang's Chinese-speaking Muslims, known as "Dungans" in Xinjiang.[44]

In discussing a similar phenomenon in Russian Turkistan, scholars such as Adeeb Khalid have emphasized the role of the Russian state in shaping "the Muslims" as a territorially bounded community with ethnic qualities.[45] While I do not see such terminology as a product of the Qing conquest, clearly Qing classifications and local self-perceptions were mutually reinforcing. Language itself bears witness to the presence of a territorialized Muslim identity during the Qing, with the term "Muslim" (*musulmān*) becoming synonymous with "Local" (*yerlik*). Muslim translators in Beijing, for example, when dealing with the Qing category of Hui, would translate it not as *musulmān* but as *yerlik*, and the Huibu as the "Locals' territory" (*yerlik aymaq*).[46] Elsewhere we find Xinjiang Muslims referring to their language as "Localese" (*yerlikchä*).[47] In the 1850s the tsarist foreign ministry sent Chokan Valikhanov on a reconnaissance mission to Xinjiang, and in his reports he treated *yerlik* as equivalent to Kashgari, the designation by which Xinjiang's Muslims were known in Russian Turkistan.[48]

On this evidence we might be inclined to treat "Muslim" and "Local" in Qing Xinjiang as ethnic, or proto-ethnic autonyms. Yet I hesitate to ascribe distinct in-group/out-group boundaries to Muslim/Local identity in Qing Xinjiang, as the confusion of these categories could equally lend a confessional coloring to "Local" identity. In the early 1880s the Russian explorer Grigorii Potanin visited the oasis of Hami and questioned its inhabitants as to their community's origins. One man described to Potanin how four acts of revelation had established the social divisions that he experienced in Hami: "God created two people, a father and a mother, and from these [two] the multitude of people were bred. They were born every day. Then God created four prophets and four books, which were sent to separate nations: the Bible, which is the law of the Russians; the Psalms of David, which is the law of the Qalmaqs; the Torah of Moses, which is the law of the Chinese; and Muhammad's Quran, which is the law of the Locals."[49] Potanin, who thought of Muslim identity in a strictly confessional sense, was confused by this account: "Local" here seemed synonymous with Muslim. If that was the case, then any Muslim might count as a Local. Potanin came away from Hami with the view that, paradoxically, the immigrant Tatars and Kazakhs from Russia that he met in Hami would also count as "Locals."

The geographic notion of a Muslim Territory (Huibu) was both singular and plural. As the "Muslim Territory" it represented the land of the Muslims, in the same way as Tibet and Mongolia were pieces in the Qing ethnoterritorial jigsaw. As "Muslim Territories" in the plural it had a more specific meaning, corresponding to the aristocratic fiefdoms that the Qing granted to local collaborators in the course of the conquest. According to historian Mulla Musa Sayrami, the Qianlong emperor (r. 1736–1796) publicly identified the Huibu as the patrimony of these Muslim aristocrats, even to Manchu officials. Sayrami describes a temple that once stood on the road leading south from Turfan to

Kashgar. In it hung the portraits of the first generation of Muslim aristocrats and a decree from the emperor: "I have made these men the guardians of the Seven Cities [of the Tarim Basin]. From now on, all officials who serve in the Seven Cities must come here and pay their respects!"[50] While occupying a prestigious position as go-betweens with the Qing emperor, these aristocrats, or *wang*s as they were known, sought to maintain the trappings of Islamic rule, and as far as possible they construed the Qing institutional context in Islamic terms. The Turfan *wang*s, for example, drew a link in their genealogy to the illustrious saint Muhammad Sharif and through him tapped into the Chaghatayid and Qarakhanid legacy. While serving in Yarkand in the 1760s, Turfan Wang Imin Khoja went by the grandiose title of "wang khan," and his sons and grandsons were called "shah."[51]

Like the Junghars, the Qing recognized the strategic importance of the Ili Valley and continued the policy of resettling Muslim peasants there from the south. The key difference in Qing policy was that these Taranchis were no longer enslaved to individual aristocrats but were incorporated into the network of Qing agricultural colonies in Ili, which consisted of garrison farms, colonies of transported convicts, civilian settlements, and Taranchi villages. The Taranchis not only survived as a distinct group within the "Turban-Wearing Muslim" population, but grew in size, a large proportion of the new influx hailing from Uchturfan, which rebelled against the Qing in 1765. By 1770 the Taranchis numbered more than six thousand households, and by the mid-nineteenth century this had risen to eight thousand. Some families were assigned to work the lands of the *hakim beg*, the local Muslim governor, while the rest fell within eight Taranchi districts, each administered by a "treasurer" (*shangbegi* or *ghaznachi*).[52]

In Qing scholarship, the identity of the empire's Muslims never became the object of study that the origins of the Manchus and Mongols did. A variety of views existed, each informed by different theories and admitting different forms of evidence. This form of ethnography linked peoples of the present to past groups described in dynastic histories according to a set of at times contradictory principles. Geographical continuity was one such principle, by which people were identified as the heirs to those who had previously occupied the same territory. Ethnographic similarity was another, linking people who exhibited similar lifestyles. Where it was possible to consult genealogies, particularly those of the aristocracy, these were also taken into consideration. Finally, the philological techniques developed by the school of "evidentiary learning" (*kaozheng*)

A prince (*taiji beg*) of Hami, a member of the Qing
aristocracy permitted to wear the Manchu queue, 1890.
(Grigorii Efimovich Grumm-Grzhimailo Collection. MAE
[Kunstkamera] RAS 643–5.)

were brought to bear in reconciling toponyms and ethnonyms, and gauging the
reliability of historical sources. These traditions provided resources for Qing and
Chinese scholars to construct a variety of theories regarding the identity of the
Muslims of Xinjiang.

   Language played little role in determining the relationship between various
peoples of the realm. The concept of "Turkic-speaking" peoples, so crucial to
Western perceptions of this region, seems not to have entered the discussion in
Qing China. For the most part, if Qing scholars drew a connection between
the Uyghurs of the past and any of the present-day empire's Muslims, it was
not with the Turkic-speaking Muslims of Xinjiang but with the Chinese-
speaking Muslim community. The early Qing scholar Gu Yanwu (1613–1682)

argued that the name of the Chinese-speaking Muslims (Huihui, or simply Hui) was derived from that of the Uyghurs (Huihu), suggesting there was a historical link between the Tang dynasty Uyghurs and the Hui.[53] Gu was cautious, though, knowing full well that the Yuan and Ming dynasty chronicles spoke of the Chinese-speaking Hui and the Uyghurs of Uyghuristan as two distinct groups, and "thus the *Huihui* and the *Huihu* came to be treated as two types of people (*zhong*) again." The Huihu > Huihui > Hui theory nevertheless proved compelling (and is probably correct), and since the Muslims of Xinjiang were similarly known as Hui, it could be extended to them too.[54]

Weighing against this etymological theory was the fact that it contradicted the principle of ethnographic similarity. As depicted in dynastic histories, the Uyghurs of the steppe were a link in a chain of nomadic groups that stretched back to the Han dynasty's great rival, the Xiongnu, and continued to the nomadic Mongols who now occupied the grasslands where the Uyghurs had originally roamed. Reconciling these contradictions was on the Qianlong emperor's mind when in 1759, on the eve of his army's final push into the Tarim Basin, he found an old bronze bowl among the collection at his summer retreat at Rehe and identified it as an Islamic work. Delighted at the coincidence, he took brush in hand to compose an inscription for the bowl, in which he reflected on the identity of the Xinjiang Muslims and their connection to the rest of his subjects. Responding to Gu Yanwu's theory of the similarity between Uyghurs (Huihu) and Muslims (Hui), Qianlong noted that Tang historians had unambiguously linked the Uyghurs to the nomadic Xiongnu, whose heirs the emperor identified as the Mongols, and he objected to Gu's (and Kangxi's) theory on these grounds: "The Muslims are not Mongols, they follow their own religion." Going on, he pointed out that while the Uyghurs of the Tang had been equestrian raiders practiced in mounted archery, "this is not something that the Muslims are capable of." He concluded that "it is simply because the words *Huihu* and *Huihui* sound similar that people connect the Turban-Wearing Muslims with [the Uyghurs]."[55] Yet the emperor was far from decided on the subject, and these ruminations did not prevent alternative views from circulating.

Qing officials in the field, working with local informants, grounded their analysis in the study of aristocratic genealogies, which they compiled both for intelligence reports and official publication. This research eschewed the sinocentric impulse to define the Muslims of Xinjiang in terms of categories derived from the Chinese historiographical tradition and linked them to peoples farther west, most commonly to Bukhara. According to one of the earliest descriptions of the Muslims of Xinjiang, "all the Muslims of the various countries originate from Bukhara."[56] It is tempting to see this association with Bukhara as in some way connected to the Russian habit of referring to all Turkistani Muslims as "Bukharans," and by extension to the Tarim Basin as "Little Bukhara," but the two do not have a common origin. Russia had a long history of diplomatic and commercial relations with Turkistan in which Bukhara figured prominently. By contrast, the Qing had only a hazy notion of Bukhara as a political actor, and I believe the link to Bukhara here reflects the fact that Xinjiang's Naqshbandi *khoja*s, with whom the Qing clashed but also collaborated, had genealogies tracing back to Bukhara, resting place of the eponymous founder of the Naqshbandiyya, Bahauddin Naqshband.

Familiarity with Chinese sources was uncommon among Xinjiang Muslims during the Qing but not completely unknown, particularly among the aristocratic families who interacted frequently with Qing officials. In the 1890s, Xinjiang's provincial governor Tao Mo (1835–1902) wrote to the hereditary *wang* of Hami inquiring into his family's origins. In his reply, the Hami *wang* demonstrated a certain familiarity with Chinese accounts of his region. As already mentioned, Ming Hami was identified as home to three different groups: the Muslims, the Uyghurs, and the mysterious Ha-la-hui. The Hami *wang* interpreted the first as referring strictly to the Chinese-speaking Muslims and traced the origins of Hami's Turban-Wearing Muslims to the remaining two: "The Uyghurs and the Ha-la-hui both professed Islam and dressed similarly. Previously they used white cloth to bind their heads and thus became known as White-Hat Muslims. Later there were others who used different colors, called Red-Hat Muslims. There is no difference between these groups, so they are all called Turban-Wearing Muslims, just as people in Jiangnan and Jiangxi are all known as Han." From within this confusing ethnic mix, the Hami *wang* specified his own family's origins as follows: "My line belongs originally to the White-Hat Muslims, and are mostly descended from Uyghurs and Muslims."[57]

Such exchanges were rare, though, and most Manchu and Chinese officials in Xinjiang did not inquire deeply into the origins of the province's Muslim subjects. Since the Turban-Wearing Muslims had no family names equivalent to Chinese *xing*, they found genealogical inquiries difficult. In the last decade of Qing rule, the dynasty called on officials to prepare new local gazetteers, requiring them to report on what "types of people" (*renlei*) were living in each county. From Xinjiang they received a wide variety of responses, showing a new sensitivity to observable ethnic traits, and a geographic frame of reference that exceeds earlier Qing descriptions, but no consistency. In these descriptions, the Xinjiang Muslims are commonly described simply as Locals (*tuzhu*), though the compilers of one held that it was in fact the Chinese-speaking Muslims of Gansu who were indigenous to Xinjiang, while the Turban-Wearing Muslims were simply "remnants of the Junghars." Most added some clarification regarding ethnic affiliation. Some describe them as of the "Arab type" (*Alabo zhong*), while others refer to them as Persians. In one, the Turban-Wearing Muslims are identified as Andijanis—a designation usually reserved for foreign Muslims.[58]

Andijanis and Kashgaris

An ambiguous sense of local (*yerlik*) identity must be distinguished here from native place solidarities and the idea that people in Xinjiang identified themselves by oasis of origin. From the nineteenth century onward, Orientalists and activists imparted negative connotations to what they saw as oasis parochialism, describing it as a reflection of the Turkistan Muslims' isolation and backwardness. Adapting the thesis to contemporary Xinjiang, Justin Rudelson has argued that the persistence of the oasis as the focal point of Xinjiang Muslims' loyalties explains the weakness of Uyghur nationalism.[59] The recent trend among Xinjiang scholars has been to reject both these positions, affirming the existence of a robust sense of protonational identity in nineteenth-century Xinjiang and a strong and widely held sense of Uyghur identity in the present day, manifested in everyday resistance as much as nationalist slogans.[60] While concurring with the second point, I am less convinced of the idea that a trans-oasis bond existed between, say, Muslims of Kashgar and Hami, that did not exist between Muslims of Kashgar and Andijan. In any case, there is no denying that oasis identities were among the most salient forms of community and solidarity in the past, as they remain today.

The tenacity of oasis identities in Xinjiang is often attributed to the isolation of oasis life, but I suggest that these boundaries were equally a product of inter-oasis interaction. In the process of conquering the Tarim Basin, for example, the Qing court appointed members of elite Hami and Turfan families to positions of authority in Kashgar and Yarkand, resulting in an influx that heightened the sense of a north/south divide in Xinjiang society. Or consider Xinjiang's trading communities, which like the Chinese traveled in networks that were shaped by native-place ties. Similar to the native-place lodges (*huiguan*) that the Sichuan, Tianjin, or Shaanxi networks established in Xinjiang, Muslim caravanserais were often identified by those they accommodated. A description of Aqsu from the 1870s, for example, records the existence of Khotani, Kashgari, Andijani, Yarkandi, and Dungan caravanserais.[61] Qing administrative practice built on these native-place ties, assigning headmen, or *aqsaqal*s, to the various trading communities. These headmen had the task of checking the paperwork of incoming goods and collecting duties. Accounts of Ürümchi in the late Qing depict the Chinese bazaar as divided into Tianjin, Shaanxi, and other native-place associations, while in Ürümchi's Muslim bazaar there were *aqsaqal*s for each of the Turfani, Aqsu and Kashgari communities.[62] As much as travel might broaden horizons, therefore, commercial competition and administrative structures required traders to locate themselves within an oasis-based network.

Beyond the bounds of Xinjiang, these oases identities were less salient, and to outsiders Xinjiang Muslims were known simply by the nearest departure point. Those who plied the mountain trails leading from Yarkand to Ladakh and India, for example, were known as Yarkandis. To the west, Kashgar was the city of the Tarim Basin most widely known among Muslims, who thus tended to be identified as Kashgari. In neighboring regions, the Tarim Basin was often referred to simply as the "Province of Kashgar," from which Russian scholars derived their term "Kashgaria." The historical record gives us many scholars and shaykhs in Islamic lands who went by the *nisba* al-Kashgari—most famous among them the eleventh-century lexicographer Mahmud al-Kashgari. Conversely, Muslims from Xinjiang's immediate neighbor, the khanate of Kokand, were known locally by the last major town they set off from—Andijan.

The roads from Kashgar to the west, one of the chief settings of this book, have been the scene of many migrations.[63] One anthropologist counted more than twenty toponyms in the neighboring Ferghana Valley bearing the name "Kashgar," or "Kashgari."[64] Such place-names also occur in the mountains to the south, where some Tajik communities trace their origins to émigrés from Kashgar.[65] Beginning in the seventeenth century, an identifiable exile community of Kashgaris emerged in the Ferghana Valley, coming under the rule of the khans of Kokand in the early eighteenth century. As struggles between rival Sufi factions in the Tarim Basin intensified, there was rarely a period in which prominent Kashgari *khoja*s and their retinues were not to be found among the Muslims of the Ferghana Valley.[66] The Qing conquest of Xinjiang only added to this exodus. Islamic sources give inflated figures for these migrations, but their impact was undoubtedly great. According to one account, on the first flight from the Qing in 1759, the *khoja*s Burhanuddin and Khoja Jahan led with them around twelve thousand families across the Pamirs to Badakhshan, nine thousand of whom eventually made their way to Kokand.[67]

From the mid-eighteenth century onward, meanwhile, Andijanis emerged as the dominant actors in cross-border commerce in the Tarim Basin, controlling the main east-west routes linking Xinjiang and Kokand. The Andijanis' economic strength was among the factors that obliged the Qing to reach a political accommodation with Kokand. Qing officials had at first assumed the right to appoint headmen among the Andijanis, as they did among all trading communities in the empire, whether foreign or domestic. Over time, though, Kokand wrested control of this position, and with it the right to collect customs from foreigners in Xinjiang, as well as household dues from mixed Andijani-Kashgari families. These *aqsaqal*s, as the Andijani headmen were known, were tax farmers, who pledged to provide a fixed annual sum to the Kokand court.[68] In turn, the *aqsaqal* in Kashgar appointed deputies elsewhere in the Tarim Basin, selling the positions for a fee depending on the level of commercial activity in the town.[69] The first *aqsaqal*s were merchants, but as the position grew more lucrative, Kokand's military class came to monopolize it. The Kokandi *aqsaqal* in Kashgar resembled an official consul, with a staff that included tax collectors, a treasurer, and other officials with policing duties. Qing concessions to Kokand also entailed elements of extraterritoriality: the *aqsaqal* employed religious functionaries to handle the affairs of Kokandi subjects according to the sharia, and where Qing statutes applied, the *aqsaqal*s encouraged Kokandis to flout them.[70] Tensions between the Andijanis and local Muslims were common, and at least once in the 1840s Andijanis had to erect barricades around their homes to defend themselves from rioting Kashgaris.

The presence of a significant population of Kashgaris in Kokand and Andijanis in Xinjiang was an important precondition for a series of *khoja*-led rebellions in nineteenth-century Xinjiang, a conflict described in rich detail by Laura Newby.[71] On at least two occasions the Kokandi *aqsaqal* was instrumental in betraying Kashgar to rebels invading from Kokand and was promoted to high rank by the victors. In the 1820s Khoja Burhanuddin's grandson Jahangir organized the first foray into Qing territory, which soon turned into a full-scale Kokandi invasion, headed by Muhammad Ali Khan (d. 1842). The defeat of Jahangir, in turn, set off a new wave of migration from Kashgar to the west. One account tells us that during the retreat from Xinjiang, Muhammad Ali

Khan compelled seventy thousand Kashgari families to accompany him.[72] Mirza Shams-i Bukhari, a participant in the second major incursion in 1830, says that on its eve around twelve thousand Kashgaris were residing on Kokandi soil.[73] Following the defeat of this second incursion, Chokan Valikhanov claims that as many as seventy thousand Kashgaris fled to Kokand and settled around Khojand or on the outskirts of Tashkent.[74] Again, in 1847, during the so-called Seven Khojas rebellion, we read that up to twenty thousand Kashgaris escaped from Qing territory.[75] Many of these died along the way, their remains lining the mountainous roads for years to come. Finally, after the defeat of Vali Khan Törä's raid in 1856, another fifteen thousand are said to have left Kashgar.[76]

Chokan Valikhanov, the best source we have on this émigré community, says that in the 1860s there were a total of fifty thousand Kashgari households living in the Ferghana Valley.[77] On this basis, some have calculated that there were as many as three hundred thousand Kashgaris in Kokandi territory in the nineteenth century—around half the khanate's entire population![78] This seems excessive, but perhaps not by much. When bands of Kashgaris escaping the collapse of Yaqub Beg's emirate flooded into the town of Osh in 1877, tsarist officials reported that half of them could be accommodated "in the houses of relatives, since almost a third of the population of Osh consists of Sarts who are natives of Kashgar and had migrated here in the Islamic period."[79]

To a limited extent there were cultural differences between the communities. Valikhanov tells us, for example, that Kashgaris were believed to be good musicians.[80] Some were struck by the way that Kashgaris called each other "so-and-so akhun"—for example, Dawut Akhun, Turdi Akhun—and started calling the immigrants "the Akhuns" (*Akhunlar*), a nickname still in use in the Ferghana Valley.[81] Such markers were not so significant, though, as to prevent the Kashgaris from blending into the local population while retaining memory of Kashgari origins. As long as the sporadic anti-Qing violence continued in Xinjiang, the Kashgaris in Kokand cultivated a certain prestige for themselves as holy warriors. "Central Asia was overrun gradually by Kashgarians," Valikhanov noted wryly in the 1850s. "They gave exaggerated descriptions of the misfortunes of their country, and of the injustice and oppression of the Chinese, and complained that the infidels carried off their wives and daughters and prohibited the free observance of their religious rites. The Kashgarians became the objects of universal respect."[82] New shrines sprang up where the martyrs of the jihad had dwelt, and rituals associated with Kashgari saints such as Afaq

Caravanserai on the Osh-Kashgar road, 1915. (Photograph by Percy M. Sykes. © The British Library Board Photo 1042/[46].)

Khoja helped to maintain these traditions. One émigré who wrote of his exile took the pen name Khoshhal Gharibi, "the forlorn happy one." His literary identity expressed both his good luck in escaping Kashgar alive and his misery at being parted from his beloved homeland (*vaṭan*): "I am struck by pain without remedy, / From my own country it has parted me. / Kashgar, that is to say, was my nation, / And for years my place of habitation. / But then Kashgar was defeated and fell, / Laid waste at the hands of the infidel."[83] Never at peace in Kokandi territory, Gharibi likened himself to Majnun, the love-struck madman of Persian poetry, wandering endlessly in search of union with his beloved Layli.

Gharibi's was a lone voice, yet his work seems to support the view that the memory of jihad and flight served to distinguish the Kashgaris from their neighbors. As Kokand fell to the Russians in the 1860s and 1870s, the notion of the Kashgaris as a bulwark against the infidel must have lost some of its currency.

For their part, Russian administrators saw little need to distinguish the Kashgari immigrants they found in the Ferghana Valley from the native population, whom they treated collectively as Sarts. For administrative purposes the significant dividing line was imperial subjecthood, and in Russian sources the term "Kashgari" seems to refer exclusively to Qing subjects. In 1897, when the tsarist empire carried out its first empire-wide census, the Ferghana Valley recorded only 14,915 Kashgaris, a far cry from the possibly hundreds of thousands of individuals of Kashgari origins.[84] This census can be difficult to interpret, relying as it did on the respondents' own notion of what their native tongue was, but subsequent population surveys support my reading. These statistics show low but increasing numbers of Kashgaris in the Ferghana Valley as economic opportunities enticed traders and laborers to cross the border: 47,388 in 1904 and 50,238 in 1906, figures that correspond well with Chinese estimates of the sojourning population.[85] Officially at least, what distinguished a Kashgari from a Sart of Kashgari background was a Qing passport.

Orientalism and the Identity of the Uyghurs

To complete this preliminary discussion, I turn to the scholarly traditions of western Eurasia, which gradually came to dominate global perceptions of the history and identity of the peoples of Asia. For Orientalists in seventeenth- and eighteenth-century Europe seeking to account for the great migrations of people in history (*völkerwanderungen*), the Uyghurs of the steppe, and of Uyghuristan, left behind traces in a wide range of historical records, providing entry points into a remote and obscure world. As John Pocock has discussed, Enlightenment Europe's interest in the steppe nomad reflected a renewed interest in notions of barbarism and civilization in Christian Europe's own past.[86] Scholars were initially little interested in clarifying the chronology or ethnic identity of the peoples they encountered, focusing instead on fitting the evidence of foreign scholarly traditions into Europe's prevailing views of postdiluvian world history and its own barbarian invasions. As Orientalism professionalized and comparative linguistics intruded on historiography in the nineteenth century, though, a picture of the Uyghurs as a historical people gradually came into focus.

French and Jesuit scholars were pioneers in the study of Asia, sometimes drawing on Chinese sources and sometimes on Islamic. Among the first European notices on the Uyghurs since the thirteenth-century missions of Friar William of Rubruck or Marco Polo to the great khans was an entry in Barthélemy d'Herbelot's *Bibliothèque orientale* (1697), where they appear as the Igur, or Aigur. Herbelot's eclectic compendium of notices on Oriental peoples and places drew heavily on the Ottoman statesman Katib Çelebi's writings on geography and hence presented a view of the Uyghurs as they appear in Islamic sources. The legend of Uyghur origins was given according to Abu'l-Ghazi Bahadur Khan's *Genealogy of the Turks*, a work that was soon published in Latin translation.[87]

Chinese sources on the Uyghurs were first introduced to Europe's scholarly community in the 1730s in the missionary Antoine Gaubil's biography of Chinggis Khan. Gaubil here described the Ouei-ou-eul (representing Wei-wu-er) of Turfan and their submission to the world conqueror. Following him, in the 1750s Joseph de Guignes discussed the Uyghurs of the steppe in his *Histoire générale des Huns, des Turcs, des Mogols, et des autres Tartares occidentaux*. Yet the link between the Uyghurs of Islamic sources and Chinese references was not immediately obvious to these scholars. Subsequent editions of Herbelot's *Bibliothèque* were supplemented by the work of the Jesuit Visdelou, who provided sinological commentary on Herbelot's entries, along with a separate *Histoire de Tartarie* in which he translated all known references to the steppe Uyghurs of the Tang dynasty without connecting these Uyghurs to Xinjiang at all. Instead, he applied the principle of geographic continuity and traced the inhabitants of Uyghuristan to the Jushi, a polity known from Han dynasty chronicles.[88]

The reconciliation of these diverse sources was the work of the polyglot Julius Klaproth (1783–1835), an enterprising and wide-ranging philologist. Acquainted with classical references to the Uyghurs, in 1805–1806 he sought out their descendants while serving on a Russian embassy to China. Passing through the Sino-Russian trading post of Kiakhta, he enquired among Muslims there as to the existence of such a people, and was told that they could be found in the vicinity of Turfan to the south. Much to his regret, Klaproth failed to enter Xinjiang, but he did succeed in tracking down a man from Turfan living in the outpost of Ust Kamenogorsk and took from him a short list of words in what he believed to be the "Uyghur" language.[89] Upon returning to Paris, Klaproth scoured Islamic, Chinese, and Manchu sources for further references to the history of the Uyghurs, first publishing his findings in 1811.[90] Klaproth argued that the Uyghurs of Islamic sources were the same people as the Huihu of the Chinese chronicles and could be identified with contemporary Turkic-speaking communities of Xinjiang. He also analyzed the Uyghur script, describing a chain of transmission leading from the Syriac script, via Sogdian to Uyghur, and eventually to the Mongolian and Manchu scripts. Klaproth's findings were well received and made their way into the works of Abel Remusat, Europe's first chair of sinology. Published in 1820, Remusat's magnum opus, *Recherches sur les langues tartares*, drew the same conclusions regarding the Uyghurs, and like Klaproth he described Uyghur as a language still spoken by the inhabitants of the lands between Kashgar and Hami.[91]

Klaproth's work was groundbreaking, but not all were convinced. His monograph drew a fierce response from an unexpected quarter—the Moravian missionary and Mongolist Isaac Jacob Schmidt (1779–1847), who penned an article in 1818 attacking Klaproth's conclusions.[92] At the time, Schmidt was working in Saint Petersburg on manuscripts of a seventeenth-century Mongolian history, Sagang Sechen's *Jeweled Chronicle* (*Erdeni-yin Tobči*), and was therefore working with an ethnolinguistic lexicon very different from that of his Western European Orientalist counterparts. The *Jeweled Chronicle*'s account of the invention of the Mongolian script differs significantly from Klaproth's Islamic sources, and to the extent that Uyghurs feature in the text at all, they do so as Buddhist nomads with Tibetan-sounding names. Rejecting Klaproth's conclusions on the Turkic identity of the Uyghurs, Schmidt argued that they were identical with the Tangut, that is, a Tibetan-speaking people of the Qinghai plateau. He ridiculed the table of letters that Klaproth had labeled as the "Uyghur alphabet" as simply "badly-written Mongolian" and dismissed Klaproth's account of its origins as a fabrication.

This was the opening salvo in the *Uiguren-Streit*, a bad-tempered fracas typical of nineteenth-century philology. To bolster his position, Klaproth published a second edition of his book, adding new linguistic materials drawn from Ming dynasty translation manuals, provided to him by the Jesuits in Beijing.[93] Schmidt held firm, continuing to insist that the theory of the Uyghurs as a Turkic-speaking people was a "chimera."[94] He called into question the authenticity of Klaproth's Ming documents and suggested that Rashiduddin's folkloric account of the origins of the Uyghurs—one of Klaproth's key texts—was a concoction that could be attributed to Rashiduddin's misreading of Mongolian sources. In reply, Klaproth ridiculed Schmidt's methodology and conclusions, summarizing his views in a piece that he optimistically titled a "definitive demonstration" that the Uyghurs were racially Turkic.[95] Schmidt, of course, was not finished, producing another book in 1826 criticizing Klaproth's views.[96] Then, in 1828, with the field divided between a majority who saw the Uyghurs

as Turks and a minority who argued for their Tibetan origins, the Russian Orthodox monk and sinologist Bichurin intervened with a third position, arguing
on the basis of geographic continuity that the Uyghurs had been Mongols.[97]

By now Klaproth could not rouse himself to prosecute the *Uiguren-streit* any
further, and from this point on the field progressed slowly. Works in Uyghur
script had been identified in libraries in the 1820s, but were not edited and published for another half-century.[98] The next breakthrough came in 1870, when
the Hungarian Arminius Vambery published Yusuf Khass Hajib's *Qutadghu
Bilig*, a didactic text written at the court of the Muslim Qarakhanids in the
eleventh century. In Europe the history of the Qarakhanid dynasty was even
less well known than that of the Uyghurs, which led many scholars to treat any
text in Uyghur script as a product of the Uyghurs themselves. Vambery thus
introduced the *Qutadghu Bilig* to the Orientalist community as "an ancient and
unique linguistic monument of the Uyghur people" and depicted the Uyghurs
as spreading across Central Asia from Gansu as far as Samarkand, which he
suggested had been founded as a Uyghur colony. Vambery was more cautious
than Klaproth on the issue of linguistic continuity, though, criticizing Klaproth's belief that the Muslims of Chinese Turkistan still spoke the language
of the ancient Uyghurs: "The lexicon out of a mouth of one of today's Turfanis,
in which the learned Klaproth delighted for some forty years, can provide no
genuine trove of Uyghur linguistic material." On this point he held a view much
closer to that of linguists today, namely that the "spiritual and physical influence of Transoxiana" had brought to Xinjiang a heavily Arabic- and Persian-
influenced form of Turkic that was remote from Old Uyghur in its phonology
and vocabulary.[99]

The Triumph of Turkology

To some, now, these questions were of more than purely scholarly interest. In
the 1860s a massive anti-Qing uprising shook northwest China and drew new
attention to the identity of China's Muslims. In response to these developments, in 1867 Russia's leading expert on Islam in China, the sinologist Vasilii
Vasiliev, gave a lecture at Saint Petersburg University, "On the Movement of
Muhammadanism in China."[100] In his speech Vasiliev argued that the rebellion
indicated the vitality of Islam in China, contrasting this with the lethargy of
China's dominant Buddhist and Confucian civilizations. This led him to the
sensational conclusion that China was on the way to becoming a Muslim

country, a prediction that soon made its way into British and French works on Islam in China.[101]

Vasiliev had served at the Russian Orthodox mission in Beijing for many years, and his views were informed by the Chinese *kaozheng* tradition. In explaining the identity of China's Muslims he endorsed Gu Yanwu's thesis of a link between the name Uyghur and the Chinese word for Muslim (Huihui/ Hui), but went further in his efforts to dispel the ethnonymic confusion. Showing the tenacity of Schmidt's theories, Vasiliev postulated that these Uyghurs, a people who had played "an insignificant role in Central Asia," were synonymous with the Tanguts. In support of this view he held that the name "Dungan" or "Tungan," by which the Hui were known among Turkic-speaking Muslims, was simply a corruption of the word "Tangut." Since the domains of the Tibetan-speaking Tangut had once stood between China and lands to its west, Muslims in China were either Uyghur/Tangut converts to Islam, or migrants from Central Asia, who had picked up the Tangut/Tungan ethnonym while traveling through Tangut domains. Further, he argued that these Muslims had exploited a similarity between the Chinese names for the Tangut kingdom (Daxia) and Arabia (Dashi), to deliberately obscure their Tangut origins and claim the more prestigious (for Muslims at least) Arab descent. Tangut = Dungan = Huihui = Uyghur. It was a triumph of Russian *kaozheng* scholarship.

Vasiliev's theories led him, like Schmidt, to deny any Turkic element in Uyghur history. This put him at odds with scholarly trends, which were increasingly privileging linguistic affiliation above all other considerations. Turkology, the study of Turkic languages and peoples, was a late-blooming field in comparison with other fields of Orientalism and historical linguistics. It was not until the 1850s that German scholars conducting fieldwork in Russia produced the first scientific descriptions of living Turkic languages, and it was a German, Vasilii Radlov (or Wilhelm Radloff), who emerged as the leading representative of this so-called new school of Russian Turkology. While working as a teacher in the Altay in the 1860s, Radlov spent his summers traveling and collecting folk stories and oral epics among the Turkic-speaking peoples of Russia, including a trip to Ghulja in 1862. Radlov's collections were not simply extensive, they had a literary quality that has allowed them to serve as the basis of many "national literatures" of the Turkic-speaking peoples of Russia.

In response to the Muslim uprising in China, in 1868 Radlov traveled back to the Ili Valley to investigate it firsthand, while fighting was still raging in

Ghulja. In his reflections on the trip, Radlov squared the circle on earlier debates by postulating the existence of two groups of Uyghurs: the "Northern Uyghurs" of the steppe and the "Southern Uyghurs" of Hami and Turfan. Like Visdelou a century before him, he traced the Uyghurs of Hami and Turfan back to the Jushi of the Han dynasty, and saw both the Chinese-speaking Dungans and the Turkic-speaking "Tatars of Little Bukhara" as their descendants.[102] Yet he did not follow Klaproth in believing that these people still were Uyghurs, or that their native tongue was Uyghur. The term "New Uyghur," which was gaining currency in scholarly circles, had no place in Radlov's linguistic recordings or dictionaries, and his texts from Ghulja were published as specimens of the "Taranchi" dialect.

In Russia the rediscovery of the Turkic past was in many ways a collaborative project between Russian and Muslim intellectuals. Radlov played an important role in mediating the relationship between Muslim reformists and the tsarist state's own plans for Russified schooling among the empire's Muslims. Following his second trip to Semireche, in 1871 Radlov was appointed inspector of Tatar, Bashkir, and Kazakh schools in Kazan, where he collaborated with pioneers of modernized pedagogy among Tatar intellectuals. This meeting of the minds led to the opening of a teachers college in Kazan for Tatar students and to the cross-fertilization of Islamic and Orientalist traditions of scholarship, as local historians seeking to construct a Tatar or Bolghar national history drew on Russian sources for their work. Such initiatives sat well with Radlov's views on the importance of rescuing Turkic folk traditions from Arabic and Persian intrusions, as well as the Kazan linguistic school's tenet that the structure of the spoken language revealed the essence of ethnic identity.[103] Similar collaborations developed elsewhere in the empire among officials and native literati. The tsarist officer Nikolai Pantusov, for example, spent many years collecting folk stories among the Taranchis in Ghulja and Semireche and also edited and published the works of Taranchi and Kashgari authors.[104]

In 1884 Radlov left Kazan and took up appointment as director of the Asiatic Museum in Saint Petersburg, where he produced his second great encyclopedic work, his dictionary of Turkic dialects (published 1888–1911), and also published an edition of the *Qutadghu Bilig* (1910). He arrived just as the great fin de siècle Turkological boom was starting, commencing with the discovery of a set of Turk and Uyghur inscriptions in Mongolia in an unknown runic script. Radlov set to work on deciphering these texts, knowing that he was in competition with the Danish scholar Wilhelm Thomson. This classic scholarly rivalry brought to the fore a methodological divide between the Western European and Russian schools, with each side playing to its particular strengths. Those in Berlin or Paris prided themselves on having access to the best libraries and the latest scientific methods, and saw these as the key to solving the philological and historical problems that the inscriptions posed. Those working in Russia, on the other hand, valued the fieldwork opportunities that Russia's many Turkic-speaking peoples provided and hoped that accumulating data from living languages would help them unlock the mysteries of dead ones. Radlov and his circle in Saint Petersburg were inclined to see links between the present and the past where others did not, and in the wave of expeditions that scoured northwest China for manuscripts and buried cities at the turn of the century, the Russians not only sent out archaeologists and geographers, but also field linguists. The first of these was Nikolai Katanov, a leading "native" (*inorodets*) intellectual in the Russian academy, who spent the years 1889–1892 traveling in western Mongolia and Xinjiang, becoming the first scholar to conduct linguistic research in Hami and Turfan.[105]

Thomsen ultimately beat Radlov to deciphering the Orkhon inscriptions. In 1893 he announced his successful reading and in 1896 published a full translation and transcription of two inscriptions, to great scholarly acclaim. In the deserts of western China, meanwhile, discoveries continued, with the focus shifting from inscriptions to manuscripts, and from Mongolia to the deserts of Xinjiang and Gansu. The Prussians organized the first expedition to the oasis of Turfan, while Aurel Stein set off from British India on the first of many expeditions scouring the Tarim Basin for buried cities. On his second expedition in 1906–1908 Stein skirted the south of Xinjiang and headed to the cave monastery of Dunhuang in Gansu, where he famously acquired the first manuscripts from its long-sealed monastic library. Sites such as Turfan and Dunhuang provided Orientalists with a veritable treasure trove of frescoes, manuscripts and text fragments, much of it shedding light on the Buddhist Uyghur society of Uyghuristan and presenting a host of new challenges for philologists.

Radlov, as a member of the Russian Committee for the Study of Central Asia in Saint Petersburg, was involved in planning and directing Russia's archaeological missions to China and all along remained convinced of his fieldwork approach to historical linguistics. At a meeting of the committee in 1910 discussing the Russian response to the flood of new texts from Xinjiang, he argued that "for the best comprehension of these texts it is necessary to dedicate the same research to the last remaining dialects that preserve linguistic features of the Uyghur language."[106] The dialects that Radlov had in mind were not those of the Muslims of Xinjiang but of the little-known Yellow Uyghurs of Gansu, a small and isolated community that preserved the name, Buddhist faith, and, Radlov hoped, language of the ancient Uyghurs. To carry out this work he recommended his most promising student, Sergei Efimovich Malov (1880–1957).

Malov made two trips to western China, the first in 1909–1911 and the second in 1913–1915, and in doing so became Russia's leading authority on the living Turkic languages and peoples of China. His trip largely dashed Radlov's hopes that linguistic fossils of Old Uyghur could be found somewhere in China's west. "I must disappoint you," he wrote to his teacher in 1910 from the mountains of Gansu, "but the lexicon of the contemporary Uyghur language is unlikely to contribute to elucidating obscure points in ancient Uyghur texts."[107] In other respects, though, the trips were a great success, not least because they yielded the first examples of previously unknown living Turkic languages such as Yellow Uyghur and Salar. Malov also collected a wide range of recordings on what he called the "Turkish dialects" of Chinese Turkistan. His manuscript finds were impressive too: from Chinese book collectors in Ürümchi he received a number of texts in Uyghur and runic script as gifts, and his visit to a Yellow Uyghur Buddhist monastery turned up a stunning Old Uyghur manuscript.

The Saint Petersburg scholar's visit must have been something of an event for Xinjiang's diaspora of Russian subjects, and while passing through Malov socialized with the local consuls and Russian-subject Muslims. On his second expedition, the linguist met in Ürümchi a Tatar named Burhan Shahidi, an entrepreneur from Kazan who had been doing business in Gansu and Xinjiang for a number of years already. Shahidi, like many Russian Muslims of the day, took a keen interest in the progress of Turkological research and reported on Malov's work among the Yellow Uyghurs for the Orenburg Tatar newspaper *Time* (*Vaqït*).[108] In terms of the twentieth-century history of Xinjiang, the chance meeting was an encounter worth noting: each in his own way, Malov and Shahidi were to figure in the emergence of Uyghur nationalism in decades to come. It also exemplifies the way in which Orientalist discourses were coming to enter the public sphere among Muslims in Russia, a theme to which I will return.

The communal narratives of Muslim identity that circulated during the Qing, and the nineteenth- and early-twentieth-century Orientalist tradition, were an interconnected and swirling mass of historical narratives and ethnonyms. The *Times* correspondent George E. Morrison, who rode a horse through Xinjiang in 1910, found his interviews with the province's missionaries, diplomats, and Chinese officials frustrating: "I have never met such a confusion of theories about the different races of these parts as those of people who ought to be authorities on the subject."[109] Had Morrison inquired among the locals, he might have found a few well-read individuals, familiar with either Islamic or Chinese historiography, who thought of themselves as descended from the Uyghurs, but the name would have meant little to the vast majority of Xinjiang Muslims.

Far from Xinjiang, though, the Uyghur legacy was emerging as a key element in a revised view of Turkic history. Orientalist circles were also discussing the idea that somewhere in western China this legacy lived on. For those who wished to do so, there was a foundation here to construct the Muslims of Xinjiang as a nation linked to the Uyghurs of the past, though that was far from the only possible conclusion that could be drawn. While some confusion persisted surrounding the question of linguistic continuity, few if any participants in the Turkological boom were willing to postulate a direct link between the Uyghurs and a people of the present. We should be wary of presuming that Qing categories of identity, or scholarly romanticism, led smoothly to the emergence of a Uyghur nation. This story is too complicated to be reduced to the top-down construction of identity or the intellectual history of the "Uyghur" ethnonym. Both of these perspectives, while necessary, leave significant gaps in explanation, not least in accounting for the way in which this developing discourse intersected with the Muslims of Chinese Turkistan. From this point on, therefore, it is necessary to step back from these narratives and look instead at social and political conditions along the great political dividing line of colonial Turkistan.

CHAPTER TWO

The Making of a Colonial Frontier

I n the late 1850s, Qing officials might still have imagined the empire's western reaches in much the same way as they had in the 1750s, when the Qianlong emperor's generals carried out their conquest of the "New Frontier." That is to say, it was still possible to maintain the fiction that the Qing was the preeminent actor in the region and that the neighboring Kazakh sultans, the khans of Kokand, and even the rulers of Badakhshan and Afghanistan were but submissive tributaries of the Son of Heaven. Of course, such claims no longer withstood close scrutiny. After a series of local rebellions and incursions from Kokand, the Qing now kept to its line of border posts and abandoned any mediating role in Central Asian diplomacy. To pacify unruly Andijan merchants from Kokand the Qing court had granted them a series of trading concessions, which some have referred to as China's "first unequal treaty." Still, this was officially nothing more than an act of imperial beneficence toward an outlying polity. The Qing did not consider its dealings with Kokand as part of the "treaty system" with which it grappled after the Opium Wars.

Twenty years later things looked very different. Severed from the empire by a major Muslim rebellion in 1864, Xinjiang was eventually reconquered in 1877, leading to its transformation into a fully fledged province of the Qing in the 1880s. Equally significant in this period was the growing strength of Russian colonialism. Just as provincialization was bringing a Chinese-style administration to Chinese Turkistan, this transition also marks the point at which Russian Turkistan became Russian. The events linked the two Turkistans in new ways, both by creating new population flows between them and by projecting new imperial loyalties onto existing diasporas. The meeting of the two empires, perched atop a Muslim population sharing much more in common with each other than with their colonial overlords, produced a frontier society that had elements in common with China's coastal treaty ports but with the dynamics of extraterritoriality shaped by the distinctive environment. While Russian consuls and Andijani merchants collaborated in linking Xinjiang to Russia's colonial periphery, their own relationship was also mediated by the structures of Russian colonialism. This led to the emergence of institutions not found on the China coast, chief among them the presence of the trading headman, or *aqsaqal*.

The Muslim Rebellion in Xinjiang

By 1864, the wave of Muslim revolt that erupted among the Chinese-speaking Muslims of Shaanxi and Gansu had spread to the Qing Empire's far northwest, sparking local rebellions that Qing officials failed to suppress. As Kim Hodong has described, local grievances against heavy taxation and maladministration fed the discontent, but in addition to this many among the Dungans of Xinjiang seem to have believed a rumor that the Tongzhi emperor (r. 1861–1875) had decreed the extermination of the empire's Muslims. Successive uprisings in Kucha, Ürümchi, Kashgar, Yarkand, and Khotan were led mostly by the local clergy and Sufi shaykhs, but the events soon aroused interest in neighboring Kokand. The rebellion of the 1860s ultimately split Xinjiang in three ways. By 1867 a Kokandi officer named Yaqub Beg had consolidated his control of Xinjiang's south, ruling an independent emirate from Kashgar, while Dungan and Taranchi rebels occupied the north.[1]

Yaqub Beg's incursion into Xinjiang from Kokandi territory was in part a repetition of earlier anti-Qing rebellions and brought with it a new representative of the exiled Kashgari *khoja* dynasty. It also reflected deteriorating conditions in Kokand itself, which was hard pressed by Russia's military advance into Turkistan. Moving south from its line of forts across the Kazakh steppe, the Russians took Tashkent in 1865 and went on to reduce the khans of Khiva and emirs of Bukhara to client status. A participant in the battle of Tashkent, Yaqub Beg led a section of the defeated army to Kashgar, where they intervened in the ongoing rebellion and founded an Islamic state along Kokandi lines. With his Kokandi and Kashgari troops, joined by a few local Chinese who survived the invasion by converting to Islam, Yaqub Beg then set about incorporating other rebel strongholds into his regime, moving first on Khotan, then Kucha. Yaqub Beg distributed these towns to loyal tax-farming deputies, the majority of whom were part of the Kokand military elite that had accompanied him on the campaign to Xinjiang.

Having stabilized his rule in the south, the amir turned his eyes north to Ürümchi, where a Sufi shaykh known as Dawud Khalifa (Tuo Ming) claimed the loyalties of Xinjiang's Dungan Muslims. By early 1865 Dawud Khalifa, assisted by troops from Kucha, had seized control of not only Ürümchi but surrounding towns and proclaimed himself an Islamic king (*qingzhenwang*). Scholars concur that Dawud Khalifa was most likely a member of the Jahriyya Sufi brotherhood, and was in this way linked to the main fighting force of the Dungan rebellion in Gansu and Shaanxi. Yet the Ürümchi rebels never succeeded in opening a line of communications to the east and soon found themselves threatened by Yaqub Beg's advancing army. In 1869, Dawud Khalifa turned to the Russians for support to fend off the Kokandi amir, pledging submission to the tsar. "With our two peoples now forming a single family," his desperate letter reads, "we desire only to unite and with common purpose and combined strength to destroy our enemy and live in peace and friendship."[2] No response was forthcoming from the Russians, and after a series of campaigns Ürümchi fell to Yaqub Beg in 1872.

In the Ili Valley, meanwhile, the Taranchis had raised up a man named Abu'l-Ala as an independent sultan. Unlike Yaqub Beg in the south, who implemented strict Islamic law and compelled remaining non-Muslims in his territory to convert, the Taranchi regime in Ili had a distinctly post-Qing flavor to it. The sultan created a hybrid administration, merging categories of the Qing *beg* system such as the *ghaznachi* (who became the sultan's chief advisers), with Ottoman-inspired Islamic institutions such as the *qadi asker* (military judge). The Taranchi sultan dressed in ceremonial Qing armor, wielded a trilingual seal in Turkic, Manchu, and Chinese, and invited representatives of the valley's bannermen elite into his court, issuing them with Qing marks of rank such as the jeweled cap button.[3] The regime's recourse to Qing symbols of authority was a product of acculturation—knowledge of Chinese among the Taranchi elite was common—but also reflected the Taranchi sultan's weakness, which was soon to be tested by his neighbors. When Yaqub Beg set out on his first campaign against the Dungans in Ürümchi in 1870, he called on the Taranchis to commit troops to his support. Instead, Sultan Abu'l-Ala sent a letter to the Dungans promising them reinforcements. Unfortunately, his letter fell into Yaqub Beg's hands, causing an irreparable breach in relations.[4] Armed conflict between Yaqub Beg and the Taranchi Sultan was now a distinct possibility, and something that worried the Russians.

Further north, Tarbaghatay and the Altay saw similar violence, but without the consolidation of any new center of authority. On Chinese New Year in 1865, Dungans in Tarbaghatay ambushed and killed the local Qing officials, whom they had invited to the mosque for talks. The rebels then besieged the Qing fort, finally storming it in early 1866, by which time most of the garrison had already fled. Backed by Kazakh allies, the Dungans then headed south and joined forces loyal to Dawud Khalifa, who were occupying the town of Manas. Qing officials returned to the vacant Tarbaghatay and directed new contingents of Mongol troops on punitive expeditions against the Kazakhs of the Altay and Dungan brigands roaming Jungharia. All was not calm, though, and a second uprising broke out in Tarbaghatay in 1875, this time among Chinese convicts whom the Qing court had resumed exiling to Xinjiang.[5]

Yaqub Beg entered into negotiations with both the Russians and the British to win diplomatic backing for his position, but these efforts ultimately failed. A trade deal signed with the Russians in 1872 acknowledged Yaqub Beg as the de facto ruler of Kashgar, but in practice the amir restricted the flow of caravans in and out of his domains, creating an impediment to good relations. Meanwhile a series of exchanges with envoys from British India led to a similar commercial treaty in 1874. This permitted Yaqub Beg to obtain a small amount of arms from India but nothing more substantial in the way of support.

Meanwhile Yaqub Beg's success in creating an independent Islamic outpost in China was arousing interest in the Ottoman Empire. "Twenty years ago, the fact that there were Muslims in Kashgar was not known," Young Ottoman intellectual Namik Kemal noted with irony in 1872. "Now, public opinion tries to obtain union with them."[6] For the Ottoman sultan Abdulaziz (r. 1861–1876), interest in Yaqub Beg was probably motivated not so much by pan-Islamic zeal as by the fact that he had failed to defend the Muslims of Bukhara from Russian invasion and now had a chance to make recompense for this. Yaqub Beg's representatives arrived in Istanbul soon after the founding of the Islamic state in Kashgar, and the Ottoman press reported on events in Xinjiang closely. Yet it was not until 1873, having failed to ingratiate himself with either Russia or Britain, that Yaqub Beg announced his state to be formally subject to the sultan. With this act of submission, Istanbul dispatched a small party of officers and field guns, and for the remainder of its existence the Kashgar emirate's coinage and communal Friday prayers proclaimed the sovereignty of Sultan Abdulaziz.

In terms of the history of Kashgar-Istanbul contacts, the enlistment of Ottoman backing was a significant event. Yet this support was limited and proved insufficient to preserve Yaqub Beg's emirate from the advancing Qing forces. In 1877, while Qing general Zuo Zongtang's Hunanese troops were securing the Hami-Barköl approach to Xinjiang, Yaqub Beg suddenly died. His regime soon splintered, and many of his Kashgari troops deserted to the incoming Qing army, allowing them to seize the rest of the Tarim Basin with hardly a fight. As Zuo Zongtang's deputies restored Qing authority to the towns of the Tarim Basin, the Ottomans sheltered a number of leading representatives of the fallen emirate, but offered no public protest.

The Russian Occupation of Ili

By this time, subjects of the Russian tsar were a familiar presence in Xinjiang. Prior to its official opening to Russian trade in 1851, Russian Muslims, particularly Tatars from the Volga or Siberia, had long been visiting the bazaars of Tarbaghatay and Ghulja. It had become standard practice for these Russian Muslims to declare themselves subject to a Central Asian ruler who was permitted to dispatch tribute missions to Xinjiang. One account from the 1820s explains how Kazakh sultans facilitated these deceptions: "Our merchants, who are unable to appear in Ghulja under their own names, assume a false identity as Andijani, i.e., subjects of Tashkent, to which the Kazakh sultans testify. They state in their letters that the caravan is subject to this [Kazakh] authority, along with which they declare that out of deep devotion to the Chinese state, and for their own profit, gifts have been sent with the caravan."[7] The subterfuge seems to have been an open secret in which Qing officials connived. In 1845 a Russian envoy made his way to Tarbaghatay and Ghulja disguised as a Turkistani Muslim, but revealed his identity upon arrival. Instead of expelling him, the Xinjiang officials received him cordially and encouraged Russia to keep sending caravans, provided of course that they crossed the border in Central Asian guise.[8]

The 1851 Treaty of Ghulja legalized this preexisting commerce in terms similar to those prevailing in the cross-border trade of Kiakhta-Maimaicheng (in Mongolia), the main difference being that trade in Xinjiang was tax-free. Only bartering was permitted, and no goods could be exchanged on credit. Trade was limited to a period between March and December in designated trading colonies, or "factories," in Ghulja and Tarbaghatay, and not even dead Russians could remain on Qing soil: corpses were temporarily interred, pending removal with the next departing caravan.[9] In 1860, the Treaty of Peking between Russia and the Qing eased some of these restrictions and freed Russian merchants and missionaries to travel throughout China. The treaty also permitted the opening of a Russian consulate in Kashgar. In 1861 local officials assigned the Russians a plot of land on the banks of the Qizil River, but the only permitted routes to Kashgar ran through the khanate of Kokand, and for the time being political instability there deterred the Russians from dispatching either consul or trading caravans.

At the outbreak of the Muslim rebellion, Russia's withdrawal of its consuls and the loss of its trading quarters in Ghulja and Tarbaghatay came as a blow to tsarist commercial interests. The emergence in Kashgar of an Islamic state with ties to Russia's enemies in Kokand was also a source of anxiety, as was the thought that the British might take advantage of Yaqub Beg's weakness to extend their Indian frontier northward. Meanwhile, Kazakh nomads were exploiting the lawless environment to launch raids on Russian caravans from what was formerly Qing territory. In contemplating events in Xinjiang, Russian officials did so within a long-term perspective for Russian progress in Central Asia. The Ili Valley, they knew, offered a cultivated oasis in the dry steppe of Semireche—a potential breadbasket that could supply much of Russian Turkistan. Russian administrators naturally felt that their form of civilizing mission was better than anything that the Qing Empire offered local Muslims, and the wide thoroughfare connecting Jungharia to the Kazakh steppe troubled those who believed in "natural borders." Intrepid Russian colonists had already established themselves in the mountains north of Ili, and many in the empire's military and geographic circles felt that it was only a matter of time before part, if not all, of Chinese Turkistan became Russian.

In 1871, Russian officers seized on the flight to Taranchi territory of a Russian-subject Kazakh accused of murder to launch an invasion of the Taranchi sultan's territory. General Kolpakovskii's Cossack strike force, reinforced by a contingent of refugee Mongol bannermen, encountered little resistance in the six-week-long campaign. On the night of July 3, the deposed Sultan Abu'l-Ala handed over to Kolpakovskii the keys to the four gates of the Muslim city of Ghulja, along with his royal insignia: a sword, a silk parasol, and his trilingual seal.[10] To the gathered locals, Kolpakovskii declared that he had come to put an end to the constant warring among the peoples of the valley. To the world, Russia announced that it would hold on to Ili for as long as it took the Qing to pacify the rest of Xinjiang. This, of course, was something that many believed the Qing would never achieve. Thus commenced a decade of Russian rule in Ili that is known in diplomatic history as the "Ili Crisis."[11]

While the Russians deported the Taranchi sultan downriver to Vernyi, they sought out collaborators among his confidants. Prior to the Russian incursion, imperial envoy Baron von Kaulbars had carried out a diplomatic mission to the Taranchi court. On his journey in and out of the sultan's realm, he was escorted by a man called Bushri Jalilov, also known as Bushri Khaufi, "Bushri the Dangerous." Bushri was a prominent member of the sultan's court and was also a *bay*, that is, a wealthy merchant (one chronicle of the Taranchi rebellion calls him the "leader of all the *bay*s").[12] When they parted, Kaulbars presented his escort with a pair of binoculars "so that he might scout out his enemies from afar."[13] It was a hint, and Bushri took it. Six months later, on the night when the Russians occupied the town of Suiding and prepared for the assault on Ghulja, Bushri snuck out and presented himself to General Kolpakovskii, informing him that the city was defenseless and the Taranchis were on the brink of surrendering.[14] The Russians had found their man.

In place of Sultan Abu'l-Ala's administration, the Russian occupation brought with it the tsarist system of "self-administration" (*samoupravlenie*). Canton heads (*volostnoi*, known locally as *bolus*) presided over the three Taranchi cantons (*volost'*), and below them a cohort of headmen, or *aqsaqal*s, for each village.[15] Similar offices existed for the Ili Valley's various Kazakh, Dungan, and other populations. In place of the ceremonial jackets, peacock feathers, and buttons of rank with which these elites had displayed their receipt of the Qing emperor's grace, Russian occupation brought with it a new system of symbolic rewards, one based on wristwatches and medallions. A Russo-Chinese-Taranchi school was set up in a building formerly belonging to the Ghulja Sultan, aiming to provide Muslim children with at least a rudimentary level of Russian.[16] To smooth its introduction, the school obtained the blessing of Ghulja's chief qadi, though like most schools of its kind in Russia it failed to attract many students.

Among the Taranchis, the head of the native administration was the *aqsaqal* of Ghulja. In theory all such positions were elective, but in the case of Ghulja at least it was evident who was the preferred candidate: soon after the consolidation of Russian control, Bushri was proclaimed *aqsaqal* of Ghulja and remained so for the duration of the occupation.[17] Still a young man, he cut an authoritative figure on the streets of the bazaar. In 1873 American diplomat Eugene Schuyler met him on his visit to Ghulja and was impressed: "all classes of the population seemed to stand in great awe of him."[18] A menacing portrait of him and his sidekicks in Schuyler's travelogue leaves little doubt that as mayor

A view of Ghulja, with the main Taranchi mosque in the foreground, 1880. (Photograph by E. Delmar Morgan. Royal Geographical Society rgs029449.)

of Ghulja, Bushri "the Dangerous" was living up to his name. Bushri seems to have played host to most foreign visitors to Ghulja at this time. He was evidently a man of cosmopolitan tastes, entertaining Schuyler with an evening of Taranchi and Chinese music, and treating the Cossack officer Khoroshkhin to a performance of Chinese opera, to which he provided running translations for his guest.[19] Soon he would find ways to make his newfound preeminence pay off, mediating an unlikely business deal between Russian grain dealers and Zuo Zongtang's advancing army.

Cross-Border Commerce and the Rise of the Rich

The collapse of Qing rule and the encroachment of Russian forts and communications links from the north enabled Muslim merchants in Xinjiang finally to revive the lapsed north-south trading network from which they had profited under the Junghar Mongols. Until the middle of the eighteenth century, Tarim

Basin traders had occupied an important position in a north-south trade linking the territory to Russia and China via Junghar domains, but in the 1750s the Junghar civil war and the Qing invasion ended this profitable business. Russian customs records show that in the seventeenth and eighteenth centuries one of the most popular exports from Turkistan to Russia was a Yarkand textile known as *irketchin*. In 1747, 150,000 rolls of *irketchin* were shipped to Siberia; but by 1752 this had shrunk by 90 percent to 15,000, and in 1753 the export came to a complete halt.[20]

In the wake of the Qing invasion some locals found a niche in the provisioning business. Yet once they were ensconced in Xinjiang, the Qing military mostly met its needs by permitting Chinese and Dungan merchants to extend their networks from Gansu and Mongolia into Xinjiang. Those few Muslim aristocrats who were obliged to make periodic trips to the Qing court carried with them trading goods to sell in the capital, but this form of "tribute-trade" was not an option for most Muslims. As security concerns mounted toward the end of the eighteenth century, strict regulations were placed on local caravans exiting Xinjiang to the west.[21] As a result, there was little scope for Kashgaris to compete with the Andijanis or Dungans in long-distance trade to the west and east respectively. Visiting Kashgar in the 1850s, the tsarist spy Chokan Valikhanov left with the impression that a distinct mercantile estate simply did not exist in Xinjiang. As he saw it, the richest man in the Kashgar district was the shaykh of the shrine of Satuq Bughra Khan in Artush, whose wealth derived from pious donations.[22]

Kashgari traders took advantage of the rebellion to establish northward links via Russian forts such as Vernyi (founded 1854) and Kopal (1847) to the trading fairs of Novgorod and Irbit. In 1874, Sir Douglas Forsyth's British mission to Yaqub Beg found that the Andijanis still held a dominant position in the Kashgar bazaar, but they were not without Kashgari rivals. A list that the British produced of the richest men in Kashgar shows that of the top fifteen, ten were Andijanis and five were locals, a number of whom had employees stationed in Russian territory. Textiles were again among the leading exports from Xinjiang: Russian statistics show that in 1876, on the eve of Yaqub Beg's downfall, 890,000 rubles' worth of a local cloth known as *mata* was shipped to Semireche.[23] The ability to gain this slim foothold in Russia in the 1870s proved decisive in the formation of a new Kashgari elite of *bays*. Forsyth's mission found a certain Akhun Bay to be the richest Kashgari in the bazaar, commanding a capital of 100,000 taels.[24] Akhun Bay's family firm (the Akhunbayevs) was to remain the wealthiest and most politically influential Kashgari import-export business for the next sixty years.

It was in the north of Xinjiang that Russian commerce presented locals with the most lucrative opportunities, as locals inserted themselves into transactions between Russian firms and the Qing army. By 1875, Qing forces had pacified Gansu, and the court was conducting its "great debate" on whether to continue the continental campaign into Xinjiang or redirect its scarce resources to China's maritime defenses.[25] Basing himself in Lanzhou, Zuo Zongtang faced the perennial problem of supplying an army in China's far northwest. Granaries in Shanxi and Inner Mongolia were running low, and shipping grain up the Gansu corridor was bound to be slow and expensive. As much as he lobbied the court to fight on, he must have realized that his supplies would not allow it. It was at this point that a solution presented itself from an unlikely quarter—a Russian scientific and commercial mission that was making its way back through Gansu to Siberia. This was the mission led by Lieutenant Colonel Sosnovskii, scouting out new trade routes though China's west. Its sponsors included Siberian merchants, who hoped to build on the Russian foothold in Ili to establish connections in the Chinese interior.

So far, the Sosnovskii mission had little to show for its efforts; in terms of deals sealed, it was returning to Russia empty-handed. With anxious investors waiting in Siberia, Sosnovskii took a risk in Lanzhou. Without informing his companions, he called on Zuo Zongtang one evening and negotiated with him a contract to ship grain from Siberia to the Qing army—a thousand tons in 1875, and half as much again in 1876.[26] To pay for the supplies, Zuo instructed his financiers in Shanghai to contract a series of loans with the Hongkong and Shanghai Banking Corporation. Sosnovskii was delighted over the deal, but Zuo was equally satisfied with the price of 7.5 taels per picul (5 for the grain, 2.5 for transport). Both the speed with which the deal was sealed and its political implications worried some of expedition's members, who argued that to supply Chinese troops would only prolong the bloodshed in northwest China, and might eventually compel Russia to give up its recent acquisitions in Ili.[27] Once they were back in Russia, the mission's scientist penned an attack on Sosnovskii entitled *The Unsuccessful Expedition to China*, which he concluded with a copy of the controversial grain contract signed with Zuo Zongtang.

Sosnovskii's chief collaborator in the deal was Ivan Feodorovich Kamenskii, a guild merchant from Tomsk. Kamenskii shared Sosnovskii's enthusiasm for making commercial inroads into western China and was initially bullish about his prospects. "The supply of grain along the entire Chinese military column," he boasted to Turkistan officials in February 1876, "is now largely in my hands." Before he completed his deliveries, he urged Saint Petersburg to wring new economic concessions from the Qing: "Each day sees the passing of great historic opportunities. A month from now, with the delay in concluding a treaty [with the Qing], Russian commerce will suffer a great loss."[28]

Despite Kamenskii's confidence, however, the necessary quantities of grain were not easily found in Siberia, and Dungan bandits roaming Jungharia preyed upon his first caravans.[29] In response to these setbacks he shifted his operations south to Ghulja, where the bazaars were well stocked. Bushri Aqsaqal smoothed Kamenskii's entry into the local grain market, and through Bushri the Russian entered into partnership with a Kashgari cart dealer by the name of Vali Bay (Yoldashev, also known as Vali Akhun).[30] With grain and transport secured, and hungry Qing soldiers now camped only a few stages down the highway at Manas, Kamenskii, Bushri, and Vali Bay were poised to make a hefty profit. With Zuo's commanding officer, the Manchu Jin-shun (1831–1886), they struck a new deal for five thousand tons of grain at 4 taels a picul, cheaper than the original contract but still highly lucrative terms.[31] According to one account, Kamenskii was buying grain on the local market at (in Russian terms) 10–15 kopeks a *pud*, and selling it to the Qing army in Manas at an outrageous eight rubles, earning himself a 6000 percent profit![32] As a key go-between in the Ghulja grain bonanza, Vali Bay soon became the richest man in town.

Russo-Qing Treaty Negotiations and the Recovery of Ili

As the Qing army pushed onward, it drove parties of refugees into Russian territory, creating political complications between the two empires. In the winter of 1877–1878, thousands of Yaqub Beg's supporters took to the roads, some natives of Kokand, others Kashgaris, who joined the already sizeable Kashgari émigré population of the Ferghana Valley. Along with these were others from further afield: parties of Dungan Muslims from the provinces of Shaanxi and Gansu, remnants of militias who had been fighting the Qing since the 1860s. One group were adherents of the Jahriyya, the Sufi brotherhood that had formed the backbone of the anti-Qing rebellion. These crossed the treacherous Bedel Pass from Aqsu and headed to Qaraqol (Przhevalsk), on the eastern banks of Lake Issiq Köl. Others fled all the way south to Kashgar, and from there took

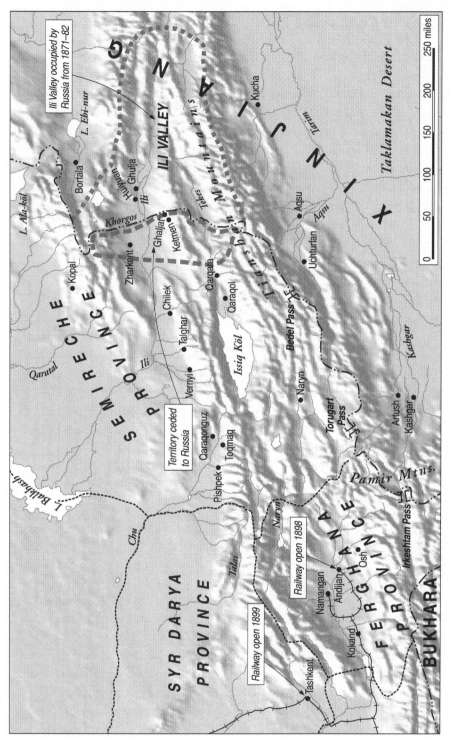

The Russia-China frontier, ca. 1900. © 2016 David Brophy.

one of two routes leading into Russian territory; a minority opted for the Irkeshtam road to Osh and the Ferghana Valley; while the biggest group, comprising some three thousand Dungans from Shaanxi, took the Torugart Pass to Naryn and eventually made their way to the Chu Valley, west of Lake Issiq Köl.[33] Zuo Zongtang and his deputies had pursued these Dungans to the edges of the empire and clamored for them to be extradited. Zuo was particularly chagrined that the Shaanxi rebel leader Bai Yanhu (d. 1881) had got away. Russia resisted these calls, however, seeing benefit in populating its new frontier with a community fiercely hostile to the Qing.

As the towns of the Tarim Basin fell to the advancing Qing forces, Qing officials insisted that Russia keep its word and hand back the occupied Ili Valley. Much of Saint Petersburg's top brass were opposed to doing so, and a fierce debate over the fate of Ili arose in Russia's diplomatic and military circles. For those in favor of retaining it, the valley offered a natural frontier, with rich mineral deposits and a ready-made irrigation network far superior to any of Russia's other Central Asian possessions.[34] Yet for Russia to break its promise to the Qing would lead to severe diplomatic, if not military, conflict and a blow to Russian commercial interests in China. Among those favoring restitution, a minority argued to hand back the entire Ili Valley in return for a huge indemnity, but the majority eyed territorial concessions—both for reasons of strategy and to resettle the anticipated influx of Ili Valley Muslims to Russian-held Semireche. Driving a hard bargain, in 1879 the tsar's negotiators secured the advantageous Treaty of Livadia, ceding to Russia much of the Ili Valley, with a compensation bill of five million rubles for the rest. Yet to the surprise of the Russians, the Qing court refused to ratify the treaty, and in 1880 both sides readied for hostilities.

Diplomatic disputes between Saint Petersburg and Beijing were complicated by ongoing quarrels in Ghulja surrounding Kamenskii's gain transactions. The Qing camp was chronically short on cash, making initial payments in exchange receipts from the Hankou Customs Bank. Kamenskii, for his part, could only supply the grain in installments, and so both sides had grounds for complaint. All the while, the Qing army was exploring new supply lines, making it less reliant on Russian imports. In Ghulja itself, Kamenskii's procurements were having a disastrous impact on the grain market, forcing prices up and creating serious shortages. In March 1878, with locals rushing to join in the boom, Ghulja's Russian authorities finally cracked down and banned the export of grain to Qing territory. A distraught Kamenskii hurried to Saint Petersburg, but his petition to carry on his shipments was rejected.[35] Soon enough, angry Qing officials were arriving in Vernyi to press for the grain still owing to them, or their money back.[36]

In 1880 Turkistan Governor-General Konstantin von Kaufman, who was tasked with supervising the hand-back of the Ili Valley, sent a commission to Ghulja to carry out a valuation of Russian property and investigate Kamenskii's dealings.[37] In these circumstances, the merchant was unlikely to obtain a sympathetic hearing. Those among Russian officials who approved of returning the Ili Valley to the Qing would see Kamenskii's obligations as a sticking point in the negotiations, while those opposed to the decision could easily link Kamenskii's grain shipments to the Qing army's rapid advance across Jungharia, which had placed Russia in such an awkward position. Not surprisingly, the commission found against him. The following year, deep in debt, and a very long way from realizing his dreams of striking it rich in the Orient, Kamenskii passed away in Pishpek (today's Bishkek).[38] The Russian imperial treasury took upon itself 40,000 rubles of his debt to the Qing, and within a few months the Treaty of Saint Petersburg was signed.

The fiasco implicated Kamenskii's local partners, Bushri and Vali Bay, and the commission summoned them both. Bushri, it was found, had an unfulfilled contract with Kamenskii, while the Russian was indebted to Vali Bay for his carts. In the end, though, both men emerged unscathed. With rival empires now competing for the loyalties of the Ili Valley's Muslims, Bushri and Vali Bay were worth much more to the Russians than Kamenskii had ever been.

The third clause of the Treaty of Livadia stipulated a period of a year in which residents of the Ili Valley could choose whether to move to Russian territory as tsarist subjects or remain on Qing soil as Qing subjects. Chinese scholarship casts this as a cynical ploy to depopulate the valley, but as Eric Lohr has discussed, the principle of allowing inhabitants of a contested territory to choose their future political allegiances was gaining acceptance in diplomatic circles in this period.[39] Russia's treatment of the Ili Valley mirrored its policy in the Ottoman Empire's eastern provinces of Kars and Ardahan, which it annexed in 1878. There, locals who wished to remain Ottoman subjects were granted a window of time in which to leave, and those who did not would automatically become Russian subjects. Both deals were tweaked in Russia's favor. In the case of Kars and Ardahan, those who migrated to Ottoman territory were forbidden from ever returning to their homes in Russian territory. In the Treaty of Livadia, though, Russia insisted that its newly acquired subjects would have the right to return to Xinjiang, with all the privileges that Russian subjects enjoyed. This stipulation was among the many points in the Treaty of Livadia to which the Qing court objected, and it was deleted from the 1881 Treaty of Saint Petersburg, leaving the status of naturalized Russian subjects who went back to Xinjiang ambiguous. Yet the main clause remained: from the treaty's ratification locals had a year in which to decide whether or not to move to Russian territory.

Russian, and Soviet, scholars have long argued that a fear of Qing reprisals drove the Taranchi migration. There certainly must have been trepidation among Muslims at the prospect of a new occupying army. Five years earlier, Zuo Zongtang had reprimanded Jin-shun for permitting excessive bloodshed in the storming of Manas to Ghulja's east, and rumors were now circulating that Qing soldiers were to be granted a free hand to loot Ghulja in lieu of a salary.[40] Yet swapping the well-irrigated surrounds of Ghulja for the dry and dusty lower reaches of the Ili River could not have been an attractive prospect for the Taranchi peasantry, and to this day Chinese scholars accuse the Russians of forcing them to leave Xinjiang against their will. Caught up in this polemic, neither side has looked closely into local political dynamics. In Ghulja at least, the decision to move to Semireche was a collective one, made at a public meeting chaired by the Taranchi ulama in June 1881.[41] It makes sense, therefore, to reexamine the exodus in light of the interests of influential men such as Bushri and Vali Bay.

From October 1879, when Russian officials first announced its hand-back policy, until 1883, when the window for migration finally closed, the political climate in Ghulja offered fertile ground for intrigue and controversy. Information was a scarce commodity, monopolized by men such as Bushri who shuttled between Ghulja and Vernyi for meetings with Russian officials. In 1880 local Muslims lodged a complaint that the *aqsaqal* was profiting from this uncertainty. Bushri, they charged, was hostile to the Russians and was spreading rumors that they would renege on the migration deal and hand the entire population back to the Qing. In his view, they claimed, the Taranchis would be better off reaching an accommodation with the Qing.[42] Vali Bay, meanwhile, was focused on expanding his business interests. Amid rumors of war in 1880, he contracted to provision the Russian troops that had been mobilized and tapped his trading contacts for intelligence on Qing deployments.[43] When talk of war subsided, Vali Bay sold off his grain to the incoming Qing garrison. In this brief window of opportunity he set about diversifying his portfolio, buying up tracts of land along the western end of Russian-held Ili. To his grain business he added contracts to supply clothing for the Qing troops and fodder for their mounts.[44] Qing officers lacked the cash to pay for these supplies and preferred not to send payment through the banks of Shanghai or Tianjin, as this would alert Beijing to the transactions. As a result, Jin-shun, the incoming Ili military governor ended up deep in Vali Bay's debt: by March 1882, he was said to owe him the enormous sum of half a million taels.[45]

When Jin-shun arrived to reclaim the Ili Valley for the Qing, the shape of postconquest Xinjiang was yet to be determined. For the time being, he set about reconstructing his local administration along traditional lines, seeking to appoint a *hakim beg* at the head of Taranchi affairs. There was a candidate from the line of local *hakim beg*s, but his family had played a vacillating role in the rebellion of the 1860s and did not inspire the confidence of Qing officials. Instead, Jin-shun reached out to Vali Bay and offered him the position, on condition that he exert his influence to prevent the Taranchis from leaving Ghulja.[46] That Jin-shun would tender this post to a merchant with no family history of service to the Qing indicates the shift in thinking that was occurring among Qing officials, a shift that would soon lead to provincialization and the abolition of the *beg* system entirely. Yet Vali Bay had reason to be wary: to stay in Ghulja would mean selling grain at prices fixed by the Qing administration, which would amount to a significant markdown, so he refused Jin-shun's offer. Subsequent events vindicated his decision. When Jin-shun next met with prominent Taranchis to appoint a *hakim beg* from among them, he reached a deal with the new *hakim beg* to sell Ili's remaining grain at the low price of 15–20 kopeks a *pud*.[47] Clearly it was in Vali Bay's interests to shift his operations to Russian territory, whence he could enforce the same advantageous terms with the Qing that he was currently enjoying.

The Taranchi Exodus to Semireche

The majority of the Taranchi population—almost ten thousand households—registered for the convoys heading west into what was now the province of Semireche, leaving some eighteen hundred families behind.[48] In the eyes of Russian officials, it was Vali Bay's advocacy that dispelled remaining doubts that many locals had about leaving Ili. Vali Bay also took important practical steps to expedite the migration. By this time, many Taranchis were deep in debt to him, and some probably saw the transition to Qing rule as an opportunity to escape these obligations. To bring these Taranchis around, in 1882 Vali Bay canceled many debts owing to him and distributed funds for transport and other aid to Taranchis who were yet to leave Ili, totaling over thirty thousand rubles. The next year he again spent thousands on carts to carry hundreds of households of impoverished stragglers.[49]

The Taranchi migration conformed to the pattern of Slavic migration elsewhere in Russia. Before the move, the heads of Ili's Taranchi and Dungan cantons toured Semireche Province to scout out land for their communities.[50] The Taranchis were resettled in two of the province's districts (*uezd*), Vernyi and Zharkent, the latter newly created out of territory ceded to Russia, with three Taranchi cantons in both. While peasants spread out in search of good farmland, Ghulja's mercantile and religious elite took up residence in the town of Zharkent, once known as Samar and home to a Sibe and Solon garrison. In 1866 rampaging Taranchi rebels had burnt this Qing outpost to the ground. They now rebuilt it as the center of the new Russian-subject Taranchi community. The migration process preserved local communities intact: Taranchi villages in Semireche such as Qazanchi ("pot-beaters") or Naghrachi ("drum makers") took their names from suburbs of Ghulja known for these crafts. In a number of locations, however, conflicts with Kazakh nomads and Cossacks prevented Taranchis from taking up assigned territories, leaving some drifting from one canton to another and to the towns surrounding Vernyi. As many as five and half thousand Taranchis and Dungans ended up registered to Russian communities, and many others were not attached to any location at all, instead roaming the province as day laborers and peddlers.[51]

One difficulty in settling the Taranchis in Semireche was that they were something of a legal anomaly. As the Kazakh steppe was gradually opened to Slavic colonization, tsarist administrators came to view provinces such as Semireche in terms of a binary opposition between "natives" (*tuzemtsy*), which was synonymous with Kazakh, and Slavic "settlers" (*pereselentsy*). As Muslim colonists from Chinese territory, the Taranchis were neither *tuzemtsy* nor *pereselentsy*, rendering them an awkward fit in the administrative landscape. According to the terms of the 1881 Steppe Regulations, foreigners and non-Christian nationalities other than *tuzemtsy* were forbidden to own land in Semireche, which if strictly interpreted would call into question Taranchi landholdings. By the 1890s, as tsarist colonization policy in Turkistan shifted to a decidedly pro-Slavic approach, the Taranchis found themselves a conspicuous minority amid a growing population of *pereselentsy* and Cossacks. In 1899 an imperial decree

The ruins of Zharkent, 1880. (Photograph by E. Delmar Morgan. Royal Geographical Society rgs029466.)

addressed this anomaly and confirmed that the Taranchis were "equal in rights with the indigenous population of the region (*krai*)."[52] In other words, they were to be treated as *tuzemtsy*. Yet certain forms of discrimination remained. Adeeb Khalid points out, for example, that sedentary *tuzemtsy* such as the Taranchis and Dungans were prohibited from voting in Semireche's elections to the First Duma.[53]

The Taranchis found themselves at the bottom of a rigid hierarchy of ethnic categories in Semireche that were inscribed on the administrative map. Taranchis lived in designated Taranchi cantons, Dungans in Dungan cantons, Kazakhs in "Kirghiz" cantons, and Slavic settlers in peasant cantons (*krestianskie volosti*). Statistics from 1902 show that an average Taranchi household held only thirty-five acres (12.8 *desiatin*) of land, much less than Semireche's Slavic settlers (eighty-seven acres) and Cossacks (two hundred and thirty acres).[54] Not surprisingly, some itinerant Taranchis ended up back in Ghulja. In many ways, the conditions of the Taranchis who had remained in Xinjiang turned out to be better than the conditions of those who had moved to Russian soil. When Xinjiang's new provincial administration was introduced in 1884, local peasants were freed from corvée service to the *hakim beg*, and tax obligations were kept low. Combined with a degree of homesickness and a desire to be reunited with family members, this led to the illicit return of thousands of Taranchis to Qing territory each year. Judging from statistics, this remigration to Xinjiang peaked in 1906, when a drop of almost ten thousand is recorded for the Taranchi population in Semireche. In 1909, statistician P. P. Rumiantsev led a detailed investigation into the state of agriculture in Semireche and found a high rate of desertion from Taranchi lands. Roughly 10 percent of Semireche's Taranchi peasants were living in Ghulja, as were almost 20 percent of the Taranchi population of Zharkent.[55]

Tsarist officials seem to have turned a blind eye to much that was irregular in Taranchi society, creating ideal conditions for men such as Vali Bay to maintain an intermediary position with the authorities. Particularly along the Chinese frontier, tsarist structures of self-administration lent a thin Russian veneer to an identifiably Qing system of village organization. In Ketmen Canton, for example, local headmen held titles such as *mingbashi* and *yüzbashi*, not found elsewhere in Semireche.[56] Much of Vali Bay's land holdings fell within this strip of newly acquired Russian territory, and he was permitted to retain possession of it, with Taranchis there living as his tenants. Vali Bay collected between a third and half of the harvest as rent, and from this he paid the canton's tax obligations himself.[57] He also employed his own private corps of functionaries who were in charge of irrigation and the collection of grain.[58] As much as these irregularities raised eyebrows on occasion, the Taranchi districts were far enough from Semireche's center of Vernyi, and Vali Bay sufficiently well-connected, that they were never seriously questioned.

From his base on the Russian side of the border, Vali Bay continued selling grain to the Qing army on his terms. To transport his shipments to Ghulja, he teamed up with an exiled Polish engineer, Jan J. Poklewski-Koziell, to order from Britain the first-ever steamship to ply the rivers of Turkistan.[59] Launched in May 1883, they christened it the *Kolpakovskii* in honor of the man who had led the Russian occupation of Ili and had since risen to the governorship of Semireche. Vali Bay kept control of the processing end of his business too, operating a mill on the outskirts of Ghulja.[60] Besides grain, Vali Bay went into

cotton farming, successfully introducing an American species into the dry climate of the Zharkent district. He also had an interest in coal, acting as consultant to Russian officials who were eyeing the rich deposits around Ghulja. By
these various means Vali Bay accumulated capital to dwarf that of any of his
neighbors. A list of electors drawn up for the district of Zharkent in 1899 records Vali Bay's personal fortune at forty thousand rubles, a sum greater than
the combined wealth of the next eleven men on the list.[61]

Creating Provincial Xinjiang

While the Taranchis were adapting to a new life on Russian soil, Qing control
was being restored in Xinjiang through reconstruction bureaus (*shanhouju*)
modeled on the institutions of the post-Taiping reconstruction of the 1860s.
New city walls and administrative buildings had to be erected, canals dredged,
and long abandoned agricultural land reclaimed. As Kataoka Kazutada has discussed, much of this work was entrusted to demobilized soldiers from Zuo
Zongtang's Hunanese army, as well as poor Chinese migrants who were enticed to Xinjiang by the farming opportunities that the reconstruction bureaus offered them.[62]

The breakdown of imperial authority in Xinjiang had convinced many
officials that drastic reforms were required to prevent a future relapse into an-
archy, and in the eyes of men such as Zuo Zongtang, these Chinese-led reconstruction efforts proved the viability of a more proactive colonial policy in
Xinjiang. Zuo and his co-thinkers were opposed to resurrecting the patchwork
of local autonomies that had previously existed in Xinjiang, blaming it for the
persistence of anti-Qing sentiment, and they were equally critical of the long-
established precedent of appointing only Manchu or Mongol officials to high
positions in the region. Zuo also recognized a need to strengthen Xinjiang's
cultural ties to the center, and he argued for the introduction of Confucian
primary schooling for local Muslim children. After a flurry of proposals and
counterproposals, in 1884 it was decided to transform Xinjiang from a frontier
dependency to a province, to be administered by a new cohort of Chinese
bureaucrats.

On the face of it at least, provincial Xinjiang was a Chinese-dominated affair, and scholars have focused on the integrating and homogenizing thrust of
the provincialization policy. Kataoka, for example, refers to the policy as the
"sinicization" of Xinjiang. Yet in a number of respects this requires qualifica-

tion. In practical terms, many reconstruction initiatives failed to produce the desired results. The supply of immigrants gradually dwindled, little headway was made in reclaiming land, and ruined Qing yamens remained derelict well into the 1880s. The economy, too, struggled to rebuild; without a good supply of silver and copper currency, Yaqub Beg's silver coins circulated for many years, and by the time they were finally withdrawn from circulation and melted down, the Russian ruble had intruded as the province's most stable currency. At the level of local administration, moreover, the concept of sinicization conceals the ongoing reality of local autonomy. Former *beg*s, now known by the Chinese title of *xiangyue*, continued to occupy an important position as intermediaries with local society. How could it be otherwise, when Chinese bureaucrats were assigned to rule vast counties with entirely Muslim populations? For some, this fact made a mockery of the notion of provincial Xinjiang. In 1891, Tao Baolian, son of Xinjiang governor Tao Mo, gave this blunt assessment of the policy: "Since dismissing the *beg*s, they have been changed to village heads (*xiangyue*), but the Muslims still call them *beg*s. The Chinese officials don't know the Muslim language or script, so they can't help but rely on the village heads. . . . Before the introduction of prefectures and counties, the Muslims hated the *beg*s, even though they belonged to the same community. Now, having created prefectures and counties, we've simply added another layer of exploitation, and all the hostility is directed at the Chinese officials."[63]

The view that Xinjiang was a province in name only was widely held in late Qing Xinjiang. Yet there is a further sense in which we should be wary of treating provincial Xinjiang as a shift to direct Chinese rule. Xinjiang became a province in the midst of an empire-wide shift in official thinking on local administration, informed by the ad hoc measures adopted during the suppression of the Taiping rebels and formalized in the postwar reconstruction process. Reliance on thinly spread bureaucratic structures was giving way to forms of local autonomy in which social forces outside the bureaucracy—primarily the rural gentry and urban merchants—performed new roles as civic activists and community leaders. In this sense Muslim involvement in local administration conforms to, rather than contradicts, the prevailing provincial model. Chinese sources give little insight into the collaborative relationship between officials and Muslim elites, and this side of provincialization has been largely neglected by scholars. No doubt, Qing officials in Kashgar or Yarkand can hardly have expected the locals to take up state-building projects as enthusiastically as had the patriotic gentry of Suzhou or Canton. Nevertheless this ideal of informal civic participation was on the minds of those advocating provincialization. In 1882, Zuo Zongtang's second-in-command Liu Jintang expressed his hope that, with the abolition of the *beg* system, the class of ex-*beg*s would not simply vanish but instead come to fulfill the function of "gentry managers" (*bangong shenshi*), to whom some of the state's previous responsibilities might be delegated.[64] As events proved, it would not be the ex-*beg*s so much as Kashgar's commercial elite who would come to occupy this position.

The Xinjiang Treaty Ports and the Russian *Aqsaqal*s

One of the most immediate consequences of Russia's arrival on the Qing Empire's doorstep was felt among the Andijanis in the south of Xinjiang, people who had never previously had any link to the tsarist empire. Upon completing its conquest of Kokand, Russia assumed the right to protect all of the Kokand khan's subjects, including these émigré Andijanis, and offered similar protections to Bukharans trading in Qing territory. Thousands of Andijanis as far afield as Hami and Khotan, who until recently had thought of the Russians as a hostile empire and Russian merchants as rivals, suddenly found themselves subjects of the "White King," as the tsar was known among the Muslims of Turkistan.

Zuo Zongtang's deputy Liu Jintang bridled at the notion of recognizing these Andijanis as Russian subjects and tried his best to prevent Russian representatives claiming them. "After all," he reasoned, "they are not real Russians."[65] In the chaos of the late 1870s, Liu expelled hundreds of Andijanis suspected of collaboration with Yaqub Beg and proposed naturalizing long-term Andijani residents of Xinjiang who had property or family on Chinese soil.[66] Yet with the conclusion of the Treaty of Saint Petersburg in 1881, such heavy-handed tactics had to be abandoned. In accordance with the terms of the treaty, Russia extended its network of consulates from Tarbaghatay and Ghulja to Kashgar, and eventually Ürümchi, and reserved the right to further representation should the growth of trade warrant it. Nikolai Petrovskii, a stalwart of tsarist diplomacy, arrived in Kashgar in 1882, and other consuls soon followed. The treaty granted Russian subjects the right to move freely throughout Xinjiang and exempted them from all Qing duties on the traffic and disposal of their goods. Under such conditions, it did not take long for the Andijanis to reestablish their dominant position in local markets, often as intermediaries for Russian firms. From this point on, as the Soviet Orientalist Rostovskii put it, "the Andijanis were agents of Russian capitalism."[67]

If men like Liu Jintang lamented the presence of so many tax-exempt Russian Muslims in Xinjiang, they might have consoled themselves with the thought that they would now be dealing with a limited number of Russian consuls instead of the Kokandi *aqsaqal*s who had spread to almost every oasis and played such a disruptive role in the mid-century rebellions. Liu resisted the reemergence of a network of *aqsaqal*s among the Andijanis, and in this he was on solid diplomatic ground. The Treaty of Saint Petersburg permitted the consul to send his employees into the field temporarily, but there was nothing in it about resident *aqsaqal*s. Yet soon after Petrovskii's arrival, men claiming to be Russian-appointed *aqsaqal*s started appearing among the province's Andijanis. In a strongly worded letter to the governor-general of Turkistan in 1884, Liu railed against this and other violations of the Treaty of Saint Petersburg, calling on Russia to withdraw its *aqsaqal*s and insisting that only consuls had the right to intervene in matters involving Russian subjects in Xinjiang.[68]

This was the tense situation at the end of 1884 when a man named Halim took up the position of Andijani *aqsaqal* in the town of Uchturfan. As he described in his reports to Petrovskii, Reconstruction Bureau officials refused to meet with him and ignored his courtesy calls. When Halim drew up a list of Russian subjects and their goods, local customs officials ignored him and continued to tax these goods as they had been instructed. Abdurahim Bay, from the Ferghana Valley oasis of Marghilan, complained about this to Halim, who forwarded Abdurahim Bay's tax receipts to Petrovskii in Kashgar. When the Reconstruction Bureau got wind of this correspondence, they hauled Abdurahim Bay in and interrogated him as to why he had lodged his complaint with Halim instead of with the Qing authorities. Next they called in the Russian-appointed *aqsaqal*. In Halim's presence, the Qing officials questioned Abdurahim Bay as to whether he was a subject of Tsar Alexander III or of the Guangxu emperor. To the *aqsaqal*'s dismay, Abdurahim stated that he was a Qing subject, and that Halim had listed him as a Russian subject without asking his permission.[69]

The Qing officials now pressed Halim to sign a confession that he had registered Abdurahim in error. Halim pulled rank, insisting that he would sign nothing without consulting with Petrovskii. At this, the official changed tack and tried flattery: "I see you are a good fellow, from now on I will discuss things properly with you . . . and whenever you send a report to the consul, make sure you inform me first." Russian subjects traveling to the nearby town of Aqsu reported the affair to the Andijani *aqsaqal* there, who invited Abdurahim Bay to a meeting with the Aqsu circuit commissioner (*daotai*). Here, Abdurahim changed his story again, stating that he was indeed a Russian subject but that the Reconstruction Bureau officials had bullied him into declaring himself a subject of the Qing.

Although vindicated by this admission, Halim Aqsaqal derived little satisfaction from showing up the Reconstruction Bureau. Shortly after this the bureau appointed a man of its own choosing as head of the Andijanis in Uchturfan named Nar Mirza. Nar Mirza initially declined the appointment, fearing to incur Petrovskii's wrath, but by the middle of 1885 he was seen going around Uchturfan drawing up his own list of Russian subjects and spreading malicious gossip about Halim. Effectively, a situation of dual headmen prevailed—one recognized by the Russian consul, the other by the Reconstruction Bureau. Nar Mirza emerged as the eventual victor in this tug-of-war. Leveraging his connections with Qing officials, he won recognition from Petrovskii in Kashgar, usurping Halim's position as official *aqsaqal* of Russian subjects in Uchturfan.

Such conflicts were to become commonplace in provincial Xinjiang. In one sense the revival of the *aqsaqal* network episode could simply be read as a case of Russia testing the limits of its treaties with China, but this would miss something important. Historians of diplomacy have identified a trend in the late nineteenth century in which consular representation came to supplant preexisting networks of trading headmen.[70] The case of China's coastal treaty ports conforms to this model, where, for example, East India Company factors were replaced by British consuls. Yet this straightforward transition did not take place in Xinjiang. The Qing, Russian, and British empires that met in Xinjiang were all ruling Muslim communities that had little in common culturally and linguistically with the colonial officials serving among them. On either side of this triangular frontier, forms of local autonomy prevailed in which a layer of Muslim go-betweens mediated between imperial administrators and the subject population. In Russian Turkistan, for example, as part of the new Russian system of colonial "self-administration," officials instituted a system of electing elders in local communities, also known as *aqsaqal*s. In Xinjiang, this system of self-administration now merged with that of consular extraterritoriality. The result was something of a paradox: by placing Russian subjects in Xinjiang under the jurisdiction of the Russian consuls, the Qing fostered an expectation among these Russian-subject Muslims that they would enjoy an autonomy from Russian officialdom similar to that which they enjoyed on Russian soil.

The Russian-subject *aqsaqal*s in Xinjiang can be thought of as a hybrid of two institutions: the Kokandi headmen, whose primary duty had been to deal with Qing officials; and the *aqsaqal*s of Russian Turkistan, who liaised with tsarist authorities. As Halim's ordeal shows, the loyalties of these *aqsaqal*s soon became the object of a contest between the desires of the "sender" state to supervise its subjects residing abroad and those of the "receiving" state to manage the disruptive presence of foreigners within its boundaries, as well as the interests of the Russian Muslims themselves in preserving a degree of autonomy from both. Halim's constituency in Uchturfan was living far from Consul Petrovskii in Kashgar, but even those in close proximity to a Russian consul preferred to appoint an *aqsaqal* rather than deal directly with the consul.[71] In Tarbaghatay the majority of foreigners were Russian-speaking Tatars, who resided in a compact trading colony where shops, houses, and the mosque all stood close to the Russian consulate. According to a local imam, Tarbaghatay's Russian subjects first elected an *aqsaqal* in 1892. He functioned for seven years without any official recognition until the Russian consul and local Chinese Qing officials finally confirmed his position.[72]

A similar process of grafting a consular system onto existing networks of headmen occurred in the case of the British. In the 1870s, when Sir Douglas Forsyth's mission traveled to Yarkand and Kashgar, they found *aqsaqal*s there among the Kashmiri and Badakhshani trading communities.[73] When the British Raj obtained the right to appoint a resident in Kashgar in 1891, he assumed control of this preexisting network of *aqsaqal*s throughout the south of Xinjiang. There was great ethnic and occupational diversity among these newly acquired British subjects in Xinjiang, a fact that made it hard for a single *aqsaqal* to represent the entire community. In some places where Indian peasants were long-term residents, a practice evolved of appointing both a peasants' *aqsaqal* and a traders' *aqsaqal*. In one case from 1918, *aqsaqal* elections in Yarkand led to the formation of five-member council, with one member each representing the Pashtun, Hindu, Kashmiri, Wakhi and Chitrali, and Balti diasporas.[74]

These *aqsaqal*s were native functionaries at the bottom of an imperial bureaucracy that offered them little prospect of advancement, yet their role in mediating disputes between Russian and Qing subjects made them influential members of local society. Given the demands of the position, the wealthiest traders did not seek the position for themselves; instead it was usually filled by middle-ranking members of the community. The *aqsaqal* in Ghulja, a Tatar by the name of Fazlullah (or Faziljan) Yunich, first came to Xinjiang as an employee of a Semireche trading company and eventually became one of the richest and most influential members of Xinjiang's Tatar community.[75] Russian *aqsaqal*s received a salary, collected from among the traders and supplemented with a stipend from the consul, which was high enough to employ a small staff. The *aqsaqal* in Tarbaghatay earned between six hundred and a thousand rubles a year, while the total income of the *aqsaqal* in Kashgar was estimated at two hundred rubles a month.[76] Russian *aqsaqal*s were equipped with seals bearing the Imperial Russian coat of arms, and British *aqsaqal*s flew the Union Jack from their dwellings.[77] Chinese officials would always insist that there was no provision in any treaty for the appointment of *aqsaqal*s, but day-to-day business in the outlying towns of the Tarim Basin lay well beyond the gaze of the circuit commissioner in Kashgar or Aqsu, and instead of combating the *aqsaqal*s, most local officials did their best to stay on good terms with them, even awarding them Qing honors.[78] One source describes a British *aqsaqal* on a visit to the Kucha country magistrate being carried in a palanquin and striding through the yamen's ceremonial central gate, where he was welcomed with firecrackers.[79]

As Russia and Britain vied for influence in the so-called Great Game, the *aqsaqal*s contributed by supplying local intelligence, monitoring suspicious foreigners, and accommodating weary explorers and officials. They were also a link in the growing traffic of antiquities, procuring items from local treasure seekers that eventually set off the great wave of Silk Road archaeology of the early twentieth century. It was Abdusattar, *aqsaqal* of Russian subjects in Khotan, who first informed Consul Petrovskii of the finds emerging from buried cities in the Khotan desert.[80] Shortly afterwards, the Indian *aqsaqal* in Khotan, an Afghan by the name of Badruddin Khan, provided George Macartney with manuscripts and fragments of fresco and stucco that locals had unearthed. Later, Badruddin Khan helped Aurel Stein provision his expeditions to the buried cities of Dandan Öylük and Niya in the Taklamakan Desert. For his services to archaeology, Badruddin earned the title of Khan Sahib and is remembered fondly in Stein's reports.[81]

Extraterritoriality and the Subjecthood Question

The colonial relationship between consul and subject in provincial Xinjiang rendered the functioning of extraterritoriality highly complex, and legal disputes between Russian and Qing subjects in Xinjiang were handled in a variety of ways. In theory, provincialization rendered local Muslims subject to the empire-wide Qing code, but forms of legal pluralism persisted, and qadi courts continued to hear civil matters according to Islamic law. In serious criminal matters involving Russian and Qing subjects, the consul and Qing authorities would try the case on consular grounds in a joint sitting similar to the hybrid courts of the coastal treaty ports. For lesser plaints, though, the *aqsaqal* might simply handle the case in conjunction with local Muslim translators. In some of Xinjiang's towns and villages, local Muslim diplomatic officials mirroring the Russian-subject *aqsaqal* emerged, bearing the title of "diplomatic *aqsaqal*" (*jiaoshe shangyue*), until a decree from Ürümchi abolished them in 1924.[82] If both parties agreed, a qadi could resolve the case according to the sharia, for which purpose Russian consuls appointed a qadi of Russian subjects.[83] Beside these practices, a specific form of extraterritoriality evolved among the Kazakhs. According to an agreement reached in Tarbaghatay in 1884, Kazakh judges (*biys*) from both Russian and Qing-subject communities held juridical congresses in Tarbaghatay and Ghulja every few years to resolve the backlog of disputes. Although Russian and Chinese officials attended these meetings, which sometimes ran for up to a month, it was only in a supervisory capacity, and they played no role in hearing cases. So successful was this system of conferencing that officials extended it to Kashgar in 1904.[84]

Given the ability of Andijanis and Kashgaris to resolve conflicts according to a common Islamic law, either through the *aqsaqal* network or qadi courts, it might be argued that consular jurisdiction in Xinjiang was not as great an imposition on the Qing as it was in the coastal treaty ports, where Qing and European law clashed directly. Yet in other respects the problems of extraterritoriality were exacerbated by the distinct environment in Xinjiang. In the coastal treaty ports, it was common enough for Qing subjects to seek advantage by faking foreign subjecthood or claiming foreign protection as a Christian, but was difficult for Qing subjects to actually pass themselves off as foreigners. In Xinjiang, by contrast, neither religion, speech, or dress distinguished Russian-subject Andijanis from Qing-subject Kashgaris, and here the problem of policing subjecthood status took on epidemic proportions.

In theory, the problem of determining the identity of foreigners was now greatly simplified. Andijanis arriving in Xinjiang were subjects of the tsar, and Russian authorities provided them with bilingual passports and customs documents. In Xinjiang's treaty ports, the Qing established trade bureaus (*tongshangju*) that issued Russian subjects with the documents needed to transport their goods elsewhere in the province and claim the tax-free status to which they were entitled. This exempted them from the *lijin*, a levy on goods in transit introduced as a response to the Taiping civil war in the 1850s and intended as a supplement to provincial revenues. In 1878, Zuo Zongtang reintroduced a tax on the transport of goods through Xinjiang, although collection was intermittent at first. In theory, the *lijin* could be applied to any shipment of goods from point A to point B, but Liu Jintang decided to focus collection on shipments of goods reaching Xinjiang from the east. He set up two *lijin* bureaus in Gucheng and Hami, the entry points for caravans arriving from Mongolia and the Gansu Corridor respectively.

Between the trade bureaus in the province's west, and the *lijin* bureaus in the east, there was ample space for complications. Russian subjects might exploit their tax-free status to buy and sell goods within Xinjiang, moving between bazaars that were far from any consul or Qing official. In such a situation they would obtain a receipt from the local Russian-subject *aqsaqal* attesting to their identity as Russian subjects and their ownership of the goods. Known as "little receipts" (*xiaotiao*), these documents were entirely in Turki with no Chinese or Russian translation, and thus incomprehensible to Chinese officials.[85] Locals could also conspire with Russian subjects to pass off their own goods as part of a foreign caravan and therefore exempt from *lijin*, or they might themselves obtain a "little receipt." The considerable advantage that attached to such outward signs of Russian subjecthood quickly spawned a black market in trading documents. For the right price, local Muslims could even buy a Russian trading permit (which were often issued blank) and thereby pass as Russian Muslims. For these reasons, Xinjiang's *lijin* income declined rapidly soon after the tax's introduction, and in 1887 Liu Jintang requested permission to abolish it. In doing so, Xinjiang distinguished itself by becoming the only province in the empire to abandon collection of the *lijin*.

This decision must have come as a relief to local officials, who had found themselves helpless to prevent the *aqsaqal* network from eroding their authority. As the scale of commerce grew, Russian-subject Tatars and Andijanis hired increasing numbers of local Kashgaris as agents in outlying towns. It was a short step for these employees to claim the protection of the *aqsaqal* network as a viable alternative to working within Qing law. In 1898, for example, the Russian consul in Kashgar drew up a document listing the fees the *aqsaqal* was entitled to collect from his constituents. In pledging to pay these fees, Andijanis affixed their seals to the document, but so too did a number of local Kashgaris. As a result, these locals took part in the election of the Russian *aqsaqal* that year—a step toward claiming Russian subjecthood outright.[86]

The thorny "subjecthood question" (*guoji wenti*), as it was known, high-lighted the fact that the Qing had only a hazy sense of the composition of its population, and in particular of the numbers and identity of foreign residents in China. This was among the issues that the Qing court sought to address in its final decade of rule, as it charted a course toward a system of constitutional monarchy. The court first instructed officials throughout the empire to compile a new series of local gazetteers, which in the case of Xinjiang provided rough figures for the number of foreign households in each county. Then in 1908 the Qing court promulgated a set of statutes that outlined plans for the first empire-wide census, which required Xinjiang officials to create a census bureau.[87]

This interest in identifying and counting the empire's population drew responses from local officials, who sought to tailor the impetus from Beijing to Xinjiang's unique circumstances. In 1909, the Aqsu Circuit Commissioner Pan Zhen (1851–1926) wrote to the court with suggestions for resolving the "subjecthood problem." He argued to commission registers of Russian and British subjects, and to strictly enforce the requirement that Qing subjects claiming foreign subjecthood first obtain release from Qing status. Such a policy held out the prospect of a financial windfall, as property held unlawfully by foreigners could be confiscated.[88] Winning the court's approval, the scheme was entrusted to the members of Xinjiang's fledgling Consultative Bureau, who tempered Pan's ambitious initiatives. Despite consensus on the need for better knowledge of the foreign population, it was evident that such surveys would be impractical without the cooperation of the Russian and British consuls, which was unlikely to be forthcoming.[89] It was also clear that fixing the boundaries between locals and foreigners would not be achieved without confronting the *aqsaqal*s and the widespread abuse of trading privileges that they facilitated.

The one place where progress was made on this front was Ghulja, among Taranchi peasants who had returned from Semireche.[90] These fell into two categories: those who regained possession of their land, and those who had lost it and were now laboring on land belonging to Qing subjects.[91] Russia initially sought to extradite these runaway Taranchis, but not everyone considered it worth the effort, particularly as they continued to pay tax to the Semireche authorities via the Russian consul. These returnees were thus subject to double taxation—both by Chinese officials and by the Russians, and given the opportunity, many were willing to discard Russian subjecthood. Karl Mannerheim, a Finnish officer in tsarist service who traveled through the Ili Valley in 1906, found that "Russian subjecthood is something to be avoided rather than coveted."[92] Not long after his trip, the two sides agreed to allow those who so wished to revert to Qing subjecthood. In 1908, a new local gazetteer noted that two-thirds of Russian subjects had reverted to their original status as Qing subjects.[93] In the end, though, this initiative only compounded the confusion. Those who compiled the register among local Kazakhs listed all family members of households taking up Chinese subjecthood. For the Taranchis, though, they only recorded the name of the household head. As a result, the Russian consul and his tax officials were still in a position to claim the wives, children, and even grandchildren, of these re-naturalized Taranchis, as Russian subjects.[94]

The Kashgari Labor Migration

The new caravan networks that gave Kashgari merchants a foothold in Russian Turkistan also doubled as channels of labor migration, as landless and indigent Kashgari peasants sought higher wages in Russian territory. The émigré Kashgari community in Russian territory was small at first: statistics from 1869 show only sixty-nine Kashgaris in Vernyi.[95] By the mid-1870s, though, the press in Russian Turkistan was carrying reports that caravans from Kashgar were bringing with them significant numbers of young men looking for work in towns such as Vernyi, Qaraqol, or Toqmaq, where the daily wage was more than ten times as high as in Kashgar. To staunch this outflow of population, Yaqub Beg tried to set a limit on number of caravans exiting his domains, but to no avail.[96]

With the arrival of Russian consuls in Xinjiang, a more stable regime of seasonal labor was instituted. To cross to the Ferghana Valley or Semireche, a prospective laborer first had to obtain the permission of his village head. Having secured this, he would then go to Kashgar and get a Qing passport, literally a "permit to exit the guard post" (*chuka zhizhao*).[97] These were bilingual, printed and filled out in both Chinese and Turki, and then endorsed with a visa and signed by the consul, with the traveler's details translated into Russian. Upon arrival in Russian territory, Kashgaris would present their documents and receive a temporary residence permit valid for up to six months.[98]

The expense involved was more than most poor peasants in Kashgar could afford, and some went into debt in order to make the annual crossing. In 1904 the fee for a Qing passport was 0.4 taels.[99] Russian visas were initially free, but in 1894 the tsarist administration introduced a levy of one and a half rubles on each passport (approximately 15 taels), a fee that gradually increased.[100] Chi-

Bazaar in Andijan, late nineteenth century. (Photograph by F. Orden. MAE [Kunstkamera] RAS 255–291.)

nese authorities, who received no corresponding income from the many Russian subjects traveling to Kashgar, resented the introduction of the fee, and in response the Kashgar circuit commissioner temporarily refused to issue new passports. Taking into account the unofficial fees required to get anything done at the county yamen or the Russian consulate, the total cost for passport and visa could be as much as five rubles (50 taels).[101] The issue caused controversy in Russia too. In 1906 the liberal daily *Russian Turkestan* criticized the fees, blaming them for slowing the supply of labor. Nikolai Petrovskii defended the practice, however, claiming that Kashgaris would earn as much as 50–60 rubles in a season of four months' work.[102]

Some migrants found ways to avoid the fees, and Russian and Chinese sources concur that there were many who crossed into Russian territory illegally, taking one of any number of poorly guarded paths through the mountains. Some of these undocumented Kashgaris avoided inspection by working on land belonging to nomads in mountainous regions. Others ran the risk in the lowlands, often borrowing someone else's Qing passport to apply for a residence permit. Policing of the system seems to have been fairly lax, and those who were caught were not necessarily deported to Xinjiang. In fact, on his inspection tour of Turkistan in 1908–1909, the privy councilor Count Pahlen found that in some cases the Semireche governor was simply granting illegal Kashgari immigrants Russian subjecthood.[103]

By the turn of the century, the Kashgari labor migration to Russia was reaching significant proportions, and Kashgari labor came to be considered an essential ingredient in the development of Russian Turkistan. In 1894 Qing diplomat Xu Jingcheng noted that each year some six or seven thousand Kashgaris traveled to Russian territory for work.[104] This accords with Petrovskii's statement that in the six months leading up to August 1903 he issued six thousand visas. These Kashgaris were driven not only by the pull of higher wages but also by the push of declining economic conditions in Xinjiang. Rent on land doubled in the first years of the twentieth century, as the Boxer indemnity led to a steep fall in official subsidies to Xinjiang. Rough estimates show that the size of the labor migration was steadily increasing: 13,000 in 1905, 16,000 in 1906, and 28,000 in 1908.[105] One scholar suggests that by the outbreak of World War I, over fifty thousand were making the annual journey.[106] The impact of these movements could easily be seen in Kashgar. A correspondent for the Tatar newspaper *Time* found Kashgar during the summer to be a ghost town. "The rich go to the countryside for the summer, the poor go to Andijan," he noted. "Only the elderly, women, and girls remain."[107]

Provincial Xinjiang saw little improvement in its communications with China, but connections to Russia were developing rapidly. By 1888 Russia had extended its Trans-Caspian Railway to Bukhara and Samarkand, and in 1899 the line connected Tashkent and Andijan. In 1906 the opening of the Orenburg-Tashkent Railway provided a more direct link from Turkistan to Russia. Meanwhile, construction had commenced on the Trans-Siberian, which eventually included the Trans-Manchurian link to Beijing. With this, the quickest journey from China's capital to Kashgar was on the Russian railway. Traders naturally benefited from these links, which consolidated Russia's position as Xinjiang's main export market. Even Chinese goods sent to Xinjiang were shipped via Russia. Kashgari merchants could now transport goods from Shanghai via ship to Batumi on the Black Sea, then by rail and ship to Andijan, with only a short caravan trip to Kashgar remaining. Seeing benefits in this rerouting, in 1904 the Russian Ministry of Finance decreed the tax-free transit of luxury goods from China through Russia to Xinjiang.[108] In reconquering Xinjiang, the Qing had achieved a degree of political integration, but socially and economically its Muslim community continued to face west.

An equally important byproduct of Russian empire building was the strengthening of ties between Muslim communities in Eurasia. To the north of Xinjiang, the majority of the Taranchi population were now Russian subjects in Semireche, forming outposts of sedentary Muslim life in a traditionally nomadic Kazakh region. Russia's trading colonies in Ghulja and Tarbaghatay were home to growing communities of Tatars, with direct links via trade routes running through the steppe to centers of Muslim intellectual and social life such as Kazan and Ufa. In the south, by contrast, Russia's conquest of Kokand had subsumed the Kashgari exile population and extended Russian subjecthood to the émigré Andijanis in Xinjiang. This north/south divide had consequences for the way in which new cultural trends manifested themselves in the early twentieth century. More so than at any point in its history, Xinjiang was now linked to the intellectual world of Russian Muslims and would absorb the same influences that these Muslims, primarily Tatars, were bringing to Russian Turkistan. At the same time, Russian railroads and steamships made it all the more feasible to strengthen old ties with the Ottoman Empire. Those in Xinjiang who benefited most from the new commercial opportunities with Russia, easily identified by their Russified family names, were also the most eager of Xinjiang's Muslims to cultivate a bond with the tsar's rivals in Istanbul.

CHAPTER THREE

Imperial and Islamic Reform between Turkistan and Turkey

At the turn of the century, three centuries-old dynastic courts in Saint Petersburg, Beijing, and Istanbul confronted the challenge to modernize in the face of the new imperialism. Situated at the intersection of these three empires, Xinjiang provides an opportunity to explore how reformist initiatives across Eurasia intersected and were appropriated by local interests. The social and economic ties that linked Chinese and Russian Turkistan ensured that intellectual trends among Russian Muslims, as well as dramatic events such as the 1905 revolution, would make themselves felt in Xinjiang. In the Ottoman Empire, too, the Muslims of Xinjiang were bound inextricably to an empire to the west. These ties were built, not with railway lines and telegraph wires, but with the religious legitimacy that Ottomans drew on and with which they sought to combat foreign encroachment on the sultan's not-so-well-protected domains. This reserve of spiritual prestige led Sultan Abdulaziz's successor, Abdulhamid II (r. 1876–1909), to strengthen his dynasty's claim to leadership in the Islamic world by reviving the title of caliph.

The focal point for much of this reform was the question of primary schooling. The *maktab* in Xinjiang drew on a curriculum that was common across Turkistan, consisting primarily of Quran recitation, catechisms, and Sufi poetry. Alongside these schools were limited efforts to introduce the language and culture of the metropole to local Muslims: Russo-native schools in Russia, and the Chinese schools (*xuetang*) that Xinjiang officials introduced in the 1880s in the wake of the reconquest. Satisfied with neither the existing *maktab* nor its Russo-native alternative, Russian Muslims in contact with similar modernizing initiatives in the Ottoman Empire came to promote a "new method" (*uṣūl-i jadīd*) or "phonetic method" (*uṣūl-i sautiyya*) of teaching the Arabic script in the *maktab*. Besides an improved pedagogy for Arabic, these schools emphasized

86

the importance of subjects such as geography and mathematics, and were associated with a broad "Jadidist" social criticism, ranging in its targets from the profligacy of the rich to Sufi mysticism and the cult of saints. Scholars have already done much to elucidate the course of Russian Muslim and Ottoman pedagogical reform, but the history of Jadidism in the distinct political and social environment of Qing Xinjiang is less well known. Here Muslim initiatives came to coincide with, and complement, the Qing Empire's own steps toward Western-style schooling.

The Ottomans and the Muslims of China

Late-nineteenth-century Istanbul had given refuge to those fleeing Yaqub Beg's fallen emirate, and at times ties between Ottoman and Xinjiang Muslims invoked precedents established during the Muslim rebellion. For most Qing Muslims, though, Ottoman prestige was chiefly a function of the empire's guardianship of the twin shrines of Mecca and Medina. Each year the annual hajj pilgrimage drew tens to hundreds of pilgrims from Qing territory, and the majority of these stopped off in Istanbul on the way. There they would usually stay in a Sufi-run lodge and participate in the weekly audience that the sultan held during hajj season. In a letter in 1906, the ulama of Hami and Turfan told the sultan that the Muslims of Chinese Turkistan "believe a visit to your lofty residence prior to making the hajj is as much of a religious obligation as the trip to the Hijaz itself, and consider a pilgrimage to the caliphal seat as the fulfillment of the hajj."[1] The sultan's standing was further enhanced by his role in dispensing holy relics, such as hairs from the Prophet Muhammad's beard. In the late nineteenth century one of these greatly prized strands made its way into the possession of Vali Bay in Zharkent, and Kashgaris petitioned the court for the same favor.[2] Historian Mulla Musa Sayrami titled his 1906 history of Xinjiang *A Hamidian History* (*Tarikh-i Ḥamidi*) in honor of Abdulhamid and praised him as the "Ottoman Sultan of this land and people of Moghulistan."[3]

The journey from China to Arabia was arduous, and in comparison with Russian Muslims, Qing pilgrims were poorly serviced along the way. There is some evidence that during the hajj certain Kashgari pilgrims known as "hajj chiefs" (*hajjbashi*) would fan out along the itinerary through Russia, evidently with some pastoral function. In Yaqub Beg's day, a Naqshbandi shaykh with links to Kashgar occupied the post of "chief of the gate" (*kapı kethüda*) in Istanbul, a quasi-diplomatic position that in theory saw to the needs of Kashgari pilgrims.[4] As Naganawa Norihiro has shown in his research on the hajj from Central Asia, there were periodic efforts to revive this position.[5] In 1893, for instance, petitions were presented to this effect, and in 1906 a certain Musa Jalaluddin was appointed to the position of *sheikh ül-hujjaj* (head of the hajis), claiming that Qing officials had approved his appointment. Yet without the diplomatic protection of a Qing consul, Chinese Muslims inevitably had to rely on Russia and the Ottomans for support. Some of those who reached Istanbul via Russia were assisted by Russian officials in obtaining an onward permit for the Hijaz. Ottoman Turkey in turn recognized the de facto right of Russian officials to protect these Qing subjects in Ottoman domains. The Russian consul in Jiddah complained that while the Kashgaris availed themselves of his services in times of crisis, for example on the death of a pilgrim, they were liable to "suddenly remember" that they were Qing subjects if they wished to evade the consul's scrutiny.[6] As Lale Can has discussed, those who found themselves in financial or administrative difficulty during their travels also petitioned the Sublime Porte for aid, emphasizing their Ottoman "spiritual subjecthood."[7]

Notwithstanding the limited Ottoman support for Yaqub Beg, the Qing court did not perceive the Ottomans as a threat to its position in Xinjiang. Among Qing Muslims, it seems it was entirely possible to position oneself as a spiritual subject of the Ottoman sultan without this taking on subversive connotations. In 1893 an Ottoman traveler in Tianjin, for example, found Dungan Muslims there pronouncing the *khutba*, the dedication in which the name of the reigning sovereign was pronounced, to Sultan Abdulhamid. In 1906 a Bukharan named Muhammad Abdurahman Effendi, said to have studied for sixteen years in India, preached to the Muslims of the Qing capital. Warning them against sectarian division and customs that were not in accord with the *sunna*, his parting gift was to teach them the *khutba* as it was then being delivered in Mecca and Medina, including a benediction for Sultan Abdulhamid.[8] This situation contrasts starkly with Russia, where officials kept a keen eye out for signs of dual loyalties among the empire's Muslims and monitored the *khutba* closely. In Xinjiang, too, the Russian consuls policed the *khutba* in mosques frequented by Russian Muslims.[9]

For their part, the Ottomans had nothing to gain by inciting the Muslims of China to revolt against the Qing. Rather than lament the plight of Muslims under non-Muslim rule in China, liberal pan-Islamist thinkers of the Hamidian period were just as likely to express solidarity with China in its struggle against unequal treaties and concessions. Orientalist and missionary accounts of Islam in China, which were an important source of information for Ottoman and Russian Muslim views, helped to square this circle by depicting Islam as a rising force in China. Far from a Muslim community in need of Ottoman guidance, these accounts gave Chinese Muslims a leading role in China's national revival. One important source of this discourse was Vasilii Vasiliev's prediction, in the 1860s, that Islam would eventually emerge as China's national faith. Vasiliev's work was first discussed in Istanbul in the 1890s and remained popular, particularly among those who were committed to the idea of pan-Islamic solidarity. In 1913 the Islamist journal *The Straight Path* (*Sebil'ür-Reşad*) published a serialized translation of Vasiliev's influential lecture on Islam in China.[10]

One of only a few Muslims from China to participate in this ongoing discussion was Abdulaziz Ghuljali (i.e., from Ghulja), a Naqshbandi Sufi who taught Arabic at the Sublime Porte. In 1899, Ghuljali wrote a series of pieces on Islam in China for the Ottoman press, introducing readers to the diversity of China's Muslims, with articles on the Salars, the Dungans (a people he likened to the Ottoman Empire's crypto-Muslim Dönme), and the Turks of Chinese Turkistan. It was the Salars, according to Ghuljali, who were the most supportive of Ottoman-style modernization. In 1891 a Salar Muslim on his way back to China from study in Istanbul and Cairo had preached in Ghulja on the need to improve schooling by inviting teachers from India or Istanbul, and had encouraged the locals to import a printing press to publish books and periodicals. While seeking to correct certain errors that derived from the European press, Ghuljali concurred with the prevailing view of the Qing state's admiration for the Islamic faith. In his opinion, the small community of Muslim aristocrats from Xinjiang residing in the Forbidden City in Beijing was particularly significant in this respect: "from the Islamic world's point of view, it is important to call attention to the fact that these Beijing Turks . . . reside within the emperor's city, while preserving the name Chantou, which is Chinese for Turk."[11]

Events at the end of the nineteenth century seemed to confirm this perception of Qing Islamophilia. In 1898, Indian and Turkish newspapers reported that the Qing court, recognizing the vitality of its Muslim population, had decided to base its military response to Europe on them. This was a distorted account of the formation of the "Gansu Braves" (Ganjun), an army of Muslims from Gansu commissioned in response to an uprising in 1895 and who joined the Beijing garrison in 1898. Necib Asım, editor of the Istanbul daily the *Intrepid* (*İkdam*), expressed pride in the achievements of his coreligionists in China:

"To learn that in this far-off country our Muslim brethren . . . make up the most progressive, most industrious, and most daring class is naturally something that we will all be delighted at."[12] This excitement soon turned to dismay, however, when the Gansu Braves led the assault on Beijing's foreign legations during the Boxer Rebellion of 1900. From Germany, Kaiser Wilhelm organized a party of Ottoman officials and clerics, blessed by Caliph and Sultan Abdulhamid, to pacify the Muslim population of China. They hoped to achieve this by making direct contact with the Gansu Braves commander Dong Fuxiang, a man widely, though incorrectly, believed to be a Muslim.[13]

This first quasi-official Ottoman mission to China in 1901, sent in the wake of the Boxer Rebellion, pursued objectives largely devised by the sultan's European allies. It suggests that Sultan Abdulhamid saw his popularity among Qing Muslims not so much as a basis for independent activity in China, but as a bargaining chip in his dealings with European powers. It was not until 1908 that Abdulhamid took concrete steps toward strengthening his contacts with Chinese Muslims. In the wake of the visit to Istanbul of an eminent Beijing imam, the Ottoman court appointed a man named Ali Riza and a Daghistani collaborator named Tahir Effendi to teach in Peking's Ox Street madrasa. Yet although the two missionaries were initially acting on the sultan's instructions and receiving a stipend from the court, Istanbul's enthusiasm for the mission to Beijing seems to have soon waned. Following the Young Turk revolution of 1908 and the deposition of Sultan Abdulhamid in 1909, the two men found themselves cut off from Ottoman direction. "The Muslims here have the deepest love and affinity for the caliphate," Ali Riza complained in a letter to Istanbul in 1911, "but the court seems not to comprehend this."[14]

Vague hints of Ottoman missions to the Muslims of Xinjiang abound in this period. In 1879 the British ambassador in Beijing warned Qing officials that Abdulhamid was dispatching secret envoys to Kashgar, an accusation that would be heard many times again.[15] While there is no evidence for any court-appointed mission to Xinjiang in this period, this did not stop British and Russian diplomats from spying Ottoman intrigues in China's far west. Usually they saw these intrigues directed not at the Qing but against their own interests, and potentially in collusion with Qing officials. In 1904, for example, the Russian consul in Kashgar raised the alarm at the presence in his jurisdiction of a suspicious Turk, a certain Ilyas Effendi, who claimed to be there on business. Ilyas Effendi, the consul noted, seemed to be on good terms with Chinese officials and was aided by an equally suspect Chinese-speaking Russian Muslim.

The consul drew the conclusion that the Ottomans, with the blessing of Qing officials, had established an underground "trading and political agency" in Xinjiang, though nothing further is heard of this supposed Ottoman outpost in Xinjiang.[16]

In the absence of formal ties, much of the story of Ottoman-Qing connections revolves around individuals who inserted themselves into the space between the two empires. The pro-Ottoman mood certainly made Qing Muslims receptive to those who brought with them the prestige of Ottoman religious learning. As there was little supervision over mosques in China, it was entirely possible for such sojourners to perform the Friday prayers; indeed, it was a matter of local courtesy that they do so. Ottoman Muslims might also gain a following within local Sufi networks, and Turkish officers passing through Hami in 1917 found there a *muazzin* who had once been employed reciting the call to prayer in the Ayasofya mosque of Istanbul.[17] Historians of the late Ottoman Empire have described an increase in the frequency of Ottoman Muslims claiming descent from the Prophet, and this fact is reflected in claims to sayyid status made by Ottoman subjects in Xinjiang. A Chinese observer passing through the town of Kucha in 1916 noted several families of Turks residing there, whom the locals all honored as sayyids.[18] A Muslim journalist found a number of Bedouin Arabs in Yarkand similarly passing themselves off as sayyids.[19]

For every freelance Ottoman missionary in Xinjiang there were also unscrupulous individuals who sought to profit from Ottoman popularity (and some who blurred the line between these two categories). Sources describe a number of incidents in Xinjiang of fraudulent fund-raising on behalf of the sultan, an embarrassing phenomenon that the Ottomans were aware of and sought to stamp out. In 1906, for example, a Russian Muslim posing as an Ottoman officer swindled more than five thousand taels out of the Muslims of Suiding.[20] In 1910 a man appeared in Ghulja in military dress soliciting donations for the Ottomans, and a rumor spread that he was a "pasha" from Istanbul who intended to establish an Ottoman consulate. Suspicious locals wired a query to Istanbul and were told that no such agent had been sent. The man, who turned out to be a French impostor, escaped with a haul of two thousand rubles.[21] Such difficulties convinced Qing Muslims of the need for better diplomatic ties between Istanbul and Beijing. Far from pursuing anti-Qing politics, therefore, Muslims in Xinjiang seeking to forge ties with the Ottoman Empire had a direct interest in strengthening, not weakening, the Qing Empire's global standing.

From the Ili Valley to Istanbul

In the late nineteenth century, as we have seen, Vali Bay's landholdings and business interests made him by far the wealthiest man in the district. To admiring Russian officials, he was the model of an enterprising self-made man. He was recognized as one of only a few "honored citizens" (*pochetnyi grazhdan*) of Zharkent and was admitted to the first merchants' guild of Vernyi. Perhaps the highlight of his career came in 1896, when he represented the natives of Semireche at the coronation of Tsar Nicholas II in Moscow. Here the one-time cart dealer found himself mingling with the leading lights of fin de siècle diplomacy, among them Qing China's own representative, Li Hongzhang, Viceroy of Zhili and imperial envoy to the capitals of Europe. As it happened, the two men met at the coronation. Li, among the most pro-Russian members of the Qing elite, evidently saw Vali Bay as a man to be cultivated and presented him with a Qing medal of honor for services rendered to the Manchu dynasty.[22] On his trip back from Moscow to Semireche, Vali Bay stopped off in Bukhara to pay his respects to the amir, who also granted him a star of honor.[23]

Vali Bay directed some of his largesse to philanthropic projects as he took on the role of local cultural patron. In 1887, a few years after the final conclusion of the migration, local Muslims petitioned him to support the construction of a mosque, resulting in the grandiose hall of worship that still stands in the town's center and is known simply as Vali Bay's mosque. What is immediately striking about the mosque is its mixed style, combining a Turkistani entrance arch with a mosque hall essentially Chinese in composition. The hall was the work of a Chinese artisan and was directly copied from the main Taranchi Mosque in Ghulja (shown on page 60). The Chinese style, much more evocative of Dungan mosques in Gansu than anything in Kashgar or Yarkand, typifies the cosmopolitan Ili Valley, where Taranchis were subject to the influence of Qing culture to a greater degree than their coreligionists in the south of Xinjiang. As a symbol it conveyed the message that, although they were now Russian subjects, the Taranchis would not simply adapt to Tatar or Turkistani norms. Its construction put on public display in Semireche an embodiment of a distinctly Qing Muslim community.

Clearly Vali Bay had an interest preserving the Taranchis as a community apart from the rest of the Russian Empire's Muslims. In many ways the rigid social boundaries of Semireche society contributed to the isolation of the Taranchis from other groups. One tsarist official who witnessed the migration from

The Vali Bay mosque in Zharkent, 1911. The man in the dark coat in the foreground is most likely Vali Bay himself. (M. Philips Price Collection. Royal Geographical Society rgsF039/0168.)

Ghulja to Semireche noted that, whereas in Ghulja the Kazakhs, Taranchis, and Dungans had all submitted to a common Islamic court, the strict boundaries between communities in Russian territory now prevented this.[24] Almost all of the Taranchi religious elite had migrated to Russia, giving the community a degree of cultural self-sufficiency at first. Yet there was no way to isolate the Taranchis completely from Russian Muslim society, as gradually the ulama dwindled.[25] In this situation, Vali Bay's position as communal patron obliged him to tap into social and cultural resources deriving from elsewhere in Russia, particularly among the Tatars, who found work as schoolteachers throughout Semireche and the Kazakh steppe. The entrepreneur's authority did not rest on the support of an entrenched ulama, and he publicly positioned himself in support of the new form of education that these Tatars brought to Semireche—the so-called New Method.[26] In the madrasa attached to his mosque in Zharkent, Vali Bay hired a Tatar named Gabdurahman Damolla b. Gataullah Muhammadi (d. 1909), who hailed from a line of Tatar madrasa instructors and was well connected to the intellectual scene in both Kazan and Bukhara.[27] Locally he became known as a champion of the New Method and attracted a following of Taranchi and Dungan students, not only from Semireche, but from Ghulja too.

As the network of Tatar-run schools in Russian territory extended into Semireche, it drew the interest of Russian Muslims residing in Xinjiang, particularly in Ghulja and Tarbaghatay. By the late 1890s, prominent Xinjiang Tatars were connected to educational reform efforts across the border in Russia, with the Ghulja *aqsaqal*, Faziljan Yunich, organizing fund-raising efforts for the Semipalatinsk Islamic Charitable Society.[28] This soon led to the first experiments with the New Method in Xinjiang itself, catering to the children of Russian subjects in Xinjiang. Reports from 1900 indicate the presence of one such school in Tarbaghatay run by the son of an imam from Semipalatinsk.[29]

Among local Muslims in Xinjiang, the first to show an interest in the New Method were the Musabayevs, a family from the town of Artush in the south who had recently established themselves in the Ili Valley. The patriarch Musa Bay's background is poorly known, though one account says that upon returning from a trip abroad he set up a tanning workshop in the Ili Valley in the 1880s. Musa Bay handed on this leatherworks business to his two sons, Husayn and Bahauddin (d. 1928), and by 1903 the Musabayev workshop was worth around 300,000 rubles. This was still a small firm by Russian standards, but was three times the size of their nearest local rival.[30] The quality of its output surpassed similar enterprises across the border in Semireche, enabling the Musabayevs to compete in Russia's leather market. From Ghulja, the brothers ran a network of stores stretching across the border to Zharkent and Semipalatinsk.[31] In their Ghulja factory, they mainly employed Kashgaris from the south, but in their shops they also hired Tatars as shopkeepers and accountants, thereby tapping into the preexisting network of Tatar trade along the steppe route to Russia.

The record of the Musabayev family of Artush as cultural patrons dates back to at least 1894–1895, when Husayn Musabayev refurbished one of Kashgar's most prestigious madrasas, the Khanliq.[32] A few years later the family sponsored Kashgar's first-ever publishing enterprise, the Sunlight Press, as Rian Thum has recently discussed.[33] The shift to Ghulja situated them in a social climate that was supportive of reformed schooling. Active in importing business practices and technology from Russia, the Musabayevs must have felt a need for better-educated employees than could be found locally, and in 1898 they decided to start experimenting with the New Method. One of the pupils in this trial was Masud Sabri, a young boy destined for a long and distinguished career in Xinjiang politics. In the 1940s, Masud recalled how he was pulled out of his *maktab* one day and had geography and mathematics textbooks thrust into his hands. Six months later, he and his classmates took an examination.[34] Evidently satisfied with the results, in early 1900 the Musabayevs turned the school that they ran into an explicitly Jadidist institution.[35] As a teacher they recruited one of Gabdurahman Damolla's students from the Vali Bay madrasa in Zharkent, a man by the name of Muhammad Masum Effendi.

This connection to Zharkent places Jadidism in Xinjiang in a line of transmission from Tatar innovations. According to Masud's account, Husayn Musabayev's inspiration to sponsor New Method schools came from a meeting with Ahmad Bay Husaynov (1837–1906), founder of the modernized Husayniyya madrasa in Orenburg, and the Musabayevs subsequently sent a pair of students to the Husayniyya. Yet before long its patrons reached out in a different direction. As was typical of early Jadidist schools, the Musabayev enterprise was on shaky pedagogical foundations, as Masum Effendi only had the training for a year's curriculum. Whether motivated by a desire to maintain independence from Tatar competitors, or simply by the prestige of contacts with the Ottoman court, in 1902 Husayn Musabayev decided to send the teacher to Istanbul for further study. Along the way, Masum Effendi stopped off in the Crimean town of Baghchasaray to visit the Tatar publicist Ismail Gasprinskii, considered by many to be the father of the New Method. The two discussed the state of the new schools in Xinjiang and the prospects for the development of Jadidist instruction in China. In contrast to Russia, where the New Method had aroused official suspicions, Masum Effendi told Gasprinskii that Chinese officials were wholly in favor of it. According to Masum, the circuit commissioner in Ili had issued a decree praising the New Method and declaring his support for the promotion of New Method schools.[36]

In 1904, after a course of study at Istanbul's Imperial School of Civil Administration, Masum Effendi returned to Ghulja and was appointed head of the Musabayev school, which from this point on was known as the Maktab-i Hamidi-i Husayni, in honor of both the Ottoman sultan Abdulhamid II and the school's patron, Husayn Musabayev.[37] According to a description from 1910, the school's curriculum was based on Istanbul methods and taught accounting as well as Russian and Chinese.[38] Next to the school was a reading room that subscribed to periodicals from Russia. Upon returning to Ghulja, Masum Effendi encouraged his patrons to send a group of students to Istanbul. He wrote a letter of introduction to the sultan for the first party of four, which included his pupil Masud, and with this recommendation the students were enrolled in Istanbul's Hamidiyya High School. Others followed this initial cohort, and by the time of the outbreak of the Balkan Wars in 1913, a total of fifteen students from Xinjiang were studying in Istanbul, including six at the Military Academy, four at the Galatasaray Lycée, one at the Imperial School of Arts, and one, most likely Masud Sabri, at the prestigious medical faculty of the Imperial University.[39]

The 1905 Revolution and the Taranchis

In 1905 a wave of peasant revolts, strikes, and mutinies struck Russia, bringing the tsarist monarchy to the brink of collapse. Central Asia, too, saw social democratic agitation in its cities and peasant militancy in the countryside, but primarily among the Russian population. For Muslim society the most significant outcome of the revolution was Tsar Nicholas II's manifesto of October 17 granting new civil rights to the empire's subjects. Among its consequences in Turkistan were the growth of a liberal press and the formation of civic associations. A new rhetoric centered on notions of "progress" and "freedom" emerged in public discourse, even in distant corners of the empire such as Semireche. Encouraged by the newfound freedoms, loose networks of Jadidist activists sought to implement a more thoroughgoing vision of social reform, but these efforts soon ran into opposition from the very people whose financial resources they were counting on, highlighting a deep contradiction in the Jadidist project.

There were by this time inchoate currents of political opposition among the Taranchis in Semireche, who resented Vali Bay's dictatorial position and the connivance of local Russian officials in his self-aggrandizement. Some historians mention groups of self-styled "progressives" in Vernyi or Pishpek.[40] In Zharkent itself, such dissidents were known as "short-shirts," for wearing short Russian-style shirts instead of long Taranchi coats. The short-shirts were marginal actors and could only resort to the weapons of the weak in their struggle against Vali Bay. In the days following the tsar's manifesto in 1905, a liberal Russian newspaper described a satirical cartoon that circulated in Zharkent depicting Vali Bay in a velvet coat; in his right pocket sat the district commandant (*uezdnyi nachal'nik*), and in his left, the local *aqsaqal*. Both try to climb out, but Vali Bay advises them: "Sit still, our pockets are warm, and the procurator's pockets are cold. If you climb out you'll freeze!"[41]

In January 1906, Gabdurahman Damolla Muhammadi announced his intention to found an Islamic Society (Jam'iyyat-i Islāmiyya) in Zharkent to sponsor educational activities. In collaboration with two outsiders, one a Bashkir from the Volga, the other a "Sart" from Kokand, Muhammadi succeeded in opening a reading room, and published its constitution as required by law.[42] These were modest initiatives, but they had the potential to create a focal point for further reformist agitation, something that worried Vali Bay. The entrepreneur had positioned himself as a patron of the New Method and won praise for these efforts in the Russian Muslim press.[43] Yet this support was centered on his mosque and madrasa, and can equally be seen as an effort to position himself at the center of intellectual life among the migrant Taranchis. He was resolutely hostile to any efforts to create alternative sources of cultural or spiritual authority in the community. To fend off the threat of Gabdurahman Damolla's fledgling Islamic Society, Vali Bay organized a petition to have the *mudarris'* two collaborators driven out of town, and the Semireche authorities obliged.[44]

Down but not out, Gabdurahman Damolla now traveled to Vernyi for the founding of its Islamic Society. The first meeting of this society was held in the city's Tatar neighborhood, and drew up a petition for a new Turkistani spiritual assembly. The petition was typical of Semireche politics in its sensitivity to communal autonomy. The signatories specifically requested that seats on the spiritual assembly be allocated to qadis from "each of the Muslim peoples (*tā'ifa*)" of Turkistan: one each for the Kazakh, Kirghiz, Sart, Qalmaq, Noghay

(i.e., Tatar), Taranchi, and Dungan peoples. (This was in contrast to the Tash-
kent ulama, who called for a spiritual assembly that would represent all
Turkistani Muslims, "whether they are Sart, Noghay, Kazakh, or Kirghiz.")[45]
Further, they argued that since the Muslims of Semireche "in terms of race (*jins*)
consist of five groups," each of the Kazakhs, Kirghiz, Taranchis, Sarts, and
Noghays should be assigned a seat in the new State Duma.

The idea of shifting the locus of Taranchi spiritual authority away from
Zharkent was a threat to Vali Bay and his allies, who were unwilling to submit
to any religious body outside their control. Two weeks later, Vali Bay responded
by convening his own assembly in Zharkent, summoning local Taranchis, Dungans, and Kazakhs who had migrated from China. Vali Bay was honorary
chair of the meeting, with secretaries drawn from leading members of the
Taranchi ulama. It had recently been announced that Zharkent District would
be entitled to two seats in the State Duma: one to be elected by the town, the
other by the countryside. Preempting the elections, the meeting proclaimed Vali
Bay as Zharkent's representative to the Duma.[46] The resolution of this choreo-
graphed event was a document that appealed to the distinct historical experience of the Xinjiang émigrés to argue for autonomy in religious affairs—not
from the tsarist administration but from Russian Muslims: "For over two hundred years under Chinese rule, we Taranchis and Dungans of Semireche Province, and Kazakhs of this province's Zharkent District, enjoyed the autonomy
given to us in China in our spiritual affairs, at the head of which we had the
high religious offices of mufti, qadi, akhund and other figures. . . . Although
we follow the same religion as the Muslims of the Russian interior, yet over time
we have established our own traditions, and we differ to some degree from the
Muslims of Russia as a distinct nationality (*natsional'nost'*)."[47]

While the resolution recognized the fact of ethnic difference among the migrants from China, ethnicity alone was not enough to ward off the centralizing
initiatives of Russian Muslim activists. Rather, it grounded its argumentation
in the Qing, and indeed Chinese, origins of this community. As is well known,
much of the post-1905 agitation among Muslims in Russia invoked the idea of
the Muslims of Russia as a nation. Here, Vali Bay was countering this with the
idea of the Muslims of China as a nation. The declaration said in words what
his mosque said in bricks and mortar: we may be living on Russian soil as
subjects of the tsar, but our communal and religious norms derive from our
experience as Qing subjects. It was a strategic invocation of diasporic status in

return for the recognition of Vali Bay's fiefdom at the center of communal authority.

Vali Bay and his critics were now on a collision course. In 1907 the Tashkent Jadidist organ *Progress* (*Taraqqi*) printed a scathing public attack on him, a letter signed only by "the Taranchis."[48] In it they condemned Vali Bay's manipulation of local elections and accused him of standing in the way of progress by closing the Zharkent reading room. Going on, they voiced deeper grievances against him: that he had compelled the Taranchis to migrate from Ghulja to Semireche for personal gain, and that by colluding with local officials to build up his land holdings he had reduced the Taranchis to poverty. This was an attack on Vali Bay's authority without precedent, and when *Progress* hit the streets of Zharkent, Vali Bay ordered the canton head Qayyum Beg to buy up all copies of the offending paper. He then summoned the district's qadis and *aqsaqal*s to a meeting. After a day of deliberation, they decided that the authors of the affront were likely to be the short-shirts. They also pointed the finger at Mamur Effendi, one of Gabdurahman Damolla's students, who had supported his teacher in 1906 and participated in the Vernyi Islamic Society. They decided to drive Mamur out of town and pursue the short-shirts with the help of the district commandant, a man whose cooperation could be relied upon. According to one account, as accusations flew back and forth between 1905 and 1910, as many as forty young Taranchis spent time in the local lockup.[49] Mamur escaped across the border to Ghulja, where he became an imam.

Vali Bay's position seemed as secure as ever. In July 1908, the tsar's inspector, Count Pahlen, stopped off in Zharkent during his tour of Turkistan. A group of Taranchi petitioners who had a grievance against Vali Bay's subordinates tried to appeal directly to the count while he was passing through, but local officials persuaded them to delay—lest they spoil the party.[50] Vali Bay received Pahlen in grand Oriental fashion in a silk tent on the edge of town, slicing with his own knife the choice cuts of a roast sheep for his guest.[51] Pahlen had little time for investigations, making a cursory inspection of the local jail and finding it in "perfect" condition before continuing on his way. Perhaps the count was not the best person to resolve conflict among the Taranchis anyway. In his memoirs of the trip, he betrays his ignorance of Semireche's history by describing Vali Bay as the "chief of the Taranchi tribe" of Kazakhs. Although he erred in equating Vali Bay with the hereditary Chinggisid nobility he had met among

Muslim dignitaries in Semireche, 1899. Vali Bay is seated, third from left. To his right is a Dungan *volost* head. (Central State Archive for Film, Photo, and Audio Documents of the Kyrgyz Republic.)

the Kazakhs, in terms of his host's authority within the community, he was not far wrong.

Merchants and Mandarins in Kashgar

Both Russia and the Qing were undergoing turbulent transitions toward constitutional rule in this period, but the process played itself out at a different pace on each side of the border. In places such as Semireche, where the wealthy elite had already positioned themselves on the side of the Jadidist discourse of progress, the agitation that surrounded the 1905 revolution brought the New Method's proponents into conflict with its patrons. In Xinjiang, by contrast, it was the late-Qing reform process that first created the conditions for reform-minded Muslims to extend the Jadidist experiments of the north to the south. From 1907 onward Kashgar became the site of parallel efforts to reform traditional pedagogies, both in the Muslim *maktab* and the Chinese *xuetang*, and in many ways these were complementary projects. For this reason it is important to situate the controversies around the issue of school reform against the backdrop of the impact of the Qing New Policies (*xinzheng*) in Xinjiang.

The New Policies were a series of initiatives launched by the Qing court in its final decade of rule leading toward the promulgation of a draft imperial constitution. Modernizing Chinese literati and military leaders such as Zhang Zhidong and Yuan Shikai provided much of the energy behind these policies. In 1902 Zhang set about organizing a modernized "New Army" (*xinjun*) in the province of Hubei, and in 1908 a unit of this Hubei army was transferred to the Ili Valley. Zhang was also a driving force in the policy of New Education (*xinxue*), decreed in 1904. The most dramatic consequence of the New Education policy—the abolition of the centuries-old examination system—meant little to Xinjiang Muslims. Far more significant was its network of empire-wide reformed schools, which introduced a scientific curriculum to the traditional, and highly unpopular, Confucian *xuetang*. These *xuetang* reached the province in 1907, to be directed by the newly created provincial superintendent of schools. Meanwhile, the adoption of a Qing constitution in 1908, and with it a blueprint for a national consultative assembly, led to the establishment of a preparatory office for a provincial consultative bureau (*ziyiju*) in Ürümchi. Elsewhere in the province, the principle of local self-government (*difang zizhi*) informed efforts to increase the involvement of local elites in policy initiatives. Despite serious funding shortfalls, officials in Xinjiang tried to act according to the spirit, if not the letter, of the New Policy decrees that reached them.

Local fiscal autonomy and the practice of tax farming deepened the relationship between local elites and Qing officials. In particular, the imposition of the *lijin* (domestic transit duty) created opportunities for merchants to work with the local bureaucracy to meet its budgetary needs. As discussed in Chapter 2, Liu Jintang had abolished the Xinjiang *lijin* for fear of pushing locals into securing Russian subjecthood, but in the wake of the crushing Boxer indemnity of 1901 Beijing's subsidies to Xinjiang plummeted, and the province had no choice but to revive it. Qing officials in Kashgar were still wary of any policies that might push locals into the arms of the *aqsaqals*, though, and initially resisted its reintroduction. While *lijin* bureaus sprang up throughout the rest of Xinjiang, the Kashgar circuit tried to meet the local financial shortfall by increasing the levy on passports for travel to Russia and through a straightforward toll on pack

The Xinjiang Provincial Consultative Bureau, Ürümchi, 1910. (Photograph by George E. Morrison. State Library of New South Wales [1010033].)

animals leaving Chinese territory—a toll that would apply equally to Russian caravans. After two years of experimentation this approach proved ineffective and *lijin* duties were reimposed. Unlike elsewhere in the province, however, *lijin* collection was presented to local merchants as a tax-farming opportunity.

Akhun Bay and his sons, Karim and Umar, still dominated the Old City of Kashgar. The Akhunbayevs dealt primarily in wool and cotton, both of which were enjoying strong worldwide demand at the turn of the century. Drawing on a network of buyers stationed throughout the south of Xinjiang, they sourced wool from Kirghiz pastoralists and cotton from the local peasantry. In Kashgar, the produce was packed and loaded onto caravans to Issiq Köl and then shipped by boat and railroad to Russia, usually headed for the trading fairs of Irbit in Siberia or Nizhnii Novgorod, halfway between Kazan and Moscow.[52] It was Umar Akhunbayev who bought the *lijin* contract for the Kashgar circuit, pledging fixed sums for each of the main trading towns, from the wealthy entrepôts of Kashgar (16,000 taels annually), Khotan (15,000) and Yarkand

(14,000), to the small bazaars of Yengisar (3,000) and Maralbeshi (2,000).[53] Contracting out the *lijin* was not only a good source of income for the Kashgari *bay*s, it also put them in a strong position in relation to Qing officials, who depended on them for their salaries. The Akhunbayevs cultivated good relations with both Qing and Russian officialdom, regularly wining and dining the circuit commissioner and the consul.

Tash Akhun, a wealthy native of Artush, offers a second example of how partnering with Chinese officialdom could be the secret to success in this period. Sent to Russia by Kashgar circuit commissioner Yuan Hongyou (1841–1912) to obtain machinery to modernize the Kashgar mint, Tash Akhun took advantage of his trip to familiarize himself with the latest dying techniques, with an eye to improving the quality of his *sargaz*—a local textile. Returning to Xinjiang he set up production in secret, and before long a new and improved "Tash Akhun *sargaz*" burst onto the Kashgar market. The entrepreneur soon found his product in demand in bazaars beyond Kashgar and became the region's main supplier of cloth for men's robes, undercutting the fashionable Russian textiles that were encroaching on the market. As the Russian consul put it in 1908, "now even commoners, town-dwellers mostly, have the ability to dress almost as elegantly in cloth of local production as in cheap Russian cottons, but much more inexpensively."[54] Tash Akhun remained on good terms with the circuit commissioner, and in August 1909 he was appointed *beg* of Artush.[55]

Kashgar's Old City merchantry and those from neighboring Artush were natural rivals. The former controlled the district's largest bazaar, with tens of thousands flocking to it on market days. The latter sat astride the Naryn–Issiq Köl trade route to Russia, the main outlet for Kashgar's exports. Competition between the two factions intensified in 1905, when the Musabayevs returned to Kashgar and tried to carve out a niche in local trade with Russia. The new arrivals made a splash by offering local sellers a higher price for their wool, sparking a bidding war with the Akhunbayevs. The Kashgaris responded to this threat by swearing before the town's qadis to exclude the Artush outsiders from the Kashgar bazaar. In the end, though, the Kashgaris decided not to ban their competitors, for fear that the Artush merchantry might in retaliation block their caravan traffic heading to Russia. To avert an all-out trade war between the neighboring towns, the two parties negotiated a truce by fixing a price for wool. For the time being, the Musabayevs conceded the popular Naryn–Issiq Köl trade route to the Akhunbayevs and instead shipped their goods over the Irkeshtam pass to the Ferghana Valley and by train to Tashkent.[56]

The division of the local merchantry into oasis-based factions and family units ran counter to the direction of late-Qing economic reforms, which encouraged the pooling of capital and the formation of companies under official oversight—a model summed up in the formula: "officials supervise and merchants manage" (*guandu shangban*). Kashgar officials did what they could to resolve the conflict between the Akhunbayevs and Musabayevs, although without great success. At a dinner in 1907, held by Yuan Hongyou to welcome Husayn Musabayev back from the hajj, Yuan urged Husayn and Karim Akhunbayev to cooperate in developing the circuit and proposed the formation of a joint-stock company to exploit local mineral resources—particularly gold deposits around Khotan. The circuit commissioner stumped up the first ten thousand taels and offered to create a cheap supply of labor for the company by halting the seasonal labor migration to Russia. In the end the company raised only twelve thousand taels, but it was enough to build a meeting hall and hire a Russian engineer to scout mineral deposits in the Khotan and Turfan areas, recruited through the Musabayev network in Russia.[57] The following year, in response to decrees encouraging local self-government, Yuan Hongyou tried to form a municipal council, hoping to enlist the aid of Kashgar's *bay*s in the various New Policy projects that the Qing court required of him. The British consul called it an "advisory council," corresponding to the Chinese *nisihui*, but locals drew on a Russian analogy and referred to it as the "Kashgar Duma." Rather than hold elections, Yuan simply instructed the wealthy traders to choose twenty members and singled out Husayn Musabayev as his preferred chairman.[58]

Yet given the rivalry between the Musabayevs and the Akhunbayevs, such collaborations were unlikely to last long. At the same time as he was trying to set up the Kashgar Duma, the circuit commissioner was overseeing the introduction of a new simplified scale of *lijin* collection, which provided new grounds for competition between the Kashgar and Artush factions. Having sold off the *lijin* to the Akhunbayevs, Yuan lacked reliable figures for the scale of trade in his circuit, and *lijin* income in Kashgar had gradually declined. By 1908, the Kashgar *lijin* contract had dropped to 200 *yuanbao* (10,000 taels). Spying an opportunity, the Musabayevs launched a bid to wrest the *lijin* collection from the Akhunbayevs, offering Yuan 300 *yuanbao* annually. The bid backfired, though, by indicating to the circuit commissioner the true value of commerce in his circuit. Instead of playing one faction off against another, Yuan decided to place control of the *lijin* back in the hands of Chinese customs officials, along the lines of Xinjiang's other circuits. In September 1908 the customs duties more than doubled, from 3 percent to 6.5 percent, drawing an angry response from Kashgar's shopkeepers, who shut their doors indefinitely.[59] In such a climate, it is not surprising that Yuan Hongyou's joint-stock company and the Kashgar Duma both failed to get off the ground.

Shami Damolla and the *Maktab* Question in Kashgar

Establishing a Jadidist school in Kashgar was not likely to be as easy as it had been in Ghulja. In Kashgar, in contrast to Xinjiang's north, there was a network of madrasas that underpinned the authority of the local ulama, whose views on the new schools would carry weight. The peripatetic Tatar schoolteachers who had been hired in the virgin lands of northern Xinjiang could not easily find sponsors in Kashgar or Yarkand, where the authority to teach was acquired in long-standing circuits of training that might extend to Bukhara or Istanbul, but not to Kazan. Given the serious commercial rivalry that the Musabayevs' return from Ghulja to Kashgar ignited between the Kashgar and Artush merchantry, furthermore, it is not hard to see how the move might also provoke a cultural clash between the two factions.

In 1907, Husayn Musabayev started holding informal gatherings in Kashgar toward the formation of a charitable society, hoping to raise funds for New Method schools similar to those the family had established in Ghulja.[60] British consul George Macartney looked positively on the initiative: "it promises to become the Muhammadan rallying point in these parts."[61] In this project Husayn Musabayev teamed up with an Ottoman Arab, Said b. Muhammad al-Asali (1870–?), who was known in Xinjiang as Shami ("The Syrian") Damolla. Shami Damolla was linked to Salafist circles in the Ottoman Empire and India, and was not a product of the Jadidist tradition. Originally from (Syrian) Tripoli in the Ottoman Empire, he gained his theological training in the madrasas of north India in the 1890s and for a while taught Arabic at an elite Muslim school in Hyderabad. At the turn of the century he returned to Istanbul, where for a few months he served as editor of the Arabic-language edition of the journal *Information* (*Malumat*). Soon, though, the publication and those associated with it found themselves the victim of Sultan Abdulhamid's crackdown on press freedom, and Shami Damolla went into exile. He headed first to Egypt and then in 1901 traveled via India to Xinjiang. On this first sojourn in the province he seems to have kept a relatively low profile, running a private hadith class in Kashgar. It was on his second trip in 1907 that he found the confidence to pronounce on religious orthodoxy and promote his preferred version of modernized Islam.[62]

These first steps toward *maktab* reform among Muslims in Kashgar coincided with the Qing policy of New Education, which also reached Kashgar in 1907. To many locals the two projects must have looked very similar, which raised the question of the relationship between them. While the new *xuetang* were in theory compulsory, they were hamstrung by a serious lack of funding and would inevitably depend on men such as the Akhunbayevs and Musabayevs for financial support. Xinjiang's provincial superintendent of schools, Du-tong .(1864–1929), himself a Manchu, was not opposed to admitting Muslim teachers to the reformed *xuetang*. Indeed, he recognized that having Muslims teach Muslims was in many ways preferable to dispatching Chinese instructors to the south of Xinjiang.[63] Kashmir circuit commissioner Yuan Hongyou seems to have held the same opinion, and instead of competing with the *maktab* reformers, he came out in support of Husayn Musabayev's society and transferred to its control a local *xuetang* that took Muslim students.[64]

This was a promising beginning, but there was trouble brewing. While he found the Musabayevs receptive to his views, Shami Damolla also made enemies in Kashgar with his frank criticism of local standards of learning. In meetings with the Russian consul he freely vented his frustration with the Kashgari ulama.[65] Early in 1908 he upbraided the locals publicly in a speech in Kashgar's main Idgah Mosque on the need for school reform. Before he had finished, one of Umar Akhunbayev's men jumped up and shouted him down, causing a scandal that went all the way to the circuit commissioner's desk. Reviewing the case, Yuan sided with the Musabayevs and sacked the chief qadi of Kashgar, a close associate of the Akhunbayevs.[66]

No doubt there was some doctrinal dimension to this conflict. The local ulama were predominantly members of the Naqshbandi Sufi brotherhood, a mystical current in Islam whose practices were at odds with Shami Damolla's hadith-centered spirituality. Yet we can well imagine how many Kashgar Muslims must have perceived the situation at this point: the cosmopolitan Musabayevs had teamed up with a dubious exile from Ottoman lands, who was seen hobnobbing with the Russian consul and the Kashgar circuit commissioner, to bring down the chief qadi of Kashgar. From this point onward, Old City sympathy for the Musabayev charitable society quickly dried up. According to the Russian consul, when members realized how much money would be required to maintain the new schools, interest in the project faltered, and the conflict with the Akhunbayevs effectively killed it off. In 1909, the acting British consul found that the Musabayev initiative had left little trace in Kashgar society: "with the exception of a few of the better read, nobody has ever heard of the 'Jamait-i-Kharia' [sic] of Kazan, and there are no ideas of inaugurating a similar institution in Kashgar."[67] The Musabayevs retreated to their hometown of Artush, where they established a small New Method school and imported a set of textbooks from a Tatar publishing house in Kazan.

As *maktab* reform ran into difficulties in Kashgar, the New Education *xuetang* stumbled on. To attract donors, Qing officials promised to create space for Islamic instruction in the *xuetang*, and in 1909 Husayn Musabayev and Umar Akhunbayev contributed three thousand taels each to local *xuetang*s, with another five thousand raised among the rest of the Kashgar merchantry.[68] Strategies to meet the funding gap elsewhere in Xinjiang proved less successful. In Khotan officials imposed a new levy on births and deaths, something unknown in Islamic tradition. Khotan's chief qadi lent the policy religious sanction, but other mullas in Khotan issued a fatwa countering his views and denouncing him as an infidel. Officials further antagonized locals by forcing them to donate building materials for the new schools.[69] Worried by these trends, the British consul in Kashgar informed the authorities in Ürümchi, who dispatched two envoys on a fact-finding mission to the south. The trip led to a modification of the *xuetang*: respected mullas would now teach alongside Chinese instructors. Kashgar officials sought to build on this compromise and consulted the chief qadi on the possibility of allowing Chinese to teach in Muslim schools, thereby merging the *maktab* and *xuetang*. The chief qadi raised no objection to this, but when the plan was announced a mob assaulted him and stripped him of his seals.[70]

Having failed in his efforts to win the Kashgaris to his vision of progress, Shami Damolla headed north, continuing to inveigh against local distortions of the sharia. Evidently troubled by the pervasive custom of shrine worship, he penned a critique of the legend surrounding one of Xinjiang's holiest shrines, that of the Seven Sleepers in Tuyuq, east of Turfan.[71] Shami Damolla's criticism was convincing enough for one local historian, Mulla Musa Sayrami, to include it in his work on the history of Xinjiang.[72] The Ottoman made a positive impression elsewhere too. On visits to Tarbaghatay he met the Russian Muslim imam Qurbangali Khalidi, who accorded him a brief mention in the biographical dictionary he was compiling, describing him as "a great man, learned and erudite."[73]

While passing through Kucha, Shami Damolla encountered the Japanese officer Hino Tsuyoshi, who invited him to visit Japan. A journey to the Far East was still Shami Damolla's intention when he met the Russian consul in Ürümchi, but at some point he changed course and returned to Anatolia via Russian Turkistan, making a pilgrimage to the shrine of the hadith scholar Imam al-Bukhari along the way.[74] Political change in Istanbul was probably what drew Shami Damolla back to the Ottoman capital. In 1908 the Young Turks had forced Sultan Abdulhamid to reinstate the Ottoman constitution and relinquish his authority, before deposing him in 1909. The turn of events must have come as a relief to Shami Damolla, even though the westernizing Young Turks were hardly likely to welcome back the exiled Arab theologian with open arms. These political sensitivities may help to explain why when Shami Damolla arrived in Istanbul he introduced himself as a representative of the Muslims of Chinese Turkistan—Kashgar's *sheikh ül-Islam* no less. The presence of this well-traveled theologian excited local religious circles, and the editors of the Islamist monthly *Explication of Truth* (*Beyan'ül-Hak*) published a speech that he delivered in the capital, in which he praised the Guangxu emperor's dedication to the cause of educational reform.[75] Sultan Mehmed Reshad (r. 1909–1918) received the visitor with great respect, granting the Muslims of Kashgar a strand of the Prophet Muhammad's beard and a collection of religious texts.

Yet Shami Damolla's triumphant return to the Abode of the Caliphate was to be short-lived. At some point a Kashgari in Istanbul denounced him as a fraud, and he was again expelled from Ottoman territory.[76] Now doubly persona non grata in Ottoman domains, Shami Damolla made his way back to Xinjiang. Arriving in Kashgar in early 1911, he fired a parting shot at his enemies in the form of a letter to the sultan, signed by a hundred and sixty-five local Muslims, refuting the accusations against him. The letter indicates that Shami Damolla's claim in Istanbul—that he was there as a representative of the Kashgaris—was not entirely groundless. Thanking the court for its gifts, they explained that "in 1910 we sent Mavlana Sayyid Shami Damolla as our plenipotentiary representative to the Holy Kingdom. . . . We have greatly benefited from his teaching, and honestly consider him a progressive member of society. Recently we hear that a reckless group has made accusations against him. We sincerely hope you will not believe this wild talk."[77] Lacking alternative means to support himself, Shami Damolla continued to court controversy in Xinjiang by collecting donations for the Ottomans.[78] In 1913, a party of Arabs informed on him to local officials, who seized the funds he had raised, as well as the strand of the prophet's beard he had brought back from Istanbul. In response, Shami Damolla's friends wrote once more to the Ottoman sultan, asking him to request the Russian consul to intervene in the affair. Shami Damolla, they explained, "is a great and learned man. For fifteen years he has been spreading knowledge in our land, and is much loved by all."[79]

It is difficult to say how much these letters represent Shami Damolla's ventriloquism and how much the genuine voice of the Kashgar community. Subsequent Turkish visitors to Xinjiang dismissed Shami Damolla as a charlatan cashing in on Ottoman prestige for his own benefit, but there is no doubt that he enjoyed a degree of local support. What this episode shows is that links between Kashgar and Istanbul relied on the initiative of individuals of various backgrounds and political outlooks, and that ructions in Ottoman politics would make themselves felt as far away as China. The religious opposition to the Young Turks, embodied by Shami Damolla, could certainly still obtain a hearing among the Muslims of China by tapping into their deep respect for Ottoman religiosity and its symbols. The question to be asked now was whether or not his Young Turk detractors, who had driven him out of Istanbul, would find a similarly warm reception in Xinjiang for their views.

A Kashgari Jadidist: Abdulqadir Damolla

The story so far has centered on patrons rather than the patronized, and we have seen few examples of native Kashgari Jadidists. Abdulqadir Damolla, a native of Artush, is one man who does qualify for this category. After schooling in Kashgar, Abdulqadir headed first to the madrasas of Kokand before enrolling in studies in Bukhara in 1891, where he remained for eight years. By his own account, he studied there the works of classical scholars such as Ibn Taymiyya and Ibn Qayyum and those of modernists such as Jamaluddin Afghani and Muhammad Abduh. That is to say, he became acquainted with reformist thinking in its Bukharan variety. After returning to Kashgar he left once more in 1906 as a pilgrim to Mecca, stopping off in Cairo for a visit to the al-Azhar, center of theological study in the Islamic world. It was at the end of this trip that he started publishing a series of textbooks for the New Method *maktab*. The first of these was a primer of Arabic, *The Key to Literacy in Arabic Comprehension*, the second a religious manual, *Jewels of Certitude*.[80] His works did not go unnoticed in Russian Muslim intellectual circles. So impressed was one reader that he doubted that the author could really have acquired such good Arabic in a Bukharan madrasa. Sabirjan Shakirjanov, a Bashkir schoolteacher, met Abdulqadir while he was passing through Vernyi and assumed that he was a Syrian or Egyptian scholar.[81] Such was the view among Russian Muslims of the state of learning in Bukhara (and by extension in Kashgar).

From Russian Turkistan, Abdulqadir headed via Vernyi to Ghulja at the invitation of the Musabayevs, who continued to profit from late-Qing reform initiatives that drew officials and local entrepreneurs into collaboration. The arrival of the New Army in 1908 had given a boost to local industry. To meet the New Army's requirements for leather goods, and to compete with the Russians, the Ili military governor Chang-geng founded the Leather and Wool Company (*pimao gongsi*), a joint-stock company with shares held by Chang-geng himself, and Ili's Mongol and Manchu banner officers.[82] The Leather and Wool Company went into partnership with the Musabayevs, investing 400,000 taels to reorganize their leatherworks as the Ili Leather Company (*Yili zhige gongsi*), with Bahauddin traveling to Germany to purchase new equipment and recruit an engineer.[83] In the first year of the new enterprise, the Musabayevs received an order for two thousand boots for the New Army, increasing to five thousand in 1909.[84] Chang-geng also ordered saddles and purchased cloth for uniforms from the factory.

Things were still looking up for Jadidists in Ghulja. On his way through, Abdulqadir Damolla took part in the activities of a charitable society in Suiding called the Service of the Religion (*khidmat-i din*), and one in Ghulja calling itself the Islamic Progress Society.[85] Apart from the strength of the Tatar diaspora, the other reason why Ghulja remained a conducive climate for such activities was that it was now the stronghold of Chinese Republicanism in Xinjiang. The head of the local New Army, Yang Zuanxu, was a revolutionary officer from Wuchang in Hubei, and since his arrival in 1908 he had launched a number of radical cultural initiatives, including Xinjiang's first Chinese-language newspaper, the *Ili Vernacular News* (*Yili Baihua Bao*), which commenced publication in 1910. One of Abdulqadir Damolla's collaborators in the Islamic Progress society, a local Tatar named Abdulqayyum Hifzi, edited a Muslim edition of Yang Zuanxu's Republican flagship, which was called the *Ili Provincial News* (*Ili Vilayatining Gazeti*), and might well be considered as Xinjiang's first Jadidist periodical.[86]

The *Ili Provincial News* was a handwritten, biweekly lithograph, in a language somewhere "between Kazakh and Kashgari" according to one account.

Coming at a time when the press in Russian Turkistan had been all but shut down, the *Ili Provincial News* was welcomed by Tatar newspapers such as *Time* and *The Interpreter*, which printed excerpts from its more noteworthy articles. While drawing on translations from the Chinese edition, it also included its own editorials, which promoted New Method schooling and mourned the lack of benevolent societies and libraries in Xinjiang.[87] The editors believed that Chinese policy was much more supportive of educational reform than was Russian. Veering into political territory that censors in Russia would not permit, the *Ili Provincial News* denounced imperialist aggression against Muslims and the Yellow Race, which included both Turks and the Chinese. On the basis of this racial unity, the diverse population of Xinjiang was encouraged to unite against "pan-Christianism" and "pan-Europeanism," and dedicate themselves to science and education. The fourth issue quoted a *hadith* commonly invoked in the Islamic world, "love for the homeland is part of faith," to recommend a patriotic stance toward China among its Muslim readers.[88]

Yet all was not as encouraging as it seemed in Ghulja. As was the case elsewhere in China, progressive initiatives on the eve of the 1911 revolution ran up against an indifferent public and an increasingly paranoid Qing court. From mid-1911 onward the court consolidated itself around a new, Manchu-dominated cabinet, which was enough to convince many anti-Qing radicals of the need for immediate action. This last-gasp recentralization of Manchu authority found its reflection in Xinjiang when the relatively popular Ili military governor, a Mongol by the name of Guang-fu, was replaced by a Manchu aristocrat, Zhi-rui, a cousin of two of the Guangxu emperor's concubines. Zhi-rui's appointment was a blow for local republicans, and he clashed almost immediately with Yang Zuanxu by withholding salaries for the New Army troops. Zhi-rui was equally hostile to reformist elements among local Muslims, and he responded to the complaints of local imams by shutting down Masum Effendi's Jadidist school. Around the same time, a lack of funds forced the *Ili Provincial News* to close, and no new publication stepped into the breach.[89]

With a showdown looming in the Ili Valley, Abdulqadir Damolla set out for Kashgar. In traveling south he was stepping into an environment that was no less fractious than Ghulja. Yet Abdulqadir Damolla was a local, and his Bukharan brand of Jadidism was much less threatening to Kashgar's Old City elite than was Shami Damolla's schismatic Salafism. For these reasons, Umar Akhunbayev proved receptive upon Abdulqadir Damolla's arrival in Kashgar, and the Akhunbayevs were among those who paid for Abdulqadir's next publications, a series of short handbooks covering the basic tenets of Islam, and Turki orthography, printed in Kazan in 1911–1912.[90] The Akhunbayevs' support for Abdulqadir Damolla shows that it would be wrong to depict cultural politics in Kashgar in black-and-white terms, pitting the progressive Jadidist Musabayevs against the reactionary anti-Jadidist Akhunbayevs. In lending his name and resources to Abdulqadir's curriculum, Umar Akhunbayev proved himself willing to support a version of reformed schooling, so long as those schools did not threaten his communal authority or financial interests.[91] In 1912, Abdulqadir Damolla succeeded in opening the first New Method school in the Old City of Kashgar. It enrolled its first students just as the revolution that toppled the Qing was spreading to the south of Xinjiang.

Although the first decade of the twentieth century in Xinjiang was witness to a new ethos of reform, when viewed collectively the initiatives described here call into question the idea of Jadidism in Xinjiang as a well-defined intellectual movement. While the Ili Valley experiment initially relied on Tatar links to the centers of Russian Jadidism, Istanbul clearly offered the more attractive model for the Musabayevs, whose own prestige was enhanced by contact with the Ottoman court. Yet it is telling that these same Jadidist patrons were equally willing to collaborate with Shami Damolla, an Arab critic of the Ottoman sultan educated in the madrasas of India. While Russian Jadidism is often described as motivated by a desire to desacralize and secularize primary education, Shami Damolla's activities in Kashgar show that the impetus for reform in Xinjiang was equally linked to scripturalist and revivalist currents of Islam that were circulating across Eurasia in this period; or indeed, that the line between Jadidism and such currents was not as distinct as it may look to scholars today. Meanwhile, Abdulqadir Damolla seems to conform to a distinctly Turkistani model of Jadidism, and his limited success built on the prestige of the traditional Kashgar-Bukhara axis.

Early reform efforts in Xinjiang floundered from skepticism and disinterest as much as from outright opposition, and in the end, none of these initiatives achieved the desired results. The late Qing environment placed local Muslim society in something of a paradoxical situation. On the one hand, the weakness of the Qing administration in Xinjiang, the province's porous borders, and the relative disinterest among local officials in issues of religion, made it a space where cultural trends from the rest of the Islamic world could penetrate easily.

The expectations of public loyalty that the Qing required of local Muslims sat easily with expressions of pious devotion to the Ottoman caliph, and the state's dire fiscal condition meant that policy directives from Beijing would necessarily be tailored to the interests of the province's Muslim elite or else remain a dead letter. To those looking on, therefore, Qing China seemed to offer the communal autonomy that still eluded Russian Muslims post-1905. "Although Chinese and Manchus are in charge of the government," wrote one Tatar from Ghulja in 1906, "in matters of religion and education there is complete freedom."[92] Yet for precisely the same reasons, it was wrong to expect that local Muslims would be politicized in the same way, and to the same degree, as the Muslims of Russia, and that they would rush to avail themselves of this freedom in the way Tatars or Ottoman Muslims hoped. Tatar praise for the benevolence of Chinese officialdom could quickly turn into sharp criticism of the benighted locals, but Kashgaris were entitled to ask: What did Russian Muslims have to show for their much-vaunted New Method?

We have seen here that Muslims from Xinjiang, when moving across imperial boundaries, freely drew on the notion of the Muslims of China as a distinct entity. In petitions for the sultan's beneficence, Kashgaris in Istanbul announced themselves as belonging to the community of Muslims of "Chinese Turkistan," or simply of China. The absence of formal Ottoman-Qing ties only increased the incentive for Muslims to present themselves as in some way representative of this remote and little known Muslim community—as men such as Shami Damolla well knew. Among the Taranchis in Russia political and social conditions were different. Yet here too, a quarter of a century since the migration to Semireche, a sense of a distinctly Qing Muslim community was alive and well. It was represented in Vali Bay's mosque and in his bold declaration that he would represent the Qing émigrés at the forthcoming Duma. In Semireche, though, the concept meant something different than it did for Kashgaris abroad. For the Taranchis, the link to the Qing was a legacy of the past, not a description of the present. Vali Bay invoked his community's Qing origins, not as way to present the Muslims of China to the world, but to keep the outside world at bay.

CHAPTER FOUR

The End of Empire and the Racial Turn

The Muslims of Xinjiang were on the margins of, but nevertheless implicated in, two cataclysms at the opposite ends of Eurasia in the early twentieth century: the 1911–1912 Xinhai revolution that dethroned the Manchu dynasty in China; and the First World War. The fall of the Qing naturally raised the question of the status of Xinjiang, a far-flung frontier region home to very few Chinese. In contrast to the Qing Empire's Mongols and Tibetans, though, Muslims did not greet the new Chinese Republic with calls for native sovereignty. Indeed, in the years following Xinhai there were points at which the province's elite proved themselves willing collaborators with Chinese Republicans, and in some places the fall of the Qing prompted renewed efforts to restart a faltering reform program. Yet the preferred modus operandi among the Kashgaris, the importation of Ottoman expertise, eventually ran afoul of the changing international and domestic circumstances. Given the province's links to both Russia and the Ottoman Empire, Russian eyes in Xinjiang grew increasingly wary as the Balkan Wars of 1912–1913 evolved into the global conflict of 1914. The outbreak of war coincided with the defeat of the Chinese Republicans in Xinjiang and the emergence of Yang Zengxin (1864–1928) and his anti-revolutionary regime in Ürümchi.

If the preceding period can be described as one in which political discussion was framed by notions of Islamic community and imperial subjecthood, these years saw the crystallization of new racial discourses on the Muslims of Xinjiang. In China, the republic declared the Muslims to be one of the nation's five constituent races (along with the Manchus, Mongols, Tibetans, and Chinese) and promised a new era of "five races in harmony" (*wuzu gonghe*). This did not go unnoticed by the empire's Muslims, and there were efforts by both Chinese-speaking Muslims and Kashgaris to invoke this slogan as grounds for greater support, or even political autonomy. It was racial thinking from the West, though, as filtered through the diaspora of Chinese Muslims in both Russia and Istanbul, that had the most significant impact in this period. The Ottoman Empire's wartime shift to a Turkist, as opposed to Ottomanist or Islamist, public presentation was one side of this process. The other was a growing interest in narratives of Turkic identity among the Muslims of Russia. These two trends had much in common, but while the first took pan-Turkic solidarity as its primary goal, the second was utilized in providing distinct national histories for the Turkic-speaking peoples of Russia. As a community with a diaspora in both Ottoman and Russian territory, the Muslims of Chinese Turkistan found a place for themselves in both discourses.

The Xinhai Revolution in Xinjiang

The 1911–1912 Xinhai Revolution, which led to the fall of the Qing and the establishment of the Chinese Republic, came late to China's northwest. The first uprisings in Xinjiang broke out at the very end of 1911, while negotiations between the Chinese Republicans and the Qing court were already under way to the east. Having been betrayed to Governor Yuan Dahua, conspiring soldiers in Ürümchi launched a precipitous mutiny on the night of December 28, 1911, which the loyal majority of the local Qing garrison put down. The governor's reprisals were swift, summarily executing some hundred Hunanese officers and soldiers suspected of revolutionary sympathies. This act made Yuan, a native of Anhui province, immensely unpopular with Xinjiang's Hunanese faction, who were still a force to be reckoned with since Zuo Zongtang had won back Xinjiang for the Qing in the 1870s.

In Ili, a territorial unit still administered separately from Xinjiang, the Republicans had better prospects. There, Revolutionary Alliance member Yang Zuanxu stood at the head of the well-drilled New Army troops. On January 7, ten days after the failed Ürümchi mutiny, Yang and other revolutionaries in Ili led a better-organized uprising that succeeded in capturing and killing Military Governor Zhi-rui and proclaimed a Xinjiang-Ili Commandery (Xin-Yi Da Dudufu) loyal to the Chinese Republic. To win the confidence of Ili's holdout Manchu garrisons, the new regime brought Zhi-Rui's predecessor, the Mongol Guang-fu, out of retirement as its figurehead. Other sections of Ili's multinational elite were incorporated into the regime too. Soon after the establishment of the Xinjiang-Ili Commandery, Guang-fu appointed Bahauddin Musabayev

The New Army in Huiyuan (Xincheng), 1910. (Photograph by George E. Morrison. State Library of New South Wales [1006006].)

as the regime's industrial consultant and commissioned the Musabayev leatherworks to outfit its new Citizens' Army (Minjun). On Yang Zuanxu's first official visit to Ghulja in March 1912, the Musabayevs hosted a reception in his honor.[1]

Before it had time to consolidate itself, Qing loyalists in Ürümchi mobilized against the Xinjiang-Ili Commandery. Throughout the first half of 1912, fighting between the two sides raged along the northern flank of the Tianshan, until pressure from Beijing compelled the warring parties to commence negotiations. South of the mountains, disaffected Chinese soldiers and secret-society members continued to run riot, carrying out a campaign of terror against Qing officials. Much of this was the work of the Gelaohui (Brothers and Elders Society), an empire-wide secret society that was first brought to Xinjiang by Zuo Zongtang's Hunanese army. The Gelaohui now included migrants from Shaanxi and Gansu among its ranks and was not exclusively Chinese in composition. The society's brief moment in the sun introduced elements of popular democracy to Xinjiang, including elections for county magistrates. The lifeless Kashgar Duma finally became the scene of genuine political debate, when Gelaohui members occupied it and used it as a forum for revolutionary anti-Qing oratory.[2]

The outbreak of the anti-Qing revolution in China was followed enthusiastically in the Russian Muslim press. Ismail Gasprinskii dedicated a front page of *The Interpreter* to celebrating the fall of the Manchus: "China has come to life!" he announced joyfully.[3] Soon, though, this press was noting troubling reports from Ghulja that Muslims in the south were opposed to the republic and had proclaimed a new khan of Kashgar.[4] This talk of restorationist sentiment among Xinjiang's Muslims disturbed Gasprinskii: "[we hear that] Muslims in the Kashgar and Ghulja regions are inclined against the system of a republic and wish for the return of the Manchu dynasty. If this is so then they are acting incorrectly."[5] Such rumors that China's Muslims supported the return of the Qing dynasty or would follow Mongolia and secede from the new Chinese nation thrived in the uncertainty of the republic's first days. Early in 1912, word reached the British consul in Kashgar of a Muslim uprising in Gansu aimed at establishing a son of the Manchu prince Duan (1856–1922) at the head of an independent "Great Western Kingdom," made up of the predominantly Muslim provinces of Shaanxi, Gansu, and Xinjiang. Another version of this rumor held that Prince Duan had already seized Xi'an and proclaimed himself emperor.[6]

The plots were simply rumors, but it is true that there was opposition to the revolution on the Qing periphery. Jadidist commentators such as Gasprinskii either failed, or were unwilling, to see that the rising tide of Chinese nationalism did not necessarily bode well for the rest of China's five races. By siding with the Chinese Republicans in the name of constitutional reform, Jadidists such as Gasprinskii were promoting a strategy that, if successful, would inevitably lead to the strengthening of minority Chinese rule in multiethnic territories such as Xinjiang, which from the perspective of Xinjiang's majority non-Chinese population might well be seen as disastrous. For all the Republicans' talk of "five races in harmony," the victory of the revolutionaries in Ili greatly disquieted the local garrison communities who stood to lose most from the fall of the Qing, and many looked nervously for fallback plans. Two weeks after the New Army mutiny, a delegation representing Ili's Sibe bannermen slipped into Russian territory seeking refuge from an anticipated anti-Manchu pogrom. Before long, fighting broke out between the Republican militia and the Chahar Mongols who resided to Ili's north. The clash resulted in hundreds of Mongols fleeing across the mountains into Russian territory, where they petitioned

for protection. When Russian officials turned them down, some journeyed onward through Siberia to newly independent Mongolia and submitted to its
ruler, the Bogd Khan.[7]

Unlike the Mongols and Tibetans of the Qing Empire, Xinjiang's Muslims
did not mobilize immediately in response to the deteriorating situation in China.
The explanation for this lies partly in the success of provincialization, which
had diminished the status of Xinjiang's residual Muslim aristocracy. These
wangs, whose position was most threatened by the revolution, did not enjoy
anything approaching the authority of Mongolia's Chinggisid aristocracy, or
Tibet's high lamas, and could only wait and watch as Chinese politics played
itself out. The province's mercantile elite, for their part, had never had any
form of patrimonial relationship with the Qing emperor and stood ready to
collaborate with Chinese officials of any stripe, as they had up until now. When
the anti-Qing revolt reached Xinjiang, officials in Kashgar moved to mollify
the mood of the bazaar and handed control of the *lijin* back to the Kashgari
*bay*s as a means of limiting the spread of unrest.[8] Finally, to the extent that
Muslim reformists in Xinjiang raised demands in 1911–1912, they were not calls
for sovereignty but for autonomy in religious affairs and the full inclusion of
Muslims in the institutions of the new Chinese Republic.

One example of this is an anonymous eighteen-point petition that circulated in Kashgar in 1912. Calling on the new Chinese Republic to guarantee
freedom and equality for Muslims in China, the petitioners proposed the formation of a centralized spiritual board in Beijing, headed by a *sheikh ül-Islam*,
that would take responsibility for the country's Islamic schools and *waqf*, with
other positions modeled directly on the hierarchy of the Ottoman clergy. They
requested the freedom for Muslims to build mosques wherever they desired, to
collect funds for such projects, and for Muslim clergy to be accorded the same
rights and privileges given to public officials. They insisted that no obstacles
should be placed in the way of the Jadidist program of schools, reading rooms,
and charitable societies, but also that Muslim students wishing to study in Chinese schools should be admitted and included in any efforts by the Chinese
Republic to send students abroad. Finally, they called on the new regime to
take measures to improve the safety and security of the nation's pilgrims:
"There should not be any restrictions on Muslims traveling abroad. For the
convenience of those Muslims going on the hajj, consulates should be opened
in certain cities along the way. Along with this, there should be an agreement
for the exchange of ambassadors with the Ottoman government."[9]

The Rise of Yang Zengxin

Radicals in Xinjiang, as elsewhere in China, lacked the social weight to topple the old regime, let alone construct a new one, creating a stalemate situation favoring the rise of a conservative force that could mediate the conflict. In this way Yuan Shikai, a stalwart of the Qing military and political elite, was able to insinuate himself between the revolutionaries and the Qing court and seize the Chinese presidency. In March, when Yuan was installed as president in Beijing, mutinies and rebellions were continuing in Xinjiang's south, prompting the resignation of Governor Yuan Dahua. With few options left, Yuan Shikai appointed Provincial Judicial Commissioner (*tifashi*) Yang Zengxin to the position of Military Governor (*dudu*) in May. Meanwhile, the Bureau of Mongolian and Tibetan Affairs sent out teams of "pacification commissioners" to investigate conditions on the frontier and convince nervous locals of the republic's benign intentions. Those sent to Gansu and Xinjiang were headed by Jin Yunlun, a prominent member of the Gansu-based Jahriyya Sufi brotherhood, an ideal link between Yuan Shikai and the Muslim communities of Gansu. He was accompanied by Yusuf Beg, a scion of Xinjiang's Naqshbandi *khoja* dynasty. Crossing into Xinjiang, these emissaries were instrumental in placating Muslim rebels in Hami, who threatened both the local Hami *wang* and Yang Zengxin in Ürümchi. Yusuf Beg continued on to Turfan, where he met with the *wang* and elicited from him a statement endorsing the republic.[10]

Yusuf Beg had his own reasons for returning to Xinjiang. Descended from the Muslim elite residing at the capital (Yusuf was related to the Qianlong emperor's Muslim concubine, Xiang Fei), he and his forebears had subsisted throughout the Qing on stipends from the state, as had other bannermen in the imperial city of Beijing. The fall of the Qing was a crisis for this group as much as it was for the Manchus, as they were forced to seek alternative means to support themselves. Encouraged to leave the capital, some headed to Kashgar, where they tried to obtain a share in the *waqf* endowment of the wealthy Afaq Khoja shrine complex. In 1915 the British consul reported that "a band of seventy of these hungry descendants, who are Muslims, but dressed as Chinese with pigtails, have arrived, and eighty more are on the way. The various *Shaykhs*, who are enjoying the revenues of the shrine are much perturbed." For his part, Yusuf petitioned to inherit a lapsed title of duke that he claimed was rightfully his, hoping to make a fresh start as a member of Xinjiang's landed gentry, but the Bureau of Mongolian and Tibetan Affairs rejected his application.[11]

Yang Zengxin's rise did to local politics what Yuan Shikai's did nationally. With the country now in the hands of conservatives who were nominally loyal to the republic, the Republicans were obliged to come to terms with people who were deeply hostile to any kind of revolutionary vision for China. The Ili leadership reached a peace deal with Yang in June 1912, but they were far from reconciled to the new reality. According to a report from the Russian consul in Ghulja, the Ili Revolutionary Alliance did not endorse the presidency of Yuan Shikai until early 1913, when they reorganized themselves as a branch of the newly formed Guomindang. Unfortunately for the Ili Republicans, they were financially reliant on Ürümchi's goodwill. The Beijing treasury assigned Ili a monthly stipend for troop salaries, but transmitted the silver through Ürümchi.[12] Control of this financial lifeline gave Yang Zengxin a crucial edge in negotiations, through which he succeeded in first neutralizing, then fragmenting, the Ili Republicans. Those among them who resisted Ürümchi's authority were gradually killed off. Over the next three years, Yang fended off military threats from newly independent Mongolia and extended his authority to the south by suppressing Xinjiang's secret societies.

More a Qing relic than a Republican warlord, Yang had years of experience in China's Muslim northwest, and he prided himself on his harmonious dealings with local Muslims. Drawing on prior experience as an official among the Muslims of Gansu, Yang set about recruiting a militia from the Dungans of Ürümchi and its surrounds, and cultivating the Muslim elite of Xinjiang.[13] His success in doing so can be seen by examining the activities of Abdulqadir Janggi Beg, an adjutant (*janggi*) in the Uchturfan *wang* administration and the only Muslim from Xinjiang sent to the 1913 National Assembly. While in Beijing, Abdulqadir lodged a petition describing the hardships endured by his fellow Muslims. He argued the need to establish Chinese-Muslim *xuetang* in Xinjiang, combining Chinese teachers with well-respected Muslim *akhund*s, to be paid for by promoting local industry. He also complained about employment discrimination, estimating that there were at least a hundred Muslims in Xinjiang sufficiently versed in Chinese language and laws to serve in the provincial bureaucracy. Only by recruiting such individuals into state service, he argued, "will there truly be Fives Races in Harmony."[14] While critical of his province's condition, though, Abdulqadir was fulsome in his of praise Yang Zengxin, stating that Yang's abolition of the New Policy levies and reduction of the land tax was evidence of his "preferential treatment" (*youdai*) of the Turban-Wearing Muslims. With talk that Yang might be withdrawn from the northwest, in 1914

Abdulqadir transmitted a letter from the chief *akhund*s of Qarashahr and Turfan that praised Yang for relieving them of the extortionate practices of the New Policy era, and pleaded: "Yang in Xinjiang is like the sun in the sky. Just as we cannot do without the sun, so too we cannot do without Yang."[15]

Adjutant Abdulqadir was not the only Muslim contemplating the meaning of Republican slogans of "Three People's Principles" and "five races in harmony" for his community in the early years of the republic, and not all were as enamored of Xinjiang's new governor. In the wake of the revolution, a number of Chinese Muslims contrasted the egalitarian promise of "five races in harmony" with what they saw as constitutional anti-Muslim discrimination. In its efforts to stave off further territorial loss, Republican China left much of the old Qing patrimonial hierarchy intact, including privileges for Mongolian aristocrats and Tibetan lamas. While Chinese provinces were assigned representatives to China's National Assembly according to population size, Inner Mongolia and Tibet enjoyed fixed quotas, which to many looked like a system of ethnic quotas. Besides this, there were dedicated organs to handle Mongolian and Tibetan affairs, and state-funded schools in Beijing for elite Mongolian and Tibetan children. In comparison, China's Muslims remained divided across various Chinese provinces, administered by Chinese officials, with seemingly no constitutional recognition of their status as one of China's five races. To those following this train of thought, Xinjiang occupied a particularly important position. While it was officially a province, Xinjiang was still home to a class of hereditary Muslim aristocrats—the *wang*s—who could be seen as analogous to the aristocracy of Mongolia and the clergy of Tibet. On this basis, it was possible to argue that the Muslim northwest deserved to be treated in the same way as Mongolia and Tibet.

As they had during the Qing, the Xinjiang *wang*s continued to make periodic trips to the capital. In 1914, Hami Wang Shah Maqsud went to Beijing to meet Yuan Shikai, and while there he was waited on by a local Muslim named Dawud Li Qian. Whether or not the two men had a previous connection remains something of a mystery. One apocryphal account suggests that Li Qian's family had formed a bond with the Hami *wang*s as early as the 1870s, when Li's grandfather served in Zuo Zongtang's Hunan army.[16] Following Shah Maqsud's visit, Li took the opportunity to intervene in Republican politics, declaring himself to be the "plenipotentiary representative" of Xinjiang's Muslim aristocracy. He used this calling card to lodge a series of petitions, requesting dedicated Muslim representation in the National Assembly and funding for a

Muslim affairs office in Beijing. In the course of his campaign, with which he persisted through the 1920s, Li emphasized the Muslim identity of the Tarim Basin, referring to it either as the "Muslim territory" or the "Eight Muslim Territories," reflecting the eight aristocratic families he claimed to represent: "The Muslims of the Eight Territories number more than ten million," he wrote in one of his petitions. "This territory from east to west exceeds four thousand li, and from north to south some three thousand li. Although it nominally belongs to Xinjiang, all of its language, script, history, and customs, are unique."[17]

Li was nothing if not a quixotic figure. His view of southern Xinjiang as the Muslim Territory clashed head-on with Yang Zengxin's efforts to centralize the province around Ürümchi and incorporate neighboring regions such as Ili and Altay. To combat Li, Yang mobilized his own representatives in the capital, including his brother Yang Zengbing. When news of Li's activities reached Xinjiang, Shah Maqsud disavowed any relationship with him, pulling the rug out from beneath the feet of his "plenipotentiary representative."[18] Was he a fraud all along? It is hard to say, but even if he was the charlatan that Yang Zengxin accused him of being, there was a certain logic to Li Qian's position, and his campaign left a mark among Muslim intellectuals in Republican China. For the time being, the disfunctionality of the National Assembly rendered these early constitutional discussions moot, but they would resurface once more in the late 1920s, when the revival of the Guomindang again raised the question of what "five races in harmony" actually meant.

The Kashgari *Aqsaqal*s

While many late-Qing reform initiatives in Xinjiang were put on hold during the early years of the Chinese Republic, the sphere of foreign affairs saw renewed activity. For much of the dynasty's existence, the court and its officials had been hostile toward Qing subjects who chose to leave the empire's bounds, but as the Qing adapted to international diplomacy at the end of the nineteenth century, officials exhibited new interest in the fate of Qing subjects abroad. This led to the repeal of anti-emigration laws in 1893, and the passing of a *ius sanguinis* subjecthood law in 1909. The Treaty of Peking (1860) accorded China the right to station representatives in Russia, and Xinjiang officials recognized the need to make this promise a reality. The objective of establishing official networks among Xinjiang Muslims abroad sat well with the provincial elite's commercial interests, and with the deeply felt need to improve conditions for

Kashgaris on the hajj. When the British consul in Kashgar sampled the views of local traders in 1911, this was among the complaints most commonly heard: "As the Russians are represented by Consulates in Chinese Turkistan, why should the Chinese be precluded from being similarly represented in Russian Turkistan?"[19]

It was not that Kashgaris on Russian soil were completely abandoned. On arrival, there were local Kashgari officials on hand to confirm their identity, which would allow them to obtain permits to stay in Russian territory.[20] The Russian system of native self-administration in Turkistan prescribed the appointment of headmen through election and confirmation by Russian officials. Where Chinese-subject Kashgaris were sufficiently numerous they were included in this system. By the 1890s, a *desiatnik* (lit. "head of ten") supervised the Kashgari community in Vernyi, and during the first decade of the twentieth century, Chinese-subject *aqsaqals* turned up elsewhere in Semireche.[21] In the course of duty these *aqsaqals* naturally entered into a relationship with Xinjiang officials. On a number of occasions the Ili circuit commissioner received requests to issue credentials to *aqsaqals* who had been elected by the local community, including an *aqsaqal* in Zharkent in 1906 and one in Qaraqol in 1910.[22] Nonetheless, these *aqsaqals* remained products of a process that took place on Russian soil under the watchful eyes of the Russian administration. They were not representative of Kashgari or Chinese interests in the way that the consuls and *aqsaqals* in Xinjiang served Andijani and Russian interests.

Xinjiang officials had occasionally tried to establish formal contact with Qing subjects in Russian territory, though with little success. In 1895, officials in the Altay district appointed a Kashgari *aqsaqal* and Chinese tax collector to supervise the small Qing-subject trading community in the town of Zaysan, but the two men lasted less than a year before being forcibly expelled from Russian territory. In 1904, during a Russo-Qing juridical congress held in Kashgar, Circuit Commissioner Yuan Hongyou drew up a plan to station *aqsaqals* in Russian territory, and local merchants set about selecting suitable candidates for the positions.[23] Again, the Russians rejected the proposal, citing Turkistan's special status as a military jurisdiction. At the fall of the dynasty in 1912, the promise of reciprocal rights to representation in Russian Turkistan was still a dead letter.

A corollary to China's weak position in Russia was the ongoing manipulation of subjecthood in Xinjiang itself. In 1911, the Russian consul was rumored to be issuing certificates of Russian subjecthood based on letters from local qadis affirming that the applicant was a Russian subject.[24] The British consul suspected that his Russian counterpart was also giving these certificates to indigent Kashgaris who presented the residence permits they had obtained during seasonal trips to Russian Turkistan. In 1912, the British *aqsaqal* in Khotan reported that the Russian *aqsaqal* there was selling Russian documents for three taels each.[25] Yet as much as the British liked to take the moral high ground on such occasions, their own policy was hardly any different. During a tour of Yarkand and Khotan in 1914, Macartney took wide license in registering British subjects, signing up Indians born in Xinjiang to parents who had never lived under British rule. To do otherwise would have resulted in an insignificant number of British subjects, which, "in the event of our wishing to have a say as to the future of this part of the New Dominion, would scarcely give us a broad basis."[26] Macartney also offered British protection to Afghans, arguing that if he did not do so, then the Afghans would seek Russian subjecthood. In years to come, cases of false identity were just as likely to involve British documents as Russian.[27]

The "subjecthood question" took a dangerous turn in mid-1912, when a riot broke out in the Chira oasis. Studies of the Boxer Rebellion of 1900 have described how outlaw Chinese in Shandong converted to Christianity in order to obtain foreign protection and evade Chinese authorities, and in doing so incurred the hostility of non-Christian neighbors.[28] Something similar seems to have been at work in Chira, where the high-handed behavior of a group of Russian subjects provoked a serious riot. The catalyst was a land suit in which the decision went against a Russian subject, Sayyid Haji. Defying the verdict, Sayyid Haji mobilized fellow Russian subjects and fortified himself in his estate, running up the Russian flag. Local Muslims and Gelaohui freebooters then besieged and torched the residence, killing dozens of men holding certificates of Russian subjecthood. This was, in a sense, Xinjiang's Boxer Rebellion and, like the Boxers, has been praised in Chinese historiography as a patriotic blow against Russian imperialism. Soon enough, the international press latched on to what was in reality a fight between two groups of Muslims and sensationalized it as a Chinese massacre of Russians.[29] In fact, most of these Russian subjects had held their Russian documents for less than a year; George Macartney believed that there were only two actual Russian subjects among the dead.[30]

These intersecting issues—the manipulation of subjecthood in Xinjiang and the lack of any diplomatic presence abroad—were painful reminders of the compromised state of Chinese sovereignty in the early twentieth century. Pressure was finally brought to bear on this front in 1912 when Zhang Shaobo (1871–?), a graduate of Ürümchi's Russian-language college, assumed the position of special envoy for foreign affairs in Ürümchi. Like many in the provincial administration, Zhang resented the terms of the Treaty of Saint Petersburg. Unfortunately, the Xinhai Revolution caused China to miss its window of opportunity for proposing revisions (which occurred every ten years), and in any case the fledgling Chinese Republic was hardly in a position to extract diplomatic concessions from the tsarist foreign ministry. Existing treaty provisions nevertheless provided Zhang with grounds to lobby for official representatives in Russia and to curtail the Russian-subject *aqsaqal* network in Xinjiang.[31] Soon, the Xinjiang administration announced a set of statutes restricting the functions of the *aqsaqal*s. These required, for example, that local trading permits be obtained solely from Chinese *lijin* officials and insisted that such permits would not count as proof of an individual's subjecthood.

Zhang's more assertive approach chimed with the thinking of the newly appointed Kashgar circuit commissioner, Chang Yongqing. In December 1913, Chang traveled through Russian territory on his way to take up his position, and along the way he noted considerable numbers of Chinese subjects living and trading in Russian territory. He estimated that there were some sixty or seventy thousand Chinese—that is, former Qing—subjects in the Ferghana Valley.[32] When he reached Kashgar, he submitted a request to the Russian consul there to officially appoint *aqsaqal*s among these Chinese subjects.[33] Chang's proposal expressed a paternalistic concern for the Kashgari sojourners: "lonely and abandoned in a foreign land, there is nowhere for them to turn." He argued that such *aqsaqal*s would be of as much benefit to the Russians as to Chinese officials. They could, he suggested, improve discipline among the Chinese subjects, take up collections to meet the outstanding debts these Kashgaris incurred, and assist the Russian authorities in conducting criminal inquiries.

Initially the Russian response to Chang's request was dismissive. The governor-general in Tashkent reaffirmed the official position that Turkistan was off-limits to diplomatic representation. Considering the poverty of the Kashgaris within his jurisdiction, the governor of Ferghana province doubted they could afford any new fees to pay an *aqsaqal*'s salary.[34] Yet at the same time the Russian Ministry of Foreign Affairs was learning of Zhang Shaobo's plan to abolish its *aqsaqal* network in Xinjiang. Knowing full well that Russia's consuls could not function effectively without these *aqsaqal*s, Saint Petersburg countered Zhang's move with an offer of reciprocity. To preserve their own in Xinjiang,

the Ministry of Foreign Affairs expressed a willingness to accept the appointment of Chinese *aqsaqal*s in Russian Turkistan. At the end of 1914, China
confirmed that Russia's *aqsaqal*s in Xinjiang would retain their existing de
facto rights, and Russia permitted the appointment of similarly empowered
Chinese-subject *aqsaqal*s in Russian Turkistan.

As a result of these negotiations, the institution of the *aqsaqal*, far from being
curtailed by China's transition from empire to nation and efforts to revise its
treaties, was instead extended to new domains. For provincial officials seeking
to deal with the subjecthood question, recognizing Russian *aqsaqal*s in Xinjiang was not the ideal solution. Nevertheless, the creation of Chinese-subject
*aqsaqal*s in Russian Turkistan was a victory of sorts, wresting control of representation among the Kashgaris abroad from Russian hands. Following up on
this success, Chang Yongqing contacted his colleagues in Ili to suggest that they
adopt similar measures toward Chinese subjects in Semireche. Here, though,
Russian authorities pointed to the preexisting, locally elected Kashgari *aqsaqal*s
to turn down Ili's request. This satisfied the Ili authorities for the time being,
and Russian officials retained control of the institution of *aqsaqal* in Semireche.
Here most Kashgaris were working on public works projects, and Russian
officials relied on a close collaborative relationship with the *aqsaqal* to maintain
the flow of cheap Kashgari labor. One such figure was the Kashgari *aqsaqal*
in Toqmaq, Turdi Akhun Almasbekov, who in 1916 was commended for his
contribution to canal works in the Chu Valley.[35]

The real winners in these negotiations were the Kashgari *bay*s. In Chapter 2
I argued that the institution of *aqsaqal* reflected a three-way contest, not only
between Russian and Chinese interests, but involving the interests of Muslims
in maintaining a degree of autonomy in commercial and communal affairs. The
Russian *aqsaqal*s in Xinjiang offered Kashgar's mercantile elite an attractive
model for a self-governing Muslim trading network functioning across an imperial frontier—exactly what they envisaged for themselves in Russia. Now not
only had they gained a set of *aqsaqal*s, they had greater control of them than
their Russian Muslim rivals. While Russian *aqsaqal*s in Xinjiang were elected
locally as the consul's deputies, there were no Chinese consuls in Russian
territory to supervise such elections. Instead, the selection took place in Kashgar,
where the *bay*s could ensure that the positions went to trustworthy representatives. In this sense these Chinese *aqsaqal*s occupied a status somewhere between
that of headman and consul, but they were as much the consuls of the Kashgari *bay*s as they were of the Xinjiang authorities. They would be accountable

to elite Kashgari interests first, Kashgar's Chinese officials second, and Ürümchi and Beijing only a distant third.

A meeting held in Kashgar in August 1914 elected five men to the position of *aqsaqal*. All of them were local merchants with experience doing business in Russian territory, and most had obvious ties to the Akhunbayevs.[36] Four of these were appointed to trading centers with substantial Kashgari populations: Osh, Andijan, Kokand, and Tashkent. A fifth was sent to the Black Sea port of Odessa, which was by now an important hub on the pilgrimage route preferred by well-to-do Kashgari hajis, where they disembarked the train and boarded the steamships that plied the Black Sea to Istanbul. The new cohort of Chinese-subject *aqsaqal*s entered Russian territory with official letters from the Kashgar circuit commissioner, displacing those who had been appointed through the Russian system of native self-administration.[37]

Tsarist officials in the Ferghana Valley were disappointed at the caliber of the Kashgar-appointed *aqsaqal*s. In a letter to Xinjiang officials they complained that "often individuals are appointed to these positions with very dubious backgrounds, with accusations hanging over them, and sometimes even deep in debt to Russian firms." Just such an unsavory character, in Russian eyes, was the chief *aqsaqal* in Andijan, Abdurahman Qari Haji Tairov. Having set himself up in Andijan, he referred to himself as a consul and instructed Kashgaris to refrain from having dealings with the Russian authorities. The Russians regarded him as a spy and suspected that he was informing the Kashgar circuit commissioner of any Kashgaris with pro-Russian inclinations. He also came under suspicion of belonging to the Gelaohui secret society, a catchall in Russian eyes for any form of conspiratorial behavior among Chinese subjects. Within a year of his appointment, the Andijan authorities brought him up on a charge of kidnapping. Although he avoided conviction, officials in Kashgar recalled him and sent a replacement.[38]

The Young Turks and the Young Kashgaris

While Xinjiang's Muslim elite was finding its feet in the new conditions of the Chinese Republic, many were equally attentive to events in the Ottoman Empire, which was struggling for its survival in the Balkan Wars. On the eve of the First Balkan War in 1912 the merchants of Kashgar and Ghulja sent a contribution of four thousand rubles to the imperiled empire, a donation for which the Musabayevs were awarded Ottoman honors.[39] In the middle of 1913, when Turkish commander-in-chief Enver Pasha recaptured Edirne (Adrianople) for the Ottomans and saved Istanbul from Bulgarian onslaught, the Muslims of Ghulja rejoiced: "all the shops in the bazaar were shut, trade was halted, and the Muslim subjects of China ran up flags along the streets."[40] Bahauddin Musabayev hosted a rally where the crowd said prayers for the Ottoman martyrs and heard a panegyric on Enver Pasha composed by the recently deceased Tatar poet Gabdullah Tuqay.

Amid the uncertainty of the early republic, Kashgari reformers redoubled their efforts to put New Method schooling on a secure footing. In the process of dispersing the revolutionary threat in Ili, Yang Zengxin appointed the New Army chief Yang Zuanxu to the position of provincial commander-in-chief (*tidu*) in Kashgar, a decision that pleased Kashgari Jadidists. Qutluq Haji Shawqi, one such local, wrote to Ismail Gasprinskii in 1913, expressing his hope that Yang Zuanxu's arrival would boost flagging reform efforts in his hometown. Shawqi described how, in his first speech in Kashgar, Yang had called on Muslims to enlighten themselves, in terms that translated easily into the Jadidist lexicon: "As long as the laws are obeyed, then you may implement reforms as you see fit, nothing will stand in the way. You should make particular efforts in science and education. If there emerge talented and qualified people among you, then they will be appointed to positions according to their ability, including even the position of governor. . . . The age of ignorance has ended—all peoples and nations must open their eyes."[41]

Hoping to take advantage of the new climate, in 1914 Shawqi, Abdulqadir Damolla, and some of the local ulama joined the Musabayevs to found the Society for the Promotion of Education (Nashr-i Ma'ārif Jam'iyyati) and started propagandizing more publicly. The society met every Friday in Kashgar after midday prayers to criticize superstitious customs. They disseminated pamphlets "for the public good" and greeting cards for religious holidays. Some of Kashgar's clerics criticized these activities as illicit innovation (*bid'a*), but it was the group's next step that proved its most controversial.[42] Through contacts in Istanbul, the society invited a Turkish teacher to Kashgar. The Ottoman interior minister, Talat Pasha, recommended Ahmed Kemal (1889–1966) for the job.

Ahmed Kemal, originally from the island of Rhodes, was a rising star in Young Turk literary circles. His most recent work was a book of bloodcurdling lullabies on nationalist themes, full of militant exhortations to resist the Slavic foe and drive tyranny from the Balkans.[43] He reached Kashgar in March 1914

Bahauddin Musabayev, Ghulja, 1910. (Photograph by
George E. Morrison. State Library of New South
Wales [1788108].)

accompanied by a group of Kashgari students who had been studying in Istanbul, then headed to Artush where he took charge of the Musabayev school.
Ahmed Kemal changed the school's name to the Union Teachers College—a
reference to Turkey's ruling Young Turk party, the Committee of Union and
Progress, of which he was almost certainly a member.[44] Credible witnesses testify that the star and crescent of the Turkish flag flew above the school, that
students sang Ottoman military marches, and that in the neighboring mosque
portraits of Turkish generals hung from the mihrab wall.[45] At the same time,
the school also drew on the resources of Turkistani Jadidism. On examination

day, students staged the recent, and highly popular, Jadidist play *The Patricide* (*Padarkush*), by the Samarkandi author Mahmud Khoja Behbudi.[46]

As a textbook for the school, the Musabayevs paid for Ahmed Kemal's *Turki Alphabet* (*Alifba-yi Turki*) to be published in Kazan, as Abdulqadir Damolla's textbooks had been. While Abdulqadir Damolla had focused on the basic Jadidist objective of an improved pedagogy for Arabic, Ahmed Kemal's work exhibits a desire to expose students to a new, modern way of life as a westernizing "effendi." To this end, students were taught words such as "watch" and "watch fob," and that "progressive and advanced nations fix the time of everything they do precisely." On this question of the nation, too, there were differences between the textbooks. In the catechistic *Essential Precepts* (1911), Abdulqadir Damolla wrote in terms of a single Muslim nation and warned students against the evils of disunity:

Q: What is the reason for the shame and ignominy of the nation?

A: There are two reasons. One is stubbornness and ignorance; the other is conflict and discord. The reason for the disgrace and decline of any people or any nation is ignorance and the lack of unity.[47]

Ahmed Kemal went much further in promoting a racialized view of Kashgari Muslims as the Turks of Chinese Turkistan, who could take pride in the fact that they resided in the heartland of the Turk nation, which he situated in Asia. A conversation between teacher and student in his textbook runs as follows:

Q: Where are you from?

A: I am from Kashgar, Sir.

Q: Do you know where Kashgar is, and in which part of the world?

A: I do, Sir.

Q: Where did you learn this?

A: I learned it at school. I didn't just learn about Kashgar, I gained a degree of knowledge about every part of the world.

Q: Can you tell me what you know about Kashgar?

A: Very well, Sir. Kashgar is a city that belongs to us, the Turks of Chinese Turkistan. The city is in the continent of Asia. It is a great place, where the Turk race, to which we belong, was born and grew up.[48]

The Society for the Promotion of Education believed, perhaps naively, that they had the blessing of Chinese officials for such a school. As they probably anticipated, the school was criticized among the Kashgar ulama.[49] More serious, though, was the anxiety it provoked among Russian diplomats in China, who feared an Ottoman conspiracy to destabilize Russian Turkistan. In 1914, Ahmed Kemal was one of a number of suspicious Turks passing through Kashgar, and some of these clearly were Ottoman spies: five Turks who belonged to Enver Pasha's intelligence unit, the Teşkilat-i Mahsusa, reached Kashgar in November 1914, and were expelled the following April.

By July 1915, the Russian ambassador in Beijing had lodged an official complaint against Ahmed Kemal's school, which he saw as a breach of China's position of neutrality in the World War. The growing disquiet put Umar Akhunbayev in a difficult position. Any hint of anti-Russian agitation in Kashgar might have damaging consequences for his export business, and in the end he too denounced the school and its initiators to Chinese officials.[50] In August, Yang Zuanxu, who had expressed his sympathy for Jadidist activities in Kashgar, was removed from his post, as Yang Zengxin set about strengthening his grip on the south of Xinjiang. The following month, after a flurry of telegrams between Kashgar, Ürümchi, and Beijing, the Kashgar circuit commissioner shut the school down.[51] Yang Zengxin subsequently issued decrees prohibiting foreigners from teaching in the province and expelling Ottoman subjects (including Shami Damolla, who was running his own school in Kucha) from Xinjiang. Following this, he widened the crackdown to Chinese subjects who were suspected of propagating pro-Ottoman views in their schools.

The expulsion of the Turks marks the point at which the political trajectory of Muslim modernizers in Xinjiang brought them into direct conflict with the Chinese authorities. For some of these "Young Kashgaris," reaching the dead end of school reform was a radicalizing experience that drew them to new forms of conspiratorial politics. According to the British consul, while he was being held by Chinese police in Kashgar, Ahmed Kemal set up a new organization. This may be the origin of what in subsequent Soviet reports was described as a Kashgar branch of the Committee of Union and Progress. A hundred members took a loyalty oath on the Quran and swore to divorce their wives in case of failure—failure to do what, precisely, was not clear to the consul.[52] Nor was it necessarily clear to the participants themselves. As inspiring a teacher as Ahmed Kemal might have been, he offered his students little in the way of a strategy for standing up to the Xinjiang authorities. For Kemal, China's anti-Turkish turn was all a terrible mistake, one that he still hoped would be corrected. Without exception, the Turkish approach to China was based on anticolonial collaboration with the Chinese, not against them. The victims of Yang Zengxin's repression, some of whom were languishing in prison, would have to seek support elsewhere. Not surprisingly, many of Ahmed Kemal's class of 1915 eventually turned to the Soviet Union, and in so doing they redefined these local battles for cultural reform as part of a struggle for national liberation.

Russian Muslim Explorations of Chinese Turkistan

The amount of writing on Islam in China in Ottoman and Russian periodicals was increasing in this period. The emergence of Japan as a global actor, and its military victory against Russia in 1905, was the primary inspiration for interest in Asia, prompting a new pan-Asianist mood among Muslim intellectuals. Although China did not offer a model of modernization in the way that Japan did, sinological theorizing (such as Vasiliev's) about the impending Islamization of China allowed Muslim authors to imagine a Sino-Muslim collaboration of a different kind. In 1916–1917, the ex-qadi of Ufa, Rizauddin b. Fakhruddin (1859–1936), wrote a series of articles on China for his journal, *The Council* (*Shura*), which he concluded by outlining three possible paths for the country's development. One was that the Western colonial powers would partition it, as they had Africa and India. Or China might submit to Japan and thereby avoid dismemberment. The third possibility was that China would come under Muslim leadership, which was the only way he imagined the country being able to save itself independently.[53]

Trade was the most common reason for Russian Muslims to take up residence in China, but political factors drove the migration too. By 1908, a backlash against the freedoms won in 1905 was in full swing in Russia, and the political climate there was becoming increasingly hostile to Muslim activism. A clampdown on "pan-Islamism" saw modernized madrasas shut, sending many teachers and students south toward Russian Turkistan or into Xinjiang. Gabdullah Bubi (1871–1922) was probably the most well-known victim of this repression to cross into China, arriving in Ghulja in 1913. The Russian consul promptly locked him up, until a crowd of local Tatars secured his freedom.[54]

Firsthand experience of life in Xinjiang evoked a variety of responses from Tatar authors. In this writing, an abstract discourse on Chinese progress mingled with ideas about ties between the Turkic-speaking peoples, and between Russian and Chinese subjects. Russian Muslims, as we have seen, were part of a privileged elite in Xinjiang. For some, the social divide was sufficiently great to cast doubt on the idea that the Muslims of China could advance along the same path to enlightenment as those in Russia. One who seems to have held this critical outlook on local society was Gabdulgaziz Munasib, a Tatar who spent five years working in Ghulja for a local import-export company in the period leading up to the Xinhai Revolution. Munasib's views during his time in Xinjiang can be seen from a pessimistic letter he wrote to the Orenburg newspaper *Time* in 1907 responding to news that the Chinese railway was to be extended to Ghulja. This was, he felt, a mixed blessing at best: "Instead of happily stating that if the railway comes to Ghulja it will be the cause of progress among the Turkic peoples, there are reasons for caution. . . . If the railway is laid, then well educated Armenians and Jews will come from all parts, the English will bring their new equipment and start farming, and the Taranchis will abandon these occupations . . . and the result will be decline."[55] In 1912, after returning to Kazan, Munasib commenced work on a novel set in Ghulja. The result, which he titled *Taranchi Girl; or, Halim's First Love*, was the first ever depiction of Muslim society in Xinjiang in narrative fiction.[56] Although he finished the book by 1915, the war set back its publication until 1918, by which time Munasib had thrown himself into activity with the All-Russian Muslim National Military Council. That he saw his book to print at such a crucial time in his life indicates something of the significance he accorded it.

Taranchi Girl drew on a trope already well established among Tatar writers, that of a young girl representing the fate of a nation. The work is a parable of the bond among the community of Russian Muslims, and the incommunicability of Jadidist notions of enlightenment to those outside this community—the Kashgaris. In his preface to *Taranchi Girl*, Munasib evinces a more positive view of the Taranchis than he did in 1907, describing them as "one of the most quick-witted and culturally accomplished parts of the Turk-Tatar nation." Munasib's fiction served him as a form of ethnography, and he emphasized the need for such research as a step toward a Taranchi cultural revival: "The Taranchis' livelihood, customs, and histories must be thoroughly investigated." To lead this renaissance among the Taranchis, he called upon the Russian-subject Taranchis of Semireche, men such as Husayn Beg Yunusov, who ran a small printing press in Zharkent; the Islamic scholar Maruf Masudi; and Muhammad Imin Zaynalov, a prominent Jadidist in Ghulja.

The hero of Munasib's story is Halim, a Tatar émigré in Ghulja, who works for a wealthy merchant (the book may be partly autobiographical).[57] Between jobs, Halim frequents the house of his neighbor Zaynab, the widow of a Taranchi imam from Semireche, where he meets and falls in love with Zaynab's grand-daughter, Janasta. Halim courts Janasta on a tour of the historical sites of the district, which takes them to the shrine of the martyrs of the anti-Qing rebellion of the 1860s, and there the two pledge to marry. When Halim's boss returns from his trip to Russia, Halim asks his permission to wed Janasta, but is tragically denied. Instead, his boss sends him on a business trip to the military governor's seat of Huiyuan to meet with Qing officials. While he is away, a thief sneaks into Zaynab's house and kills both her and Janasta. At the novel's conclusion the thief, a Chinese-subject Kashgari who has been terrorizing the community for years, is caught and executed. Halim is relieved to see justice done, but he knows that he will never love again.

In this way *Taranchi Girl* posits a deep divide between Russian and Qing Muslims, one based not only on subjecthood, but also on class. The romance between the Tatar Halim and the Taranchi Janasta is a union between two Russian Muslims living in China: Janasta's family migrated to Russia before returning to Ghulja, and she remains a Russian subject. Cultural boundaries here are easily surmounted: Halim speaks the Taranchi dialect fluently, and as the courtship begins Janasta starts to learn Tatar. *Taranchi Girl* taps into traditions of anti-Qing resistance among the Taranchis and is dedicated to those who fell in the Muslim uprising of the 1860s, but the anti-Qing or anti-Chinese edge of the novel is blunted by Munasib's depiction of Qing officials, who are remote from day-to-day life in Ghulja and are primarily men with whom to do business. The villain of the piece is undoubtedly the Kashgari criminal who disrupts the harmonious Tatar-Taranchi union. He represents the wave of land-hungry migrants from the south of Xinjiang who had settled in Ghulja following the Taranchi migration to Russian territory. By the early twentieth century these Kashgaris outnumbered the remaining Taranchis, and Ghulja's Russian-subject elite clearly saw them as a disruptive element.[58] Other Kashgaris in the story invariably occupy low-status positions: the hooded executioner at the end of the novel, for example, is a Kashgari. So too are the mean folk who cater to travelers along the road between Ghulja and Huiyuan. When Halim stops among them for refreshments, they serve him tea from a filthy teapot.

Gabdulgaziz Munasib's circumscribed vision of a Tatar-led revival among the Taranchis was in many ways consistent with prevailing Jadidist opinion. In

Russian terms, it was politically correct to emphasize links among Muslims within the tsar's domains, but not with those beyond it. Yet not all Russian Muslim intellectuals were satisfied with this Russia-centered approach, and consciousness of a global Islamic or Turkic community drew some toward travel and travel writing. The new genre of the serialized travelogue was a vehicle well suited to commenting on the affairs of Muslims abroad. Ismail Gasprinskii had published accounts of his trips to Turkistan and India in *The Interpreter*, but by now the name most associated with this genre was the Tatar publicist Gabdurashid Ibrahim (1857–1944). In the course of a famous journey via China to Japan and back, Ibrahim published a number of articles in the Turkish and Tatar press, as well as book-length accounts of the trip in 1909 and 1911.

Among those inspired by Ibrahim's globe-trotting was a young Tatar named Nushirvan Yavshev (1885–1917) from the Belebei district of Bashkiria. In 1913, having already spent time teaching on the Kazakh steppe, Yavshev set off on a journey south into Russian Turkistan, which took him first to Samarkand. While there he befriended some of the local intelligentsia, including the writer Sadruddin Ayni, who encouraged him to continue his journey east into Xinjiang. From Samarkand, Yavshev headed to Semireche, and then traveled up the Ili Valley and entered Chinese territory, making the towns of Suiding and Ghulja his first ports of call. From the Ili Valley, he followed the highway east to Ürümchi, then south to Turfan, and around the rim of the Tarim Basin. Judging from his articles, Yavshev reached Kashgar by the middle of 1915. Later that year he followed the road to the southeast via Yarkand and Khotan, reaching as far as Keriya by the spring of 1916 before returning to Kashgar. During his three years in the province, he kept up a prolific output, penning more than a hundred and fifty articles for various Tatar publications and Turkistan's own fledgling Jadidist press.

Yavshev in Xinjiang sounded themes similar to those expressed by Tatar visitors to Russian Turkistan. Crossing the border into Chinese Turkistan, he was shocked by the streets of Ghulja: "the buildings are chaotic and dirty, the streets are extremely filthy, the bodies of dead dogs or dead donkeys are thrown into streams and canals that people drink from."[59] Occasionally he blamed its Chinese administration for the province's run-down condition, but more commonly he pointed the finger at local Muslims. "While there is freedom in every matter in China, the Muslims don't know the value of that liberty." Local schools he found to be either dysfunctional or bastions of obscurantism. Turfan, for

Yavshev, was a "second Bukhara," with all of the negative connotations of scholasticism that this implied.[60] It wasn't just the local Muslims who exhibited these deleterious traits: while passing through Ürümchi he found Russian Muslims to be divided on the question of the New Method. Things seemed to get worse as he headed south. "No one here knows what education is," he wrote from Aqsu, "they don't know anything apart from saying prayers and making the hajj." Superstitious devotion to saintly shrines was rife in the province, and Yavshev devoted several articles to debunking the myths that surrounded these holy sites.

Yavshev's experience tested his faith in the applicability of the Jadidist program to China, as he found few locals who shared his reformist concerns. From Kashgar in 1915 he dispatched an article to *Time* calling for the creation of Russian-style spiritual boards (*idāra-i sharʿiyya*) in Chinese Turkistan.[61] A few months later, the article returned to Kashgar in published form, but the response was disappointing. "The Chinese Muslims did not pay the slightest attention to that article, since they don't know what a spiritual board is. After that article appeared in Kashgar, people were going around asking 'what is a spiritual board?'"[62] Nevertheless, he believed that the province's wealthy patrons still had the wherewithal to rescue local Muslims from their plight, if only they would stop frittering their money away on wedding feasts and parties. Instead, Kashgar's *bay*s needed to pool their capital and form an economic society to exploit local resources and compete with Russian imports. They would also need to reorganize Xinjiang's *waqf*, pious donations of land whose revenue was allocated to shrine complexes and saintly families. Yavshev estimated that confiscating and renting out Yarkand's *waqf* would produce enough funds for all levels of Islamic schooling in Xinjiang, with a surplus to support new technical schools. He was confident that the Chinese authorities would support the measures he advocated.

Yavshev's writings stand in a tradition of using the travelogue as a vehicle for social criticism, but this was not the only purpose of his trip. Excited by the exploits of European archaeologists and philologists in Xinjiang, Yavshev intended to make his own contribution to the rediscovery of the Turkic past. "My goal in coming to Chinese Turkistan," he wrote from Kashgar in 1915, "was to find ancient works about Turkistan's history."[63] Among the Manchu-speaking Sibe in Ili, he acquired a set of historical works in Manchu, and from a qadi in the village of Qaraqash he obtained a late-seventeenth-century chronicle of the Chaghatayid khans of Yarkand.[64] From July 1916 onward his serialized précis of this work (which had simultaneously been discovered in Tashkent by the Bashkir scholar Ahmad Zaki Validi) was published in *The Council*.[65] In Kashgar he discussed the merits of the ancient Uyghur script with a Swedish missionary, likely to have been the linguist Gustaf Raquette. In a similar spirit, Yavshev adopted an ethnographic standpoint at various points in his journey. He dabbled in field linguistics, offering his readers a comparison between Sibe and Turkic vocabulary; in the village of Ayköl on the outskirts of Aqsu, he described a "spirit-summoning" ritual, a custom that was of particular interest to Russian scholars of the period.[66]

In some of his reports from the field Yavshev adopted the dispassionate tone of the Orientalist, but his goal of rewriting Turkic history was equally inspired by romanticism. If there was a redeeming quality to Xinjiang for Yavshev, it was its timeless significance as the heartland of Turkic civilization. Here he struck notes not found in Munasib's writing, of a trans-imperial solidarity premised on Turkic unity. In his account of his visit to the shrine of the Qarakhanid Satuq Bughra Khan in Artush, Yavshev was scathing about the local shaykhs who preyed on superstitious pilgrims but reverent toward the shrine itself. Here he imagined himself conversing with the saint, who revealed to him the glories of the Turkic past and the decline that he had witnessed since his death: "The schools and madrasas filled up with Persian and Arabic books and stories, and the Turk spirit completely disappeared. In the place of Turkism and heroism, the customs of dervishes and qalandars triumphed. In short, from that day until now there have been many changes, but these changes have not been beneficial, they have been harmful. If the changes had led to improvements, then the Easterners would not have fallen behind the Westerners. Instead they would have advanced beyond them."[67]

The vignette paid homage to a 1906 story by Ismail Gasprinskii, the "Conversation of Sultans," and invites comparison with it.[68] Here Gasprinskii imagined a visit to the crypt of Amir Timur in Samarkand, when suddenly the tombs break apart and Timur and his teacher Sayyid Baraka emerge. The gathering soon swells with the arrival of nineteenth-century monarchs such as Nasiruddin Shah of Iran, Nasrullah Khan of Bukhara, Ismail Pasha of Egypt, Khudayar Khan of Kokand, and Yaqub Beg of Kashgar. Stunned by the decline of the Muslims since his days of world-conquering, Timur questions the sultans as to how this disastrous situation could have come about. As they struggle to excuse themselves, the pan-Islamist theorist Jamaluddin Afghani (d. 1897) joins in the interrogation, roundly condemning the monarchs' complacency in the face of aggressive European modernity. Though Yaqub Beg in Kashgar and Sultan Mahmud in Istanbul had made some efforts towards reform, Afghani identified the Caucasian rebel leader Shaykh Shamil as the only Muslim leader who had made a dent in Europe's colonial armor.

For Gasprinskii, the encounter with the ghosts of sultans past was a way to criticize the nineteenth-century Islamic world's inability to keep pace with Europe's technological and political progress. The morality tale that Yavshev placed in the mouth of Satuq Bughra Khan sounded a different theme, one better suited to the militant Turkist mood that the First World War aroused among some Russian Muslims. The rot had not set in in the nineteenth century, Satuq Bughra Khan told him, but centuries earlier, when the heroic traditions of the Turks were diluted by the corrupting influence of Arab and Iranian culture— particularly Sufism ("the customs of dervishes and qalandars"). While there is no evidence that Yavshev thought of himself as an atheist, he clearly regarded the conversion to Islam as the catalyst for the decline of the Turks. In a 1917 article on "Islamic identity and nationhood" he elaborated on this, pointing the finger squarely at Iranian mysticism: "the Persian axe . . . completely uprooted the tree of Turkism."[69] Yavshev situated this decline narrative within a broad East versus West paradigm, showing how Turkist thinking on Xinjiang blended with pan-Asianist views on China, justifying his call for collaboration between progressive Muslim Turks and Chinese Republicans.

The idea that Muslims in Russia might make common cause with China or Chinese Muslims, or even that China might become an Islamic state, might seem farfetched, but the thought worried sections of Russian officialdom. The fall of the Qing came at a time of heightened paranoia regarding cross-border contacts among Russian Muslims.[70] In 1912, while the tsarist military mobilized for possible conflict with China, secret police were on the lookout for any signs that the instability might spread. Among the Taranchis, police spies focused their attention on the Jadidist short-shirts, depicting them as a threatening conspiratorial organization with seditious links to China. According to one report from 1912, "the society pursues anti-government goals, and awaits only external complications to bring their activity into the open."[71] In this environment, the authorities kept close tabs on Jadidist publications, and at the end of 1912 they thought they had a smoking gun when the *The Council* ran an article on the history of the Turks of Chinese Turkistan. Signed pseudonymously by the mysterious Mr. "Upright" (*Toghru*), it dealt with Yaqub Beg and his emirate in Kashgar, and in conclusion touched on the recent anti-Qing revolution in

China. Not concealing his enthusiasm for the fall of the Manchu dynasty, Upright ended with a call to his fellow Muslims: "it is time for us to strive toward enlightenment along with the Chinese." The police commissioned a hasty, and incorrect, translation of the article, which made its closing line sound like a threatening call to arms: "it is time for us to start things like the Chinese."[72] These twisted words were enough to spark a witch hunt for the seditious Mr. Upright.

Upright was Nazarkhoja Abdusamadov (?–1951), a Taranchi from the town of Ghaljat. He was indeed part of the small and marginal circle of reformists known as the short-shirts, who were certainly in no position to spread the Xinhai Revolution to Russia. By Abdusamadov's own account, the police roundup in 1912 hit Taranchi progressives hard, and many New Method schools in the Zharkent district were closed.[73] Finding little audience locally, men such as Abdusamadov instead sought co-thinkers in the world of letters by writing for Jadidist journals, seeking to educate the Muslims of Russia on the Muslim community of China. Like many Jadidists, Abdusamadov admired what seemed to him an enlightened laissez-faire approach to Islam in China, using it as a foil for indirect criticism of Russian policy. "One cannot help but feel," he wrote in his first essay for *The Council* in 1911, "that in not a single one of the civilized countries of Europe are Muslims given this degree of freedom."[74] He titled this piece "An Appeal Regarding the National History of the Sarts of Chinese Turkistan," and in it he asked the journal's editors to consider the "thirty million" Turks of Chinese Turkistan, whose history was so poorly known. "While a degree of information is provided on the Buriats and Tungus," he complained, "not a word is written about the Taranchi Turks in Chinese and Russian Turkistan." The editors, in his view, did not appreciate the size of the Taranchi population. By his calculations, if there had been twenty thousand households of Taranchis in the 1860s, then by now there should be as many as four hundred thousand Taranchis.[75] Later, he was distressed to read that there were only fifty-five thousand Taranchis in Semireche, leading him to worry that the Taranchis were a people in decline.[76]

Ghaljat was a sleepy town nestled in the mountains south of Zharkent, but even here Abdusamadov was not entirely cut off from the literary scene among the Russian Empire's Muslims. In 1913 a young Tatar by the name of Zarif Bashiri (1888–1962), who was teaching at the school of a Taranchi entrepreneur in Kopal, took a trip south to Ghaljat and looked up Abdusamadov. The village was, as Bashiri put it, one of "the darkest corners of Central Asia," but he was pleasantly surprised to find in Abdusamadov a well-read and accomplished scholar. "He has achieved great things in studying the lives and history of the Central Asian peoples," he noted with approval. Equally impressive was Abdusamadov's familiarity with ongoing controversies among the Tatar literati, some of whom were Bashiri's close friends. Abdusamadov expressed his admiration for the poetry of Majid Ghafuri, but had his reservations: "Lately Majid Ghafuri has become too left-wing, and the more left-wing he becomes, the more of an atheist he becomes!"[77]

The encounter between Abdusamadov and Bashiri was in many ways a meeting of the minds and marked the beginning of a collaboration that would last well into the 1920s. Bashiri took a lively ethnographic interest in the Turkic peoples of the Russian Empire, and was already something of an expert on the Chuvash, neighbors of the Tatars. This interest had resulted in an ethnographic work on the Chuvash, and also a romantic short story, *Anisa, the Chuvash Girl* (1910).[78] Tatars such as Bashiri expressed solidarity with these peoples of the empire, not by emphasizing a monolithic Turk identity, but instead by fostering the study of the particularities of each branch of the Turkic family—a stance that was inherent in the Tatars' own national project. Among the Taranchis, he sought out similar opportunities to record folk songs and collect manuscripts— even hoping to track down a copy of the Qarakhanid classic, the *Qutadghu Bilig*. Contacts such as this must have inspired Abdusamadov to continue delving into Taranchi history, a process that increasingly led him beyond the two-hundred-year history of the Taranchis to the Islamic history of the Tarim Basin. In 1913 he wrote a piece on the Qarakhanid monarch Satuq Bughra Khan and his conversion to Islam. The following year he lobbied the editors of *The Council* to publish the *Qutadghu Bilig* in serialized form.[79]

Abdusamadov's turn to history reflected his disillusionment with reformist politics centered on New Method schooling. Out of favor with the local elite, Abdusamadov stood on the sidelines while Jadidist schools sprang up among the Taranchis, and he came to view these schools as part of a cynical struggle between factional interests. Commenting on local qadi elections in 1910, he noted that both sides spent large amounts of money in bribes, but also publicized their contributions to educational reform in the Taranchi cantons: "although it is most unfortunate that both sides are engaging in all sorts of corrupt deals for the sake of winning, the good news is that in order to satisfy the people they have also been obliged to establish schools."[80] As Abdusamadov willingly conceded in 1915, "among the Taranchis, the *uṣūl-i jadid* was accepted without any fuss."[81] As such, further progress required a critique of Jadidism, and he lashed out at what he saw as a stultifying and fake progressivism among the Taranchis, identifying the Zharkent *mudarris* Gabdurahman Damolla Muhammadi as one of a number of local clergy whose Jadidism left room for all sorts of superstitious Sufi customs. This attack on the Zharkent ulama drew a response from a local mulla, who defended the *mudarris* and his students' record as champions of New Method schools. Finding little support for his views, Abdusamadov felt obliged to make a public apology.[82]

In the summer of 1914, Abdusamadov decided to observe life among the Muslims of Xinjiang firsthand, and took a trip across the mountains to Aqsu. He took with him to Xinjiang similar sensibilities to those of Yavshev, finding local society incorrigibly backward. Yet the prescription he offered was not the standard Jadidist program of schools and reading rooms. As he explained to readers of *The Council*, he had heard of the progressive Musabayevs and the work of Abdulqadir Damolla in Kashgar, and went to Xinjiang still holding out some hope for a Jadidist revival sponsored by the province's wealthy *bay*s. Yet he soon realized that such hope was misplaced. The problem that was holding back the Muslims of Chinese Turkistan, as he now saw it, was one of lost identity: "If you ask a local Turk 'Who are you?' he will say, 'Kashgari' or 'Khotani.' If you say, 'What about the name of this place?' he will just say, 'I'm a Muslim.' If you say, 'No, I didn't ask you your religion,' he will be dumbfounded and say, 'I'm a Turban-Wearing Muslim.' Those who live together with the Kazakhs and Kirghiz will say, 'We're Sarts.' That is to say, they don't even know who they are. Such ignorance!"[83] Upon his return from Xinjiang, Abdusamadov began to sign himself as "Uyghur's child."

The Uyghurs and the Turks of Turan

Where did Abdusamadov find the inspiration to style himself in this particular way? The war years witnessed a rapid shift in the Muslim world from a focus on a cultural reform within existing imperial boundaries to racial narratives that transcended these boundaries. As I discussed in Chapter 1, the scholarly rediscovery of the Uyghurs dramatically revised the standard Orientalist view of Turkic history, and this had immense significance for nationalists among Turkic-speaking peoples. In Anatolia, the word "Turk" had connotations of backwardness that the Ottoman elite associated with the nomadic lifestyle. Radlov's comparative dictionary of Turkic languages, for example, gives the definition of "Turk" in Ottoman as "uncultured, brigand, vagabond" and informs the reader that "because of this meaning the Ottomans do not like to call themselves Turks." For those interested in promoting any kind of Turkic nationalism, this was obviously a serious problem.

Turn-of-the century Turkological discoveries caused a stir among Ottoman scholars, who were excited at the recovery of a long-lost Turkic past. The runic inscriptions consolidated a view among such thinkers of the Uyghurs as exponents of the most ancient Turkic civilization, which elevated the Uyghurs from the minor part they had played in the traditional ethnogenetic narrative centered on Oghuz Khan to a position of preeminence as Eurasian culture bearers. Necib Asım, a historian and editor of the Istanbul newspaper the *Intrepid*, was the first to comment on the discoveries, and he went on to write a monograph on *The Oldest Turkic Writing* (1899). Şemseddin Sami, an Albanian intellectual and Necib Asım's collaborator, incorporated these new findings into his 1899 dictionary of Ottoman Turkish, where the entry on "Uyghur" reads: "A great tribe of Turks who spread to the north and east of Transoxiana, and were the first to attain civilization and make use of an alphabet to write Turkish. Because of this, Old Turkish has become known as the Uyghur language, and its script as the Uyghur alphabet. In the wake of Chinggis Khan's conquests they blended with the Mongols who had adopted Islam and took the name 'Chaghatayid.' "[84] Among this small circle of Turkist theorists, a new paradigm had emerged, centered on the Uyghurs and endorsed by the leading Orientalists of the day.

As the Ottoman Empire's mobilizing ideology shifted from Ottomanist or pan-Islamic emphases toward Turkic nationalism, activists in Anatolia seized on the Uyghurs as an abstract and deterritorialized symbol of the civilized Turk—something that any Turk could rightly be proud of and aspire toward. The word "Uyghur," according to this view, was synonymous with urban and civilized, and any Turkic nation that had attained a high level of civilization were Uyghurs. This glorification of the Uyghurs, or "Uyghurism" as we might call it, was an integral part of late-Ottoman Turkism and Turanism (an ideology premised on racial kinship between Turkic and Uralo-Altaic peoples). In his 1914 manifesto *Turan*, Ahmed Ferit Tek identified his Ottoman forefathers as a particularly refined species of Uyghur: "We should regard the Ottomans, Hungarians, and particularly the Finns, who are the most literate people in the world, as among the most advanced Uyghurs (*en mükemmel Uygurlardan*). . . . The primitive and nomadic Turks were shepherds who engaged in rudimentary industry. . . . The Uyghurs who lived in cities were naturally more advanced in this field."[85]

Muslim scholars in Russia likewise accorded pride of place to the Uyghurs in the new Turkic civilizational history. In 1909 Hasangata Gabashi published his *Comprehensive History of the Turkic People*, including a chapter on the Uyghurs, whom he depicted as uniquely civilized among the Turkic peoples, "on a par with the Iranians and Chinese."[86] From traditional genealogical narratives linking the Uyghurs to Oghuz Khan's confederation, he postulated that the Uyghurs were among the Oghuz tribes of Turks, who were the first to leave the steppe and migrate into Slavic and Islamic lands. In the course of their peregrinations, the Uyghurs had provided the stock for the Oghur-Bulghar peoples, as well as the Bashkirs and Magyars, even the Avars and the Finns. In Central Asia, the Uyghurs were seen as founders of both the Buddhist kingdoms of Uyghuristan, and of the Muslim Qarakhanid dynasty. While Gabashi's narrative up to this point had much in common with his Turkish counterparts, his view of the Uyghurs had greater historical specificity. He explained how the Uyghur language became known as Chaghatay, and the Uyghurs lost their identity, coming to be known as "Kashgari Turks" or something similar. His loose association of the Uyghurs with his Kashgari contemporaries brings him close to an incipient Uyghur national history.

These writings imparted to the Uyghur historical legacy both universal and particular meanings. One version of Uyghurism imagined a Uyghur golden age as part of the heritage of all Turkic-speaking peoples. Given its connotations of "civilized Turk," it is not surprising that Abdusamadov was far from the only Muslim in Russia to take "Uyghur" as a pen name in this period. This broad pan-Turkist interpretation of the Uyghur past reached its apogee in the flurry of linguistic invention in 1930s Turkey, when Kemal Atatürk ordered linguists to purge the Turkish language of Arabic and Persian elements. In Atatürk's new Pure Turkish (*öz Türkçe*) lexicon, the name "Uyghur" was adopted as the word *uyğar*, substituting for the Arabic *madani*, meaning "civilized."[87]

By contrast, Gabashi's vague identification of the Uyghurs with the Kashgari Turks points toward a second sense of Uyghurism, one in which the Muslims of Xinjiang had a privileged claim to the Uyghur legacy. In the predominantly Tatar intellectual milieu in which Taranchis like Abdusamadov functioned, the idea of constructing a pan-Turkic identity was losing ground to the Tatarist project favored by young radicals.[88] It was Abdusamadov's adaptation to this trend that led to his romantic rediscovery of the Uyghurs as a symbol of Taranchi identity. In a 1919 poem addressed "To the Toiling Taranchis," he personified Uyghur as a mytho-genealogical link between the patriarch Turk and his own Taranchi community: "Great Turk is your grandfather, Uyghur is your father."[89] In making this connection Abdusamadov believed he had hit upon something that was holding back not only the Taranchis of Russia but the Muslims of Xinjiang, with whom he imagined sharing this common Uyghur genealogy. This is not enough to make him a Uyghur nationalist, but Abdusamadov's interest in reclaiming a lost identity, and his effort to foster a sense of the Uyghurs as a link in the communal genealogy of the Taranchis, were important steps in the articulation of the new Uyghurist project.

This was an intellectual trajectory that made sense in the Semireche context, but not necessarily in Xinjiang itself. Neither intellectual rivalry with the Ottomans nor political pressure from Chinese officials required local Muslims to distinguish themselves from the Ottoman Turks by constructing a distinct racial genealogy for themselves. As already discussed, Chinese Republican politics centered on the "Muslims" as one of the nation's five constituencies, and it was on these terms that Xinjiang Muslims engaged in Chinese politics. For those drawn to a sense of Turkic identity, the shift from thinking in terms of the Muslims of Chinese Turkistan to the Turks of Chinese Turkistan could equally be reconciled with Chinese politics. The founding text of Chinese Republicanism, Sun Yat-sen's *Three People's Principles* referred not simply to the "Muslims" as one of China's five races, but specifically to the "Turks who profess Islam" (*Huijiao zhi Tujue*). Amid the heightened tensions created by the war, the Kashgaris in Istanbul, and those who were drawn to Ahmed Kemal during his stay in Kashgar, would have seen no reason not to take up the militant Turkist rhetoric that the Young Turk leadership was propagating. The difference in emphasis between the pan-Turkist and Semireche Uyghurist projects was minimal at first, but would be exacerbated soon enough, as theories of racial identity among the Xinjiang Muslims were fashioned into mobilizing tools, and the Russian Revolution threw the Taranchis and Kashgaris into new collaborations.

CHAPTER FIVE

Rebellion, Revolution, and Civil War

After two years of illness, Vali Bay died in 1916. The *Semireche Provincial News* mourned the loss of the man they called the Taranchi Harun al-Rashid, likening him to the Abbasid caliph whose name was a byword for untold wealth. Here was a man, his eulogist wrote, "who had created his enormous wealth out of literally nothing, who occupied a leading social position, who personified the entire Taranchi and part of the Dungan population of the province, and who won for himself a place in the pages of the history of Semireche and neighboring Chinese territory."[1] The timing of his death was probably for the best, as he would not have enjoyed the turn that events took later that year. Vali Bay's passing was a harbinger of the coming rebellions and fall of the tsar. In 1916 his eulogist expressed a hope that Zharkent would turn one of Vali Bay's small botanic plantations into a commemorative park, but there was to be no such memorial to the entrepreneur. The coming revolution wiped out the Taranchi elite that had risen to prominence through the Russian occupation of Ili and the migration to Semireche. Their place was filled by the likes of the short-shirts, who had bitterly denounced Vali Bay and all his works.

Up to this point, I have described the structure of representative authority within the trading networks that spanned the border, the contestation of community leadership among the Taranchi migrants in Semireche, and the growing radicalization of aspiring educational reformists in Xinjiang itself. From now on these distinct narratives start to intersect. I begin my account of this convergence by examining the consequences of the 1916 anti-tsarist rebellion in Russian Turkistan, the revolutions of 1917, and the Civil War that ensued, from the various perspectives that have been introduced so far: those of the Taranchis of Semireche, the Kashgaris in Russian Turkistan, and the Muslim community of Xinjiang.

In June 1916, with the tsarist army suffering a serious shortage of manpower in World War I, Tsar Nicholas II issued a hasty and ill-considered decree drafting non-Russians in the Kazakh steppe and Turkistan to labor on the front. The decree was greeted almost immediately with riots and attacks on tsarist officials, spreading from the Ferghana Valley east and north into Kirghiz and Kazakh districts. Nomadic raids on Russian settler communities were followed by tsarist reprisals, as martial law was declared throughout Turkistan. Of the Kirghiz and Kazakhs, who mounted the stiffest resistance to the mobilization decree, many eventually fled to Chinese territory. By early 1917 well over a hundred thousand had crossed into Xinjiang, creating an emergency for Chinese officials. Of these runaways, thousands died crossing the mountains in the wintry conditions, and many thousands more perished from hunger and disease in Xinjiang. The story of nomadic rebellion and the flight to China is a key chapter in the history of the Russian Revolution in Turkistan, and features in various national histories in post-Soviet Central Asia.[2] In comparison, the fate of others whose stories intersect with China is less well known. The Taranchis and Kashgaris of Semireche lacked the mobility of the Kazakh and Kirghiz nomads who escaped to Xinjiang, and found themselves caught between the rebels and the reprisals.

The Taranchi Tragedy

Among the Taranchis there was some resistance to the tsar's conscription decree of 1916—a total of nine men were executed for agitating against it. The opposition was considerably less than among Semireche's Kazakhs, though, and when the anti-conscription rebellion had subsided, the mobilization was carried out in Zharkent.[3] In the first batch of November 1916, six hundred Taranchi workers boarded the train to the front, with Vali Bay's close associate, the merchant Husayn Beg Yunusov, sending them off with a rousing patriotic speech and hurrahs.[4] Statistics on the recruitment of émigré Kashgaris are harder to come by, but Kashgari Communists later claimed that tens of thousands of Kashgaris were sent to work on the front.[5]

Russian officials in Semireche generally saw the province's Taranchis as passively loyal, the Tatars of the province actively so.[6] This stands in stark contrast to the case of the Dungans of Issiq Köl, who mobilized against both nomadic predations and Russian reprisals. Later analysis linked Dungan militancy in 1916 to the activities of the Gelaohui, the Chinese secret society that Zuo Zongtang's Hunan army had brought to Xinjiang. From Xinjiang, the Gelaohui had sought allies among the Semireche Dungans, where tsarist officials had first detected Chinese secret society activities in the 1890s.[7] Although wary of such activity, officials saw the Gelaohui as an exclusively anti-Manchu organization, and not a direct threat to Russian interests. Now, though, the conspiracy seemed to be aimed against the tsar. According to testimony gathered in the aftermath of the uprising, in 1915 the organization had sent activists to the urban centers of Semireche, where they established societies of both Russian- and Chinese-subject Dungans. One such group briefly seized control of Qaraqol in August 1916, during the height of the conflict. In the same month, Russian troops detained four men for spreading propaganda among the Dungan population of Qaraqonguz (now Masanchi, Kazakhstan), advocating "an uprising against the Russian authorities, the expulsion of Russian authorities from the Turkistan Territory, and the formation of separate khanates led by individuals from the Muslim population." Some police investigators went so far as to suggest that "the uprising of the Kirghiz [here meaning Kazakhs] is the result of the activity of the Gelaohui society."[8] These events gained for the Gelaohui a reputation that would soon recommend them to Russian radicals.

Barely had the tsar's officers suppressed the rebellion when news reached Turkistan of the February 1917 revolution and the fall of the Romanov dynasty. Events in Russia inspired a range of new representative bodies in Semireche. The key political actors to emerge were the committee of Provisional Government commissars, local soviets of peasant deputies, and the Cossack military assembly (*voiskovyi krug*). Besides these, a range of national representative bodies sprang up in the provincial center of Vernyi, which were loosely affiliated to a Muslim congress known as the Quriltay. The most significant of these was a committee of Kazakh intellectuals aligned with the Alash Orda party, proponents of Kazakh autonomy. There was also a branch of the Islamic Union (Shura-yi Islamiyya), organized by a delegation from its headquarters in Tashkent, as well as a Taranchi group calling itself the Taranchi Committee, which was led at first by a wealthy Taranchi businessman, and later by a member of the Taranchi ulama, Maruf Masudi. In the summer of 1917 the committee admitted a Dungan into its leadership, thereby becoming the Taranchi-Dungan Committee. At this point, the Taranchi-Dungan Committee could only claim to represent Taranchis and Dungans in Vernyi and its surrounds. In Zharkent, a rival Taranchi-Dungan committee came into being under Husayn Beg Yunusov. Located in the heartland of the Russian Taranchi community, these

Zharkent elites saw themselves as its natural leadership and were unwilling to submit to the authority of a Vernyi-based organization.[9]

Outside the cities, the land question dominated politics in Semireche. Many of the province's able-bodied Slavic peasants had been called up to the army in 1917. Now demobilized, these men returned to Semireche with their colonial outlook steeled by the militant revolutionary mood. Among these Slavic settlers, the desire for revenge against the Kazakh and Kirghiz rebels of 1916 was strong, and many sensed an opportunity to finally resolve the long-standing contest between steppe and sown. Apart from the Kazakhs, this hostility was also directed against the Cossacks, who enjoyed the biggest and best allocations of land in the province, and against Taranchi immigrants from Xinjiang. Taranchis in Semireche were generally much worse off in terms of land than either Slavic settlers or Cossacks, but as Muslims from China they were widely viewed as intruders in a zone of colonization now reserved for the "Slavic element." In comparison with the well-armed *stanitsa*s (as Cossack settlements were known), moreover, the Taranchi villages were a soft target. Not surprisingly, anxious Taranchi elites came to see the Cossacks as guarantors of their security.

In January 1918, Soviet authority was established in Pishpek, and in February the Second Congress of Peasant Deputies in Vernyi passed a resolution endorsing the October revolution. That month the two Taranchi-Dungan committees held a combined congress in Vernyi. Besides thrashing out its position toward the revolutionary events taking place around it, the congress brought out many other lingering controversies in Taranchi politics: inequalities in the distribution of land, whether or not the locus of spiritual authority among the Taranchis should be in Zharkent or Vernyi, and methods of instruction in Taranchi schools. The more conservative Zharkent faction, led by Husayn Beg Yunusov, won the day, and the congress declared its continuing support for the Provisional Government. In doing so, however, the Taranchi-Dungan committees were endorsing a lost cause: within a few days of the congress's conclusion, the Second Semireche Cossack Division mutinied, and Vernyi passed into the hands of a newly formed pro-Bolshevik Military-Revolutionary Committee. At this point, wealthy supporters of the Quriltay emptied Vernyi's banks and fled the city, and leaders of the Taranchi-Dungan Committee such as Husayn Beg Yunusov and Maruf Masudi headed to the Taranchi cantons surrounding the city. Yunusov eventually escaped to Ghulja, but Masudi was killed in the subsequent fighting.[10]

That April, Red Army reinforcements were sent to Vernyi to disarm the district's Cossacks and requisition grain, only to be repelled by Cossacks belonging to the army's remaining anti-Bolshevik divisions. Soon all the *stanitsa*s south of Vernyi rose in revolt and commenced a siege of the provincial capital, with the Taranchi cantons around Vernyi becoming the epicenter of the White counterattack. These rural communities were headed by the *volostnoi*, positions that were in theory elected but in reality were monopolized by wealthy Taranchis whose relationships with Russian officials often dated back to the occupation of the Ili Valley in the 1870s. Head of the Qarasu canton Jamaluddin Bushriev, for example, was the son of Bushri Jalilov, *aqsaqal* of the city of Ghulja during the years of Russian occupation. Jamaluddin had already served two terms as *volostnoi* of the Qarasu canton and retained an ex officio authority in the district. He mobilized local Taranchi labor to reinforce the siege of Vernyi and recruited a small Taranchi fighting force of around fifty men. In an assault on Vernyi, the Cossacks drove these poorly armed Taranchis ahead of themselves as human shields, and they were all but wiped out. Tragic events such as this heightened Bolshevik suspicions that the Taranchis were siding with the counterrevolution.

In May, Turkistan's Central Executive Committee and Council of People's Commissars dispatched the Red Army officer Muraev to Semireche to relieve Vernyi.[11] Throughout the month, Red soldiers took control of Cossack *stanitsa*s in Vernyi District and proceeded to raze nearby Taranchi villages, massacring many of the inhabitants. Later White reports describe gruesome scenes of Taranchi peasants being forced to dig their own burial pits before being mowed down by machine guns.[12] The violence resulted in an exodus from Vernyi District east along the Ghulja road, heading toward the border with China. The initial response of the Chinese authorities was to shut the crossing, resulting in a buildup of refugees at the Khorgos River. White officers briefly regrouped in Ghaljat, setting up a makeshift command center and recruiting refugees for an assault on Zharkent, including a unit of some three hundred Taranchis. The Whites succeeded in taking Zharkent on the night of May 24, but the Bolshevik response was not long in coming. Muraev advanced eastward and wrested Zharkent from the Whites by the middle of June, a victory that resulted in further revenge attacks on the locals. The mobile Kazakh population of Zharkent District fled, as they had in 1916, with many crossing the border to China. Local Taranchis were forced to flee too, adding to the throng of asylum seekers at Khorgos. When Ili officials eventually permitted them to cross, they were disarmed and sent to an internment camp on the banks of Lake Sayram, to Ghulja's north. Eventually Beijing intervened and instructed the Ili authorities to admit the refugees to the Ili district itself and provide them with basic relief supplies.

It is unknown how many people died at the hands of these punitive expeditions, which local memory records as the "Taranchi tragedy," or "shooting tragedy" (*atuv paji'äsi*). Ilya Shendrikov, a member of the Provisional Government's Turkistan Committee who joined Admiral Kolchak in Omsk, estimated the Taranchi dead at four thousand.[13] Whites in Ghulja, clearly exaggerating, put the toll at thirty thousand, while Uyghur Communists in the 1920s believed it to be above ten thousand.[14] After the civil war, the Bolsheviks admitted that "kulak" elements (i.e., wealthy peasants) had engaged in revolutionary violence for not-so-revolutionary ends, but any direct criticism of the party was avoided, and the events themselves were not closely investigated. In the 1960s, de-Stalinization allowed greater scope for public reflection on the historical experience of the community, but even here there were limits. In its original 1968 Uyghur edition, Mashur Ruziev's *The Uyghur People Reborn* gives a graphic depiction of the events of early 1918, blaming the killing on "local colonial kulaks who had armed themselves with the cloak of the Reds." However, the editors of the book's Russian versions substantially edited and weakened this section.[15] To this day, many Uyghurs regard the full details of Muraev's terror and the "Taranchi tragedy" as secrets waiting to be revealed.

Red and White Diplomacy in the Ili Valley

Xinjiang was not only a sanctuary for the revolution's victims. Although remote from the strongholds of Russian social democracy, news of the events of February and October 1917 found a sympathetic hearing in some parts of the province. It is a little-known fact of Chinese history that the first public rallies in support of the Russian Revolution were held, not in cosmopolitan Shanghai or the nation's capital of Beijing, but in the treaty ports of Xinjiang, where stirrings of revolutionary activity were felt among Xinjiang's Tatar and Russian community. As early as August 1917, tsarist officials in Tarbaghatay complained to the Ministry of Foreign Affairs in Saint Petersburg about the activities of Bolshevik agitators in the trading colony and asked that they be expelled.[16] In March 1918, International Women's Day was celebrated in Tarbaghatay, with a local Tatar teacher making a rousing speech to the crowd. Soon a youth organization calling itself Unity came into being, again with a largely Tatar membership. Inflammatory leaflets were distributed on the streets of Ghulja in 1918, calling on the peoples of the district to unite and rise up against their oppressors.[17]

In April 1918, the newly established People's Commissariat of Foreign Affairs (NKID) in Moscow declared all foreign representatives of the tsarist government dismissed and announced the appointment of its own consuls throughout China.[18] However, since China was yet to recognize the Soviet state, Beijing's Foreign Ministry allowed Xinjiang's tsarist consuls to stay put. In Ghulja the White consul was Viktor Liuba, a veteran of imperial diplomacy in Mongolia and Xinjiang. Throughout 1918–1919, Liuba remained in close contact with White centers in Russia and published an anti-Bolshevik newspaper, *Free Word* (*Svobodnoe slovo*) on Husayn Beg Yunosov's printing press. Liuba's first rival as Soviet consul was his former secretary, Ananii Pavlovich Zinkevich. He proved to be a poor choice for the job. Upon Zinkevich's arrival, Liuba gave him three days to leave before he would have him assassinated. Zinkevich requested, and received, an escort from Chinese officials back to Russian territory. Liuba was equally effective in closing off other lines of communication between Xinjiang and Soviet Turkistan. In August he communicated to Beijing complaints against two employees of the Russian telegraph office in Ghulja who had been transmitting messages between the Ili authorities and the Bolsheviks. Within days, the Chinese Foreign Ministry had the two men expelled from Chinese territory.[19] In November 1918, when a pro-Bolshevik demonstration marking the anniversary of the Russian Revolution was held in Ghulja, Liuba responded by arresting those he suspected of harboring Bolshevik sympathies and repatriating them to Russia.[20]

As the civil war in Semireche neared Xinjiang, White diplomats such as Liuba lobbied for Chinese intervention against the Reds. In negotiating for Chinese support, White leaders held out the prospect of redressing historical grievances along China's shifting border with Russia. In May 1918, when the first high-level Cossack and Muslim delegation reached Ghulja to request Chinese support, they offered to give back to China the fifteen thousand square miles of territory ceded in the Treaty of Saint Petersburg of 1881.[21] Chinese officials, particularly those close to events in Semireche, were certainly frustrated that Xinjiang's position of neutrality in the civil war seemed to mean turning a blind eye to disturbing reports of violence against Chinese subjects that they were receiving from Russian territory. Unfortunately for the Whites, these complaints were just as frequently directed against the Semireche Cossacks as against the Bolsheviks. Much to Liuba's chagrin, in August 1917 Ili Circuit Commissioner Xu Guozhen actually proposed an intervention to protect émigré Dungans from Cossack attacks.[22]

Chinese and White sources concur that somewhere between fifty and sixty thousand Taranchis escaped to Chinese territory, although an initial Bolshevik investigation in 1918 produced a total of only twenty thousand. Soviet population statistics confirm that the exodus was in the tens of thousands, registering only 45,547 Taranchis and Dungans in Semireche in 1920, a decrease of over 40 percent from 1913.[23] As a result of the overcrowding in Ghulja, the prices of food and accommodation skyrocketed, and disease also threatened.[24] In collaboration with Liuba, Taranchi leaders organized a provisioning committee, which received from the consul an initial fund of 120,000 rubles plus a supply of cloth issued from confiscated goods. Survival needs tied Liuba, his Taranchi allies, and the refugees in tight bonds. At the stroke of a pen, those who offended the consul could be struck off the provisioning committee's list of relief recipients.

Given the conditions in Ili, is not surprising that some were willing to risk returning to Red Semireche. In July 1918, Liuba sent a telegram to the Turkistan NKID in Tashkent announcing that the refugees were willing to return to Russian territory on condition that they be granted amnesty, that stolen property be returned, and that those responsible for "murder and robbery of citizens" would be called to account; by this Liuba presumably intended Muraev and his partisans.[25] The local soviet in Zharkent, no doubt dismayed at the decimation of the district's peasantry, consented to the proposal, but authorities in Vernyi would not hear of it.

Acting on instructions issued by one of Moscow's representatives in Turkistan, Extraordinary Commissar Pavel Chegodaev, Muraev continued his advance toward Chinese territory, intending to cross into Xinjiang and arrest Liuba.[26] In this he failed, but he did succeed in holding a meeting with Circuit Commissioner Xu in his seat of Huiyuan. Two accounts of this meeting exist, both drawn from the unpublished memoirs of one of Muraev's deputies, an officer named Melnikov. According to one retelling, at this meeting the Bolsheviks pledged to protect Chinese subjects in Semireche in return for access to Ili's grain market.[27] A second, more revealing account says that the Bolsheviks offered to keep the circuit commissioner supplied with Semireche opium in return for his cooperation in disarming the Whites and preventing raids into Soviet territory.[28] The meeting seems to have been kept secret from Ürümchi and Beijing, and is not mentioned in any Chinese sources, but this account is consistent with White complaints that Ili officials were conniving with Bolshevik contrabandists and receiving shipments of opium from Semireche. Chinese officials certainly had an interest in restoring trade relations with Russia. Garrison Commissioner (*zhenshoushi*) Yang Feixia was the major shareholder in a Chinese firm that Liuba accused of receiving confiscated goods in lieu of cash payments from the Bolsheviks.[29]

It was economics, not politics, that dictated early Soviet priorities in Xinjiang. By the end of 1918, famine conditions threatened Semireche, and for the first time in its history the province had to import grain, with the Ili Valley offering the most convenient supply. A series of trading delegations followed up Muraev's first contact, setting up shop in Ghulja to buy grain and other goods, but these trading missions all encountered stiff resistance from Liuba. In November 1918, the ex-consul personally assaulted the first envoy, Muraev's deputy Melnikov, before the Chinese expelled him to Soviet territory. The next "Red consul" to try his hand had an equally brief stay on Chinese soil. Frustrated by these failures, the Bolsheviks' resolve stiffened. In February 1919 they sent a threatening note to Ili demanding that at the very least a Soviet commercial agent be admitted.[30] In swift succession two such agents were dispatched, but got no closer to Ghulja than Zharkent.[31] In September 1919, the Turkistan NKID in Tashkent communicated to Ili that it intended to appoint the Socialist-Revolutionary Pavel Chegodaev as its consul. The Ili circuit commissioner rejected this request too, pleading that he still had no instructions from Beijing.[32]

As an anticipated anti-Bolshevik uprising in Semireche failed to eventuate, and relief funds started to dry up, White hopes in Ghulja increasingly turned north to Siberia, to the newly established Russian government of Admiral Kolchak in Omsk. In March 1919 a mission was sent to Omsk, headed by Liuba's consular secretary Vorobchuk and including the prominent Taranchi Husayn Beg Yunusov. Vorobchuk and Yunusov presented to Kolchak's Ministry of Foreign Affairs a set of reports on the worsening situation in Ili and introduced the admiral to the history of the Taranchis, emphasizing a tradition of loyalty to Russia and its tsar. As they described it, so strong was Taranchi devotion to Russia's White King (*aq padshah*) that not even medical sedation could restrain it: "At the end of 1917, Doctor Tseravskii in Zharkent performed a serious operation on a poor Taranchi woman. The patient was treated with chloroform.

At the time of the operation itself, when the patient was supposed to be undergoing hellish torments, she kept repeating: 'Oh poor White King! Poor Tsar! Where is the poor White King?' "[33] Vorobchuk and Yunusov submitted a request for ten million rubles toward refugee relief and organization, but received only two million. What happened next is not entirely clear, but these relief funds seem to have been lost on the way back to Ghulja. According to one account, Kolchak's donation was spent buying up trading goods in Omsk to be sold on return to China. When they arrived, the emissaries claimed that the Bolsheviks had robbed them.[34]

Although it failed in its relief mission, Vorobchuk and Yunusov's trip to Omsk drew White attention to the potential of Ghulja as a base of operations. The Cossack ataman Annenkov, then based in nearby Semipalatinsk, was already considering the possibility of a diversionary attack on Semireche from Xinjiang, and in April 1919 he sent his deputy Colonel Sidorov to Ghulja. In the face of Chinese opposition, Sidorov succeeded in recruiting a unit of around five hundred Russian Muslims. Meanwhile, Kolchak's government requested permission from Beijing to officially enlist Russian Muslims in China and dispatched two representatives, General Lieutenant Kartsev and Sub-Colonel Briantsev to Xinjiang. By the time Kolchak received Beijing's reply in the negative, Kartsev and Briantsev were already well on their way to Ghulja.

In October 1919, Kolchak's White regime in Omsk collapsed, and the admiral fled to Irkutsk. From his headquarters in Semipalatinsk, Annenkov announced the formation of a new Semireche Army, ordering the mobilization of all Russian subjects, including those in China. This rang alarm bells among Xinjiang officials, who recalled the tsar's mobilization decree of 1916 and worried about the potential for similar unrest. "If they carry out this plan," Yang Zengxin agonized from his desk in Ürümchi, "then the disastrous turmoil that previously occurred in Qaraqol will be repeated in China's own Ili!"[35] Luckily for Yang and his fellow Chinese officials, the arrival of Annenkov and Kolchak's subordinates in Xinjiang provoked a clash with the diplomatic corps, as the White officers tried to remove consul Liuba from Ghulja. From Beijing, the tsarist ambassador Prince Kudashev complained to Kolchak and instructed his consuls not to cooperate with the White call-up.[36] In the end, it seems Liuba was happy to comply with Chinese requests to halt the conscription.

The falling out between the tsarist diplomats and White officers reflected the ailing fortunes of the White cause in Russia itself. As White resistance ebbed, the Bolsheviks in Moscow reestablished communications with Turkistan, and in late 1919 Lenin's Turkistan Commission made it through to Tashkent. As Soviet Russia's plenipotentiary organ in Turkistan, the Turkistan Commission enjoyed wide-ranging powers, including in the sphere of foreign affairs. In April 1920 representatives of the commission traveled to the Khorgos River for negotiations with Ili officials. Circuit Commissioner Xu found himself in a position of strength, and in return for opening Ili to Soviet trade representatives, he won the termination of privileges enjoyed by Russians in northwest China since the Treaty of Saint Petersburg. With the signing of the Ili Protocols in May 1920, the Soviets finally succeeded in opening a foreign trade mission in Ghulja.[37] Seeking to reestablish their position against the threat of foreign competition, Soviet representatives entered into new contracts with local Muslim merchants, including the Musabayevs and also a number of former *aqsaqal*s who were in a good position to exploit their cross-border connections. One of these was Faziljan Yunich, previously the *aqsaqal* of Ghulja's Tatar community and now a Chinese subject.[38] Another was Turdi Akhun Almasbekov, until recently the *aqsaqal* of Chinese subjects in Toqmaq, who had returned to Xinjiang during the revolution.

Neither Moscow nor Beijing were well informed of these early negotiations along the Khorgos River, but they were the first steps toward Sino-Soviet rapprochement and the beginning of the end for tsarist diplomacy in China. Liuba left Ghulja in May immediately following the signing of the Ili Protocols. In September, Beijing announced that it would no longer recognize tsarist representatives and encouraged Prince Kudashev to step down as Russian ambassador.

Abdullah Rozibaqiev and the Uyghur Club

The exodus of anti-Bolshevik forces from Vernyi left the various national groupings that had affiliated themselves to the city's Quriltay depleted and divided. This created a leadership vacuum among the city's remaining Muslim residents, including the Taranchis, which new groups of young revolutionaries formed to fill. Vernyi's Kazakhs founded an association called Sunlight (Säule), while a Turkistani Muslim group took the designation "Turan," possibly affiliated to the Turan cultural society founded in Tashkent by the Jadidist Abdullah Awlani.[39] Local Tatars called their organization Tuqay, in honor of the poet Gabdullah Tuqay. Similarly, in February 1918 the Vernyi Taranchis founded a club they called "Uyghur," the first time anyone in Semireche had publicly invested the Uyghur symbol with political meaning. Although long since forgotten, in the 1920s the date of the club's establishment (February 2) was celebrated by the Soviet Uyghur community with speech making and cultural evenings.[40] The short-shirt Nazarkhoja Abdusamadov—Uyghur's Child— was one of its founding members. Other members were local Taranchi students. These included Ismail Tairov, who had studied under the exiled Tatar *mudarris* Gabdullah Bubi in Ghulja, and was now enrolled in a teacher-training course in Vernyi. Another was Muzaffar Yarullabekov, a student in Vernyi's Russian gymnasium. Of the group's small membership, though, the man who would emerge as the leader among Semireche's radical Taranchis was Abdullah Rozibaqiev.

Born in Kiyikbay, a village to the east of Vernyi, Abdullah Rozibaqiev had moved to the city in 1900 with his father Ahmad, who ran a school and served as imam of Vernyi's Taranchi mosque. Known as a man of progressive views, in 1909 Ahmad became chair of a local charitable society, with his brother Hidayat serving as secretary.[41] Like many such organizations, the charitable society at times aroused the suspicion of tsarist officials, particularly in 1913 when it donated a hundred rubles to an Ottoman officer. In other respects, though, Ahmad was a loyal member of the empire's Muslim clergy. In 1914, for example, when conflict broke out among the Taranchis over the requirement to hang the portrait of the tsar in schools in Semireche, Ahmad was a leading defender of the new statute. For taking this stance, he received a robe of honor from the tsarist authorities and death threats from other Taranchi mullas.[42] Growing up in the midst of such controversy must have been a formative experience for the young Abdullah. (Later his political rivals would accuse him of being a tsarist spy.) Abdullah completed Russian school in Vernyi in 1914, and in 1916 he graduated from an accounting course, taking up a position as a clerk in the city bank.[43]

In 1917 Rozibaqiev participated in the activities of the Vernyi Taranchi-Dungan Committee and also became involved with a small group of Muslim socialists who called themselves the Union of Muslim Workers of Vernyi. With an initial membership of seventeen, including two Taranchis, these socialists staged a demonstration of around a hundred in May 1917. At first, Rozibaqiev's socialist leanings seem not to have interfered with his position on the Taranchi-Dungan Committee. At the combined Vernyi-Zharkent congress of February 1918, Rozibaqiev and his allies lobbied for a position of neutrality in the confrontation between the Bolsheviks and the Cossacks. Although he was defeated

Abdullah Rozibaqiev (*seated, left*) and family. (Central State Archive of Film, Photo, and Audio Documents of the Republic of Kazakhstan.)

in this vote, he continued to occupy an important position on the committee as secretary of its executive National Council (Milli Shura). He also collaborated with the Tatar Zarif Bashiri, now residing in Vernyi, to edit the committee's organ, *Voice of the Taranchi* (*Ṣada-yi Taranchi*).[44] It was the establishment of Soviet authority in March that finally split the committee, with Rozibaqiev siding with the revolutionaries and remaining in Vernyi. When exactly Rozibaqiev joined the Bolshevik party is unclear, but after a re-registration of party members in 1918, he was among forty-five remaining in Vernyi, one of only five from Turkistan's non-Slavic nationalities.[45] The Left Social-Revolutionaries were still the most popular revolutionary party among the city's Muslims. In August 1918, they dominated the Vernyi District Congress of Soviets, a meeting at which Rozibaqiev served as secretary.[46]

Little is known about the activities of the Uyghur Club during this period, but no doubt it had much in common with prerevolutionary Jadidist cultural societies. The local Muslim press reports, for example, that in the middle of

1919 the club put on a Taranchi version of the *The Patricide*, Mahmud Beh-budi's popular Jadidist drama.[47] Another fleeting mention of the club describes how it organized accommodation for Turkish soldiers who were passing through Semireche on their way south from the Siberian POW camps.[48] *Voice of the Taranchi* only survived for six issues, but Rozibaqiev and a number of other Taranchis also frequently contributed to Vernyi's Muslim socialist press, which was written in a heavily Tatar-inflected language that was intended to be read by all local Muslims. It was in the *Semireche Workers' Reporter* that Rozibaqiev, writing under the pseudonym "Chantou," published the Taranchi Communists' one and only public response to the "Shooting Tragedy." Pinning the blame for the violence on the Cossacks who had lured Muraev's punitive expedition to Semireche, he lamented that the Taranchis "fell victim to their own ignorance and backwardness. . . . There is nothing about spilling innocent blood in the Bolshevik program."[49]

Rozibaqiev's defense of Bolshevik vigilantism was probably cold comfort to the Taranchi refugees in Ghulja, and to many of those who had remained behind. It was hard for Muslim Communists to deny the fact that the Bolshevik leadership remained steadfastly pro-Russian in its orientation during this pe-riod. Often these Turkistani Bolsheviks had an antagonistic relationship even with Muslim socialists such as Rozibaqiev. In seeking to remedy this situation, Muslim Communists founded their own organizations, which in March 1919 combined to form the Muslim Bureau (Musbiuro) of the Central Committee of the Communist Party of Turkistan.[50] Chaired by the Kazakh Turar Risqulov (1894–1938), the Muslim Bureau extended its network throughout the Com-munist Party of Turkistan and sought to rally the various non-party Muslim organizations of Turkistan behind its pro-Bolshevik leadership. During its brief existence, Rozibaqiev served as deputy chair of the Muslim Bureau's Semireche branch, which according to his memoirs brought Vernyi's various national organizations, including the Uyghur Club, within its purview. The Muslim Bureau also claimed leadership of the revolutionary movement in regions neighboring Turkistan and recruited foreigners into its ranks. These initiatives drew support from the Bolshevik leadership in Moscow, which was now seeking to reestablish its control in Turkistan and reverse the colonialist policy of the Bolsheviks in Tashkent. When Lenin's Turkistan Commission descended on Tashkent, it sidelined the Turkistani Bolsheviks (now known as the "Old Bol-sheviks") and encouraged Muslim Communist ambitions.

The temporary ascendancy of the Muslim Communists was a mixed blessing for the Semireche Taranchis, who were still reeling from the blows of the civil war. Initiated by Muslim Bureau chief Turar Risqulov, decolonization efforts in Semireche were aimed primarily at wooing back Kazakh and Kirghiz runaways from Xinjiang and privileged these nomadic groups at the expense of the Taranchis, many of whom were still in Ghulja. The policy highlighted once again the Taranchis' anomalous position as "native-immigrants" in Semireche, falling between the two key categories of *pereselentsy* and *tuzemtsy*. In late 1919, the Turkistan Central Executive Committee issued an amnesty to Russian-subject Kazakhs and Kirghiz in Xinjiang, and in February 1920 it dispatched a commission to Semireche to expel any colonists who had seized land since 1916.[51] While some of this land had originally belonged to Taranchis, in practice the redistribution was guided by slogans of returning land to the Kazakhs. In Zharkent, according to one account, an ex-member of the Kazakh nationalist party Alash Orda headed the survey teams, a fact that inevitably soured relations with local Taranchis. These Taranchis would later complain that when they returned from Xinjiang, they were met with the retort "Go home to Ghulja!"[52]

Boosted by the rout of the Old Bolsheviks, in early 1920 Muslim Bureau leaders such as Risqulov articulated an explicitly Turkic nationalist vision for Soviet Turkistan. They proposed the formation of a "Muslim Red Army" and passed resolutions transforming the Communist Party of Turkistan into the "Turkic Communist Party." Such moves far exceeded the bounds of the emerging Soviet nationalities policy and brought the Muslim Bureau into conflict with the Turkistan Commission. The Turkistan Commission eventually invoked its executive authority to disband the Muslim Bureau, thereby consolidating Moscow's grip on Turkistan. The attack on the Muslim Bureau brought about the downfall of some of its leading members, but not Rozibaqiev, who complied with the center's directives.

Rozibaqiev still had little to show his community for his collaboration with the Bolsheviks, and the small group of Taranchi Communists meeting in Vernyi's Uyghur Club needed a new strategy. Semireche land policy continued to disadvantage the Taranchis, who suffered from the perception that they were immigrants from China. In September 1920 the Ninth Congress of the Soviets of Turkistan confirmed that lands seized by Slavic settlers were to be restored to their original occupants. In February 1921 the Turkistan Commission instituted its own land reform policy, but the principle of "prioritization" (*ocherednost'*) still gave Kazakhs precedence in claiming agricultural land.[53] Yet while they were stigmatized by the association with China, there were also opportunities here for the Taranchis to exploit. The imperative of spreading the revolution abroad at times led Soviet officials to implement preferential policies toward border-crossing communities. This "piedmont principle," as Terry Martin calls it, offered a way for the Taranchis to turn their immigrant status to advantage in Soviet politics. By repositioning the Taranchis as part of a trans-imperial community of Chinese Muslims, and the Taranchi Communists at the vanguard of a new revolutionary push into Asia, they might also prompt a rethinking of Soviet priorities in Semireche itself. The romantic invocation of a link to the Muslims of China that the "Uyghur" Club represented now took on practical meaning as Rozibaqiev turned his hand to cross-border work.

Among the measures it took in disbanding the Muslim Bureau, the Turkistan Commission established a new organization for foreign revolutionary activity, which it called the Council of International Propaganda in the East (Sovinterprop).[54] The Sovinterprop included activists from tsarist Russia's protectorates of Khiva and Bukhara, Turkish and Iranian Communists, as well as "Chinese" representatives. Abdullah Rozibaqiev, the Russian-speaking Taranchi who had never set foot in China, was appointed to the Sovinterprop in this latter capacity.[55] Like the Muslim Bureau, the Sovinterprop was a short-lived organization, being absorbed into the Comintern within a year of its founding. The inclusion of Rozibaqiev was significant, though, as it heralded the entry of Taranchi Communists into the field of Xinjiang policy and was soon to bring them into contact with radicals among the Vernyi Kashgaris.

Organizing the Kashgari Diaspora

From the outbreak of the anti-conscription revolt in 1916, Chinese subjects in Russian territory were struck by both nomadic militancy and Russian reprisals. The violence hit the Xinjiang trading community in towns such as Qaraqol particularly hard, a toll recorded in lives as well as property. A certain Ahmad Bay, who fled to Xinjiang from Qaraqol, reported that his fellow Artush merchants there had lost a total of five million taels. "We regularly suffer mistreatment at the hands of the Russians," he stated in an impassioned plea to Ürümchi, "and not a few have become Russian subjects. Yet we have always been Chinese subjects (*Zhongmin*), and cannot forget our roots. Now that we have fallen on hard times, who will take pity on us?"[56] From late 1917, requisitioning and the imposition of price controls also led to significant hardship. In October 1918, Soviet decrees shut the Vernyi bazaar and ended private trade in the city, dealing the Kashgari trading community in Semireche a major blow.[57]

Elsewhere local Soviet authorities were not averse to simply plundering the vulnerable foreigners. The Osh Soviet raided and burnt down the city's Kashgari caravanserai, an attack in which Umar Akhunbayev lost a million rubles.[58] Those who tried to transport their trading goods back to China risked having them confiscated at the border, where Soviets kept an eye out for rich families sending their wealth to China.

Yang Zengxin communicated his concerns to Beijing's Department of Foreign Affairs, but was told that they could do nothing to prevent attacks on Chinese subjects in Soviet territory, and that his only course of action was to engage in informal negotiations with local Russian officials.[59] For Yang, this meant drawing on the network of Kashgari *aqsaqals* in Russian Turkistan. It was the *aqsaqals* who provided Ürümchi with detailed reports on losses suffered by Chinese merchants and conducted the first negotiations for redress. In 1919 a Kashgari mission reached Tashkent, led by *aqsaqal* Ibrahim Akhun.[60] The local press was eager for signs that the Soviet Union was gaining diplomatic recognition, and notwithstanding Ibrahim's lack of Chinese diplomatic credentials they announced his arrival as the visit of the "Chinese ambassador." One result of Ibrahim's negotiations was a novel suggestion for Kashgaris: to fly the Chinese flag from their caravans and wear badges indicating their nationality.[61]

The plight of Kashgari émigrés in Russian Turkistan at this time had much in common with the experience of Chinese subjects residing along other stretches of China's lengthy frontier with Russia. According to one scholar's calculations, in 1910 in the Russian Far East alone there were between 200 thousand and 250 thousand Chinese, many of them working on contract in the mines and on the railroads.[62] Apart from laborers and traders, the Chinese community in Russia also included a sizable influx of refugees from natural disasters in China. Some of these vagrants were organized into roving bands of brigands known as Red Beards (*Khunkhuzy*), who were recruited by various actors in the civil war.[63] By the time of the Russian Revolution, there were also many thousands of Chinese performing manual labor on the front in western Russia. One Chinese émigré estimated that there were 60 thousand of his compatriots digging trenches in European Russia in 1917.[64]

The first organization to emerge among Russia's Chinese diaspora was the Union of Chinese Citizens in Russia, founded in April 1917 by Chinese students in Saint Petersburg, with a branch soon opening in Moscow and in Ukraine where Chinese were laboring on the front. Not by any means a radical organization, the union aimed to meet the welfare needs of Chinese left stranded in Russia and assist those who wished to return to China—an offer that thousands took up. After the October Revolution, the Chinese embassy itself left Russia, entrusting the union with responsibility for protecting the rights of Chinese citizens. The union now took a new political direction, renaming itself the Union of Chinese Workers and issuing a proclamation to the Chinese people denouncing the warlords who dominated politics in Beijing.[65] In line with the early Soviet Union's revolutionary approach to citizenship, an NKID decree of March 1919 recognized the union's right to protect Chinese citizens and represent them in Soviet courts and tribunals. According to the union's leader, Liu Zerong, Lenin personally endorsed the letter investing the union with full legal authority in matters concerning Chinese citizens in Russia. Nevertheless, the precise status of the Union of Chinese Workers remained in doubt, and the People's Commissariat of Justice rejected the idea that organizations of foreign workers could adopt quasi-diplomatic functions.[66]

Soon enough, the leaders of the Union of Chinese Workers themselves started leaving the Soviet Union and returning to China. While some traveled by rail across Siberia, other returnees headed through Turkistan and along the way became involved in organizing Chinese subjects there. In 1919 the Kashgari *aqsaqal* in Tashkent reported that a group of five Chinese had recently arrived in the city claiming to be representatives of the Chinese embassy in Moscow.[67] The arrival of these activists coincided with that of the Turkistan Commission and its new organization for revolutionary work among foreigners, the Sovinterprop. In April 1920, the two groups collaborated in establishing a branch of the Union of Chinese Workers in Tashkent, and within a few months its membership of Chinese and Muslims from Xinjiang had risen to a hundred.[68] At the Sovinterprop's initiative, similar organizations of Chinese subjects sprang up in the Ferghana Valley, some with Communist cells.[69] Reflecting the mixed Chinese-Muslim composition of these organizations, they changed the designation "Union of Chinese Workers" to "Union of Kashgari-Chinese Workers" (Soiuz Kashgaro-Kitaiskikh rabochikh). By early 1921, it was reported that the union's Andijan branch had a hundred and fifty members, nineteen of whom were Communists, and was regularly sending records of its activities to a secretariat in Tashkent. A branch in Kokand reported that it had thirty members, and the Osh branch registered fifty.

Soviet papers carried news of these and other organizations of Chinese subjects, and articles reporting their revolutionary pronouncements made their way via Kashgar or Ghulja to Yang Zengxin's desk in Ürümchi.[70] While disturbed at their contents, which spoke of freedom and the expulsion of Chinese officials from Xinjiang, Yang was equally concerned with legal niceties, such as whether or not these organizations had the right to represent Chinese subjects on Soviet soil. Xinjiang officials wired Tashkent to inform them that, as these unions had not received any official recognition from the Chinese government, they did not have any right to enter into negotiations with the new Soviet authorities.

Qadir Haji and the Contest for the Vernyi Aqsaqalship

Among the Kashgari community in Russian Turkistan, it was the caravan leaders and bazaar traders of Semireche who were particularly hard hit by the revolution and civil war, and this prompted a politicization that brought some of them into contact with Soviet authorities. Qadir Haji (1891–1938?), a native of Kashgar, was one such individual. Prior to the revolution, Qadir had accompanied his father Hashim on the pilgrimage to Mecca. On the way back in 1916, Hashim Haji decided to leave his son in Russian territory to expand his business network, and Qadir Haji set himself up in Vernyi, where he became a mid-level bazaar trader. He was among dozens of Kashgaris in Vernyi whose business suffered through the revolution and civil war, recording a loss of two-and-a-half thousand rubles on a register compiled by the local *aqsaqal* of Chinese subjects.[71] To defend themselves against further attacks, from 1918 onward Kashgaris in Vernyi organized what they called a "Committee of Poor Chinese Subjects."[72] Among its activities, the committee ran a sharia court for local Kashgaris and communicated petitions to the Vernyi branch of the Muslim Bureau, thereby coming within the orbit of Soviet institutions. By the end of 1920, Qadir Haji had risen to the committee's leadership.

In setting out to organize local Kashgaris, Qadir Haji and the Committee of Poor Chinese Subjects was rivaling the authority of the *aqsaqal*. Like communities elsewhere in Russian Turkistan, the Vernyi Kashgaris valued the role of the *aqsaqal* network in communicating their complaints to the Xinjiang authorities. At the same time, they found the levies for the *aqsaqals'* salaries exorbitant and resented the collusion between the *aqsaqal* and Xinjiang authorities to exert political pressure on the émigrés. The Vernyi *aqsaqal* Hafiz Iminov required fees to endorse travel permits, as well as civil documents attesting to

Qadir Haji Hashim Hajiev, Moscow, 1926. (Russian State
Archive of Socio-Political History 495/226/77.)

marriages and divorces. He also levied his own tax on goods brought by Kashgari traders to Vernyi. His enemies even accused him of collecting bogus "donations for the front" and misappropriating alms collections for the Kashgari
mosque in Vernyi.[73] With a showdown looming, taking control of the position
of *aqsaqal* became Qadir Haji's primary objective, and early in 1920 his committee instigated a challenge to Hafiz Iminov's position. At the Kashgari mosque
in Vernyi around four hundred men gathered under the supervision of a member
of the Revolutionary Military Council—suggesting that the move was at least
endorsed, if not encouraged, by Soviet authorities.[74] There they elected a member
of the Committee of Poor Chinese Subjects as the community's new *aqsaqal*.
In a new, more democratic twist on the institution, they also elected a five-
member committee to supervise his activities.

Of course, the incumbent *aqsaqal* Hafiz Iminov derived his authority not
from any Soviet seal of approval but from the confirmation of the Ili circuit
commissioner, and there was no way for the Committee of Poor Chinese Sub-

jects to force him to relinquish his authority. The Kashgari community of Vernyi had no choice but to address a submissive letter to Circuit Commissioner Xu Guozhen, in which they outlined their case against Hafiz Iminov. They asked Xu to disregard Iminov's claim that his opponents were Communists: "We have heard that [Iminov] addressed a complaint against us to you. He said that we have become Communists. In what way have we become Communists? Would he clarify this, and show where we have become Communists? If we have registered anywhere as Communists, we are ready for any kind of punishment, we are happy for him to shoot us even."[75] The actions of the Vernyi Kashgaris backfired, and led the Ili administration to take steps to increase its presence across the border. Circuit Commissioner Xu also submitted a request for the extradition of members of the Union of Chinese Workers, accusing them of betraying their country.[76] What resulted was a situation of "dual power," in which there were two *aqsaqal*s among local Kashgaris—one elected with Soviet backing, the other appointed directly from Ili.

This tug-of-war in Vernyi was part of the background to the signing of the Ili Protocols of May 1920. As well as sanctioning a Soviet trading agency in Ghulja, the protocols granted China the reciprocal right to appoint its own representative in Vernyi, the first such Chinese official to be sent from Xinjiang. The first appointee was Zhao Guoliang, a Dungan county magistrate and graduate of Beijing's Russian-language academy.[77] Zhao's arrival in Vernyi in September 1920 strengthened the hand of the original Ili-appointed *aqsaqal*. Not only did successive Chinese representatives maintain Hafiz Iminov in office, they extended the reach of Xinjiang officials into other areas of local Kashgari society. No doubt much of this influence was imperceptible to the Soviets, but occasionally the conflict erupted into public view. To give an example of this, in 1923 Vernyi's Kashgari mosque was the scene of a major brawl, which broke out when activists accused the imam of colluding with the Chinese trading mission. When the dust settled, it emerged that the imam had been issued with a seal identifying him as "qadi of Chinese subjects" and was using his connections with Chinese officials to discourage Kashgaris from joining revolutionary organizations.[78] Thus, while the Ili Protocols have been considered a diplomatic victory for the Bolsheviks, they proved to be a serious setback for revolutionary organizing among émigrés from Xinjiang in Semireche.

In Soviet thinking such ties to Xinjiang were a major obstacle to establishing Soviet authority among Turkistan's Chinese subjects, and they recognized the need for a concerted "struggle with *aqsaqal*dom" (*bor'ba s aksakal'stvom*). Yet for diplomatic reasons the Soviets refrained from confronting the *aqsaqals* head-on, preferring to build up competing centers of authority without directly threatening the Chinese appointees. The task of redirecting the Vernyi Kashgaris fell to the city's Taranchi Communists. During its campaign around the position of *aqsaqal*, Qadir Haji's Committee of Poor Chinese Subjects had formed links with the local branch of the Sovinterprop, headed by the Taranchi Abdullah Rozibaqiev. Rozibaqiev and the Taranchi Communists took it upon themselves to "revolutionize" the struggle over the *aqsaqal*, by which they meant redirecting it away from diplomatically sensitive issues toward more orthodox Communist goals. They suggested that Qadir Haji instead focus his organization's energies on uniting Kashgaris under the banner of the Sovinterprop's Union of Chinese Workers, which was now spreading throughout Turkistan.[79] Thus, by the end of 1920 a group of politicized Kashgari migrants in Vernyi, under the leadership of Qadir Haji, were moving closer to collaboration with their Taranchi neighbors from the Uyghur Club, and closer to the Communist Party.

Would the East Be Red?

What of Xinjiang itself? The coherence of early Soviet policy toward China's northwest has been greatly overstated. Lars-Erik Nyman has written, for example, that there was "a highly synchronized Soviet policy regarding Xinjiang."[80] In fact there was hardly a policy to speak of at all. In the chaotic early years of the civil war, Soviet organs in Moscow and Turkistan, as well as authorized individuals, adopted a variety of standpoints toward Xinjiang that were rarely coordinated and often contradictory. Conflict over Xinjiang policy was not merely a turf war but reflected the very real predicament in which the Bolsheviks now found themselves, caught between the project of intensifying and spreading the revolution and the security interests of the Soviet state in a hostile capitalist world. This problem of the relationship between internationalism and domestic stabilization ran deeply through the various bodies that had by now declared an interest in the Soviet Union's policy toward Xinjiang. Even among those Soviet actors who were in favor of a revolutionary intervention in Xinjiang there was no consensus as to the identity of the province's revolutionary subject. Indeed, because of the ethnic complexity of western China and the shifting conceptions of anticolonial revolution in Soviet Turkistan itself, the Xinjiang question arguably brought together more conflicting interests than any other of Turkistan's political fronts.

The 1919 May Fourth demonstrations in China's major cities signaled to the Bolsheviks the possibility of striking a blow against imperialism in East Asia and led to the first dispatch of Soviet envoys to make contact with Chinese revolutionaries. As a gesture of goodwill, Soviet diplomat Lev Karakhan issued a manifesto in which the Soviet Union pledged to withhold support from forces hostile to China.[81] In theory this precluded supporting an anti-Chinese struggle in China's periphery, but would a revolution in Xinjiang necessarily be anti-Chinese? In 1919, as we have seen, Bolshevism in Turkistan remained a largely Russian affair. The Old Bolsheviks in Tashkent were still studiously ignoring Lenin's directives that national self-determination be the centerpiece of Soviet policy in the tsarist empire's Muslim borderlands. Looking at Xinjiang, therefore, Russian Bolsheviks in Turkistan were not predisposed to see a struggle between oppressed natives and Chinese colonizers. Indeed, given the poor state of relations between the Old Bolsheviks and the Muslim Communists in Turkistan itself, they were just as likely to be hostile to such a notion. Initially the group that most interested the Turkistani Bolsheviks was not any of Xinjiang's non-Chinese nationalities but an organization that they thought provided a ready-made revolutionary network stretching from Xinjiang deep into China proper—namely, the Gelaohui.

There is no evidence that the Bolsheviks ever intended to stage an uprising in Ili; there was, however, a widely held belief that unrest was likely, and hence to be prepared for by making contact with local activists. The Malinin trading mission in 1919 was the first to seek out links with the Gelaohui, but it failed spectacularly. A Tatar Bolshevik introduced Malinin to a Dungan by the name of Yahya Liu Wangfu, whom they believed to be a leading member of the Gelaohui. In fact, Yahya had for years been in Liuba's pay, and he informed the consul immediately of Malinin's approach. Liuba encouraged him to go along with it, and at Malinin's invitation Yahya crossed to Zharkent for talks, where Malinin outlined to him the Bolshevik program and showed him the draft of an agitational leaflet. Yahya returned to Ghulja with a copy of the leaflet and claimed that the Bolsheviks had given him funds and a proclamation with which to launch an uprising.[82] The discovery of the "plot" caused Ili officials to close the border and send reinforcements to protect it. Malinin admitted to his superiors that he had been careless in his dealings with Yahya but protested that he had been the victim of a White provocation, and Vernyi reiterated that they had no hostile intentions toward Xinjiang. Spies sent to Zharkent confirmed that there was no sign of an impending invasion, and traffic across the border resumed.

Chastened by this experience, the Soviets sent out feelers in other directions. Throughout 1920, the amount of uncoordinated, and mostly unauthorized, Bolshevik agitation going on in Ili increased. Staff functioning as employees of the People's Commissariat of Foreign Trade (Vneshtorg) set up intelligence stations in the towns of Zharkent and Qaraqol. The mission that negotiated the Ili Protocols in 1920 included as its secretary a Tatar spy named Agidullin, who remained stationed in Ghulja with secret instructions to establish contact with Muslim organizations. To his surprise, Agidullin found a number of Chinese Communists from Russia already present in the town. One of these Chinese activists had been dispatched by the Turkistan Front command in Semireche, whose political section included an Eastern Department for work among foreigners. Of the remaining three, one had been through a short training course run by the People's Commissariat of Nationalities, while another had experience as an agitator for the Samara branch of the Union of Chinese Workers.[83]

The rise of the Muslim Bureau and the arrival of the Turkistan Commission foregrounded the anticolonial dimension of the revolution in Turkistan and brought with it a shift in official thinking on Xinjiang. Moscow's control in Turkistan was, initially at least, a result of its coalition with local Muslim Communists, who favored an active policy toward Turkistan's neighbors. The Muslim Communists who were now being elevated into prominent positions in Turkistan's Communist Party and Soviet bureaucracy naturally tended to see politics in Chinese Turkistan as an extension of the conflict in Russian Turkistan, and considered Xinjiang's Muslim Turks as the priority for Soviet activities. So long as Moscow held executive authority in Turkistan, though, carrying on such a forward policy was potentially compromising for Soviet diplomacy. To obtain a degree of deniability toward revolutionary outbursts along Turkistan's borders, the Soviet state ceded part of its authority in Turkistan to the Comintern.

Rethinking Xinjiang as part of the revolution in the Islamic world increased the province's significance in relation to India. In 1919 Trotsky famously argued that the revolutionary tide in Europe was receding, and that the road to London and Paris now lay through "the towns of Afghanistan, the Punjab, and Bengal."[84] Rather than a bridge to China, some Comintern analysts argued that Xinjiang could equally serve as a stepping-stone to the British Raj.[85]

Officially, the Anglo-Soviet Trade Agreement of March 1920 committed the Soviets to refrain from any destabilizing actions in British India, and the NKID was staunchly opposed to any Comintern activities in Turkistan. Nonetheless, in October 1920 a new Turkistan Bureau of the Comintern (Turkbiuro) set up shop in Tashkent, subsuming the Sovinterprop and taking on responsibility for revolutionary work on the "Eastern Front," which included Iran, Afghanistan, India, and Xinjiang. Although officially closed in the spring of 1921, the Turkbiuro continued its work illegally and concealed from the NKID. Headed by the Latvian Bolshevik Jānis Rudzutaks, the Turkbiuro identified Kashgaria and Jungharia as two distinct spheres of activity. It appointed plenipotentiaries on both fronts and started dispatching its own representatives for "trans-cordon" work in Xinjiang.[86]

The Turkbiuro's Turkistan-centric view of Xinjiang cast developments there in terms of Russian Turkistan's own recent trajectory of radicalizing Jadidist intellectuals being drawn to revolutionary politics. This perspective dovetailed with reports that it received from the province, which depicted its small Jadidist circles as a revolutionary party-in-the-making. One of the first accounts of local politics in Xinjiang to reach the Turkbiuro's desk was by a young man named Yaqub Aliev (d. 1928), a native of Artush who had been one of Ahmed Kemal's pupils.[87] At the school's closing, Aliev had headed north to Ghulja and in 1920 crossed into Semireche. He then enrolled in a short training course at Moscow's Communist University of the Toilers of the East (KUTV) in Moscow, before being sent to Tarbaghatay in 1921. In his account of the situation in Xinjiang, Aliev described the province as fertile ground for agitation. As he saw it, there were large revolutionary organizations in the towns of Khotan (200 members), Bay (100), Qarashahr (90), and Turfan (300), all of whose members were said to be in favor of Bolshevism. In Ghulja he counted as many as four hundred revolutionaries, though he admitted they were lacking organization owing to the sharp eyes of the Chinese secret police. In Ürümchi, Aliev identified the leader as Burhan, almost certainly the prominent Tatar businessman Burhan Shahidi. In Turfan, Aliev's informant was one Abdulkhaliq, probably the same Abdulkhaliq who would win renown in the 1930s as a nationalist poet, styling himself Abdulkhaliq Uyghur.[88]

Clandestine organizations leave little record of themselves, and Soviet intelligence is our only guide to the political situation in Xinjiang in this period. Some reports described these Jadidist groups as "Ittihadist," that is, affiliated to (or simply inspired by) the Young Turk Committee of Union and Progress, and oriented toward the former Ottoman commander-in-chief Enver Pasha, who was now in exile from Anatolia and seeking allies in Germany and Russia. There is some evidence that while Enver Pasha was in Moscow in 1920, Unionists discussed the possibility of instigating an uprising and forming an Islamic republic in Kashgar.[89] Enver Pasha's contact point in Kashgar during this period was the Jadidist Ali (or Ila) Haji Noruz Hajiev. According to subsequent accounts, in 1920 Ali Haji teamed up with a certain Jirjis Haji from Ghulja to found an organization called the East Turkistan Society.[90] The East Turkistan Society evidently sent Jirjis Haji into the Soviet Union to contact fellow revolutionaries, but he was detained in the mountains of eastern Bukhara. Xinjiang Muslims were also in contact with Turkish POWs who were filtering south from prison camps in Siberia. Some crossed from Xinjiang into Soviet Turkistan with false Chinese passports, while others lingered on Chinese soil.[91] As in Soviet Turkistan, Turkish POWs in Xinjiang supported themselves by teaching. Istanbul-educated Masud Sabri, who returned to Xinjiang in 1914, recruited such POWs for his school in Ghulja.[92]

While the question of revolutionary strategy toward Xinjiang divided Soviet officials, they were nevertheless united on the need to combat the lingering White threat. Throughout 1920, Xinjiang saw an influx of White soldiers fleeing the battlefield of the civil war in Turkistan.[93] When Admiral Kolchak's Siberian front collapsed, General Annenkov led the remnants of his Semireche Army from Semipalatinsk into Xinjiang. Following Annenkov, the Montenegrin General Bakich (1877–1922) occupied first Tarbaghatay, then Altay (now part of Xinjiang). Meanwhile, Ataman Dutov set up his headquarters in Suiding in the Ili Valley. While Annenkov decamped east toward the Chinese interior, Bakich and Dutov looked for opportunities to rejoin the fight in Semireche.

In June 1920, the Red Army garrison in Vernyi mutinied, and the suppression of the revolt saw renewed Bolshevik attacks on Cossack *stanitsas* in the district. The instability prompted the final White incursion from Xinjiang. In November 1920, Annenkov's representative in Ghulja, Colonel Sidorov, led troops as far as the outskirts of Vernyi, but was eventually repulsed by the Red Army, including the 58th Semireche Cavalry—a Dungan unit. This defeat was the beginning of the end for the White holdouts in Xinjiang. Annenkov ended up imprisoned in Ürümchi, while his ragtag troops dispersed throughout Xinjiang and Gansu. In Ghulja, Dutov and Bakich fell out over Bakich's confiscation of a shipment of silver, and in February 1921 Tatar and Taranchi assassins shot Dutov in Suiding.

The military scenario in Xinjiang looked strikingly similar to events in Mongolia, where the Red Army had intervened to root out the White Army. Notwithstanding Lev Karakhan's 1919 manifesto to China, the Mongolian intervention led to the establishment of a new pro-Soviet regime in Urga with de facto independence from China. For some Soviet strategists, in sheltering the Whites Xinjiang had likewise become a theater in the civil war. At first, the Bolsheviks directed their activities toward the refugee White soldiers, which included units of Chinese Red Beards from Manchuria. Early in 1921, Communists in Ghulja made contact with a Chinese White officer and his battalion, who were part of Annenkov's forces. Together they organized a mutiny in Suiding, which loyal Whites suppressed. The Bolsheviks were not discouraged, though, and continued to send Chinese agents to work among the military.[94] Eventually, through negotiations with Ürümchi, the Bolsheviks were able to launch a direct military intervention against the Whites in Xinjiang in May 1921. With Ürümchi's permission the Red Army crossed into the province and forced Bakich out of Xinjiang into Mongolia, where he was captured and handed over to the Bolsheviks.[95]

The 1921 intervention provided the backdrop to Moscow's first high-level discussions of revolutionary strategy toward Xinjiang. The Soviet debate on China was developing into a confrontation between the Comintern on the one hand and the NKID on the other. The Red Army's occupation of Mongolia had given Moscow's Mongol allies broad license to denounce "Chinese colonialism" in Mongolia, which shifted Bolshevik discussion of the Chinese borderlands toward the Comintern's preferred terrain of national liberation. At the same time, such steps threatened major complications in Soviet-Chinese relations. A few weeks after the Red Army entered Xinjiang, Turkbiuro chairman Jānis Rudzutaks returned from Tashkent to Moscow and submitted to the Bolshevik Central Committee a proposal for the establishment of Soviet authority in Xinjiang. Reflecting the Turkbiuro's division of labor into northern and southern fronts, Rudzutaks envisaged dividing the province into the Soviet Republics of Jungharia and Kashgaria. We lack the full text of his plan, but we know that it was strongly opposed at the meeting by Georgi Chicherin, the People's Commissar for Foreign Affairs. In the Soviet diplomat's view, any gains made in Xinjiang would be detrimental to the progress of Soviet diplomacy in China: "in light of our general policy of friendship with China and our estimates of Chinese democracy, we must try to maintain good relations with the Chinese authorities." The majority of the Central Committee sided with Chicherin.[96]

The weeks and months following the Central Committee meeting saw a flurry of correspondence between Chicherin and NKID representatives in Turkistan, and in Xinjiang itself, seeking to ascertain what, if any, basis there was for Rudzutaks's ambitious plan to sovietize Xinjiang. The reports Chicherin received were unanimously critical of the Turkbiuro. In Tashkent, the NKID's plenipotentiary argued that, while "the objective situation in Xinjiang is revolutionary in light of the contradictory interests of the ruling Chinese colonizers and the mass of the Muslim population, who suffer national and economic oppression, subjectively the situation in Xinjiang is by no means revolutionary. Society is too amorphous, and the anti-Chinese forces hopelessly weak." An NKID representative stationed in Ghulja cautioned that any propaganda activities there must be careful weighed, "so as not to bring about the swift fall of the Chinese authorities in the Ili district." One official expressed the view, which would increasingly gain support in the corridors of the NKID, that the Soviet Union's best interests lay in shrewd diplomacy toward Yang Zengxin and his bureaucracy: "for me, the instructions to 'orient to the Mandarinate' are more to my liking than carrying out a revolution in Xinjiang."[97]

There was, within the NKID at least, a degree of unanimity on this point. Yet as the forgoing discussion has shown, no single Soviet body had exclusive control over the situation along Turkistan's frontiers. This was not the end, but only the beginning, of the political confusion surrounding policy toward Xinjiang. As "amorphous and weak" as Xinjiang's anti-Chinese forces may have looked to the NKID and other Bolshevik leaders in Moscow, the Comintern and émigré activists along the border continued to see things differently. At precisely the same time as Lenin and his colleagues on the Central Committee were voting against a move to spread the revolution to Xinjiang, delegates were converging on Tashkent for the inaugural congress of the Union of Kashgari and Jungharian Workers, where they would declare their intention to free the toiling masses of Xinjiang from Chinese tyranny.

CHAPTER SIX

From Party to Nation

Shifts in Soviet and Chinese politics, and in Sino-Soviet relations, require us to distinguish a number of phases in the contestation of the Uyghur legacy as a mobilizing tool in the 1920s. The first coincides with the high point of Soviet-Muslim unity in 1921, in which the twin streams of Bolshevism and pro-Turkish militancy temporarily converged. This process was facilitated in Soviet Turkistan by the Turkbiuro of the Comintern, which sought to direct the revolution in the Islamic world from Tashkent. When this avenue reached a dead end, in 1922–1923 Taranchi activists took the lead in inserting themselves into the Comintern's China policy, all the while hoping to win the favor of the Moscow-based body that was directing affairs in Soviet Turkistan—the Central Asia Bureau (established in 1922). These considerations drew them away from Muslim politics and into collaboration with Mongolian Communists, who shared an interest in the fate of Xinjiang. Then, in 1924, Sino-Soviet rapprochement brought a halt to any precipitous move into western China.

Within Soviet bodies there was still a lack of clarity regarding the goal of work among the Xinjiang Muslims on Soviet territory: Was it to win Soviet influence in contested regions of Turkistan, or as a stepping-stone to China? And if the Soviets had both ends in mind, what was the relationship between the two? This dilemma mapped neatly onto the two key constituencies in Soviet organizing along the Xinjiang frontier: the Kashgaris and Taranchis. In the background to this meeting were the divergent views of the Muslims of Chinese Turkistan described at the end of Chapter 4, but the problem of ethnicity or nationality is not the only lens through which to view these early years of organizing. We should also approach these groups in terms of sociological composition and political interests, in which they differed in three important respects. The Kashgaris were Chinese subjects, while the Taranchis belonged to Russia, and now the Soviet Union. The two communities were on very different economic footings: one made up of seasonal laborers and bazaar traders; the second, a predominantly peasant population. These differences in turn gave rise to political leaderships whose methodologies differed significantly: one relied on the network of Kashgari traders to win influence; the other, on the more orthodox credentials of party seniority and cultural avant-gardism.

As we have seen, a notion of Uyghur communal genealogy had already emerged in the prerevolutionary period, and a small group of activists tapped into this by rallying around the Uyghur Club in Vernyi, hoping to steer a course for their community in collaboration with Soviet authority. In the turmoil of revolutionary Semireche, creating such a rallying point brought in its train a second sense of Uyghur identity, that of party affiliation. To be a Uyghur in this sense was to belong to the Uyghur club and support its activities, and by extension to be pro-Soviet, perhaps even a Communist party member. For these Uyghurist Taranchis, scaling up to the Uyghur framework was a way to highlight their community's significance as a bridge to China. Yet there was a risk to this strategy. By associating themselves too closely with politics in Xinjiang, they might well confirm the opinion of local Kazakhs that the Taranchis were foreign colonists in Soviet Turkistan. An equal risk was that the more they emphasized the need for revolutionary work in Xinjiang, the more they played into the hands of the Kashgaris who claimed, with some justification, that they were the activists best placed to lead the revolution in Xinjiang.

If it is correct that in many eyes being a "Uyghur" was a question of party affiliation, then its efficacy as an organizing model depended on the success of the Uyghurists in winning political leadership and gaining an institutional foothold in the evolving party and administrative structures of Soviet Turkistan. In the middle of the decade these structures were radically transformed by the policy of national delimitation, which created out of Soviet Turkistan a series of new national republics containing smaller units of territorial autonomy. Linked to this was the process of establishing official nationality categories in the lead-up to the first Soviet census. These initiatives imposed a new orthodoxy on the question of what constituted a nation to which those hoping to work within the Soviet system had to adapt: the Stalinist theory of a nation as defined by a "common language, territory, economic life, and psychological make-up manifested in a common culture."[1] As Soviet policy evinced an increasing "ethnophilia," to borrow Yuri Slezkine's term, those who had seen value in a loose appropriation of Uyghurist rhetoric were obliged to clarify what it all meant. Through this process, some who had previously been skeptical of any notion of a Uyghur unity other than as a political coalition learned to speak the language of Uyghur nationhood.

The Rise and Fall of the Uyghur Revolutionary Union

In early 1921, the Turkbiuro of the Comintern announced the convening of a Turkistan Congress of the Union of Chinese Workers, an initiative to merge the disparate organizations of Chinese subjects in Turkistan. It was not intended as an explicitly Muslim rally. Indeed, when the convening committee first met on March 1, 1921, there were no Taranchis, Kashgaris, or Dungans present at all. The Turkbiuro's plenipotentiary for Kashgaria, an Armenian by the name of Nazariants, headed the three-man group, which also included a Chinese activist. It was nevertheless decided, "in light of the prevailing Muslim, and not Chinese, elements in Turkistan," to maintain independence from the headquarters of the Union of Chinese Workers in Moscow.[2] The third meeting of the committee suggested renaming the forthcoming congress, replacing "Chinese Workers" with "Kashgari and Jungharian Workers"—that is, from southern (Kashgaria) and northern Xinjiang (Jungharia)—to better reflect the geographic origins of its participants. Soon the composition of the organizing committee itself changed. After the fourth meeting, the Chinese member left and was replaced by Abdurahman Mahmudov, a Kashgari affiliated with the Turkbiuro.[3]

Mahmudov's arrival on the scene reflected a shift in the union's orientation toward Muslim politics. Little is known of his background, but at the time of the Russian Revolution he was living in the oil town of Baku on the Caspian Sea. There he completed a course at the local party school and in 1919 joined the Communist Party. It is likely, though I cannot confirm this, that he participated in the First Congress of the Peoples of the East in 1920, known as the Baku Congress. This event, an initiative of the Executive Committee of the Comintern, has gone down in history both as the high point of Comintern policy toward the Muslim world and as a harbinger of a crisis in that policy. The congress was a hastily convened propaganda exercise, with little vetting of delegates. The multinational gathering was beset by linguistic confusion, rendering the speeches little more than set pieces delivered to a mostly inattentive audience. At the congress, the chair of the Comintern executive Alexander Zinoviev famously roused the Muslim delegates—the bulk of whom were from Iran, Azerbaijan, and Turkey—to a jihad against imperialism. Yet Zinoviev was upstaged by men with better claims to be leading a jihad, such as the Turkish war hero Enver Pasha, who was invited to Baku for the rally.

Baku provided a platform to Muslim nationalists of various stripes whose aspirations had temporarily coincided with those of the Comintern but who would not be dictated to by the Bolsheviks. Enver Pasha's Islamic nationalism was well attuned to the mood of the event, and he stole the show, feted by participants wherever he went. The prevailing sentiment at Baku had implications for the forthcoming Congress of Kashgari and Jungharian Workers in Tashkent, as Enver Pasha had his own following among the "Xinjiang constituency" in Turkistan—both among the Kashgaris and the Turkish POWs who were a common sight on the streets of Tashkent.

Baku signaled the intensification of Comintern activity in Asia, to be directed by the newly formed Committee on Action and Propaganda in the East. As an organ of the Comintern Executive, the committee naturally saw its sphere of interest as extending to Central Asia. While the Turkbiuro had jurisdiction in Soviet Turkistan, the Committee on Action and Propaganda in the East took the lead in organizing activities in the new People's Soviet Republic of Bukhara, which came into being through a Red Army assault on the city in 1920. In Bukhara, the committee helped to set up a branch of the Union of Kashgari-Chinese Workers, and Kashgari Red Army recruits in the nearby town of Kerki on the Amu Darya also affiliated to this organization.[4] This Bukharan group of Kashgaris initially planned to hold its own rally but was persuaded to join with the Union of Chinese Workers in Tashkent, and Mahmudov's inclusion in the convening group was probably part of this unification process.

The Comintern's objectives for the Tashkent congress were modest: to organize educational work, draw female émigrés into political activity, and promote the formation of "laborers' councils" (*trudovye soveti*) among Chinese subjects to undermine the influence of the Chinese-appointed *aqsaqal*s in Soviet territory. Beyond this, the convening committee was undecided on a number of points and circulated a questionnaire at the event soliciting views on the most appropriate course of action for Chinese subjects in Turkistan. They asked, for example, whether Muslims and Chinese should join in a single organization, or whether they needed separate bodies; whether the union should impose class restrictions on membership or open its doors to all those with ties to China, from migrant laborers to wealthy merchants; and finally, whether or not to conduct revolutionary activity in Xinjiang, and how.

In the political climate of early 1921, preparatory work for the Tashkent Congress was difficult. Soviet authority still reached little farther than the outskirts of Turkistan's urban centers and the main lines of communication between them. Given the dangers of pro-Communist agitation in the midst of the anti-Bolshevik Basmachi insurrection, activists heading to the Ferghana Valley to hold delegate elections had to be armed. When it finally opened, the congress would hear how in some places it had proved impossible to organize a local meeting owing to the interference of the local *aqsaqal*.[5] Delegation to the conference was set at one representative for every ten members, and in its resolutions the congress claimed to represent a total of 1,500 members throughout Turkistan. In the end, however, only 117 delegates (115 men and two women) made it to Tashkent, and it is likely that few were properly elected from functioning union branches. Of those in attendance, fifty were Communist Party members, while sixty-five were unaffiliated. Eighty-three, or roughly three-quarters of participants, were Kashgaris, with the rest made up of various other groups: thirteen Taranchis, ten Dungans, three Chinese, three Tatars, two Kirghiz, and one Turk. The lone Turk was an ex-POW by the name of Sabir Ahmed, a lieutenant (*mülazımısani*) in the Ottoman army and reputedly an influential figure among the Kashgaris. Forty percent registered their occupation as "artisan," with smaller numbers of peasants, laborers, and intellectuals, and ten from the Red Army.[6]

Planning took longer than expected, and the congress was postponed from April 15 to June 1, eventually opening on June 3. At its first session, the conference heard speeches from representatives of the Communist Party of Turkistan, the Turkistan Central Executive Committee, the All-Union Council of Trade Unions, and a Russian Bolshevik from the Council of Propaganda and Action in the East. A certain Ismailova spoke in the name of the women of Kashgaria and Jungharia, and greetings were relayed from the 58th Dungan Cavalry. Over the course of a week, the congress discussed the international situation and the state of affairs in Xinjiang and received reports from the convening committee and local branches. Delegates approved the Turkbiuro's theses on the organization and tasks of the union, and determined that the struggle against the *aqsaqals* would be its first priority. A circular issued before the congress had envisaged that the union "would assume for itself the legal defense of the interests of émigrés from China." Yet the influence of the *aqsaqals* still rested on their semiofficial status and ties to the Xinjiang authorities, and it would be difficult to supplant them without provoking some sort of diplomatic conflict. In its final declaration, the union weakened its formulation: "Unions should not under any circumstances arrogate to themselves consular functions, but should defend the interests of Union members." Alongside the union would be established "laborers' councils of Chinese subjects, regardless of nationality," which would provide necessary legal protections.[7] The congress also set itself the task of forming a party of peasants and laborers in Xinjiang, incorporating revolutionary elements of the petit bourgeois intelligentsia.

These objectives reflected the fact that the congress had been convened on the basis of subjecthood, not ethnicity. Yet this focus on Chinese subjects sat awkwardly with the presence there of significant numbers of Taranchis and Dungans, all of them born on Russian soil. The well-organized Taranchi contingent from Semireche played a particularly prominent part in the proceedings. Abdullah Rozibaqiev was elected to the presidium and delivered a number of speeches, clearly positioning himself as a leader among the Xinjiang émigrés. In his first address he roused congress participants to "the struggle to liberate our toilers from the Chinese yoke," striking the first note of anti-Chinese militancy at the event. For Rozibaqiev to occupy such a leading position, though, the union would need to be put on a different basis, one not strictly linked to subjecthood. The main thrust of the Taranchi intervention, therefore, was to redefine the union in national terms. As the Taranchi Communists conceived it, it would represent the interests of three groups of Muslims from China: the Taranchis, Dungans, and Kashgaris—groups that, in their eyes, shared a common Uyghur ancestry. On the second day of the event, a letter from Taranchi students in Tashkent was read out: "Although we are called Taranchis, we are all children of one father, and one mother: 'Uyghur.'" In his next speech, Rozibaqiev presented the example of his Semireche Uyghur Club as the way forward for the union: "Three years ago the Taranchi socialist youth were organized into a union called 'Uyghur' [quotation marks in original]. This organization 'Uyghur' realized the need to unify the Kashgaris, Taranchis, and Dungans under its leadership, and hastened to carry out this revolutionary work. 'Uyghur' has now achieved this goal. Since all the 'Uyghur' toilers have united, it makes no sense for young Taranchis to have a separate organization." Rozibaqiev concluded this speech by introducing a resolution to merge his Semireche Uyghur Club with the Union of Kashgari and Jungharian Workers. "Keeping in mind the historic name 'Uyghur' of the peoples of Kashgaria," he proposed a new name for the organization: the Revolutionary Union of Altishahri and Jungharian Workers—Uyghur.[8]

This resolution has important implications for the history of Uyghur nationalism, but it was manifestly not the vote to revive a long-lost national identity that it has been depicted as. What Rozibaqiev proposed was an organizational merger motivated by what in his view was a successful case of collaboration between the Taranchis, Kashgaris, and Dungans in Semireche. By now, some Taranchis may have started to explore the idea of Uyghur identity as nationality, but this did not form part of Rozibaqiev's proposal, which referred only to the "historic name" of the Uyghurs. According to his vision, this was not to be the Uyghur Revolutionary Union, or the Revolutionary Union of Uyghurs. He was not suggesting that membership in the union should be restricted to those who thought of themselves as Uyghur by nationality (few would have remained in the hall), nor was he arguing that all members of the union were in fact Uyghurs. Uyghur here remained the name of an organization, as it had been in Semireche. Many official documents in this period put the term in quotation marks, as "Uyghur."

Far from imposing a vision of national unity on the meeting, Rozibaqiev remained sensitive to distinctions between the Taranchis and Kashgaris in his proposal. He did this by emphasizing the notion of "Altishahri" identity at the expense of "Kashgari," and by changing the union's name to the Revolutionary Union of *Altishahri* and Jungharian Workers. On the face of it there seems nothing particularly noteworthy about this. All present would have been aware that Altishahr (the "Six Cities") was simply an alternative designation for Kashgaria. Yet the concept of Altishahri identity served a subtle but important purpose for Rozibaqiev. It allowed him in his speech to review the history of the original Taranchi migration from the Tarim Basin, and thereby to confirm the Taranchis' long-standing historical ties to Xinjiang, while avoiding the implication that the Taranchis were simply a subgroup of Kashgaris—something that would play into the hands of his Kashgari rivals. Instead he told the congress that the Taranchis were "Altishahris who migrated to Ghulja, where they took the name Taranchi."

With this merger, an organization of Chinese subjects took on a new coloring as a tripartite alliance of Muslim groups with a connection to China: the Taranchis, Kashgaris, and Dungans. This shift was reflected in the election of the congress's three representatives to the upcoming Third Congress of the Comintern in Moscow: the Taranchi Ismail Tairov, the Dungan Red Army officer Masanchi (Ma Sanqing), and the Kashgari Mahmudov. Other interests remained represented on the union's Central Committee, which included Rozibaqiev as secretary, a Tatar named Galiev, the Turk Sabir Ahmed, the Bukharan Jadidist Osman Khoja Polatkhojaev, and a handful of other Taranchis and Kashgaris.[9]

The Turkbiuro of the Comintern seems not to have noticed the shift, reporting that the union had elected a central committee composed entirely of Communists (it had not) and was pursuing orthodox goals such as sending students to Moscow for study.[10] Had the union remained in Abdullah Rozibaqiev's hands, it might have continued in this vein. Within a fortnight of the congress's closing, though, Rozibaqiev's party duties intervened, and he returned to Vernyi to serve on the Semireche Provincial Revolutionary Committee. Others were similarly drawn away from Tashkent, leaving the Communists on the Union's Central Committee in a minority. Tensions regarding the union's nature and purpose now emerged, as the Turkish lieutenant Sabir Ahmed and his allies tried to expel the remaining Communists from its leadership. This faction saw close cooperation with the Bolsheviks as limiting the union's efficacy among Kashgari Muslims. According to Abdullah Rozibaqiev's account, Mahmudov argued that members of the union "should not join the Communist Party, their business is to carry out a revolution in Xinjiang—and they don't like Bolsheviks there."[11] What had started out as the Union of Chinese Workers now veered in a decidedly Turkic nationalist direction, a case of Muslim revolutionaries commandeering a Comintern body for their own ends.

Strictly speaking, the Revolutionary Union was already an illegal organization. With the conclusion of the Anglo-Soviet pact in March 1921, the Comintern Turkbiuro in Tashkent had been officially wound up, and it is possible that Soviet diplomats had no knowledge of its continued existence. In October, Turkistan Commission member Adolf Joffe lodged a detailed complaint to the Executive Committee of the Comintern on the Turkbiuro's ongoing activities, noting that its work among Xinjiang émigrés could only strain relations with China.[12] This may well have been true, though the Turkish lieutenant Sabir Ahmed was leading the union in not so much an anti-Chinese direction as an anti-Soviet one. When Enver Pasha reached Bukhara from Moscow in November, Sabir Ahmed, Osman Khoja, and other members of the union's Central Committee left to join him.[13] In due course Enver Pasha broke with the Bolsheviks and rallied Turkistan's Muslim nationalists to his cause, striking out for the highlands of eastern Bukhara. Sabir Ahmed and his "Uyghur" allies followed him, swelling the ranks of the anti-Soviet Basmachi guerillas. The union's turn to pan-Turkist militancy must have confirmed its critics' deepest suspicions, and at the end of 1921 the Communist Party of Turkistan voted to disband its Central Committee.

The Three Uyghur Peoples

Up until this point, the Uyghurist framework had served the Taranchi Communists well—winning them a seat at the Comintern Congress—and they must have been reluctant to abandon it. Yet the implosion of the Revolutionary Union of Altishahri and Jungharian Workers was a major blow for the party members associated with it and left a legacy of suspicion among Soviet officials. There was now little prospect of the Communist Party of Turkistan or the Comintern endorsing a united-front collaboration between Taranchi or Kashgari Communists and non-party émigrés from Xinjiang. Only in Semireche, where the union's membership consisted mostly of Russian-born Taranchis, was the Revolutionary Union permitted to keep functioning.[14] As an organization, though, the Revolutionary Union was poorly suited to meet the needs of the local Taranchi peasantry. Given its Comintern origins, there remained a perception that the union had been exclusively tasked with revolutionary work in Xinjiang. Local agricultural organs viewed it as an organization of foreigners, who did not enjoy rights to the land, and the union could do little to assist its members through the process of land reform.

The Taranchis, Kashgaris, and Dungans still hardly registered in the administrative bodies of Soviet Turkistan, which left them no obvious alternative to working through the Revolutionary Union. Turkistan's own Commissariat of Nationalities did not include them in its national-minority subdivisions, rendering them practically invisible from the state's point of view. At the end of 1921, though, an opportunity presented itself when Abdullah Rozibaqiev was invited to Tashkent to take up a position in the Communist Party of Turkistan Central Committee's sub-branch of national minorities.[15] This party body took responsibility for political work among a diverse range of groups in Central Asia, and its divisions were not always defined in strictly national terms. It included sections for local, "Bukharan" Jews; Polish and Hungarian sections, comprising former POWs; a Tatar-Bashkir section, uniting a long-standing diaspora in Russian Turkistan; and also an Iranian-Azerbaijani section, continuing the Comintern Turkbiuro's work among these émigrés. With Rozibaqiev's arrival,

Uyghur Communist sections and Uyghur Communist Youth organizations were added to this list.

These Uyghur sections were to be attached to party bodies throughout Soviet Turkistan and to recruit among Taranchis, Kashgaris, and Dungans. Initially the leadership of these sections was entrusted to the Uyghur Communist Section attached to the Semireche Provincial Committee. The sections still hoped to influence émigré politics elsewhere in Turkistan, and to this end Rozibaqiev lobbied for permission to create a Turkistan Regional Bureau (Kraibiuro) of Uyghur Communist Sections, to be based in Vernyi, that would pick up where the Revolutionary Union had left off and reach out to progressive circles in Xinjiang. The Regional Bureau of Uyghur Communist Sections was officially launched in March 1923. Having put Uyghur organizing work on a new footing, Abdullah Rozibaqiev proposed collapsing the Revolutionary Union into the Ploughman Union (Qoshchi), an organization catering to the needs of Soviet Turkistan's poor peasants. At a conference of the Revolutionary Union in 1922, Rozibaqiev's resolution passed, with only Qadir Haji speaking against it.[16] With its last remaining branch liquidated, the activities of the Revolutionary Union of Altishahri and Jungharian Workers—Uyghur ground to a halt.[17]

Rozibaqiev's new orientation was a partial success for the Taranchis. Addressing Taranchi complaints, a provincial congress of the Ploughman Union reversed previous policy and determined that Taranchis should enjoy the same rights to land as the Kazakhs. Along with this, a Taranchi farming cooperative was established in Vernyi. The peasant organization offered little for Kashgari traders and laborers, though, and Qadir Haji saw the liquidation of the Revolutionary Union as a blow for his constituency.[18] Although Qadir Haji was appointed head of the Kashgari cells within the Ploughman Union, he naturally saw this as a significant step down from his previous status as chairman of the Semireche Branch of the Revolutionary Union.[19]

The creation of Uyghur party sections did not immediately shift the terms of debate on the meaning of Uyghur identity. The Regional Bureau of Uyghur Sections still saw itself as representing the interests of three groups—the Taranchis, Kashgaris, and Dungans—and worked closely with Muslims of other backgrounds, most notably Tatar activists in Vernyi, such as Zarif Bashiri. In its reports, the Regional Bureau of Uyghur Sections spoke in terms of not one but three Uyghur peoples (*Uigurskie narodnosti*). Registers of Uyghur Communist sections show that members still hailed from diverse backgrounds, making such sections similar to local branches of the Revolutionary Union.[20] Yet from

an administrative point of view, the existence of Uyghur party sections entailed that the Uyghurs would be treated as a single entity, with resources designated for Uyghur, as opposed to Taranchi or Kashgari, initiatives. Not surprisingly, this soon became a source of contention. When the Regional Bureau of
Uyghur Sections opened a school in Vernyi in 1923, they insisted that it was a
Uyghur school, taking both Taranchis and Kashgaris, as well as children of
other nationalities.[21] However, the Kashgari cell of the Ploughman Union complained that it was nothing but a Taranchi school, and lobbied to establish a
Kashgari school of its own.[22] Such local quarrels did nothing to allay the bad
blood between the Taranchi and Kashgari leaderships.

In many respects the Uyghur Communist sections in Semireche carried on
where the Uyghur Club had left off and served as a vehicle for the Taranchi
Jadidists-cum-Communists. The Uyghur Club continued to be a focal point
for political activity, though with certain modifications. Like the Soviet Houses
of Culture that now sprang up throughout Turkistan, its schedule of activities
blended political indoctrination with cultural forms pioneered by prerevolutionary radicals. The short-shirt Nazarkhoja Abdusamadov's writings on
Taranchi history remained an inspiration, and in 1922 the Provincial Bureau
of Uyghur Communist sections directed some of its limited resources to publishing his *History of the Taranchi Turks* (*Taranchi Türklärning Tarikhi*), which
synthesized his writings for prerevolutionary Jadidist periodicals. They also published Abdusamadov's long poetic rendering of *Nazugum*, the story of a female
heroine in the Ili Valley and her resistance to foreign tyrants.[23] These same ex-
Jadidists also set about reviving the newspaper *Voice of the Poor* (*Kämbäghällär
Awazi*), the first issue of which had come out as a handwritten lithograph to
coincide with the Tashkent Congress of the Revolutionary Union in 1921. In a
meeting of the Regional Bureau of Uyghur Sections in September 1923,
Abdullah Rozibaqiev was appointed editor-in-chief, with an editorial committee
including Abdusamadov, his long-standing Tatar collaborator Zarif Bashiri, and
Sabirjan Shakirjanov, a Bashkir schoolteacher who had also written frequently
for the Jadidist press.[24]

As the first issues of *Voice of the Poor* rolled off the press, the Taranchi Communists launched a new united-front organization called Progressive (Täräqq-
ipärvär), which held its first conference in April 1924.[25] Progressive invoked the
name of a short-lived Jadidist network that had come into being in Semireche
around 1905.[26] It set itself the familiar goals of pedagogical reform and criticism of superstitious anomalies in the faith, hoping "to unify and activate the

ideologically progressive Jadidists . . . who had earlier worked to improve education, for collaboration in cultural-enlightenment work among the Uyghurs . . .
and carry out a struggle against the perversion of the sharia by faithless
imams and mullas." An initial list of Progressive's members totaled thirty-five,
including Abdullah Rozibaqiev and Nazarkhoja Abdusamadov. Its activities
included raising financial support for local schools and for students in Tashkent,
running literacy courses, and creating a Spiritual Board (*Ruhanilar idaräsi*) of
pro-Soviet mullas. Members were expected to pay monthly dues, and to subscribe to periodicals such as *Voice of the Poor*.[27] A second route to influence for
the Communists was via the *mashrab*, communal gatherings that involved both
music, song, and moral instruction, often with a religious dimension. Soviet
officials saw the *mashrab* as potentially subversive and prohibited it in Semireche until the end of 1923. The new Soviet *mashrab* was required to publish
its "plan of work" and subscribe to at least two newspapers: *Turkistan*, the
central organ of the Communist Party of Turkistan, and *Voice of the Poor*.
These Red Mashrabs had their own elected administrations and collected weekly
membership dues.[28]

The prevailing notion of Uyghur identity in the early 1920s derived from a
conception of the Muslims of China as genealogically linked to the Uyghurs.
In actuality, though, such an idea was still not widely held, and the linguistic
case for unity was equally important. At Semireche's first Provincial Congress
of Uyghur Communists in 1922, it was argued that "the view that it is inap-
propriate to combine the Taranchi, Dungans, and Kashgaris into one Uyghur
section is incorrect, insofar as the Taranchis were originally Kashgaris (Uyghurs), and the Dungans, although they speak a language of their own which
is close to Chinese, probably belong to the Uyghurs, and they all speak the same
Uyghur language."[29] Not surprisingly, the status of the Chinese-speaking Dungans in this three-way alliance became a topic of some debate at this point. A
month after this meeting, Sabirjan Shakirjanov penned an article for *Voice of
the Poor* on the "Dungan Turks" and Bai Yanhu, the famous rebel who had led
his followers to Russian territory in the 1880s. Presenting various accounts of
Dungan origins, Shakirjanov concluded that, despite superficial indications to
the contrary, in essence the Dungans were still the ethnic brethren of the Taranchis and Kashgaris: "there is no doubt that they are Mongolized and Sinicized
sons of Turk."[30]

This idea of the Uyghurs as a historical reference point uniting all the Muslim
Turks of China gave rise to a new sense of China's Muslim northwest as

Uyghuristan—the land of the Uyghurs. In light of the national delimitation that was to come in 1924–1925, it is common to think of Uyghuristan as simply a corollary to the other national -stans—for instance, Kazakhstan or Kirghizstan. Yet the first invocations of Uyghuristan appeared well in advance of the national delimitation process. Throughout this period a variety of terms was used to refer to Xinjiang. The 1921 Tashkent congress, as we have seen, was convened with the twin territories of Altishahr and Jungharia in mind, while Chinese Turkistan, or Eastern Turkistan, were still common designations for the whole of Xinjiang. In a piece published in 1920, Abdullah Rozibaqiev referred to "Kashgaristan," no doubt inspired by the Russian "Kashgaria."[31] In poetry, though, Uyghuristan dominated the geographic imagination of Xinjiang. In 1922, for example, Abdulhayy Muhammadi, a Taranchi student studying in Tashkent, published his poem "My Young Heart" (*Yash Yürigim*) in the student journal *Young Uyghur*: "My heart trembles and cries 'Uyghuristan, my country!' / But it cannot escape its narrow cage and fly."[32]

Given the dominant view of Uyghur identity at this point, it is premature to think of Muhammadi's Uyghuristan as some kind of ethnonational republic based on a Stalinist conception of the nation. Rather it should be seen as a counterpart to Turkistan—one the land of the Muslim Turks of Russia, the other the land of the Muslim Turks of China. It follows that in early expressions such as this, Uyghur nationalism is better thought of as something akin to Turkistani nationalism, which prompts us to rethink the relationship between forms of Turkic and Muslim nationalism, and Soviet-style ethnonationalism. Cold War scholarship depicted a stark clash in the 1920s between these two competing forms of nationalism. Most recent work has rejected the implicit privileging of Turkistani nationalism as more genuine, or authentic, and with it the divide-and-rule view of Soviet nationalities. There is still a tendency, though, to see official Soviet nationalities as something very different from prerevolutionary national projects. The case of the Uyghurs cautions us against such a clear dichotomy, as Uyghurist discourse evolved from a form of Muslim nationalism into a Soviet category of nationality.

There are parallels here between the case of the Uyghurs and that of the Uzbeks. In a revealing analysis, Arne Haugen has shown how in the course of the national delimitation process, ethnic Tajiks initially raised no objection to being included in the new Soviet Socialist Republic of Uzbekistan. Persian-speaking Tajiks did not view the shift in terminology from "Turkistan" to "Uzbekistan" as significantly changing the basis of the community to which they belonged—that of the sedentary Muslims of Russian Turkistan. The discourse of Uzbek nationhood was, initially at least, as much a continuation of the Turkistani national project as it was a break with it. It was only when the category of "Uzbek" took on exclusively Turkic ethnic connotations that a small group of Tajiks started agitating for a republic of their own. As Adeeb Khalid points out, many Persian-speaking Communists were enthusiastic participants in the "Chaghatayist" project that lay behind the construction of Uzbekistan.[33] Just as radicals in Vernyi believed that the Dungans were on the way to assimilating to the Turkic Muslim mainstream, so too these "Chaghatayists" felt that the Tajiks would eventually merge with the Turkic-speaking community.

It is not surprising, therefore, that for some the pairing of Uyghuristan and Uzbekistan was synonymous with Chinese and Russian Turkistan. In his memoirs of the early Soviet period, *Turkistan's Sorrow*, the Islamic scholar and politician Alikhan Törä (1884–1976) mourns for his country in just such terms: "What has happened Uyghuristan, open your eyes! / Open your eyes, Uzbekistan, and look at yourself!"[34] Alikhan Törä was a complex individual, who fell out with the Soviets in the 1920s and fled to Xinjiang, then served as the first president of the Moscow-backed East Turkistan Republic in the 1940s. Throughout his memoirs, he speaks consistently of the Uzbeks and Uyghurs as "the Turkic peoples of the two Turkistans." Viewed through the lens of Soviet orthodoxy on national identity, all this might be seen as evidence for Uzbek parochialism on Törä's part, but in the light of my discussion here I believe this would be wrong. Uzbek, for him, simply meant a Muslim Turk of Russian Turkistan, and Uyghur, a Muslim Turk of Chinese Turkistan.

Muslims, Mongols, and the Comintern

Although the turn toward party sections was a step back from the optimism of 1921 it was not entirely a turn away from work in Xinjiang. How could it be? The best case for the allocation of resources to work among the Taranchis or Kashgaris in Soviet Turkistan rested on the border-crossing significance of the community. The Semireche Provincial Congress of Uyghur Communists in 1922 spelled this out explicitly: "The importance of work among the Uyghurs in the form of national minority sections led by party organs consists of the fact that the Communist Party, if not today then tomorrow, will have to grapple with the question of Kashgar."[35] As the Revolutionary Union had done the previous year, in 1922 the Semireche Uyghur Communist sections elected three delegates to the upcoming Fourth Congress of the Comintern, to be held in June–July. Once again, one each was sent for the Taranchis, Kashgaris, and Dungans: Abdullah Rozibaqiev, Qadir Haji, and Masanchi.[36]

Although it had been less than a year since the Central Committee had sided with the People's Commissariat of Foreign Affairs (NKID) and expressed its opposition to any move against Chinese interests in Xinjiang, the Bolsheviks were still far from achieving their diplomatic goals in China, and there was still room to lobby the Comintern to support revolutionary work in China's northwest. This party of three from Semireche were not the only revolutionaries heading to Moscow with this objective in mind. On the train from Vernyi, they were joined by a Mongol, a man by the name of Lavaryn Demberel (1891–1938).[37] Demberel had grown up in the Ili Valley and was part of the community of Chahar Mongols who had fled the province in 1912 after clashing with the Ili Republicans. Most had eventually returned to Xinjiang, but Demberel's elder brother Sumiyaa had led the holdouts onward to Mongolia, eventually settling in the vicinity of Kiakhta. In Mongolia's new Bogd Khan regime, Sumiyaa obtained the aristocratic title of *beise* and led Mongolian forces in battle against the Chinese along the Inner Mongolian front. In the course of the 1921 Mongolian revolution, Sumiyaa became a prominent member of the Mongolian People's Party, and his brother Demberel received a wide commission for revolutionary work in Western Mongolia and Xinjiang.

On declaring independence from the Qing in 1911, the Bogd Khan and his court had hoped to include the Altay in the new Mongol nation but had been restrained by tsarist Russia. In the early 1920s Mongolian revolutionaries in Urga (Ulaanbaatar) hoped to revive claims to the Altay, which in 1918 had been incorporated into Xinjiang, and even to the Ili Valley. In 1922, Demberel traveled to the Ili Valley, where he met with Mongol elites and the spiritual heads of the Buddhist community and delivered a speech at a local monastery. At the conclusion of his mission he crossed into Semireche, where he joined the Uyghur Communists heading to Moscow. On the train they discussed politics in Xinjiang and agreed to coordinate any activity involving the province's Muslims and Mongols.[38] Demberel also transmitted a letter from the Ili Valley Mongols to Mongolian Communist leaders. "We Mongols of the western Ili district hope that Outer Mongolia will not neglect us," they wrote, "and will show concern for us and take us into their protection." From Urga, the Buriat revolutionary Rinchino (1888–1938), chairman of Mongolia's Military-Revolutionary Council, added his own commentary to Demberel's reports. Rinchino was a leading proponent of a forward strategy on China's periphery, and he outlined the significance of the Xinjiang Mongols for Soviet policy in Asia in terms of the close ties between the Xinjiang Mongols and Tibet. These ties meant that the Xinjiang Mongols were at risk of being drawn into British intrigues in Tibet, but equally that they might act as a conduit for Soviet penetration of Tibet, and thus India.[39]

For the Communist Party of Turkistan to sponsor representatives of Uyghur party sections to the Comintern Congress was slightly unorthodox. Only one (probably Rozibaqiev) was given consultative voting rights; the other two were admitted as guests.[40] There was little discussion of the "eastern question" at the Fourth Congress, and needless to say policy toward Xinjiang did not make it onto the agenda. Rozibaqiev nevertheless made good use of his time in Moscow, approaching various sources of support for his vision of a renewed Soviet push into Xinjiang. He submitted reports to the Eastern Section of the Comintern Executive and the Bolshevik Central Committee, as well as penning a personal letter to Stalin, who was now head of the People's Commissariat of Nationalities.[41] The party leadership evidently gave Rozibaqiev a good hearing. The Central Committee apportioned funds for a weekly newspaper, which went toward reviving *Voice of the Poor*, and referred his other petitions to its newly created Central Asia Bureau, which appointed Rozibaqiev as its "plenipotentiary for cross-border work among the Uyghur peoples."[42]

Rozibaqiev was not the only one to receive a commission for work in Xinjiang in 1922. Umar Qari Islamov was among the "Young Kashgaris" from Ahmed Kemal's Artush school and had crossed into Russia during the civil war. He was one of the first Kashgaris to study at the Communist University of the Toilers of the East (KUTV), an institution that was established in 1921 to train revolutionaries from Asia. Following this, Islamov took up work for the Communist Youth International (KIM), which first sent him to Xinjiang in the middle of 1922. Like Yaqub Aliev before him, Islamov returned from Xinjiang depicting the province's small Jadidist circles as the nucleus of a revolutionary party. He identified the leaders of the Turfan organization as Abdulkhaliq ("Uyghur") and Maqsud Muhiti, an entrepreneur who had sponsored schools in Turfan and hired Tatar teachers from Russia.[43] At the end of 1922, Islamov took part in the KIM's Third Congress in Moscow, where he put forward a motion to "Recognize the youth movement in Kashgaria and Jungharia as a national-liberation movement, seeking national liberation from both the despotic Chinese regime, and from the influence of English imperialism."[44]

By 1923, therefore, things were again looking up for the Xinjiang revolutionaries, allowing them to strike a note of confidence. On February 17, Zarif Bashiri's article on the "Revolutionary Movement in Chinese Turkistan" occupied the front page of Turkistan's main Turkic-language daily, and in it he described the struggle in Xinjiang as "gaining strength by the day."[45] Taking up his new responsibilities, Rozibaqiev devised a plan for an underground conference of revolutionaries from Xinjiang, intending to summon delegates from all but the province's most remote parts. Chief among his objectives for the meeting was to acquaint Xinjiang's radicals with Soviet perspectives on the revolution in Asia and to unify the most "healthy" elements in a single party. He even went to the trouble of drafting a program for the party, in which he sought to reconcile his vision of national self-determination with Soviet diplomatic goals in Xinjiang. While he listed as the party's primary task the "struggle against Chinese and English imperialism" directed toward the creation of a Soviet republic in Xinjiang, he also noted that one of its tasks would be to cultivate in Xinjiang "a decisive public opinion in favor of establishing permanent trade and diplomatic relations with Russia."[46] To carry out this program Rozibaqiev pinned his hopes on the province's Jadidists, and he called for agitation among Xinjiang's madrasa students in the Jadidist spirit (while avoiding what he referred to as Jadidism's "pan-Islamist tendency"). His program highlighted the unfinished business of prerevolutionary activism: the need to popularize the new-style Jadidist *maktab* and appropriate *waqf* income to fund education. The Central Asia Bureau endorsed the proposal and assigned fifty thousand rubles to fund a meeting in July at the Qarqara trading fair, a popular prerevolutionary bazaar that had just reopened.[47]

Meanwhile, as Rozibaqiev lobbied the Central Asia Bureau, the Buriat revolutionary Rinchino was also holding talks with the Comintern, hoping to win support for further work among the Xinjiang Mongols. The Comintern approved his plan, too, and appointed two further plenipotentiaries to Xinjiang: Lavaryn Demberel and the Buriat revolutionary Siren Arabdynovich Natsov (1898–1938), who was working as a Comintern representative in western Mongolia.

The extent to which these various plenipotentiaries collaborated is hard to say. At this point, unfortunately, my sources fall silent, and much of this planning seems to have run into opposition from the NKID. Moscow was now providing support to the Guomindang in Canton, and the Far Eastern Bureau of the Comintern's enthusiasm for agitation on China's periphery was being checked by the NKID and increasingly by the Joint State Political Administration (OGPU), the Soviet Union's secret police. Rozibaqiev's clandestine conference, if it occurred, produced nothing in the way of results, and the same can be said for Demberel and Natsov's mission to Xinjiang in 1923. In 1924 an NKID official reported to the OGPU in Semireche that rumors were circulating in the Ili Valley of an impending invasion by armed partisans of the Uyghur Union, led by Abdullah Rozibaqiev. Given the weak state of Uyghur organizations, he speculated that these rumors had been concocted either by the Chinese themselves or by the Soviet Union's imperialist enemies—all of which placed Rozibaqiev in a highly compromising position.[48] Natsov remained in Xinjiang until early 1924, but his reports show a marked sensitivity to the NKID's growing hostility to pan-Mongolism.[49] In a long report submitted in 1925, Rinchino mentions a conference of Mongol and Muslim revolutionaries, scheduled for autumn of 1924, that "for some reason" never occurred.[50] For the time being, the window for Muslim-Mongol collaboration in Xinjiang had closed.

Tashkent 1924: The Split

Domestically, too, the Uyghur Communists were struggling to make headway. Affiliated to the Semireche Provincial Committee, the Regional Bureau of Uyghur Communist Sections had little influence beyond the bounds of Vernyi. From there it took up to three weeks to travel to Tashkent, the political heart of Soviet Turkistan, and it was even farther to the significant Kashgari population in the Ferghana Valley. At a meeting in January 1924, the Regional Bureau expressed its concern over the "almost complete lack of party work among Uyghur workers and laborers" in the Ferghana Valley.[51] The same meeting noted that just across the mountains to the south the Uyghur Revolutionary Union was continuing to function illegally, in its original multinational form. In Pishpek, they heard, it was far exceeding its original remit by confiscating and redistributing land among local Kashgaris.[52] The looming process of national territorial delimitation threatened to compound this isolation, as Kazakh Communists lobbied for Semireche to be split off from Turkistan and incorporated into the Kazakh Autonomous Soviet Socialist Republic.

The most troubling indication of the Semireche Communists' limited reach was the continued strength of the Chinese-appointed *aqsaqal*s in Turkistan. Despite having identified the "struggle with *aqsaqal*dom" as the first priority for

Uyghur Communists, they had made little progress on this front. Soviet authorities never recognized the *aqsaqal*s, but avoided attacking them directly, and on occasion entered into negotiations with them as representatives of the Xinjiang authorities. Particularly in remote parts of Turkistan, the *aqsaqal*s thrived in the new environment. On a reconnaissance mission for the Comintern in Qaraqol in 1921, one official was shocked to find the *aqsaqal*, a man named Hashim, carrying out quasi-consular functions to a greater degree than any other *aqsaqal*s he had witnessed. "He has an official sign," he reported, "like that of a diplomatic representative, and occupies a section of the best real estate in town. He has guards, conducts semiofficial relations with his government, and has a whole series of documents regarding diplomatic immunity. . . . Simply put, he is more or less an official spy of the Chinese government."[53]

Soviet discourse was reluctant to admit it, but many Kashgaris benefited from the presence of *aqsaqal*s on Soviet territory. The *aqsaqal*s provided an institutional skeleton to the Kashgari community that enabled them to validate their presence on foreign soil, prove their identity as Chinese subjects, and protect their interests in an often dangerous environment. Disturbed by accounts of the *aqsaqal*s' suspicious dealings, in 1922 the NKID decreed that they were to be stripped of official functions and that documents they issued would have no legal validity.[54] In response to the NKID's decision, five men calling themselves the "plenipotentiaries of the Chinese-subject Kashgaris in Tashkent" penned a letter of protest. They did not assert a distinctive Kashgari, let alone Uyghur, identity; rather, they described themselves as Uzbeks from Chinese Turkistan, which meant that they were indistinguishable from locals in Tashkent. Many of their community, they went on, had been unable to obtain passports from the Chinese authorities for some time, and without the testimony of the *aqsaqal* Chong Akhun it would be impossible to prove that they were Chinese subjects. Chong Akhun, they explained, had played an important role in translating political goings-on for them: "As we are illiterate we have not had the opportunity to acquaint ourselves with the resolutions and decrees of the Republic of Turkistan's governing bodies, not knowing where to turn in matters or to which institution. In such circumstances we always made recourse to the *aqsaqal*, who assisted and guided us."[55]

To compete with the *aqsaqal*s, and remedy the neglect and chaos they saw at work among the Xinjiang émigrés, the Regional Bureau of Uyghur party sections needed to break out of their isolation. To this end, the bureau decided to hold its next convention of party sections not in Vernyi, but in Tashkent. Among the items of business at the convention would be a proposal to relocate the Regional Bureau permanently to Turkistan's capital.[56] Tashkent made sense as a base for work, as it was home to representatives of each of the various groups that the bureau claimed to represent. In the nineteenth century Kashgari refugees from Qing Xinjiang had established a neighborhood there, and since then the trading diaspora of Chinese-subject Kashgaris had also grown. The city's new role as the center of higher learning in Central Asia was also drawing Taranchi and Kashgari students. These students had organized themselves into a Uyghur section of the local Komsomol, and in 1921 had issued a short-lived journal called *Young Uyghur*.

Yet while the Regional Bureau presented the convention as a bid for unity, some of its members were agitating for a split. For Qadir Haji, the bureau's lack of contact with its constituents elsewhere in Turkistan had nothing to do with geography, but reflected the Taranchis' reluctance to devote resources to work among the Kashgaris. He was critical, too, of Rozibaqiev's failures in cross-border work, which he attributed to Rozibaqiev's ignorance of conditions in Xinjiang. This wrangling placed the Regional Bureau in an awkward position. It needed to expand its reach into Kashgari communities, but the member of the bureau's leadership in the best position to do so was Qadir Haji himself. He was sent out twice in 1924, first to Pishpek, and then to the Ferghana Valley, ostensibly to strengthen local Uyghur Communist sections in preparation for the forthcoming convention.[57] Freed from the constraints of work in Semireche, Qadir Haji instead took the opportunity to build up his support among Kashgaris and mobilized a contingent from the Ferghana Valley to back up his intervention in Tashkent.

The Regional Bureau's convention met in May 1924, following the conclusion of the eighth, and last, congress of the Communist Party of Turkistan. The order of business included reports from the Regional Bureau, discussion of the state of Uyghur Communist sections, agitation and propaganda work, education, and publishing—none of which gives an indication of the real issues at stake.[58] The Kashgaris from Ferghana rejected the leadership of the Taranchis, calling instead for the formation of their own Altishahri party sections. The Tashkent students tried to mediate the conflict, but when it came to a vote, the frustrated Taranchis joined the Kashgaris in endorsing a split, with only the Tashkent representatives voting for unity. Qadir Haji's group declared their independence from the Semireche leadership and formed a regional bureau of Altishahri-Jungharian Communists affiliated to the Central Committee of the

Communist Party of Turkistan. "Although the path of Communists of all nationalities is the same," he explained in justifying his actions, "the complete divergence of interests of the mass of Altishahris and Taranchis does not allow them to follow the same path, and it is still too early for unity and collaborative work." The Tashkent group refused to join either of the feuding regional bureaus, and instead organized their own provincial bureau, bringing the total number of bodies to three.[59]

Events in Tashkent raised the vitriol between the warring parties to new levels, as both sides jostled for official backing, and in the process assailed each other with potentially damaging accusations. Rozibaqiev clearly saw Qadir Haji as a demagogue more interested in collaborating with non-party men of influence than with genuine Kashgari Communists. He mocked "Qadir Haji and his disciples (murīd)" as conservative pan-Islamists, and accused him of fraternizing with dubious religious figures such as the Syrian Shami Damolla (who was now teaching hadith in Tashkent), and even with the Basmachi. Others raised accusations of Chinese espionage against the Kashgaris. The Kashgaris responded in kind, calling attention to Rozibaqiev's petit bourgeois class background. A letter written by Qadir Haji's supporters from Ferghana revived old anti-Jadidist themes, that they were working for the Russians (it accused him of spying for the tsarist police), and reminded authorities that Rozibaqiev's father had been a loyal tsarist mulla: "This Rozibaqiev was raised by the haram upbringing of this priest father of his."[60] They accused Rozibaqiev of "wearing a Uyghur mask . . . to interfere and stifle for his own ends the policies and actions of our leader [Qadir Haji] Hashim Hajiev." In 1924, such accusations might still be considered overheated rhetoric, but in years to come they would resound to much more serious effect.

The other consequence of the rift in 1924 was that the Dungans now left the coalition and went their own way, as a national minority in their own right. The Dungan leader Masanchi had served on the Regional Bureau of Uyghur Communists until 1924, but in the wake of the split, the Dungans established their own local party organizations.[61] With impeccable timing, Voice of the Poor printed an article in late 1924 by Zarif Bashiri criticizing Sabirjan Shakirjanov's earlier appraisal of the Dungans as Sinicized Turks, arguing instead that the Dungans were "purely Chinese" and accusing those who thought otherwise of wanting "to fool people with historical science."[62] Bashiri may have had a direct hand in the split too. Sean Roberts records a story that in the 1920s the Vernyi Taranchis offended local Dungans by putting on a concert lampooning them as allies of the Qing. This may correspond to Bashiri's play *Sadir Khonruq*, which glorified a Taranchi hero of the nineteenth-century anti-Qing rebellion in the Ili Valley and was first performed in Vernyi in 1923.[63] Whether or not this was an aggravating factor, it seems that such a split was likely to occur sooner or later. The Dungans had brought with them to Russia the distinct historical narratives that they maintained in China, which must have set limits on how far they would be willing to collaborate with the Uyghurist project. Today, neither Dungan nor Uyghur accounts of the Soviet 1920s make mention of the time when the Dungans were considered one of the three Uyghur peoples.

National Delimitation and the
Threat of Assimilation

The national delimitation of Central Asia was the centerpiece of Bolshevik nationalities policy in Turkistan. The project had two aspects to it: the codification and rationalization of nationality categories (in preparation for the census of 1926), and the delineation of territorial units that best reflected the national composition of Turkistan's regions. The idea of dividing Turkistan into national republics had been floated as early as 1920, but the exigencies of the civil war had seen it postponed. Beginning in 1923, autonomous provinces had been carved out of the republics of Bukhara and Khorazm, but this only hinted at the more drastic changes to come the following year, which saw the creation of Soviet republics of Uzbekistan, Turkmenistan, and Kazakhstan, and autonomous provinces for the Kirghiz and Tajiks. Throughout the delineation and for years to come, debate raged surrounding the identities of contested population groups and the boundaries that would either include or exclude them from the new territorial units.

For national minorities, the Soviet system of "nested" autonomy held out the prospect of circumscribed forms of autonomy within the new republics. For the Taranchis and Kashgaris this raised the question of how to obtain the best outcome for themselves. On the one hand, the policy created an incentive to emphasize unity among the Uyghurs so as to play up the size and significance of the community. In 1924 the Semireche Taranchis' effort to shift the center of Uyghur organizing to Tashkent was motivated by a desire to represent the broader community of Xinjiang émigrés in Turkistan and prevent themselves from ending up isolated in Kazakhstan. On the other hand, the prospect of a campaign for some form of territorial autonomy would inevitably exacerbate existing tensions between the Taranchis and Kashgaris, as the question would immediately arise: Where to locate that autonomy? In the relatively compact Taranchi cantons of Semireche, or in the Kashgari heartland of the Ferghana Valley?

The splintering of the Regional Bureau of Uyghur Communist Sections freed each faction to lobby for its own vision of autonomy. Qadir Haji and his Regional Bureau of Altishahri Communists directed their energies toward Ferghana, where they laid claim to the descendants of the nineteenth-century emigration. Many of these refugees from the anti-Qing jihad had already blended in to the local community, well before anyone thought to ask them whether they considered themselves to be "Uzbek" or "Uyghur." An ethnographic survey of the region in 1917, which informed the national delimitation process, argued that "in their way of life, language, and ethnographic type [the Kashgaris] in no way differ from the rest of the Ferghana Uzbeks."[64] In 1925 a *Voice of the Poor* correspondent from Semireche made a tour of the Ferghana Valley and found two thousand of these Qing-era migrants in the village of Kashgar Qishlaq near Osh working in cotton cultivation. He was distressed to see that "the language and customs of the Kashgar Qishlaq Uyghurs, especially among the young, have changed. [Only] among the elderly is our own language used and can our old customs be found."[65]

Population figures were now the currency of politics, and the case for autonomy rested on the identity of these Kashgaris, who were residing in some of the most hotly contested territories of the national delimitation, and Qadir Haji was not the only one interested in claiming them. The stenographic record of a meeting of the Territorial Commission discussing a group of Uzbeks living along the proposed border between Uzbekistan and the Kirghiz Autonomous Province records the following interjection:

From the floor: I am interested as to whether the interests of the Kashgari population who live in Naryn and Ferghana are being considered. They form a whole with the Kashgaris of Qaraqol, Naryn and Kokand.

Chair: We have received your suggestion . . .

From the floor: The fact is, among the 120,000 Uzbeks who are being discussed, more than half of them are Kashgaris.[66]

In August 1924, Qadir Haji's Altishahri Regional Bureau held a meeting on the delimitation policy. They communicated their concerns to the Central Asia Bureau that Kashgaris in the Ferghana Valley were being fought over by the Kirghiz and Uzbeks, who were each registering the Kashgaris as their own.[67]

In establishing his Regional Bureau of Altishahri Communists, Qadir Haji had initially turned his back on Uyghurist rhetoric, which he criticized as a thinly veiled form of Taranchi nationalism. Instead he claimed to represent the Altishahris or Kashgaris, of whom he reckoned there were a half-million in the Ferghana Valley.[68] Yet there was a risk to this approach. For Soviet ethnographers, identifying oneself by native place was a category error, and they freely classified self-professed "Andijanis" or "Samarkandis" as either Uzbek or Tajik. "Kashgari" could easily be treated in the same way, while "Uyghur" would be more resistant to such assimilation. There was, furthermore, little to be lost in switching to the discourse of Uyghur nationhood, as those who had already done so still located the majority of the Uyghurs in the Ferghana Valley. Statistics presented by the Tashkent Uyghurs in 1925 offered a figure of 600,000 Uyghurs in Turkistan, made up of 300,000 in Uzbekistan, 70,000 in the Kirghiz Autonomous Province, 115,000 in Kazakhstan, and the remaining 15,000 in Turkmenistan and Tajikistan.[69] In *Voice of the Poor* a student in Tashkent went further: "If we collected all the Uyghurs in Soviet Turkistan," he wrote, "they would amount to more than a million."[70]

Facing an assimilationist threat in the Ferghana Valley, Qadir Haji swung around behind the Uyghurist position. Not only did he appropriate the Taranchi discourse of Uyghur genealogy, he went further in arguing that the Uyghurs constituted a nation in their own right. As Arne Haugen has described, Qadir Haji's Regional Bureau of Altishahri Communists held a meeting in Osh, which passed a resolution reproducing Stalin's definition of the nation to show that the Uyghurs exhibited a "common language, territory, economic life, and psychological make-up manifested in a common culture," and arguing for the creation of an autonomous Uyghur district in the Ferghana Valley.[71] From this point on Qadir Haji started to speak in terms of two nationalities: the Uyghurs (formerly Kashgaris), and the Taranchis. To distinguish the naturalized nineteenth-century Kashgari diaspora from more recently arrived Chinese subjects, he coined the terms "Old Uyghurs" and "New Uyghurs."

We see here how the weak boundaries between the Kashgaris and their neighbors in the Ferghana Valley created an incentive for Kashgari leaders to adopt the rhetoric of Uyghur distinctiveness. In Semireche, by contrast, the

Taranchis lived in islands of settled communities surrounded by nomadic Kazakhs, and there was no such threat of assimilation. While the Taranchi Communists had pioneered Uyghur nationalist rhetoric, and continued to organize in Uyghur party sections, the heightening of national tensions in Semireche around the delimitation policy obliged them to fall back on familiar notions of Taranchi history and identity. The campaign for autonomy in Semireche was firmly grounded in the claims of Taranchis as an established community with historic grievances surrounding land rights.

In 1925, following the creation of the Kazakh Autonomous Soviet Socialist Republic, the Yettisu (as Semireche was now officially known) Bureau of Taranchi Communist Sections in Vernyi submitted a lengthy report to the local party leadership, detailing the hardship they had suffered through the land reform process and requesting the formation of an autonomous *okrug* centered on Zharkent, uniting the Taranchi cantons in Zharkent District with those to the east of Vernyi.[72] They complained that dozens of Taranchi households had been evicted since the implementation of Soviet land reforms; water resources previously allocated to Taranchis now went to neighboring Kazakh lands, which had led to a decrease in land under cultivation; and livestock confiscated from wealthy Taranchis in Ghaljat was driven long distances and given to Kazakhs, instead of being distributed among poor locals. As a result, famine continued to threaten the Taranchis throughout the 1920s.[73] The creation of Kazakhstan had only led to new grievances. By a resolution of the Yettisu Gubernia Committee (Gubkom) in August 1925, the lone Taranchi cooperative had been dissolved on the ground that there were not to be any national cooperatives.

The local party leadership responded harshly to this petitioning. In February 1926, the Yettisu Gubernia Committee discussed what it called the "Taranchi question," noting that "a series of Taranchi workers have directed their activity toward the separation of the Taranchi population into an autonomous unit." To this end, these Taranchis had been agitating among both party members and non-party individuals, with a network reaching into the rural cantons. The meeting found the formation of a Taranchi *okrug* "inexpedient and impossible," and envisaged the need to further educate its Vernyi and Zharkent organizations on nationalities policy and to remove some Taranchis from leadership positions.[74] Yet this did not put an end to the agitation. In 1927 a Tatar schoolteacher in Zharkent sent a letter directly to the president of the Soviet Union, Mikhail Kalinin, arguing for an autonomous Taranchi republic, or at the very least a Taranchi province, basing his case on the fact that "our local Taranchis

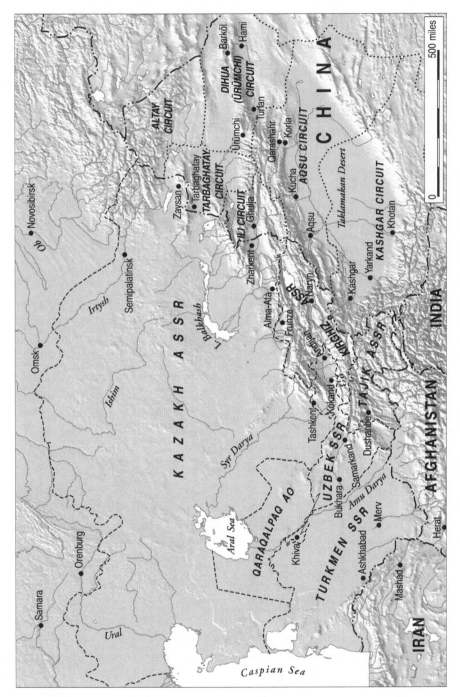

Soviet Central Asia and Xinjiang in the late 1920s. © 2016 by David Brophy.

are related to the Taranchis in China, and have connections with them. Among Turkic peoples there is a tradition of watching one's neighbors, taking pride in them and imitating them. If the local Taranchis provide an example, the Chinese Taranchis will respond enthusiastically."[75] Eventually, in 1927, a Taranchi National Canton was delineated to the south of Zharkent, but before this came into being the process of "rayonization" (raionirovanie) intervened. This led to the formation of two Taranchi raions in the Alma-Ata (formerly Vernyi) Okrug: Chilek and Zharkent.[76]

On the Uyghur question, circumstances had compelled the Kashgari and Taranchi leaderships to switch positions. The situation must have been extremely confusing for those tasked with finalizing a list of ethnic categories for the up-coming union-wide census of 1926. A 1924 questionnaire for party cadres in Semireche offered space to identify as Uyghur, but with a follow-up question in brackets: Dungan? Kashgari?[77] In 1925 the Commission for the Study of the Tribal Composition of the Population of Russia noted two trends among the Xinjiang émigré community: while recognizing that some Kashgaris and Taran-chis had begun to call themselves Uyghurs, they also found that in some re-gions "Kashgari" was being given greater ethnic significance. Hence this body decided to treat the Taranchis and Kashgaris as separate nationalities.[78] The census ended up classifying the Uyghurs as an "ethnographic group" (etnogra-ficheskaia gruppa), one of several groups who had yet to meet the criteria for full nationhood. As Francine Hirsch has described, census takers were instructed that if someone supplied their nationality as "Uyghur," they were to inquire fur-ther as to whether they were "Kashgaris, Dungans, Kalmyks, or Taranchis."[79]

This mode of questioning reflected the prevailing skepticism toward the Uy-ghurs as a full-blown nationality. The census also offers a rough measure of the relative popularity of these terms in the mid-1920s, the best guide to the con-sequences of this period of intense debate surrounding national identities and political boundaries. In Uzbekistan census takers recorded 31,941 Uyghurs and 4,421 Kashgaris. This suggests that, as expected, many thousands of pre-revolutionary Kashgari émigrés ended up classified as Uzbeks, but that among those who did not—probably Chinese subjects for the most part—proponents of Uyghur identity had made considerable headway. In the Kirghiz Autono-mous Province, where the penetration of party organizations was at its weakest, only 73 individuals registered as Uyghurs compared with 7,467 Kashgaris. Finally in Kazakhstan, 10,510 Uyghurs were counted, as opposed to 51,803 Taranchis, 8,455 Dungans, and 1,121 Kashgaris.[80] Here only around

May Day rally of the Ploughman (Qoshchi) Union, Zharkent, 1927. (Central State
Archive of Film, Photo, and Audio Documents of the Republic of Kazakhstan.)

15 percent of the three putative "Uyghur nations" registered themselves as Uyghurs, with the great majority of Taranchis still identifying as Taranchis. Thus
while Qadir Haji had failed to influence the naturalized Kashgari émigrés of
the nineteenth century (his "Old Uyghurs"), he had nevertheless succeeded in
making the Ferghana Valley officially home to Soviet Turkistan's largest population of Uyghurs.

There was a difference, of course, between registering the Uyghurs as an official Soviet nationality and creating such a nation in reality. Territorial autonomy for the newly classified Uyghurs of the Ferghana Valley was minimal—a
handful of village soviets around Andijan—and the allocation of resources to
Uyghur institutions still depended on the whim of local officials.[81] A 1926
survey found seven "Uyghur" schools in the Ferghana Valley with a total of
around three hundred students, but that the textbooks and language of instruction in these schools was no different from those of Uzbek schools. "These
schools should not be regarded as Uyghur schools," noted the report, "but rather
as centers of national assimilation. This hardly accords with our well-known

slogan on the self-determination of nations."[82] In this case this was seen as a problem: "It seems to me that we must pay the most serious attention to the Uyghurs, as a nationality of great revolutionary significance in relation to China." Elsewhere, though, officials were happy for Uyghurs to blend in with their Uzbek neighbors. The editors of *Turkistan* expressed a typical attitude in 1924, applauding the opening of a joint Uyghur-Uzbek school in Qaraqol: "Collaboration between the Uyghurs and the Uzbeks in the sphere of education and culture is to be desired, as they are very close to one another in language and history."[83] In the Kirghiz Autonomous Province, one official noted that work among the Uyghur national minority was going well, because "this nationality, especially in the Osh district, has lost its national outlook and independence and merged with the Uzbeks, thanks to which on most occasions they carry out work together with the Uzbeks."[84]

Such sentiments can be read as a desire on the part of Uzbek Communists to pursue an incomplete national project by assimilating neighboring Turkic-speaking peoples. In 1928, during an inquisition into "Uzbek nationalism" among party intellectuals in Central Asia, one of the accusations raised was that the Uzbek state publishing house was refusing to print textbooks in Uyghur, arguing that "Uyghur is basically Uzbek."[85] Yet Qadir Haji would probably not have objected to such "Uzbek nationalist" propositions. The 1927 census revealed that in Uzbekistan, among those who identified as Uyghur, only one-third registered their mother tongue as Uyghur, while two-thirds said that they spoke Uzbek.[86] Although Qadir Haji and his allies were capable of reciting the Stalinist theory of the nation when it was required of them, his Uyghur nation was essentially a Communist twist on the idea of the Muslim Turks of Chinese Turkistan as a nation, mirroring the idea of the Uzbeks as the Muslim Turks of Russian Turkistan. The two groups had many historical and cultural reference points in common, and both saw themselves as heirs to Central Asian high culture and the Chaghatay literary legacy. Among the Kashgaris at least, the idea that as Uyghurs they should distinguish themselves culturally from the Uzbeks was a still a novelty at this point, and one that would provoke debate in the years ahead.

Uyghurists into Uyghurs?

Events moved fast in the early 1920s, and strategic decisions in the heat of political infighting had lasting consequences. The commonly held view that Muslims from Xinjiang voted in 1921 to resurrect the Uyghur ethnonym as a full-blown national identity is incorrect, but by 1926 a blueprint for such a Uyghur nation had come into being. What occurred in Tashkent in 1921, I have argued, was a bid by the young Taranchi Communists from Vernyi to seize the reins of organizing work that was based on Chinese subjecthood—local Kashgari groups at first, superseded by the spread of the Union of Chinese Workers into Turkistan. Gathering these Chinese subjects within a single organization provided a forum for the Vernyi Taranchis to project a Uyghurist approach to politics across a much larger constituency. At the time, none of the Revolutionary Union's leaders were arguing that the Uyghurs constituted an actually existing nation. Yet at the end of a series of twists and turns occasioned by shifts in Soviet policy, both Abdullah Rozibaqiev and Qadir Haji were making precisely this claim. The only problem was that they disagreed on where the boundaries lay, with Qadir Haji envisaging a Uyghur nation of Chinese-subject Kashgaris, and Rozibaqiev insisting on his view of Taranchi-Kashgari unity.

As much as this case supports a view of the early Soviet Union as an environment conducive to national construction, the outcome of the 1926 census provides evidence of the resilience of preexisting forms of community. The results clearly show that it was difficult for Uyghurists to break through communal bonds established in the tsarist period and revise these in-group boundaries. Kashgaris who had settled in Russian territory ended up in the same category as the Sarts they had long lived among (i.e., Uzbek). The Taranchis, a legally enshrined nationality of tsarist Semireche, mostly remained Taranchis. Rather than ethnicity, subjecthood ended up providing the strongest basis for a distinct Uyghur nation, as shown by Qadir Haji's success in branding the Chinese-subject Kashgaris as Uyghurs. Now he at least had some facts with which to prove the existence of his version of a Uyghur nation. Rozibaqiev, by contrast, was obliged to base his case on objective reasoning. Writing in Moscow, where he was sent for a period of study in 1925, he argued that "there is not a single distinguishing feature, neither in economic or daily life, nor in language, nor in the history of the Taranchis and Kashgaris. To this one must add that they occupy the same territory, the same Chinese province and colony. What more must we show to prove that the Kashgaris and Taranchis comprise one nation?"[87]

With internal debates and external pressures both unabating, the ambiguous outcome of the national delimitation process was only the beginning of the construction of the Uyghur nation, not the end. On the Soviet side of the border the terms of the discourse had now been set by Stalin's definition of the nation; what remained was to add flesh to the bones that this theory provided. Ironically, those who were most successful in registering themselves officially as Uyghurs were the least interested in carrying out this task of cultural construction. It was the Semireche Taranchis and their Tatar fellow travelers who would take the lead on this front. Meanwhile, on the Chinese side of the border, new challenges were about to present themselves, as the eyes of the Bolsheviks turned increasingly toward China and the road to Kashgar opened.

CHAPTER SEVEN

Between the Chinese Revolution and the Stalin Revolution

I n May 1924, the same month in which Qadir Haji led the Kashgari walkout in Tashkent, Lev Karakhan and Wellington Koo concluded the Sino-Soviet treaty of recognition. With this, the Soviets positioned themselves as the champions of Chinese sovereignty in a hostile imperialist world, further constricting the scope for action in Xinjiang. At a meeting of the Vernyi branch of Qadir Haji's Altishahri and Jungharian Communists, activists who had been looking forward to getting their hands on China passed a resolution endorsing the Soviet Union's "Hands Off China" society, and sent a telegram of greetings to Guomindang (GMD) leader Sun Yat-sen.[1] Yet Sino-Soviet friendship was not entirely a blow for these Xinjiang Muslims, at least for those who were Chinese citizens. After all, Yang Zengxin ruled independently of Beijing, not to mention the GMD, which was still based thousands of miles away in Canton. For both the warlords of north China and the Chinese Nationalists of the south, collaboration with the Soviets was primarily a means to unify the country, which might well mean dislodging Yang from Xinjiang. Far from stabilizing cross-border relations in Central Asia, therefore, Sino-Soviet friendship had the potential to heighten instability in Xinjiang.

From 1924 to 1927, the outbreak of Communist-led workers' revolt in Shanghai and Chiang Kai-shek's Northern Expedition put China at the center of Soviet debate on global revolutionary strategy. Whether in collaboration with the GMD or through independent action, the Kashgaris hoped that in the midst of the revolutionary fervor in China there might be a role for them to play. Instead, by the end of 1927, they found themselves in the eye of a perfect storm of Soviet anti-British paranoia and fears of domestic Muslim rebellion, all compounded by the defeat of Stalin's policy in China and Chiang Kai-shek's anti-Communist turn. With the prospect of anti-imperialist victories in Asia now diminishing, and the inner-party conflict intensifying, Stalin directed a turn from the relatively laissez-faire New Economic Policy toward the new goal of collectivization and top-down economic planning. In Central Asia, the arrival of Stalin's vision of Socialism in One Country brought with it an antireligious and anti-Jadidist turn, rendering the exploration of national identity the site of increasingly heated polemics. It was in this changing environment that the Semireche Communists directed their energies toward the cultural construction of the Uyghur nation.

Xinjiang in the Soviet Shadow

Famine conditions in parts of Soviet Turkistan in the early 1920s made the resumption of cross-border trade with Xinjiang a priority. Yet despite the opening of the Ili Valley in 1920, the flow of commerce only picked up slowly, and reports on Soviet activities hinted at early setbacks: the People's Commissariat of Nationalities explained that "the Vneshtorg agents were not entirely adjusted to the process of free bazaar trading." In fact, conditions in Ili were anything but those of a free-wheeling oriental bazaar.[2] On the Chinese side only officials and a select group of wealthy monopolists—including the Akhunbayevs and Musabayevs—were permitted to do business with the Soviets. The real sticking point seems to have been the unit of currency. In the first contract signed with the leather and felt dealer Hasan Babashev, Semireche officials pledged to pay in tsarist bills of credit and banknotes issued by the Provisional Government (so-called *kerenki*). As the value of these notes plummeted in 1922, they rejected Babashev's request to renegotiate the deal. The next round of contracts for wool was settled in the local Ili currency.[3] With such complications, doing business with the Soviets must have been seen as a risky proposition, and the volume of trade remained well below prewar levels. In 1923 the total turnover was only 701,000 rubles, compared with two and a half million rubles in 1913.[4]

Looking further ahead, analysts saw the reopening of the Xinjiang border as essential to economic development in Soviet Turkistan. They understood that without the food and raw materials that Xinjiang could provide, plans for economic development in Central Asia—most importantly the expansion of cotton cultivation—would face serious obstacles. They also knew that in the intervening years they had lost ground to foreign competitors: European and American firms were the main cause for concern, but the arrival of an Afghan trading agent in Yarkand in 1923 was equally seen as a sign of growing competition.

They were worried, too, that the Chinese were developing transportation links to the east. Commenting on plans to build a freezer facility in Hami, the Soviet Orientalist Afanasiev-Kazanskii expressed his concern that "the cultivation of cotton in Ferghana will not develop without Xinjiang's livestock. In case of the realization of this Chinese plan, [this livestock] might all go to the east, and the Sart in Ferghana, left without meat, will graze his livestock and sow wheat on the cotton plantations."[5]

Ongoing lobbying led to the opening of the Irkeshtam road to Kashgar, but the real breakthrough came with China's recognition of the Soviet Union in 1924, paving the way for the exchange of consuls and the full resumption of trade with Xinjiang. In Ürümchi, Yang Zengxin feared the implications of this decision for provincial stability, but he also recognized the need to increase China's diplomatic presence in Soviet Turkistan. In October 1924 the Soviet Union issued its resolution on Soviet citizenship, stipulating that all those who could not produce valid foreign citizenship documents would be naturalized as Soviet citizens. The thought that many Chinese citizens sojourning in Soviet territory might be cut off from returning to Xinjiang troubled Yang, and he complied with Beijing's rapprochement with Moscow. In 1925 the former tsarist consulates in Xinjiang reopened as Soviet consulates, and Moscow reciprocated by allowing the posting of five Chinese consuls in Turkistan. These were nominally appointed by the foreign ministry in Beijing, but the process was left entirely in Yang Zengxin's hands. In January 1926 Yang appointed Zhang Shaobo, the Chinese Foreign Ministry's representative in Xinjiang, as consul to Tashkent. The consul in Andijan was Chen Deli, a county magistrate from the south of Xinjiang, who took with him a translator called Isa Yusuf (better known as Isa Yusuf Alptekin).[6] In two other cases, Yang was guided by nepotism: in Zaysan, he appointed his son, and to Semipalatinsk he sent Liu Changbing, his son's father-in-law. Finally, the Sibe official Ujala Saracun (1885–1960) was appointed to Vernyi, returning to the city where he had studied Russian two decades earlier as part of a late-Qing "study abroad" program.

Soviet consul Maks Dumpis arrived in Kashgar in 1925, having already served postings in Iran and Afghanistan. The choice of a man of his background shows the extent to which Soviet diplomacy still considered Xinjiang as part of the Islamic, and not the Chinese, world. Judging from his reports, Dumpis's initial focus was very much on local Muslim society, where he sought to win friends among the "progressive ulama." Besides his consular staff, he brought to Kashgar a series of Soviet representatives. These included agents of trading organs such as the Chief Cotton Committee (Glavkhlopkom) to handle exports of Xinjiang cotton to the Soviet Union, but also from the state steamship agency (Sovtorgflot), which was seeking to attract Xinjiang's pilgrims back to the once-popular Russian route to Mecca and Medina.[7]

Among Dumpis's first tasks was to re-register tsarist subjects in Xinjiang as Soviet citizens. Between 1920 and 1925, this Russian Muslim diaspora had lacked the protection of a consul, and Chinese officials had fielded numerous requests to take up, or revert to, Chinese citizenship.[8] Dumpis freely acknowledged that most who claimed Soviet citizenship in Xinjiang were not émigrés from Russian Turkistan but locals who had previously acquired Russian documents for economic gain. "Whenever a new *aqsaqal* was appointed at a particular place," he explained to Moscow, "if at first there were only two or three Russian subjects there, soon enough they would report that there were now between thirty and forty Russian subjects." Dumpis's approach differed little from that of his tsarist predecessors: "for purely political reasons, we must recognize that it is desirable and necessary to confirm them as citizens of the USSR." To do otherwise, he reasoned, would be to antagonize a significant community of Muslims on the borders of the Soviet Union and hand an easy victory to the British. A new cohort of *aqsaqal*s was necessary too, to carry out the registration of Soviet citizens, defend their interests, and provide economic and ethnographic data on Xinjiang. Dumpis nevertheless hoped to avoid the excesses of the tsarist period and keep a check on their powers, and their salaries.

In 1924 the People's Commissariat for Foreign Trade formulated a set of policies toward "Asian" capitalists, whom they saw as vehicles for spreading a positive image of the Soviet Union in the colonial world and hence to be enticed by preferential tariff policies. Among these measures, the Commissariat announced the free import of various raw materials into the Soviet Union from western China.[9] Gradually, Xinjiang Muslims began returning to the annual fairs that they had visited in prerevolutionary times. After a failed attempt to hold the Nizhnii-Novgorod fair in 1918, it successfully reopened in 1922, as the New Economic Policy freed up restrictions on private enterprise. Xinjiang firms returned to Nizhnii-Novgorod in 1925, when eleven sent representatives.[10] They liked what they saw, and in 1926 the number jumped to seventy-seven. By 1928, Nizhnii-Novgorod was drawing merchants not only from the old treaty ports of Ghulja and Tarbaghatay but from all parts of Xinjiang, including

Korla and Hami.[11] Closer to Xinjiang, the first fair at the Qarqara bazaar was held in 1923, and by 1925 it had a turnover well in excess of prerevolutionary levels.[12]

While the New Economic Policy revived certain features of the prerevolutionary economy in the Soviet Union, in Xinjiang the environment had changed dramatically. Soviet trading agencies held a monopoly on the export of Soviet goods and the purchase of local products, bringing to an end the long-standing dominance of the Andijanis. There was some resistance to these new methods, and particularly in the south the Soviet trading agencies found conditions difficult. Shipments of silver sent by Soviet banks to purchase local cotton, for example, were withheld. Dumpis criticized Chinese officials, but the chief obstacle in his view was the strong position of Umar Akhunbayev, still the wealthiest man in the Kashgar bazaar. Responding to the opportunities that the new era of Sino-Soviet friendship presented, Akhunbayev reorganized his firm at the beginning of 1926 into what he called the Kashgar Trade and Industry Import-Export Company and stationed representatives as far afield as Moscow.[13] Akhunbayev not only dominated the export business in Kashgar, he also controlled local customs (as he had since before the 1911–1912 revolution).

Dumpis outlined a plan of attack on Akhunbayev, proposing an embargo on his exports until he became more compliant.[14] This may account for the fact that in early 1926 restrictions were placed on Chinese citizens exporting livestock and hides to Soviet territory, leading to a new round of negotiations with Yang Zengxin.[15] Dumpis's second strategy was to cultivate a layer of petty traders as a way to break the Akhunbayev stranglehold. According to Isa Yusuf, translator at the Chinese consulate in Andijan, the Soviets would surreptitiously recruit agents to buy products directly from peasants and nomads for export to the Soviet Union at a discount. They also paid locals to import Soviet goods in their own caravans and subsidized a row of shops in the Kashgar bazaar where they were sold. "In those days," Isa Yusuf recalled, "it wasn't uncommon to see someone who one day had been cutting deals in the money-changing bazaar to open a shop the next day and start doing business."[16] As Soviet imports of light industrial goods increased and the balance of trade shifted in the Bolsheviks' favor, they found new ways to exert their influence. According to British reports, one Soviet practice was to sell a large quantity of goods to a wholesale buyer, and then a few months later dump the same goods at a significant discount, sending the first buyer bankrupt.[17]

The reopening of the Xinjiang border in 1925 brought with it a new exodus of seasonal laborers from Kashgar. As Justin Jacobs has discussed, Yang Zengxin was nervous at the prospect of thousands of Kashgaris spending the summer on Soviet soil, subject to Communist indoctrination. "If I let Xinjiang's Turban[-Wearing Muslim]s cross the Soviet border with impunity and without any restrictions whatsoever," he agonized, "the ten thousand seasonal expatriate laborers of today will become the ten thousand agitating returnees of tomorrow."[18] Certainly some effort was made to raise the political level of these migrants during their sojourns in the Soviet Union. So-called Red Teahouses were set up along the routes of the labor migration from Xinjiang, in bazaars, and in some cases in the collective farms where they lived and worked. Apart from tea, the Red Teahouse served up weekly lectures on politics.[19] In Andijan, besides a Red Teahouse there was also a Laborer's House (*dom batraka*) set aside specifically for the use of Kashgari migrants.[20] The caravanserai was another site where political work could be carried out. There were two "Red Caravanserais" on the road from Kashgar—one in Osh, the other in Özgand—designed to provide accommodation for migrant laborers in a healthy political environment.[21]

Yet the idea of cultivating a radical Kashgari proletariat was hardly a priority for Soviet planners. They knew that prerevolutionary development had relied on the supply of cheap Kashgari labor, and that it would be essential for future cotton and construction projects. Given the years of interruption, competition was strong among the Central Asian republics to tap into the new supply. At first, Kashgari workers crossed from Irkeshtam and congregated at Osh, where they would be met by recruiters from the various Soviet republics, as well as from individual state farms (*sovkhoz*). As competition intensified, recruiting agents were sent farther ahead, first to the Irkeshtam pass, and then to Kashgar itself. A system came into being of workers being recruited in Kashgar by private collectives (*artel'*), and traveling directly to the place of work in large parties. Such parties were admitted across the border with a single "group pass" rather than an individual pass with the employee's photograph (as required by the Central Asia Bureau). Recruiters usually relied on local intermediaries, paying between twenty-five kopeks and one ruble for each recruit.[22] These touts accompanied their men to the place of work, where they were responsible for supervising them and distributing their pay, sometimes keeping as much as 40 percent for themselves. For the rural Kashgari labor force, therefore, the Soviet Union was no working man's paradise. The annual trip from Kashgar to Ferghana has gone down in popular memory as a struggle to survive: "I went and had a look at Andijan," runs one ditty, "you can only just survive there" (*körüp käldim Änjanni, aran saqlaydikän janni*).[23]

Every Sixty Years a Major Rebellion?

In the mid-1920s, Soviet strategy on China was a focus of political controversy, eventually turning into a major battleground between Stalin and Trotsky's left opposition. Having instructed the Chinese Communist Party to work within the Guomindang in south China, the Soviets also sought out potential allies among the warlords of the north. Chief among these was the "Christian Warlord" Feng Yuxiang, who had risen through the ranks of the Zhili faction of militarists. Feng burst onto the political scene in October 1924 by occupying Beijing, deposing the president of the Chinese Republic and expelling Emperor Puyi from the Forbidden City. The coup resulted in a standoff between Feng and the Manchurian warlord Zhang Zuolin—arch enemy of the Soviet Union—and both withdrew to provincial strongholds, seeking to influence politics in the capital remotely. Known to be sympathetic to Sun Yat-sen's vision for the country, Feng's camp soon hosted a party of Soviet advisers. These advisers brokered a collaboration between Feng and the GMD, who sent activists to work in the Citizens' Army.

Prior to his assault on the capital, Feng had received the title of Superintendent of Northwestern Defense (*Xibei bianfang duban*). Fearing that Feng might claim Xinjiang within his jurisdiction, Yang Zengxin objected vigorously to this appointment and mobilized Xinjiang's Muslim and Mongol aristocracy, as well as its provincial assembly, to send Beijing letters of protest.[24] While Feng did not take the appointment seriously at first, in early 1925 he became military governor of Chahar and Suiyuan (formerly Inner Mongolia) and shifted the headquarters of his Citizens' Army (Guominjun) to Kalgan (Zhangjiakou, in the north of Hebei Province). Here he commenced a series of ambitious frontier development and reform projects. In August 1925 Feng extended his reach farther west by having himself appointed superintendent of Gansu. This push into Gansu met with resistance from local Chinese strongmen, but the Muslim warlords in the province's west, who lined the border with Xinjiang, were seemingly content to obtain ranks in the Citizen's Army in return for de facto independence.

While by no means his first priority, Xinjiang attracted Feng as a potential source of revenue and a secure communications link with the Soviet Union.

His approach to Xinjiang drew on the precedent of GMD policies in Inner Mongolia, where administrative reorganization and colonization had brought frontier regions more securely under Chinese control. As part of his designs on Xinjiang, Feng and his co-thinkers devised a similar plan for Xinjiang, which would see it divided into three new provinces.[25]

Feng's encroachment on Xinjiang seems to have elicited its first echo in 1924, when the provincial commander-in-chief (*tidu*) in Kashgar, Ma Fuxing, defied Yang Zengxin and ceased delivery of tax receipts to Ürümchi. In response, Yang succeeded in dismissing and killing Ma Fuxing and abolished the position of commander-in-chief, but he paid a heavy price for doing so. As rumors spread of an impending invasion from Gansu, Yang found himself unable to rely on the loyalty of the province's Dungan troops.[26] He initiated a purge of the army and instead mobilized the Torghud Mongols of Qarashahr to garrison the Gansu front.[27] In the end, only the outbreak of war between Feng Yuxiang and his Manchurian rivals at the end of 1925 provided relief for Yang. Faring poorly in the conflict, Feng resigned his position as Superintendent of Northwestern Defense and withdrew into Mongolia to tend his wounds. From there, he headed to Moscow for talks.

Uyghur Communists were doing their best to keep up with the complicated course of events in China, but Moscow was the only place where they had direct contact with Chinese political parties. Since late 1924 there had been a circle of students at the Communist University of the Toilers of the East (KUTV) calling themselves the Revolutionary Students of Altishahr-Jungharia, which included in its ranks Kashgaris, Taranchis, Dungans, Mongols, and Kazakhs. According to its records from 1925, the KUTV circle consisted of twelve students, two of whom were Mongols from Xinjiang, while the rest were from Soviet Turkistan. They held meetings to discuss topics such as the history and geography of Xinjiang and the national question in China, and occasionally heard lectures from Soviet Orientalists.[28] In 1924, Soviet collaboration with the Guomindang, as well as the split between the Taranchis and Kashgaris in Tashkent, seem to have divided this group too, and in late 1925 a small group of Chinese-citizen Kashgari students joined the Chinese student circle at KUTV. Initially the chair of this Kashgari circle was Abdumumin Hasanhajiev, a student from Artush. At one of its first meetings, the members resolved to start reading Chinese periodicals, participate in KUTV discussions on events in China, and contribute to the Chinese students' journal.[29]

In the second half of 1926, Qadir Haji was sent to KUTV for a semester of study and assumed the leadership of this Kashgari circle, continuing its orientation to Chinese politics. Qadir Haji arrived in Moscow too late to meet Feng Yuxiang, but he did contact other Chinese revolutionaries, among them the Cantonese Communist and GMD executive member Tan Pingshan, who was in Moscow for a Comintern meeting. In a report he wrote for Tan on conditions in Xinjiang, Qadir Haji expressed his skepticism about the possibility of direct collaboration with either the Chinese Communists or Nationalists, both still based in Canton: "How can we establish links with the Chinese Communist Party or the Guomindang? There are enemies between us—Zhang Zuolin and Wu Peifu. There is no railway connection between us. We still don't know what policies the CCP are implementing, its objectives and its tactics, or the resolutions of its congresses." Feng Yuxiang's army seemed to offer Qadir Haji a more realistic scenario: "There are forty to fifty students here from different nationalities of East Turkistan, who since graduation have been occupied with various tasks in Soviet territory. Some of them wish to return to their homeland, with the goal of uniting the various national organizations of East Turkistan into a single people's party in preparation for the coming revolution—along the lines of Feng Yuxiang's Citizen's Army." Qadir Haji concluded his report on Xinjiang by endorsing the need for collaboration with the Guomindang and the CCP, but asked: "Feng Yuxiang's army is close to us: would it not be desirable for us to link up with him?"[30]

Little did Qadir Haji know that there was a growing sense among Soviet China specialists that such contact would be far from desirable. Feng Yuxiang had received Moscow's support in north China, but the Bolsheviks' initial excitement about the warlord's progressive tendencies was fading as he restricted GMD activities within his army. Viewing the situation in Gansu, NKID officials came to the conclusion that any move west by the Citizen's Army would not result in GMD control of Xinjiang, but would likely hand it, and possibly the rest of China's northwest, to Dungan militarists. NKID plenipotentiary in Tashkent, Andrei Aleksandrovich Znamenskii, wrote to Georgi Chicherin in early 1926 and argued that "the Muslims of Northwest China seem to truly expect the opportunity to establish for themselves an independent territory, and only on this basis support Feng." Chicherin was convinced: "the development of internal conflict in western China is undesirable, for it is untimely and creates complications. . . . Any effort to create new national states there will lead to impossible complications, and we may appear before the Chinese national movement in the most difficult position. We must not under any circumstances induce the Dungans forward. Feng's penetration into western China is extremely dangerous."[31]

Chicherin invoked what was by now a boilerplate response: the Soviet Union must not be seen to be stirring up non-Chinese aspirations on China's periphery. Yet the NKID had new concerns too. Beginning in late 1924, Anglo-Soviet relations deteriorated rapidly, and the specter of British meddling quickly colored thinking on Xinjiang. Znamenskii intimated in his letter to Chicherin that Britain had sought to take advantage of Ma Fuxing's confrontation with Yang Zengxin in 1924.[32] Military analysts amplified the accusation, claiming that Britain had entered into negotiations with Ma Fuxing to extend the frontier of Tibet to its northwest and had helped to undermine him when he rejected the proposal.[33] If this scenario had any basis in reality, it lay in British India's claims to the disputed Aksai-Chin region (south of Khotan), but some went so far as to suggest that Britain sought to bring the entire Khotan oasis within its sphere of influence.[34] In 1924 the perceived threat of a "Greater Tibet" expanding into Xinjiang was no doubt linked to intelligence coming from Tibet itself, where the Soviets believed that Britain was trying to depose the Dalai Lama and install its own preferred candidate to rule the country.[35]

Whatever the truth of these accusations, Soviet diplomats were correct that Feng's rise in western China had indeed created a platform for Dungan ambitions toward Xinjiang. At the end of 1926, a letter reached Tashkent bearing the seal of the Gansu-Xinjiang branch of the GMD—an unknown organization, almost certainly operating within the Citizen's Army in Gansu. The letter described growing tensions in Ürümchi. At the end of the holy month of Ramadan, Yang Zengxin, fearing an insurrection, had positioned cannons along the city wall facing the main Dungan mosque. In words that call to mind China's great Muslim uprising of the 1860s, the GMD activists reported that "talk of massacring and exterminating the Muslims was heard everywhere." In appealing for Soviet support, they outlined a strategy ostensibly aimed at resisting the anti-Soviet warlord Zhang Zuolin and the British, but equally clearly designed to precipitate Yang Zengxin's downfall. To the east, they explained, one of Ma Anliang's sons commanded the loyalties of the Salar Muslims of Gansu. From the west, they looked to the Soviet Dungan Red Army officer Masanchi, who they said "enjoys a great reputation in Gansu and Xinjiang." They requested that Tashkent dispatch Masanchi to Xinjiang on a fact-finding mission, though this was almost certainly intended to be the spark for an uprising.[36]

Judging from this communication, had Qadir Haji and the Kashgaris succeeded in establishing contact with Feng Yuxiang's Citizen's Army in Gansu, they probably would have been disappointed with the result. There was little room in this Dungan plan for local Turkic-speaking Muslims: "The Kashgaris are connected to England and only know how to do business, they have no idea what a revolution is." The comment highlights the difficult position in which Xinjiang Muslims in the Soviet Union now found themselves. Orthodoxy required that they frame their activities as part of a Chinese revolution. Yet the most likely scenario for the spread of the Chinese revolution to Xinjiang—via GMD-aligned warlords and the Dungans—seemed to leave little room for the Kashgaris. This left two choices. One was to continue to emphasize orthodoxy— Abdullah Rozibaqiev's preferred option. In 1926 he again drew up a platform for a revolutionary party in Xinjiang. As he had in 1923, he envisaged a party of the progressive trading class and Jadidist clergy, but now avoided all talk of "Chinese imperialism." Instead he advocated "the closest possible ties with the CCP, Guomindang, and other Chinese proletarian organizations." The goal of such a party, as he saw it, was to be the creation of a People's Republic in Xinjiang "that will serve the interests of all nations and tribes within it, and be closely bound in its fate to that of the whole Chinese people."[37] The other option was to work in the margins, making use of Soviet resources and rhetoric where possible but pursuing a course of action that was increasingly in conflict with Soviet policy. This was the path the Kashgari Communists took.

Cross-Border Contacts and the 1927 Crackdown

With the normalization of relations between Xinjiang and the Soviet Union, Chinese consuls superseded the *aqsaqal*s as chief go-betweens across the Soviet-Xinjiang frontier but did not replace them entirely. Some *aqsaqal*s sought confirmation from the incoming consul, while others found employment as consular staff. Others simply continued to function alongside the consul. The arrival of the consuls was a serious blow to Uyghur organizing, as Chinese citizens now depended on the consuls to legitimize their presence in Soviet Turkistan. The process was a gift to the Xinjiang authorities seeking to exert pressure on members of Uyghur political organizations, as Qadir Haji complained in 1925: "The administration requires all Chinese citizens to acquire national passports from the Chinese consulate, despite the fact that many are members of the Party and the Ploughman Union. It is shocking that these citizens, who are mortal enemies in the eyes of the Chinese government, must go before the Chinese officials to receive their passports. This administrative absurdity strikes a decisive blow against Uyghur Communist organization, and serves as grounds for victimization from the Chinese government toward these citizens, and all the more so toward those living in China."[38]

Yet despite the increased surveillance, the opening of the road to Kashgar and the influx of thousands of Kashgari laborers also created possibilities for Uyghur Communists. When Qadir Haji and his collaborators split with the Semireche Taranchis in 1924, one of his chief aims for the new Altishahri Regional Bureau was to build up revolutionary cadres among Muslims from Xinjiang by placing students in Soviet institutions. Qadir Haji and Umar Qari Islamov, the one-time plenipotentiary for the Communist Youth International, invited radical Kashgaris to join them in the Soviet Union, offering them study and political training. In this way, the two men sought to position themselves as unofficial leaders of cross-border activity.

If Enver Pasha's militant pan-Turkism had been attractive to Xinjiang's Jadidists in the early 1920s, by now such attraction was waning. After the Ottoman generalissimo's death in Bukhara in 1921, his collaborator Haji Sami had assumed the leadership of Enver's diminishing band. In 1922, he wrote from Kabul to Ali Haji, the leader of the Old City Jadidists in Kashgar. Haji Sami remained wedded to the pan-Turkist goal of an anticolonial bloc with China and reminded his contacts in Kashgar that "[t]he Chinese will never be the enemies of Islam like the Westerners. It is always possible for the Muslim world and the Turks to reach accord with the Chinese."[39] By 1924, though, Haji Sami and the ex-Ottoman militants were a spent force, and repression in Xinjiang was increasing. In December, Islamov, along with the Andijani Uyghur Communist leader Ibrahim Qurbanov, reached out to Ali Haji and invited him to the Soviet Union. The Kashgari Jadidist was wary of Islamov's claim that Soviet officials were supporting his activities: "At first," he wrote in a letter to the Comintern, "we thought that what these comrades were saying would come to nothing, as had earlier communications." He nevertheless decided it was worth the risk, and in March 1925 he crossed into Kirghizstan for talks, falling into the hands of suspicious Soviet border guards. He remained coy about his goals, stating only that he had come to learn about the work of Xinjiang émigrés in the Soviet Union, and was briefly jailed.[40]

From 1925 onward, a steady stream of representatives from Xinjiang followed Ali Haji into Soviet territory and directed petitions for support through

Uyghur Communist channels. In September 1925 a group calling itself the
Turan Revolutionary Union held a meeting in Yarkand, where they chose three
envoys to send across the border carrying appeals to the NKID and the Comintern.[41] Signed by eleven members of the organization, these and other similar texts were almost certainly composed in collaboration with Soviet-trained
Kashgaris. Such collaboration helped the new arrivals couch their requests in
terms most likely to win favor and enabled Kashgari cadres to depict the activity of these Xinjiang radicals as consistent with Soviet goals in Asia. Opening
with "Workers of the world unite!" the Turan Revolutionary Union described
themselves, in clichéd terms, as Young Kashgaris radicalized by the Russian
Revolution: "From 1915 to 1918 . . . in most of our work we relied on and anticipated liberation from Turkey, but the spread of the red glow of the great October
Revolution has brought about a dramatic shift in the thinking of Uyghur revolutionaries, and strengthened our hopes for independence (*samostoiatel'nost'*)."
New was the letter's Uyghur nationalist rhetoric, tinged with Marxist historical
analysis. "Several centuries ago the independent Uyghur state," it explained,
"was among the world's most advanced countries in its culture, politics, and
economy, but owing to changing social dynamics it fell into decline and
came under the yoke of the Chinese colonists, deprived of its great historical
significance."

While these first envoys awaited a response from Soviet officials in Tashkent, the Turan Revolutionary Union met again in Uchturfan. In light of the
growing political crisis in China, they voted unanimously to dedicate all their
energies to preparing for an uprising in Xinjiang. Two leaders of the group,
Ahmad Haji Siddiqov from Kashgar and Muhammad Akhun Salih Akhunov
from Uchturfan, now crossed into Soviet territory themselves, asking not only
for support and leadership but that the Kashgari Communists be given full authority to direct the coming revolutionary upsurge in Xinjiang. This, like the
previous petition, seems to have fallen on deaf ears, and the two men joined
the growing body of restless Muslim revolutionaries from Xinjiang now stuck
in limbo in Soviet territory.

With Qadir Haji studying in Moscow, Umar Islamov took the lead in organizing the new influx of Kashgaris. In early 1925 he was in Vernyi setting up a
training program for Kashgari activists that he called Liberation of the East
(Shärq Azadlighi).[42] Moving on to Frunze (formerly Pishpek), he formed a
revolutionary committee which called itself Liberation (Qutulush), and started

publishing a newspaper under the same name. Despite his disdain for the Kashgari leadership, Abdullah Rozibaqiev saw the formation of Liberation as a positive step, describing it as the "only healthy group" in Kashgari politics. Others, however, did not see things this way. That year the NKID complained to the Central Asia Bureau that illegal organizations were smuggling arms across the border to Xinjiang, sparking an investigation into "cases of provocation" among the Uyghurs. The inquiry found the title of the Kashgari paper *Liberation* to be suspicious and blocked its distribution. Islamov was transferred to the Ferghana Valley, but controversy dogged him. In late 1926, a report was submitted to National Minorities officials in Tashkent that raised concerns about the existence of non-party organizations in the district, pointing in particular to Islamov's work among the Kashgaris. He was now referred for disciplinary investigation.[43]

During this period many leading Bolsheviks believed that war with Britain was imminent, and the "war scare" of 1926–1927 led to the implementation of much tighter controls along the Soviet Union's borders in Asia. The final straw for the increasingly nervous party leadership came in January 1927, when an uprising in the Ili Valley was suppressed by Chinese forces. This led to a definitive crackdown on cross-border activities. The secretary of the Central Asia Bureau in Tashkent, Isaak Abramovich Zelenskii, wrote a report to Ambassador Karakhan in Beijing, and Karakhan shortly afterward lobbied the Bolshevik Central Committee to curtail any support being given to activists in Xinjiang: "The Xinjiang problem . . . cannot be resolved by forces from Xinjiang without support (that is, from the Guomindang or Feng [Yuxiang]), but now is not the time for posing such a question."[44] Meeting in February to resolve the issue, the Central Committee considered a proposal jointly submitted by Zelenskii and Karakhan, and agreed on the following points:

1. To stop the Comintern's dispatch of Uyghur agents to Xinjiang without their vetting by the Central Asia Bureau;
2. For the OGPU to stem the flow of arms and armed Uyghurs across the border;
3. For the Central Asia Bureau and Kazakh Regional Committee (*kraikom*) to carry out a review of the composition of the leadership of Uyghur sections, purging them of individuals with connections to the Uyghur movement in Xinjiang;

4. To entrust the Peoples' Commissariat of (Foreign) Trade with directing Central Asian organizations to outline measures to revive and strengthen the Soviet Union's economic ties with Xinjiang;

5. To regard any agitation toward splitting Xinjiang from China as entirely harmful and impermissible.

It was a decisive verdict in favor of the status quo in Xinjiang.

The pronouncement from the center accompanied a sharp crackdown along the border. The town of Andijan at the eastern end of the Ferghana Valley was home to the largest community of Soviet Uyghurs. As such, it was the best place to find new recruits for revolutionary organizations, and also the best place for Xinjiang officials to keep tabs on the community. A Chinese citizen crossing from Kashgar would need to present himself to Xinjiang officials in Andijan at least twice during his stay on Soviet territory: the first time to receive his temporary ID card; and the second to obtain an exit visa to return to China. At first, the *aqsaqal* Karim Puchuk fulfilled this function: "Laborers and traders from China have to come and get Karim Aqsaqal's blessing," wrote a *Voice of the Poor* correspondent in 1925, "otherwise they can't do anything."[45] When Chinese consul Chen Deli arrived in Andijan in 1926, his translator, Isa Yusuf, collaborated with Karim Aqsaqal to monitor Communist activities among the émigrés. In his memoirs Isa Yusuf describes how he ran a teahouse in the courtyard of the consulate building, where he would "take the pulse" of the seasonal laborers.

Isa Yusuf moved in the same social circles as the Uyghur Communists of Andijan and was likely sympathetic to their aspirations. When the Jadidist Ali Haji was detained by Soviet border guards, it was Isa Yusuf who secured his release, and in his memoirs he praises the Kashgari Jadidist as "the best of the nationalists." Instead of trying to bypass the likes of Isa Yusuf, who were in a good position to facilitate subversive activity in Xinjiang, the Communists in Andijan sought to turn them into allies. Isa Yusuf describes how the leading Kashgari Communists in Andijan, men such as Ibrahim Qurbanov (chair of the local Uyghur Communist section), would invite him to their gatherings and flatter him as a "patriot." The differences between them centered not so much on whether they were for or against Chinese rule in Xinjiang, but on their view of Soviet policies in Turkistan and the desirability of Soviet-style modernization in Xinjiang. When Isa Yusuf heard rumors that the Soviets were arming local Uyghurs such as Qurbanov for an incursion into Xinjiang, he informed the Chinese consul, who lodged a complaint with the local NKID representative. Whether or not there was any truth to the rumors, the Soviet secret police sprang into action, rounding up Qurbanov and dozens of others and shipping them off to the gulag.[46] In a macabre scene, Isa Yusuf describes how the Soviets timed the prison train to coincide with the Chinese consul's trip to Moscow, allowing Chen Deli to personally witness the exile of the Uyghur Communists at the Andijan station.[47]

Such acts were intended as a display of good faith to the Chinese, but in China itself, Stalin's policy was rapidly falling apart. In April 1927, Chiang Kai-shek turned on the Communists in Shanghai. By the end of the year, all factions of the GMD had severed ties with Moscow and the Chinese Communists were on the run. This defeat in China coincided with a series of radical economic and social campaigns in Central Asia, which prompted some ex-Basmachi to take up arms against the Bolsheviks again. The twin crises were enough to convince many Soviet officials that the Soviet Union was threatened by imperialist plots across Asia. One of these rebels was Janibeg Qazi, a man who had fought in the first Basmachi revolt, but had surrendered in 1922 and sided with the Red Army in the final pacification of the Ferghana Valley. Janibeg revolted again in April 1927 in the south of Kirghizstan. Attracting little response to his call to arms, the rebel leader fled to Kashgar, while small bands associated with him continued to roam the Kirghizstan-Xinjiang borderlands. According to OGPU reports, one group affiliated with Janibeg consisted of Kashgaris belonging to an organization calling itself Rebirth (Tirilish).[48] To such analysts, Janibeg's retreat to Kashgar all but confirmed the existence of a dangerous Basmachi-Kashgari coalition. Officials in Osh reported to the Central Asia Bureau that Muslims in Kashgar had promised to support Janibeg against the Soviets if he would aid them against the Chinese.[49]

Equally troubling in this respect were Kashgar's connections to Afghanistan, where a number of Basmachi leaders had originally fled. While the Afghan emir Amanullah Khan was a reformist monarch and Soviet ally, the NKID was wary of his trade representative in Yarkand, who arrived in 1923. In 1925 Maks Dumpis noted that this self-styled "consul" was directing local political activity away from the Soviets toward Kabul, and on a pan-Islamic basis. Sometime around 1926–1927, two Kashgari Jadidists, former students of Ahmed Kemal's school, traveled to Afghanistan to meet with Amanullah Khan. While in Mazar-i Sharif they revealed to the Soviet consul that they had also met with the Basmachi leader Qur Shirmat (Sher Muhammad), who was then residing in Kabul. They then naively chose to return to Kashgar via Soviet territory, where they were detained and interrogated.[50] The two men obviously thought such associations were harmless and not worth concealing, but for nervous officials in Tashkent support for Qur Shirmat among Kashgaris was a troubling scenario, particularly as cross-border traffic was increasing. "Have we really checked," Znamenskii asked, "whether or not those coming from Kashgar are not connected to the former Basmachi leaders in Kabul?"[51]

The widening OGPU sweep in 1927 caught a large number of Xinjiang émigrés, both long-standing Communists and recent arrivals. Qadir Haji was implicated in various ways, but since his return from Moscow he had been working in Samarkand (capital of Uzbekistan from 1924 to 1930) and thus avoided direct incrimination. Islamov was found to be maintaining suspicious ties with the Chinese consul in Tashkent, for which he was interrogated and expelled from the party.[52] His Liberation of the East circle was identified as a subversive anti-Soviet network, and it and other Kashgari organizations were purged or disbanded.[53] Some activists, such as the former Moscow student leader Abdumumin Hasanhajiev, were detained but released. Young men such as Hasanhajiev could flee across the border to Xinjiang, but those who were already well known in Kashgar—including Ali Haji—could not return for fear of arrest and execution. They found themselves stranded in Soviet territory, sitting ducks for the next round of OGPU inquisitions in the early 1930s, which were driven by an ever-increasing paranoia toward pan-Islamic and pan-Turkist conspiracies against the Soviet Union. For a while, Ali Haji eked out an existence running a small eatery in Tashkent, but was detained again in 1931 and eventually executed. In the Soviet Union at least, it was the end of the road for the Young Kashgaris.[54]

Semireche: From Cultural Front to Cultural Revolution

The Taranchis in Semireche were largely bystanders in this course of events. While the Kashgaris tried to establish the Uyghur nation by practical means, those in Vernyi sought to do so in theory. Cultural politics remained the focus here, as the Semireche intellectuals grappled with the challenge of constructing a new Soviet Uyghur language and culture that could satisfy the requirements of Soviet national policy. At its most basic, there was a need to codify a new literary standard for Uyghur—one sufficiently distinct to establish the Uyghurs as a nation in their own right but sufficiently broad to satisfy the various constituencies that were thought to belong to this nation. This early work of cultural engineering among the Uyghurs carried on from prerevolutionary Russian and Jadidist ethnography. Much of its inspiration came from linguists and folklorists such as V. V. Radlov and the tsarist official Nikolai Pantusov, who had collected Taranchi songs and stories in Semireche.[55] Yet as much as ethnography and linguistics could be the tools of national construction, there was an inherent tension between the descriptive approach of scholarship, which tended toward further subdivision, and the normative impulse of nation building, which strived for unity.

At first, *Voice of the Poor*'s editors avoided the term "Uyghur" and announced it instead as a publication in the "Taranchi-Kashgari language," marking the first effort to give written form to the vernacular of Xinjiang. It is sometimes argued that Soviet linguistic engineering fostered artificial differences between the Turkic languages of Central Asia, but the case of *Voice of the Poor* shows that the desire to create a new and distinct literary standard was equally present among Central Asian intellectuals. The Chaghatay Turkic of the manuscript tradition differed little across Turkistan, while the prerevolutionary and early Soviet publications to which Taranchis had contributed were written in a pan-Turkic idiom intended to be comprehensible to all Turkic-speaking Muslims. In breaking with this uniformity, *Voice of the Poor* sought to put as much distance as possible between its script and those of its neighbors, adopting an orthography that looks radical in comparison to today's Standard Uyghur (SU). Among the innovations that the newspaper exhibited, some had previously been implemented among script reformers, including a proposal that Arabic and Persian loanwords be written according to local pronunciation and vowels be fully represented. New was *Voice of the Poor*'s effort to represent the peculiarities of the Xinjiang vernacular, including vowel raising and the dropping of consonants /l/ and /r/ (e.g., *boghan* instead of SU *bolghan*). In September 1923 these principles were codified by a Scientific Commission, which included Abdullah Rozibaqiev, Qadir Haji, Sabirjan Shakirjanov, and Nazarkhoja Abdusamadov.[56]

As might be expected in the fractious political climate of the 1920s, efforts to popularize *Voice of the Poor*'s approach to script and lexicon outside Semireche met with opposition from those who saw them as imposing Taranchi norms on Kashgaris. In 1924 the Regional Bureau of Uyghur Communists printed two primary-school readers, one of which was Latif Ansari's alphabet manual *First Knowledge* (*Birinchi Bilik*), in which he offered a description of the "Uyghur alphabet."[57] Zarif Bashiri gave the book a positive review in the Tashkent daily *Red Uzbekistan*, but a Kashgari critic pointed out that the book contained many words that were simply unknown in Xinjiang.[58] Not to be put off, *Voice of the Poor*'s editors proceeded to adjust its masthead in 1925 to announce itself as a newspaper in the "Uyghur language." The same year saw the publication in Moscow of a book titled *Uyghur Folk Literature* (*Uyghur Äl Ädäbiyati*), as much an attempt at an ethnography of the Uyghurs as a literary work. Citing Radlov and Pantusov's recordings as a model, the Semireche authors included songs, poetry, folk sayings, and riddles that they had collected in field trips in 1922 or that had been sent in by Kashgaris studying in Tashkent. A few of the songs had been lifted straight from Pantusov's prerevolutionary publications. In an effort to represent a literary tradition encompassing all Uyghurs, the compilation also included a set of workingmen's songs from Xinjiang, an ode to the Artush entrepreneur Tash Akhun, and a rendering of a romantic epic (*dastan*) from the oasis of Hami.[59]

Uyghur Folk Literature was the first work to posit the existence of a single "Uyghur" literature. Yet in striving for breadth it offended those whose focus was on developing a consistent, and standard, form of written Uyghur. The publication drew the ire of Sabirjan Shakirjanov, the long-time Bashkir collaborator in Taranchi publishing, who published a strongly critical review of it in *Voice of the Poor*: "never have so many mistakes been seen in a book!" Not only was its orthography riddled with Uzbek and Tatar intrusions, in Shakirjanov's eyes the editors had ignored the differences between the Taranchi and Kashgari dialects, combining the two in an artificial way: "half of one song is in the Taranchi dialect, half of it is in Kashgari. There is half a song in Uyghur, half in Uzbek." For Shakirjanov, these dialects were simply too far apart to combine into a single written language: "no-one can deny that there exist two dialects that create a large divide among the Uyghurs. One of these is the Uyghur-Kashgar dialect, the second is the Uyghur-Taranchi dialect. . . . Although the Taranchis were originally Kashgaris, in a hundred and sixty-seven years they have carved out a separate history and dialect for themselves. The environment and natural conditions in which the Taranchis lived were completely different. . . . In future it would be more scientific for works to be published either in the Kashgar or the Taranchi dialect."[60]

Although he was criticized for his skepticism, Shakirjanov's insistence on scientific accuracy was consistent with the *Voice of the Poor* approach to linguistic construction. If it was true that the written language should mirror the spoken, then Shakirjanov's conclusion was correct: there was no way that exactly the same orthography could be applied to the Taranchi and Kashgari dialects, minor though their differences were. Yet as critics were quick to point out, if there had to be two literary standards to account for the divergence of the Taranchi and Kashgari dialects of the Soviet Union, then the Uyghur language would be split into, not just two, but potentially many more variants, to account for all the shades of difference in pronunciation and grammar existing across Xinjiang.[61]

Theory aside, there were other obstacles to projecting any vision of Uyghur language or culture across a wider constituency. Chief among them was the chronic underfunding of Soviet schools, particularly for minority groups. Not without justification, the Uyghurs of Tashkent could write in 1925 that "in all the Uyghur regions of Central Asia, with the exception of Semireche, there is not even a single normally functioning primary school."[62] Maybe this was to be expected in Uzbekistan or Kirghizstan, where children of Xinjiang émigrés often went to schools that did not distinguish Uyghur from Uzbek. Yet even in Semireche the exigencies of the strict New Economic Policy, which drastically reduced school funding, limited the reach of the Uyghur Communists. As a result, these cultural experiments and discussions took place in a narrow circle of party intellectuals and had little impact beyond them.

The failings of Soviet schooling took on new dimensions in 1926, as religious schools started competing for students. In the town of Qoram, for example, two state-funded Taranchi schools came into being in 1925, but had dwindled to one by 1926. To fill the gap, a man by the name of Ahmad Akhun and established his own school in the town, funded by an organization called the Religious Union. Soon Ahmad Akhun's Religious Union was running no less than four schools in Qoram, even taking students who were members of the local Komsomol.[63] The ulama who now regrouped around the Religious Union showed themselves skilled in adapting to the new style of mass-membership organizations with which they were in competition, recruiting people out of official bodies such as the Ploughman Union and announcing plans to campaign for the upcoming Soviet elections.[64] In a few short months the Religious Union had spread throughout the Taranchi villages of Semireche, counting among its leaders men who had fled to Ghulja at the time of the revolution.[65] According to hostile accounts, the union let it be known that anyone who did not join it could not be called a Muslim, and wielded a range of tools to ostracize their enemies from local society. If someone did not sign up for the Religious Union, for example, they would not be able to find a mulla to perform an Islamic wedding ceremony.[66] Critics of the union liked to poke fun at it, but such articles were written anonymously, under pseudonyms like "Truth-teller" or "Young Worker," suggesting that the critics lacked the confidence to identify themselves.

The growth of the Religious Union shows that Islamic opposition in Turkistan was not entirely a figment of a paranoid Communist Party's imagination. Antireligious propaganda had been gradually intensifying since 1923, when religious courts in Semireche were abolished and policies implemented restricting the use of *waqf.* In 1927, Soviet authorities shifted from marginalization of the ulama and mild atheistic propaganda to an all-out assault on Islam, commencing with the *hujum* ("attack") against veiling, formally launched on International Women's Day, March 8 1927. In the Taranchi villages of Semireche, where veiling was uncommon, the mass antireligious campaign took the form of Circles to Struggle against Religious Superstition, which were set up throughout 1927 to combat the Religious Union.[67] Any remaining sharia courts and religious schools were closed, *waqf* was abolished, and mosques were converted into social clubs, with some imams ending up in prison.[68] The pages of the Soviet Uyghur press reported on village mosque employees who were abandoning their profession, providing readers with instructive quotes from the men who had turned over a new leaf. "Last year Ahmad Akhun appointed me *mutavalli* at Sultan Qurghan," ran one such confession, "but now that I realize his thievery, I have given up this job."[69]

The Soviet antireligious campaign successfully sidelined the Religious Union, but the radical turn claimed other victims too. The clash with the Taranchi ulama highlighted the failure of earlier efforts to cultivate a pro-Soviet "progressive clergy," and the reconstituted Jadidist organization Progressive fell by the wayside during the antireligious campaign. Although Progressive had denounced the harmful influence of backward imams and mullas, it had still envisaged a place for Islamic law—something that now ran counter to Soviet policy. Other cooptation strategies were abandoned too: one activist called for a clean break with the *mashrab* tradition, arguing that instead of calling them *mashrab* such meetings should be known as "evenings of acquiring knowledge" (*bilim elish kechisi*).[70] Soon, party leaders in Central Asia were denouncing the Jadidists themselves, depicting them as the ideological counterparts of the insidious NEP-men, who were reviled for exploiting the political and economic laxity of the early 1920s.[71]

The attack on Jadidism obliged the Uyghur Communists to identify the "old intellectuals" in their ranks, and the spotlight fell on Nazarkhoja Abdusamadov. The "Uyghur child," whose writings had served as inspiration for the original Uyghur Club and had been reprinted as recently as 1923, now came under sustained criticism—much of it at the hands of Abdullah Rozibaqiev. Rozibaqiev's attack on Abdusamadov served two purposes. The first was to signal a break with the Jadidist legacy in cultural politics. Second, it also allowed Rozibaqiev to forward his revisionist approach to Taranchi identity, in which he sought to divest the term "Taranchi" of any lingering sense of national identity. Rozibaqiev reviewed Abdusamadov's *History of the Taranchi Turks*, and while acknowledging the historical value of its sources, he found it seriously deficient as a scholarly work. Instead of analyzing social forces, the author had praised the *beg*s and *akhund*s who had founded the Taranchi sultanate in the nineteenth century, locating political divisions in individual rivalries instead of class conflict in Ili Valley society.[72] Rozibaqiev took particular issue with one of Abdusamadov's poems, which seemed to glorify the prerevolutionary traditions of the Taranchis. In this piece, a stubborn peasant speaks of his loyalty to rural Taranchi ways:[73]

> Companions (*yaran*), Taranness is our path (*mäsläk*),
> Taranness is our religion, our creed (*mäzhäb*),
> There is no turning back, even if we die,
> Such is our old custom.

Such a positive invocation of the old Taranchi ways, suffused with Sufistic terminology (*yaran*, *mäzhäb*) had no place in the new Soviet Uyghur canon.

In reply, Abdusamadov mounted a brave defense of his views but conceded the main thrust of Rozibaqiev's criticism, namely that being a Taranchi was not in any way a form of national identity. Instead of defending his writings on the Taranchi as a contribution to the growth of Uyghur national history, he retreated into semantics, arguing that he had never used the word *taranchi* in anything other than its strict etymological meaning of "peasant."[74] Far from petit bourgeois ideology, his invocation of Taranchi identity was simply a celebration of the virtues of the hardworking peasantry—surely not a crime in the Soviet Union? It was a clever move, but one that only bought him enough time to abandon the field of Uyghur literary polemics and escape across the border to Ghulja.[75] One among many victims of the attack on the Jadidist legacy in these years of Stalin's cultural revolution, Abdusamadov's fall from grace highlights the distance between his early, tentative explorations of the Uyghur past and the social transformation with which the notion of Uyghur national identity was aligned by the end of the 1920s.

Latinization and Linguistic Orthodoxy

Vernyi, renamed Alma-Ata in 1927, was not the only place where blueprints for a new Uyghur language were being drawn up. In Moscow, too, KUTV students were working out ways to best adapt the Arabic script to the sounds of Uyghur. The product of the Moscow circle was the publication in 1926 of Abdulhayy Muhammadi's *Principles of Uyghur Orthography* (*Uyghurchä Yeziq Yolliri*). As Muhammadi stated in his introduction, despite a long-running debate, the problem of orthography was yet to be resolved. Discussing the state of Uyghur publishing, he lamented that "each word appears in ninety-nine different forms."[76] Yet instead of seeking the best of existing models, Muhammadi chose to add yet another to the mix, producing an idiosyncratic orthography with a number of features that now look odd to us (his use of vowel diacritics, for example, is the opposite of the way they are used in Xinjiang today). In his book, Muhammadi also called for a purification of the Uyghur lexicon, purging it, not of Chinese or Russian terms, but of words from neighboring Turkic languages that did not belong. He saw the Tatar literary tradition as the main source of these errors, but also noted the pernicious influence of classical Chaghatay and Uzbek.

A third contender for the new literary standard appeared in 1927, when Qadir Haji returned from studies in Moscow and requested funding from the Central Asia Bureau for a periodical in "Altishahri-Jungharian Uyghur," that is, the language of Xinjiang. In November 1927, *Liberation* began publication in Tashkent, taking its name from Umar Qari Islamov's banned Frunze organ. Fortnightly at first, *Liberation* became weekly in 1929, and biweekly in 1930. The first issue led with an article by Qadir Haji reviewing the decade's achievements.[77] In this programmatic piece he laid out his approach to the Uyghur question, claiming the name as the exclusive preserve of émigrés from Altishahr, the Chinese citizens who had first been mobilized by the Union of Chinese Workers and who were living in Uzbekistan and Kirghizstan. On this basis *Liberation* told the Taranchis to stay out of Uyghur politics: "Instead of the Taranchis getting involved in the cultural, educational and other such affairs of the Chinese Uyghurs, they should mind their own business. . . . The liberation of Uyghuristan should never be tied up with people living in another country."[78] Predictably, Alma-Ata intellectuals criticized the publication as excessively influenced by Uzbek, but *Liberation* had little time for the vernacularist zeal exhibited by *Voice of the Poor*. "The primary task of literature in the Uyghur language," one contributor responded, "is to use literary methods to accustom the Uyghur toilers to the name 'Uyghur.'" This required an orthography that would be familiar to Muslims in Xinjiang, where Chaghatay remained the standard.

As Arabic-script prototypes for Uyghur multiplied, the launch of the Soviet Union's Latinization campaign offered a way to break the deadlock. Latinization among the Uyghurs was announced with the same excitement as elsewhere in the Soviet Union, with great claims made for its role in liberating the Union's non-Russian peoples from linguistic backwardness.[79] The campaign to abolish the Arabic script and shift all of the Soviet Union's Turkic languages to Latin letters was the result of the First All-Union Turkological Congress held in Baku in 1926, where the Uyghurs were represented by a single student.[80] In the debate on orthography among the Alma-Ata, Moscow and Tashkent prototypes, the Latinization campaign presented an opportunity to reset the clock, and a series of proposals was soon forthcoming. In Semireche, Latif Ansari came up with a thirty-three-letter alphabet, while a proposal from Uyghurs in Kirghizstan had twenty-eight letters. Yet it was the Tashkent faction who took the lead in implementing the orthographic reform. In April 1928 they organized a conference to draw up plans for the Latinization of Uyghur in far-off Samarkand, making attendance from Alma-Ata almost impossible for party intellectuals busy with other tasks.

The Samarkand Latinization conference drew fourteen delegates, a majority of them from Tashkent. Not surprisingly, the meeting provided a rousing endorsement of *Liberation*'s approach, praising it for proceeding along a "broad path," as opposed to the "narrow" approach exemplified by *Voice of the Poor*. Delegates approved the basic scheme of the Baku Latinization conference and worked out the details of the new alphabet's application to Uyghur. In the process they consciously steered away from features specific to the Taranchi dialect. For instance, they rejected the use of the consonant *zh* in initial position, which characteristically occurs in place of *y* in the Taranchi dialect (e.g., *zhil ~ yil* "year"; *zhurt ~ yurt* "home"). Delegates also criticized the Semi-reche style of dropping consonants, insisting that roots and suffixes be pre-served in their grammatical (and traditional) forms: "It is not *bomaydu*, *bomitu*, *bomidu*, or *bommaydu*, it has to be *bolmaydu*."[81] Reporting on the conference's resolutions, Abdulhayy Muhammadi cautioned the Alma-Ata fac-tion not to step out of line: "At the conference a plan was adopted, and with this the planning is finished. People should give up going around drawing up plans. We must implement the one that has been adopted." Of course, this was wishful thinking. The Semireche Uyghurs were initially receptive, electing their own New Alphabet Union to liaise with the linguists in Tashkent. Before the month was out, though, Latif Ansari was publicly ridiculing the *Liberation* group's criticisms, saying that *Liberation*'s language was 90 percent Uzbek and declaring defiantly that "Semireche won't speak *Liberation*ese!"[82]

The Latinization campaign heralded the arrival of a new attitude toward cul-ture in Central Asia, in which the relics of Jadidist discourse were drowned out by the language of class struggle in all spheres. The debate on orthography was increasingly subjected to such a transvaluation, as positions were reinterpreted along class lines. Abdulhayy Muhammadi made this explicit in a 1929 article "On the Language and Orthography Questions," in which he identified both left and right deviations on the issue of script reform. To the left were the Semireche linguists Sabirjan Shakirjanov and Latif Ansari, who held that the written language should be as close as possible to the spoken, to the extent that they were willing to countenance divergent literary standards be-tween Taranchis and Kashgaris. Rightism was characterized (or caricatured) as the position that "we should write every word according to its root, paying no attention to the features of the living language," an approach attributed to unnamed Tashkent intellectuals. This, Muhammadi contended, was the language of the mullas, and could not possibly serve as the basis for a litera-ture of the people.[83]

The Tashkent linguists had pulled off something of a coup in Samarkand, but their advantage was only temporary. The Alma-Ata intelligentsia re-sponded by organizing a second conference, this time on home soil. The Second Language-Orthography Conference in Alma-Ata in 1930 drew a heavyweight team of linguists, including two of the Soviet Union's leading Turkologists, Aleksander Samoilovich and Sergei Malov. Malov brought with him the authority of years of field research in Xinjiang and Gansu. Those ex-peditions had sought out the linguistic relics of ancient Uyghur, not among the Taranchis or Kashgaris, whose speech he referred to as the "Turkish dialects of western China," but among the Yellow Uyghurs of Gansu.[84] As recently as 1926, at the Turkological congress in Baku, Malov had discussed his research on the "modern Uyghur language," by which he meant the language of the Yellow Uyghurs.[85] To preserve some sense of Turkological credibility, Malov addressed the Alma-Ata conference on the Yellow Uyghurs, but this was a topic irrelevant to the questions at hand. "Uyghur," in the Soviet Union at least, would refer to the language of the Xinjiang Muslims, and Malov was presented with a fait accompli. He made his only public comment on this issue in 1934, justifying the new terminology in terms of "the wish of the Turkish population of Xinjiang, and . . . the scientific tradition that now exists." Yet the scientific tradition he cited was a thin one—of the scholars he listed, Julius Klaproth was the only one who had actually described the inhabitants of Xinjiang as Uyghurs.[86] Of the two factors, then, it was the act of linguistic self-determination that created modern Uyghur. Linguists such as Malov were occasional collaborators in the process, but by no means in control of it.

Thanks in part to Sergei Malov's scholarly breadth, the discussion of dialects at this event went beyond the narrow Taranchi-Kashgari divide to consider which of all the Xinjiang dialects might serve as the basis for a new Uyghur standard. Some naturally felt that the Taranchi dialect, the language of the most "advanced" section of the Uyghur population, was the best choice. Others applied a criterion of linguistic purity and suggested that less contaminated dialects were to be found across the border in Xinjiang. Some argued that Turfan offered the best specimen; others preferred the speech of Kucha. Not surprisingly, the Kashgar dialect was found wanting, as it was too close to Uzbek. Likewise, the Yarkand dialect was rejected for the presence of Hindi influence. Some went so far as to suggest that the dialect of the Dolans, a people of obscure origins living on the edge of the Tarim Basin and in Lop Nur, exhibited the least foreign intrusions and was the most appropriate model.[87]

Yet the real question, as participants knew, was the possibility of unity between the Taranchis and the Kashgaris. "Are the Taranchis and Kashgaris one nationality?" wrote Abdullah Rozibaqiev from his posting in Qizil Orda on the steppe. "To raise this question again in 1930 is ridiculous." Rozibaqiev's contribution to the conference stressed that the liberation of the proletariat could not be achieved without raising their cultural level, and hence "the struggle for a unified literary language is a class struggle."[88] Affirming this push for unity, the conference requested that Soviet administrative bodies cease using the words "Kashgari" and "Taranchi" in their decrees and publications.

On orthographic questions, unsurprisingly, the Alma-Ata intellectuals came out victorious. Malov threw his weight behind the *Voice of the Poor* orthography, recommending that *Liberation* be brought into line with the Semireche publication. Finding himself in a minority, *Liberation*'s editor did his best to defend himself: "To say that *Liberation* is completely Uzbek is a slur."[89] The new Soviet Uyghur standard received a scientific stamp of approval, but it came at the expense of those Alma-Ata intellectuals whose commitment to scientific linguistics had made them skeptical of the possibility of linguistic unity. For these "leftist" deviations, Sabirjan Shakirjanov and Latif Ansari were forced to make public self-criticisms. "Up until today," Shakirjanov confessed before the conference, "I had my own views on language. After participating in the Fourth Plenum of the New Turk Alphabet Committee and the Uyghur Language-Orthography Conference, I realized my errors. From now on I promise to abandon my mistakes, look broadly at the language-orthography question, and walk hand-in-hand with the Uyghur linguists. I am ready to devote all my energy to setting straight the culture of the Uyghur proletariat."[90]

For a man who had been a crucial intermediary in the relationship between Russian Turkology, the Jadidist literary world, and Soviet Uyghur publishing, this must have been a humiliating experience. Shakirjanov survived the Stalinist chill that descended in the 1930s and lived out his life teaching Arabic in Alma-Ata's pedagogical institutions, but the wounds of that period never fully healed. He kept up a correspondence with Malov, who like him managed to survive the purge of the academy (his colleague Samoilovich, who also attended the 1930 conference in Alma-Ata, was not so lucky). Between 1934 and 1946 Malov was unable to publish his work, but the postwar years allowed him to recommence editing his linguistic recordings from Xinjiang. In 1954 he produced a book on the dialect of Hami and sent a copy as a present to his friend Shakirjanov in Alma-Ata.[91] By now in his seventies, Shakirjanov was delighted by the gift, and his thoughts turned immediately to the polemics of the 1920s. "You may recall," he wrote in reply to the Russian (in Uyghur), "that in the 1920s certain know-nothings went around attacking me because I said that there were Taranchi and Kashgari dialects in the Uyghur language. Your work on the Hami dialect has vindicated me, as it proves that there are several dialects of Uyghur."[92] A quarter of a century after his falling out with the Uyghur

Communists, Shakirjanov's Jadidist faith in the compatibility of scientific dialectology and national cultural construction remained intact.

Soviet nationalities policy, far from consolidating the Uyghurs into a nation, had set the Kashgaris and Taranchis on divergent trajectories. Both found value in the language of Uyghur nationhood, but while the former sought to substantiate this idea through action in Xinjiang, the latter did so through nation building on Soviet soil, drawing both on the Jadidist template of the folkloric nation and the new Stalinist orthodoxy. We might say that by 1930 there was not one Uyghur nation but two: one founded on the basis of citizenship, and the other on conformity with the Soviet criteria for nationhood. In neither case can it be said that Soviet officials provided support for the nation-building process, let alone that the Soviets "created" the Uyghur nation, as is sometimes suggested: far from it, in the case of the Kashgaris the Soviet Union had killed or imprisoned some of the most dedicated believers in the Bolsheviks' declared mission of national liberation.

Among the Taranchis too, the Stalinist turn had been bruising, but here at least they had something to show for it. Having legislated a Uyghur language into existence, some of the administrative confusion surrounding the basis for a Uyghur nation was dispelled. While Uyghur as a category had been treated with skepticism in the 1926 Soviet census, it was confirmed as an "ethnographic group" in 1937 and upgraded to a "national group" in 1939—still a far cry from a full-blown nation (*natsiia*), but no longer subject to queries and doubts. Yet in achieving this the Taranchis had largely cut themselves off from Xinjiang, as Soviet foreign policy required of them. Throughout the 1930s, emphasis was increasingly placed on the specifically Soviet quality of the new nation. In 1937 Uyghur teachers in Kazakhstan held a conference in Alma-Ata, where they offered a vote of thanks to Sergei Malov for his work. Identifying themselves as "representatives of the Soviet Uyghur nation," they lauded his "great achievements in the field of collecting, archiving, and publicizing the most precious records of ancient Uyghur culture and writing, and in creating and developing a new Soviet Uyghur literary language."[93] It was in these days of high Stalinism that the category of "Soviet Uyghur" was born.

What, then, of the other Uyghur nation? Bolshevik leaders had decreed unambiguously against support for revolutionary activity in Xinjiang, and the 1927 purge had hit the Kashgaris hard. Yet the Soviets were not so ruthless as to do away with all means of influencing the course of events in Xinjiang, particularly as the outcome of Chinese politics remained in doubt. The fact that at the end of 1927 Qadir Haji was permitted to launch a new version of *Liberation* in Tashkent was, I believe, a distant echo of the rout of the Chinese Communist Party in Shanghai. As the Chinese Communist Party retreated to the mountains, and Chiang Kai-shek proceeded to unify the country on an anti-Communist basis, the Soviet Union no longer felt bound to its pledge to withhold support from anti-Chinese activists along its borders. Chen Deli, the Chinese consul in Andijan in 1927, was promoted to the Tashkent post in 1931. On arriving there he was outraged to find that Qadir Haji's *Liberation* was still being published and was seeking to draw sojourning Kashgaris into revolutionary politics.[94] After more than a decade of thrashing out the implications of the Russian Revolution for the Muslims of Xinjiang, many questions still remained. The answers to them would only be found in Xinjiang itself.

CHAPTER EIGHT

The Battle for Xinjiang and
the Uyghur Nation

Governor Yang Zengxin's commitment to national unity, and to retaining Chinese control in Xinjiang, required him to keep his distance from the national unifiers of his day. When Chiang Kai-shek established his capital in Nanjing, Yang had no interest in bringing Xinjiang into the GMD fold and jealously guarded his own authority. He had his own reasons for doing so, but he also feared that his hard-learned lessons for governing Xinjiang would be lost in the drive for modernization emanating from the interior. Maintaining independence in the new climate was no easy task, though, and eventually made Yang too many enemies to keep at bay. The man who replaced him in 1928 as provincial chairman, Jin Shuren, also kept the Nationalists at arm's length but endorsed the GMD goal of modernizing frontier administration. Jin's efforts to abolish the province's remaining institutions of non-Chinese autonomy set off an uprising in Hami in 1931 that soon spread throughout the province, leading to the creation of the first East Turkistan Republic. The 1931–1933 rebellion, the Soviet response to it, and the fate of Uyghur nationalism in republican Xinjiang provide the focus of this final chapter.

A number of scholars have described the events of the early 1930s in Xinjiang, from the first sparks of the Muslim rebellion to the rise of a new pro-Soviet warlord, Sheng Shicai (1897–1970).[1] Instead of retelling the entire story, I concentrate here on the experience of the province's Muslim actors. In many ways this revolt was a reprisal of themes already developed in the 1920s: the possibility of a Soviet-aligned national Communist coalition between Xinjiang's non-Chinese (primarily its Muslims and Mongols); the ambitions of Dungan leaders in Gansu and Qinghai to turn Xinjiang into a Muslim territory nominally aligned to the GMD; local conflicts between factions of the Kashgar merchantry; and the paranoia of Soviet authorities regarding the potential for

these divisions to be exploited by imperialist meddling. Yet along with these
familiar factors the early 1930s presented new conditions. In the Soviet
Union, fear of war with the imperialist West was compounded by alarm at the
threat from Japan. Just a few months after the outbreak of the uprising in Hami,
Japan carried out its plan to occupy Manchuria and set about constructing the
puppet monarchy of Manchukuo. In Central Asia, meanwhile, collectivization
and the intensification of cotton production were provoking opposition, resulting in a flight from Soviet territory into Xinjiang. New, too, was the scale
of the unrest, drawing a response from all corners of the province, including
communities that have played little role in the story until now, such as the Muslims of Khotan.

Echoes of the Northern Expedition

In December 1927, a man by the name of Ali Ding Xicheng arrived in Nanjing, three months after it had been declared the new capital of the Republic of
China. Ding carried with him letters from Ibrahim, the hereditary duke
(*gong*) of Uchturfan in Xinjiang, as well as a declaration to the citizens of China.[2]
Ding claimed to have met Ibrahim while the duke was serving as one of Xinjiang's representatives to the National Parliament in Beijing in the early 1920s.
When Duke Ibrahim returned to Xinjiang, he invited Ding to accompany him
to inspect social and political conditions in the province. In the documents he
submitted to the parliament, and in a series of meetings with National Government Chairman Tan Yankai, Ding lamented Xinjiang's backward condition,
which had seen little change since the Qing, and urged the GMD leadership
to pay greater attention to revolutionary work in the nation's northwest.

Each flush of national revolution in China breathed new life into the otherwise stale Nationalist slogan of "five races in harmony." In the wake of the
Xinhai revolution, Muslims in China such as Li Qian had considered the implications of this slogan for themselves and fashioned an intellectual case for
greater Muslim autonomy in western China. In 1927, when Chiang Kai-shek's
victory revived discussion of constitutional visions for China, history repeated
itself, and voices calling for greater recognition of the Muslim presence in China
could again be heard. Ding's relationship with Ibrahim mirrored that between
Li Qian and the Hami Wang Shah Maqsud in 1914. Ding knew of the precedent, and in his submissions he cited Li Qian's earlier campaigning efforts and
drew on similar rhetoric. As Li had argued, Ding held that China's Muslims

suffered discrimination in comparison with the nation's Mongols and Tibetans, in violation of the Republicans' professed commitment to "five races in harmony." When the Nanjing assembly announced the convening of a new Mongolian and Tibetan Committee, Ding lobbied for it be expanded to include Muslim representatives.[3]

In February 1928, Muslim dignitaries in the city of Wuhan invited Ding to pay them a visit, and from there he headed north to Henan Province for a meeting with its new governor, Feng Yuxiang.[4] In 1927 relations between Feng and the Dungan warlords of Gansu had soured, and the Gansu and Qinghai Muslims had revolted against Feng's Citizen's Army, leaving the warlord's claims to be defending the interests of China's Muslims in tatters. Withdrawing from the northwest, Feng threw in his lot with Chiang Kai-shek and received the governorship of Henan. The outcome of the meeting between Feng and Ding was a proposal that Nanjing send the Gansu Dungan leader Ma Fuxiang (1876–1932) to inspect affairs in Xinjiang. Ma Fuxiang had previously served in the Qing military in Xinjiang and collaborated with Feng's Citizen's Army in Gansu. For this, he too was forced out of Gansu in 1927, and when Ding met him he was on the verge of joining the GMD. Meanwhile, Ding was appointed to a group conducting preparatory work toward the creation of a GMD party branch in Xinjiang.[5]

As Yang Zengxin well knew, this combined push from Feng Yuxiang, Ma Fuxiang, and Nanjing was aimed squarely at dislodging him from Ürümchi. Scrambling to fend them off, he suddenly announced his willingness to restructure his administration along GMD lines and raise the Nationalist flag in Xinjiang. In offering this compromise, Yang might have succeeded in deterring his rivals in the interior, but he had enemies close at hand too. Within a few days of these overtures to Nanjing, he was shot dead, assassinated at a graduation ceremony. Yang's successor, Jin Shuren, who had previously served as county magistrate in Kashgar, quickly secured the scene and pointed the finger at Fan Yaonan, a long-serving foreign affairs official in Ürümchi. Not surprisingly, many have suspected Feng Yuxiang of involvement in the plot, though it seems unlikely that Feng would have organized an assassination when political momentum was going his way. In Ürümchi, there seems to have been little interest in investigating the murder, and it has never been fully accounted for.[6] Soon after Yang's death, Ding received a curious letter from contacts in Ürümchi encouraging him to return to Xinjiang, but with the proviso that "we must retain this current administration, no one should be permitted to take advantage of this."[7] Ding announced that he was leaving for Xinjiang, but when he reached Beijing, Duke Ibrahim suddenly sent word that he had never appointed Ding as his representative and would take no responsibility for any of his actions.[8]

Again we see that Ding's story mirrors that of Li Qian. In 1914, Yang Zengxin had mobilized his representatives in the capital (and no doubt intrigued in Xinjiang too), and soon enough Shah Maqsud disavowed any relationship with Li Qian. Jin Shuren seems to have succeeded in similarly outmaneuvering Ding. What had happened? Was Ding an impostor all along? Had Jin Shuren sufficiently consolidated his position to lean on Ibrahim directly? Neither of these scenarios seems likely. Most probably what caused Ibrahim to balk was the strong antagonism toward Feng Yuxiang among the Muslims of the northwest. Having thrown Feng's Citizens' Army out of Gansu, the province's Dungan warlords were in no mood to allow Feng to reestablish himself in neighboring Xinjiang. In the middle of 1929, a telegram signed not only by the Dungan military elite of the northwest, but also the Muslim aristocracy of Xinjiang (including Ibrahim), listed Feng's crimes in Gansu and denounced him in the most militant terms: "in the interests of both the nation and of self-defense, we rise as one to condemn [Feng]. We Muslims, in serried ranks 500,000 strong, will summon our strength and struggle onward, confronting the guns and cannons with our flesh and blood."[9]

This was a sharp rebuke to Feng Yuxiang, but it was by no means a vote of confidence in Jin Shuren. The view of Li Qian and Ding Xicheng—that Nationalist China's vision of five races in harmony entailed an autonomous Muslim territorial unit in northwest China—was probably widely held among Chinese-speaking Muslims who followed national politics. With any immediate GMD push into Xinjiang now looking unlikely, local Dungan leaders were obliged to look elsewhere for support for such autonomy. In early 1930, Kashgar Circuit Commissioner (now known officially as "chief administrator" [xingzhengzhang]) Ma Shaowu approached the Soviet consul with a request for arms, offering to root out Basmachi holdouts in the surrounds of Kashgar, but also expressing his desire to create a new Muslim province centered on Kashgar, stating that the Soviets would thereby obtain in the Tarim Basin "what the Japanese have in Manchuria." The NKID rejected the proposal, but a few weeks later, when Ma's officials were caught in Tashkent trying to buy arms on the black market, the Soviets seized the opportunity. In return for concealing the arrests from Ürümchi, Tashkent demanded the opening of new border crossings and extensive trading privileges in Kashgar.[10]

This incident gives a clear indication of Soviet priorities in Xinjiang, which were focused on obtaining a more extensive trade deal with Xinjiang so as to secure the province as a reliable base of raw materials in the event of war with Britain and its allies. A week after Ma's emissary was caught in Tashkent, a high-level NKID meeting held on the Turkistan-Siberia railway resolved to strengthen ties with Jin Shuren, permitting the sale of arms to Ürümchi in return for trading rights.[11] It took a further eighteen months of diplomacy to seal the deal, and in October 1931, Jin signed the secret "Agreement on Economic Relations between the Government of Xinjiang Province and the USSR."

The Hami Uprising and the Mongols

Yang Zengxin ruled Xinjiang through a carefully constructed patrimonial network among the province's non-Chinese elite, a set of constituencies that he kept in check by never allowing a single one of them to provide his sole base of support. The Russian mystic Nicholas Roerich met Yang in 1926 and marveled at his ability to manipulate the locals: "sometimes he calls into life the Dungans; now the Moslems; again the Kalmucks and then the Kirghiz."[12] By the time of his assassination, though, these tactics were reaching the end of their effectiveness. Wary of relying on Dungan support since the mid-1920s, Yang turned to the province's Mongols, garrisoning his eastern front with Torghud cavalry from Qarashahr.[13] Yet complications soon emerged in this Mongol policy, as conflict in the Altay saw troops from the Mongolian People's Republic probing Xinjiang's defenses. To prevent the possibility of local Mongols linking up with these raids, Yang leant toward the Kazakhs of the Altay, arming them to repel the Mongol incursions. When American explorer Owen Lattimore crossed from Inner Mongolia into Xinjiang in 1927, he witnessed bands of gun-toting Kazakhs moving south toward Gansu and Qinghai.[14] The arming of the Kazakhs in turn led to conflict among rival members of the Kerey Kazakh aristocracy, which threatened to spread from the Altay south to the Tianshan.[15]

The corollary of Yang's "ethno-elitist" approach to Xinjiang (to borrow Justin Jacobs's term) was his strong opposition to the Nationalists' land reclamation and colonization policies in frontier regions. At Yang's death, incoming deputy provincial chairman Liu Wenlong penned a letter to Nanjing, in which he argued for a continuation of Yang's policies and warned against any steps that could antagonize the province's non-Chinese aristocracy. "Lands that have long belonged to the nomadic Mongols and Kazakhs still belong to the Mongols and

Kazakhs," he cautioned, "and no matter what, we cannot confiscate them in the face of opposition, and forcefully convert them into agricultural land."[16] Yet Chairman Jin was committed to the Nationalist approach of homogenizing, and in effect sinicizing, the administration of China's periphery. In 1929–1930 he set about dismantling residual Qing institutions among Xinjiang's nomadic groups, appointing Chinese officials to the Ili Valley and downgrading the position of the Ili garrison commissioner. These policies were not to the liking of the district's Kirghiz, Kazakhs, and Mongols.[17] In the case of the Kerey Kazakhs in the Altay, the Kazakh *wang*s were strong enough to expel the Chinese, but in Qarashahr the local Torghud Mongols were compelled to "petition" for the appointment of provincial officials, which proceeded without a hitch.[18] Pushing ahead with the policy, in 1930 Jin abolished the Hami *wang* administration and set about dividing the fiefdom into counties, imposing new taxes, and resettling poor Chinese immigrants from Gansu in the oasis. This proved to be a step too far, and in early 1931 the local Muslim population took up arms in revolt.

What little we know of the Hami rebel camp suggests that it was home to a mix of political tendencies, including Hami aristocrats seeking to restore their hereditary rights, but also men with Jadidist backgrounds and/or pro-Soviet inclinations. It is probably unwise to assign political distinctions too much weight at this early stage in events; the immediate question for the rebels was how to obtain the necessary arms and ammunition to resist Ürümchi's reprisals. The uprising initially looked to Gansu, inviting the incursion of Dungan troops of the Nationalist army's 36th Division, led by a charismatic young officer named Ma Zhongying. This alliance inflicted a series of defeats on the provincial army in the summer and fall of 1931, before Ma was injured in a clash with Jin Shuren's White Russian mercenaries and withdrew to Gansu.

As winter set in, the rebels took refuge in the mountains north of Hami. From there, it was only a short journey to the Mongolian People's Republic, where they next looked for support. A Kazakh from the town of Barköl named Qasim, who may have been an employee of Mongolia's national minorities bureau, acted as the initial go-between in this relationship.[19] This led to Mongolia dispatching a fact-finding mission to the rebels, which crossed into Xinjiang in December 1931. The Mongolian agent entrusted with this mission was none other than Lavaryn Demberel, the same revolutionary who had traveled to the Ili Valley ten years earlier and had accompanied Abdullah Rozibaqiev and Qadir Haji to the 1922 Comintern Congress in Moscow.[20]

By the time Demberel and his party arrived, leadership of the uprising had fallen to a man named Khoja Niyaz Haji, a well-traveled Hami native who had previously been in the service of the Hami Wang. Demberel did not reveal his mission at first, arousing suspicions that he was a Chinese spy. When his purpose eventually became known, some expressed opposition to collaborating with the Mongols, having heard disturbing reports of political conditions in Communist Mongolia. Nevertheless, Demberel won Khoja Niyaz Haji's trust and eventually presented an offer of military support. Early in the new year, the Mongol emissary returned to Ulaanbaatar, taking with him a trio of Muslims from Hami, Turfan, and Kashgar. The party reached the capital in March 1932 and delivered an appeal for arms and military counsel signed by Khoja Niyaz Haji and the leaders of the insurrection.[21]

The turn to Mongolia obliged Khoja Niyaz Haji to depict his uprising in terms most likely to win Communist backing. Instead of presenting the revolt as a Muslim undertaking, the Hami leaders described it as a national uprising of the "Chantou peoples." Khoja Niyaz Haji introduced himself as the "head of the Central Committee of the Chantou People's Republic" (*Chanto khalqlarning jumhūriyatkhananing töfäyerining bashliqi*), and Demberel's reports concurred in depicting the rebels as a revolutionary party-in-formation. The letter described a network of contacts reaching as far as Kashgar and Khotan and referred to the Torghud Mongols in Qarashahr as allies.[22] It made only cursory reference to the Dungan incursion of 1931 and hinted at bad blood between the two groups, complaining that Ma Zhongying had carried off the Hami partisans' arms and ammunition and abandoned them to Jin Shuren's counterattack.

Khoja Niyaz Haji's appeal to Mongolia bore fruit, and in April 1932 Demberel and Qasim coordinated a shipment of weapons, uniforms, and cash to Hami. Not surprisingly, many have seen in this the direct hand of Moscow. It seems the Hami representatives did meet with Comintern officials along the way, but conclusive proof of Moscow's involvement is lacking. Galindeviin Myagmarsambuu's account, based on Mongolian archives, describes only the Mongol People's Revolutionary Party secretaries Shijee and Genden as approving the arms shipment, allowing for the possibility that the Mongolian Communists were acting independently.[23] The negotiations for aid took place during a wave of anti-Communist uprisings across Mongolia, which were subsequently blamed on the Comintern's "leftist" errors. In mid-1932, all Comintern representatives were withdrawn from the country, signaling the end of Comintern activities in Mongolia. Unfortunately for the rebels in Hami, the 1932 uprisings also ruled out any possibility of ongoing support for those fighting in Xinjiang. The turn toward more cautious policies in Mongolia would leave no room for dangerous cross-border operations in Chinese territory.

South Turkistan Autonomy and the East Turkistan Republic

In the spring of 1932, Ma Zhongying's deputy Ma Shiming led units of the 36th Division back to Xinjiang, restoring a tentative alliance with local Muslims. Bolstered by the new arrivals, Khoja Niyaz Haji evicted provincial troops from Hami, but insisted on consolidating his position in Hami first, before heading west. This led to a falling-out between him and Ma Shiming, who marched on the Turfan oasis in December 1932. The arrival of the Dungans in Turfan coincided with a series of uprisings in the region. The Turfan uprising was led by Khoja Niyaz Haji's collaborator Mahmud Muhiti, scion of a wealthy local family who ran a cotton business with Soviet Russia and had a Jadidist pedigree stretching back twenty years. Ma Shiming assigned the leaders of these local uprisings ranks in the 36th Division, placing them nominally within the Nationalist Army command. In Turfan, Mahmud Muhiti became Mahmud Shizhang (division commander), and the *beg* of Bügür, Temür, became Temür Lüzhang (brigade commander). By January 1933, most of the Turfan oasis was in rebel hands.

Events to the south prompted a changing of the guard in the capital. In the early days of the rebellion, Jin Shuren had relied on provincial troops and White Russian mercenaries, but in early 1933 the Soviets repatriated into Xinjiang around ten thousand Chinese soldiers who had fled into Soviet territory from fighting the Japanese in Manchuria. Locals referred to these newcomers as the Red Beards—the same name given to Chinese bandits that roamed the Russia-China frontier. The arrival of the Red Beards turned the tide in Ürümchi's favor and coincided with a breakdown of relations between Ma Shiming and the Turki rebels in Turfan. A campaign led by a Red Beard officer named Sheng Shicai soon restored provincial authority in the Turfan oasis. Yet despite this success, Governor Jin's troops lacked faith in his ability to defeat the insurrection, and in April 1933 his White Russian recruits, supported by the Red Beards, turned on him and carried out a coup. In his place, they installed Yang

Zengxin's close associate, Liu Wenlong, as acting provincial chairman, but real power fell into the hands of Sheng Shicai.

Driven out of Turfan, some of Khoja Niyaz Haji's allies headed south. Temür Lüzhang's militia was reinforced by Dungans recruited from the town of Qarashahr, led by Ma Shiming's deputy, Ma Zhancang. This gave these two men sufficient strength to seize Kucha and Korla and set out toward Kashgar. As Temür and Ma Zhancang descended from the north, Kashgar Circuit Commissioner Ma Shaowu adopted two strategies to ward off the rebels, both of which backfired. One was to commission a Kirghiz militia under an officer named Osman Ali, who belonged to the border guard stationed to the city's west. Unfortunately for Ma Shaowu, when these Kirghiz were dispatched to confront Temür and Ma Zhancang's troops, they switched sides and joined the rebels.[24] Ma Shaowu's second move was to broaden the base of his administration. At the end of April 1933, he convened a new municipal council (*shanghui*), with Umar Akhunbayev as chairman. (One witness says that Ma Shaowu actually tried to resign his position and appoint Umar Akhunbayev as circuit commissioner.)[25] Instead of organizing the defense of the city, though, the Kashgari assembly decided to send a party out to greet the advancing coalition.

In terms of Kashgar's Old City politics, Temür Beg's arrival was a victory for the Artush faction, led by a man named Noruz Bay, who had established contact with Khoja Niyaz Haji as early as the spring of 1932. Temür and Noruz Bay founded a new political party calling itself Liberation of East Turkistan and abolished Umar Akhunbayev's municipal council. In its place they organized a new assembly, to be chaired by Noruz Bay, which announced itself as the National Islamic Council of Kashgar. It did not prove easy to marginalize the Kashgar old guard, however, and Temür's group soon fell apart. In its place a combined local assembly was established, dominated by the Akhunbayev faction but including supporters of Noruz Bay and representatives of the Kirghiz.[26]

Tensions remained high among the various militias in Kashgar. Osman Ali's Kirghiz had entered Kashgar first, and set about plundering Chinese property. These attacks on Chinese antagonized the Dungans, but Temür Beg took a position of neutrality toward them, which led in turn to conflict between the Dungans and the Kashgaris in the Old City. In the wake of renewed street fighting, a tentative accord was reached between the parties, with Temür appointed commander-in-chief, Osman his deputy, and a pair of circuit commissioners: Yunus Beg Saidi (1902–1938) and Su Jinshou. The former was a graduate of Ürümchi's Institute of Russian, Law, and Politics and an ally of Temür from

Turfan; the latter was Ma Zhancang's chief of staff. Both were Russian speakers, and both expressed an intention to carry out Guomindang policy in Kashgar.[27] Local Jadidists such as Qutluq Haji Shawqi, who twenty years earlier had corresponded with Ismail Gasprinskii about the need to develop local publishing, hijacked the Swedish mission's printing press and started publishing a paper called *Life of East Turkistan*. As Temür's organ it held a pro-Khoja Niyaz Haji position, lauding him as a warrior for the faith.

Meanwhile, a party of survivors from Turfan had regrouped with Khoja Niyaz Haji in Hami, including the cotton entrepreneur Mahmud Muhiti. In April, Khoja Niyaz led his troops back to the Turfan oasis, making rapid headway during the coup in Ürümchi. For the time being, a semblance of unity among the province's rebels held. In June, they wrote to the Administrative Yuan in Nanjing, announcing themselves as the "Xinjiang Citizens Revolutionary Army" and defending their actions as a justified response to Jin Shuren's tyranny.[28] Khoja Niyaz Haji was among the signatories to the letter, as were the two newly appointed Kashgar circuit commissioners. At its head, though, with the title of commander-in-chief, was the heir to the *wang*'s fiefdom in Hami, Bashir. Two other provincial aristocrats were listed as division commanders, giving the revolutionary army a decidedly restorative coloring: Iskandar in Turfan, whose family's hereditary title of *wang* had just been abolished, along with the *wang* of Kucha. To secure the Kucha *wang*'s collaboration, Khoja Niyaz Haji signed off on a series of conditions according the aristocrat civil authority in Kucha and surrounding counties.[29]

Although the rebels seemed on the verge of taking Ürümchi, Khoja Niyaz Haji's united front with the Dungans was on shaky foundations. Conspicuously missing from the signatories to this letter to Nanjing was Ma Zhongying, who was now approaching the provincial capital from the east, sweeping along the flank of the Tianshan. Seeking to drive a wedge between the factions, Ürümchi initially contacted Ma Zhongying, offering him military supremacy in the Tarim Basin. Khoja Niyaz Haji's anxieties about Ma's ambitions were compounded by conflicts surrounding arms and ammunition, which was in desperately short supply among the rebels. This discord eventually led to a severing of ties between the Muslim leaders. Capitalizing on the breach, Sheng now entered into negotiations with Khoja Niyaz Haji. In June, a party of Sheng's representatives—including Muslims in Sheng's service but also Chen Deli, who after lengthy diplomatic service in Soviet Turkistan had now been appointed Sheng's head of foreign affairs—met with Khoja Niyaz in the town of Fukang to Ürümchi's north. As recorded by Khoja Niyaz's secretary, Hamidullah Tur-fani, the Fukang accord provided for the partition of Xinjiang into north and south, with Hami, Turfan, and the south to be administered by local Muslims. On this basis Khoja Niyaz signed off on the deal, and on his way south he received Soviet arms and sent representatives to Tashkent for talks. By July, Khoja Niyaz was signing himself as the "Head of the Local Government of South Turkistan" (*Janūbī Türkistān yerlik ḥukūmat bashliqi*).[30]

Khoja Niyaz Haji's decision to break with Ma Zhongying was unpopular among his allies in the province's aristocratic milieu, who had close ties to Chinese politics and were in favor of collaboration with the Dungans. These included men such as Yolbars Beg, the Hami *wang*'s majordomo (*ordabegi*), who professed in his memoirs to be horrified at the thought of enlisting Communist support, and now set himself up independently in Hami. The Turfan *wang*, too, lent support to Ma Zhongying.[31] Prominent voices among Xinjiang's Soviet émigrés also sided with the Dungans. In his memoirs Alikhan Törä, who was living in Ghulja when the revolt broke out, glorifies Ma Zhongying and mourns the fact that Khoja Niyaz Haji's allies failed to keep faith with him. Yet Dungan ambitions in Xinjiang, as we have seen, left little room for the intellectuals and entrepreneurs represented by Khoja Niyaz Haji and his network. These were people whose own fate was tied to the Soviet Union in various ways (many had spent time there in the 1920s) and who now decided to bind the province to it, too.

The events in the north had serious repercussions in Kashgar, as the ruling triumvirate of Osman, Temür, and Ma Zhancang fell out among themselves. Osman withdrew to the mountains, where his ranks were gradually swelled by anti-Soviet Basmachi fighters, along with a more recent influx of Kirghiz refugees from Soviet Kirghizstan, where collectivization policies were provoking violent opposition.[32] Ex-circuit commissioner Ma Shaowu now found common cause with Ma Zhancang, and the two withdrew south to Kashgar's New City. Luring Temür out of Kashgar, Ma Zhancang succeeded in capturing and executing him, leaving the seat of authority in the Old City vacant.

To Kashgar's south, meanwhile, a new rebellion had erupted in Khotan. There, the mobilization was led by a group of self-styled amirs, who advocated the founding of an independent Muslim Republic. These men took control of Khotan in February 1933 and dispatched troops westward toward Yarkand. They also sent Sabit Damolla, a respected Islamic scholar, to Kashgar for talks. As Temür Beg's star faded in the Old City, the Khotan amirs stepped in to fill the gap, and a new coalition developed around Sabit Damolla. His support rested on part of Temür's faction, sections of the Kirghiz, along with a new set of Turkish-educated nationalists who had recently arrived in Kashgar to join in the uprising. These included locals such as the poet Muhammad Ali (Mämtili) Effendi from Artush, as well as émigrés from Soviet Central Asia and Turkey, who founded the "Independence" (Istiqlal) Association.[33] In November, the Independence Association announced the formation of the East Turkistan Republic (ETR), with Sabit Damolla as its prime minister. In a surprising step, they appointed Khoja Niyaz Haji, who was then in Aqsu and theoretically aligned with Ürümchi (and by extension with the Soviets), as president in absentia.

In insisting on the ETR's independent and Islamic character, the Independence Association went well beyond the autonomous "South Turkistan" envisaged in the Fukang accords. The multinational composition of the Independence Association has led scholars to describe the ETR as a sharp turn to pan-Islamist or pan-Turkist politics in Kashgar, though in its composition the ETR exhibited significant continuity with local reform efforts of the past.[34] The ETR's minister of education, for example, was Abdulkarim Khan Makhdum (or Makhsum), who twenty years earlier had helped found the Society to Promote Education that had sought to establish Jadidist schools in Kashgar.[35] The minister of finance was a member of the Musabayev family. There was some continuity, too, with Temür Beg's short-lived administration. On receiving the invitation to serve as president, Khoja Niyaz Haji requested that the ETR appoint Temür's circuit commissioner, Yunus Saidi, to the position of interior minister. Given these continuities, it is not hard to see why Khoja Niyaz Haji chose to assume the presidency. He must have realized the risks but still hoped to steer developments in a direction likely to win Soviet backing.

If this was Khoja Niyaz Haji's strategy, he was soon to be disappointed. Shortly after he reached Kashgar the president was summoned to a meeting with Soviet officials at the Irkeshtam pass, where they upbraided him and instructed him to prove his reliability by seizing the ETR's anti-Soviet prime minister, Sabit Damolla. Finding himself caught between a rock and a hard place, Khoja Niyaz Haji obliged and rendered the prime minister up to his executioners.[36]

A Uyghur Rebellion?

These transient political formations left little written record of themselves, and it is hard to delve much deeper than the political narrative I have provided here. Yet for the purposes of this book it is necessary to ask what role, if any,

Uyghur nationalist politics played in these events. As we have seen, the first political statements to emerge from the uprising adopted traditional terminology. The Hami rebels announced themselves to the Mongolian People's Republic as representatives of the "Chantou" (Turban-Wearing) peoples, speaking for a "Chantou People's Republic." Chantou, of course, was the Qing designation for Xinjiang's Turkic-speaking Muslims, and it was also the name by which Muslims from Xinjiang were known in Mongolia. This fact may have influenced the choice of terminology, but just as likely the Hami rebels were comfortable with this self-designation.

In raising the rebel flag, Khoja Niyaz Haji and his allies needed unambiguous terms, and "Uyghur" was not yet a popular rallying point. In Xinjiang, the connotations of "Uyghur" were primarily political, not national. A vivid illustration of this is given in a story from the mid-1920s by Nazarkhoja Abdusamadov, in which he imagines two old men discussing politics in the Kashgar bazaar. Although a fictional interaction, it gives us a good sense of what the word "Uyghur" actually meant in Xinjiang:

> Tell me, what's the news?
> There's uproar in the bazaar!
> Why? What's going on?
> Right now nothing much. But there are rumors going round that the Uyghurs are about to rise up.
> Why would they rise up? Surely not!
> No, it seems to be true, my friend. The short-shirts have got very active lately.
> Those short-shirts still haven't come to their senses. In Tsar Nicholas's day they couldn't sit still in Central Asia. Since the Bolsheviks have come along they're still being stubborn. They don't get along with any of them! Well, the Bolsheviks gave them what they deserved. So they've forgotten that already!
> I know what you mean. But who are these "Uyghurs" anyway?
> The "Uyghurs" are these short-shirts we're talking about.

When Abdusamadov's collaborator Zarif Bashiri published a Tatar translation of this story in 1931, he had to add a footnote here explaining that "among the Uyghurs of Chinese Turkistan, the idea that 'we're Uyghurs' is not widespread, instead they say 'we're Muslim.' Because it was the Jadidists and nationalists who discovered the fact that they were Uyghurs, they call Jadidists and national revolutionaries 'Uyghurs.'"[37] Of course, by now the prerevolutionary short-shirts were mostly card-carrying Communists, and not surprisingly the Soviet consul in Kashgar observed in 1931 that "in Xinjiang the word 'Uyghur' is almost identical with the word Bolshevik."[38]

This does not mean, though, that ideas of Uyghur nationhood, and of Uyghuristan, had no place in the uprising. In Jadidist circles in Xinjiang that looked to the Soviet Union for support, engagement with romantic invocations of Uyghur mytho-genealogy can indeed be found. The Turfan Jadidist Abdulkhaliq, who is said to have spent time in the Soviet Union in the mid-1920s, mimicked Nazarkhoja Abdusamadov in adopting "Uyghur" as his nom de plume and wrote poetry drawing on themes similar to the Uyghur Child, invoking Uyghur as the personified progenitor of his community. Abdulkhaliq's poem "Don't Want To" (*Istimäs*) mourned the fate of his community in these terms:

> Today not one of Ham's descendants [the Europeans] remains enslaved,
> Yet Uyghur's sons have never tried to understand why this is.
> They make themselves sick consuming poison, they are in grave danger,
> But even at death's door my people don't want to cure themselves.[39]

Such poems seem to have struck a chord locally. Legend has it that in Turfan in late 1932 Abdulkhaliq Uyghur wrote out on white sheets and hung up in the streets his poem "Awake!" (*Oyghan*), which begins "Awake poor Uyghur, you've slept long enough!"[40]

The Uyghur symbol's association with Soviet politics must have made some supporters of the East Turkistan Republic wary of it. In his inaugural speech, ETR prime minister Sabit Damolla proclaimed that "the blue flag with moon and star has been adopted for the whole of great Turkistan (*bütün ulugh Türkistan*)."[41] Certainly there were many in Kashgar who had an interest in emphasizing pan-Turkic or Muslim unity, most notably the émigrés from the Soviet Union. For these, maintaining a united front either with the Dungans or with the Kirghiz was essential to staving off a Red Xinjiang, and all that it would entail. In the ETR's journal *Independence*, Tughrul Beg Rahimi from Margilan, warned against division:

> Never call people "city-dweller," "Andijani," or "Kirghiz."
> We are all sons of the same father, and members of one nation.[42]

Yet the concept of Uyghur-as-descent (as opposed to Uyghur-as-nation) was by no means incompatible with such talk, and supporters of the ETR also made use of Uyghurist symbols. There was, it would seem, some confusion within the ETR as to the best name for the state: its coins were stamped either as the Republic of East Turkistan or the Republic of Uyghuristan.[43] The poet Muhammad Ali Effendi was among the students from Xinjiang who returned to Kashgar from Istanbul to greet the founding of the republic. His 1933 poem "We Are Uyghur's Children" (*Biz Uyghurning baliliri*), spoke in terms similar to those of Abdulkhaliq Uyghur:

> We are Uyghur's children, our hearts are bright.
> Glorious is the long road of life we have traveled.[44]

Many of these issues have been reinterpreted through the lens of conflicts that were yet to come, and we cannot be sure to what extent questions of identity divided the rebel camps. On this issue, Xinjiang was still a decade behind the Soviet Union, and in this sense the early 1930s in Xinjiang correspond to the early 1920s in the Soviet Union. Various parties to the conflict made use of romantic notions of Uyghur genealogy, or of Uyghuristan, but neither Khoja Niyaz Haji nor the Khotan rebels formulated their political claims in terms of the rights of the Uyghurs as a nation. Rhetoric of Turkic or Muslim unity, I suggest, should be seen as primarily expressing a political position within shifting coalitions of Dungans, locals, Kirghiz, émigrés, and Chinese, and not a theoretical stance on the ideal boundaries of the nation. That is to say, the time had not yet come when strictly defined national categories would form the basis for provincial politics. That time, however, was not far away. Just as 1924 and the national delimitation policy had seen a sharpening of these issues in the Soviet Union, 1934 would see them posed in a new way in Xinjiang.

The View from across the Border

By the early 1930s, contradictory trends were influencing Moscow's view of Xinjiang. On the one hand, the Comintern was now much more an instrument of Soviet state interests than it had been in the 1920s, giving the NKID the upper hand in policy deliberations. In Xinjiang policy this was confirmed in 1927 when the Politburo resolved to "orient to the mandarinate" in Ürümchi, leading to the roundup of the Uyghur Communists in Andijan. On the other hand, Chiang Kai-shek had severed ties between China and the Soviet Union, freeing the Bolsheviks to experiment with policy options that had previously been avoided for diplomatic reasons. One example of this newfound flexibility in China policy was a resolution from the Sixth Congress of the Chinese Communist Party, held mid-1928 in Moscow, "On the National Question in China." Here for the first time was recognized the existence of oppressed minorities in China deserving of the right to national self-determination. The resolution was tentatively worded, calling only for further discussion on the topic at the Seventh Congress (not held until 1945), and for this reason scholars have tended to see it as a dead letter. Yet while Chinese Communists showed little interest in investigating the issue further, Soviet experts on China deemed it a topic worthy of study.

Pavel Mif, a leading member of the Comintern Executive, was rector of the Communist University of the Toilers of China (KUTK, also known as Sun Yat-sen University). He also directed research on China in the Institute of Global Economy and Global Politics, part of Moscow's Communist Academy. Mif's Scientific Research Institute on China commenced work in 1931, just as the revolt in Hami was breaking out, and in its first year of existence it undertook two projects with significance for Xinjiang. One was to study the national composition of China, aiming at a comprehensive description of its non-Chinese nationalities. This ethnographic work was considered particularly urgent given the likelihood that Japan would push the Chinese resistance into the nation's southwest, known to be heavily populated by poorly studied national minorities.[45] The other undertaking involved fieldwork: a scientific expedition to the Sino-Soviet frontier in Central Asia to study the Xinjiang émigré population and its political orientation. In 1931 two parties set out toward Xinjiang—one to study the Dungans of Issiq Köl and Frunze, the other to work among Kashgari migrants in the Ferghana Valley. The research teams were tasked with investigating the socioeconomic motives for the migration, connections that migrants had with politics in Xinjiang, and factors that might be producing anti-Soviet sentiment among them. The mission to the Kashgaris was to be the first of three expeditions to the borders of Xinjiang in 1931, 1932, and 1933, each of which produced differing results and recommendations. These three expeditions allow us to trace the shifting Soviet position toward events across the border.

The motivation for these missions was a growing sense that the Xinjiang émigrés were hostile toward the Soviet Union—an impediment to influencing politics in China's west. The 1927 crackdown on the Uyghur Communists, it seems, had consequences for social conditions along the border. With many of those activists working among the Kashgari labor migration now purged, control of the labor supply was effectively handed to the *aqsaqal*s and Chinese consuls.[46] In Kashgar itself, Maks Dumpis's idea of cultivating support in the lower echelons of the bazaar had been abandoned, as the Soviets reached a modus vivendi with Umar Akhunbayev. In 1930 the Soviet consul in Ürümchi, Moisei Adolfovich Nemchenko, expressed his view that economic pursuits were compromising the Soviet Union's political interests: "Soviet organizations in western China are completely isolated from the local population," he wrote. "Trade is conducted exclusively with the colonizing group, which was established by the Qing and is artificially maintained by the local Chinese administration, which seeks thereby to isolate Soviet organizations from local national elements. As a result the local national groups, exploited by the Chinese and this colonial elite, redirect their dissatisfaction toward Soviet organizations and the system of Soviet trade."[47]

Having recently returned to Moscow from his posting as consul, it was Nemchenko who led the 1931 expedition. On this first trip, he focused on gaining a picture of the Tarim Basin's rural society and its class composition, but along the way he found serious shortcomings in the treatment of the Kashgari laborers on Soviet soil. He reported on these to the Central Asia Bureau in Tashkent, which passed a series of resolutions to improve the health and well-being of the Kashgari migrants, calling for more Red Teahouses, medical stations, and food distribution points along the roads that they traveled. When Nemchenko returned to Moscow he submitted his findings to the Comintern's Eastern Secretariat and also published a piece on Xinjiang in Pavel Mif's journal, *Problems of China*. Here he argued that the rebellion against Ürümchi was not only an anti-Chinese uprising, but had a progressive class dynamic to it: "the pauperized peasantry's bondage to the feudalist and exploiter is continually increasing and leads to the growth of an agrarian movement alongside the national-liberation movement."[48]

Nemchenko evidently succeeded in persuading Karl Bauman (1892–1937), head of the Central Asia Bureau, of his positive appraisal of the Hami uprising as a national-liberation struggle deserving of Soviet support. In September, Bauman submitted to Moscow a proposal to send Soviet-trained Communists into Xinjiang to direct the uprising, but when the Politburo discussed the plan, Lev Karakhan from the NKID intervened to block it.[49] At the Comintern, meanwhile, Pavel Mif was receiving reports that contradicted Nemchenko's version of events, and he remained unconvinced of the ex-consul's analysis. Mif and his fellow China specialists directed Nemchenko to conduct further investigations, recommending that he form a commission at the China Institute to study events in western China. The second member of the commission was to be P. I. Fesenko, a Xinjiang specialist at KUTV, who regularly participated in discussions on Xinjiang politics with the university's Kashgari students. The other two members were to be the Uyghur Communists Abdullah Rozibaqiev and Ismail Tairov. (At the time, Tairov was working in Moscow, while Rozibaqiev was still in Kazakhstan.)

While Nemchenko and Fesenko traveled back to Central Asia to meet the next wave of seasonal migrants in 1932, the Politburo continued its deliberations on Xinjiang. In June, the party leadership asked the NKID to propose directives for Xinjiang work, which were submitted and approved in August. While these directives ruled out raising anti-Chinese slogans and endorsed friendly relations with Jin Shuren in Ürümchi, they also entertained the possibility of decentralization and national territorial autonomy in Xinjiang, particularly "where there was no basis to fear the success of English or Japanese imperialism."[50]

That summer, researchers delved further into social and political conditions in Soviet territory than they had in 1931, studying the Red Teahouses and caravanserais, as well as local Uyghur Communist sections. I cannot confirm whether Nemchenko and Fesenko ever met with Rozibaqiev and Tairov, but the two Russians maintained a supportive stance toward the uprising in Xinjiang, a position that far exceeded the bounds set by the NKID. At the end of this second expedition, Nemchenko wrote to Georgi Safarov, head of the Eastern Secretariat of the Comintern, arguing for full support of the uprising and the need to create a popular-revolutionary party to lead it. He suggested a list of slogans for such a party, condemning imperialism and the Chinese bourgeoisie and envisaging Xinjiang as an independent people's republic with provision for national autonomy, linked to Outer Mongolia and the CCP's soviet bases in China. For the Dungans, whose militancy the NKID greatly feared, he raised the possibility of "unity with the revolutionary movement in Gansu." Meanwhile, Fesenko recruited a new batch of Kashgari students to take back to KUTV for training.

Nemchenko was evidently optimistic about events in Xinjiang, but what he discovered among the émigrés in 1932 was nothing short of scandalous. To secure the necessary labor supply, he found that Soviet officials were turning a blind eye to the highly exploitative conditions in which the Kashgaris lived and worked, and had effectively handed control of the labor supply to predatory Kashgari intermediaries. Nemchenko broke the migration into three phases. Roughly 90 percent undertook the journey between February and May, almost all on foot and often lacking sufficient supplies for the journey. Then, between May and June, when the workers had already earned some money, a wave of "exploiters" crossed from Xinjiang: moneylenders, money changers, gamblers, contrabandists, village officials, imams, mullas, and Sufi shaykhs.[51] Soviet institutions offered little in the way of protection. It was found that up to 80 percent of Kashgari migrants were staying in private caravanserais, where besides expensive accommodation they fell prey to these exploitative elements and exposed to anti-Soviet agitation.[52] This was not even the worst of it. It was found that many of the laborers were sent by "masters" in Xinjiang, usually a local *beg*, to whom they would hand over their earnings after returning to Kashgar.[53] To enforce this system, cooperatives and collective farms were tolerating the presence of Kashgari village heads, and even Chinese police, to monitor the workers. Nemchenko pinned the primary blame for these outrageous conditions on the recruiters, who collaborated with all manner of class enemies to meet their quotas, but also criticized local officials who had failed to act on previous instructions to improve conditions for the migrants.

In the fall, as parties of Kashgaris started dribbling back to Xinjiang in a disheveled state, Chinese officials were shocked at what they saw. Forbidden to transport silver out of the Soviet Union, the Kashgaris had been forced to convert their cash into textiles and shoes, which they bartered for bread along the way to Irkeshtam. As a sign of how far things had deteriorated, Kashgar Circuit Commissioner Ma Shaowu, a staunch reactionary in Soviet eyes, now rose to the defense of these Kashgari proletarians, many of whom were crossing back into Chinese territory after a season of work with nothing to show for it. In a protest note to the Soviet consul, which he must have taken great delight in writing, Ma Shaowu expressed his astonishment at these abuses, "for the Soviet Government has always upheld the principle that workers should enjoy special privileges." This was highly embarrassing for officials in Tashkent. NKID plenipotentiary Garegin Apresov called on the Workers and Peasants' Inspectorate to take "all measures to expose and punish those individuals who have twisted party directives and permitted the most outrageous treatment of the Kashgari workers."[54]

Such recriminations were an admission that anti-Soviet sentiment in Xinjiang was at least partly the fault of Soviet policy. Yet by now the official narrative on Xinjiang was moving in a different direction. Vague hints of contacts between Ma Zhongying and the Japanese, or between the Khotan rebels and the British, provided Soviet officials with an exculpatory account of the anti-Soviet mood that Nemchenko found among the Kashgaris. Despite the fact that the ETR failed to win recognition, let alone support, from any state in the world, the dominant Soviet analysis now emerging was that the rebellion was an imperialist plot. By the middle of 1933 the finger of blame for anti-Soviet sentiments among the Kashgaris in the Soviet Union was being pointed not at official wrongdoing but at the Uyghur Communists, who were thought to be in league with the rebels in Xinjiang. The summer of 1933 saw Nemchenko sidelined, and in his place a colleague from the Communist Academy, I. I. Akhmatov, led the expedition to the Ferghana Valley. This was no scientific expedition, but a political inquisition, interrogating almost two hundred Uyghur party members and assisted by the local OGPU wherever it went.

So far, the Soviet Uyghur press had been largely silent about the uprising. It was not until March 1932 that *Voice of the Poor* saw fit to report on it, describing it as if it were a peasant revolt in a far-off country, whose outcome had nothing to do with Soviet policy.[55] Yet despite the media blackout, rumors flowed freely across the border, and events were discussed widely among Uyghurs in Soviet territory. As one put it, "when four or five Uyghurs get together in the evening for tea or *laghman* [a noodle dish], they traverse the whole of Xinjiang, from Ürümchi to Kashgar."[56] As the official line shifted in 1933, and the Soviet press started denouncing the uprising as an imperialist plot, cross-border Uyghur Communist links continued to give Uyghur party members confidence to express solidarity with the uprising, as this transcript of an OGPU interview from August 1933 shows:

> **Baratov (Uyghur):** Previously I never thought that in such a backward country, such a great mass of people was capable of rising up in revolt.
>
> **Rahmatov (OGPU):** How do you know about the uprisings?
>
> **B:** I know about it from the newspapers.
>
> **R:** And what is written in the newspapers?
>
> **B:** The newspapers say that the movement is developing, and that England and Japan are leading it.

R: Is it possible, in your opinion, to say in relation to its internal class dynamics that this movement has some kind of revolutionary perspective, and what are these perspectives?

B: Right now it's hard to say about perspectives, the movement is still very young. But among the rebels there's a bourgeois-democratic tendency, and there are, without question, leftist tendencies. They are led by students and others who ran away from here, who lived in Soviet territory for a long time. Among them are Shamsuddinov, a KUTV student and teacher in Andijan. He stands at the head of a sizeable armed force in Kashgar. Even if at present he is yet to achieve his goals, I'm sure that in the future he will implement his plan. Undoubtedly there are signs of national liberation appearing in the movement. This can be seen from the fact that the Chinese regime has been overthrown and has passed into Uyghur hands.

R: If this is, as you say, a national-liberation movement, then how does it struggle with imperialism?

B: The question of the struggle with imperialism has not yet been posed.

R: If this tendency, as you say, is bourgeois-democratic, then I am interested as to how it deals with the land question.

B: The land question, as far as I know, has not yet been raised.

R: See how it works out with you. A bourgeois-democratic movement, but without posing the agrarian question. A national-liberation movement that doesn't carry on a struggle with imperialism and doesn't orient to the USSR. Let me ask you another question: what is the nature of this movement—reactionary or revolutionary?

B: The leadership of the movement is still for the feudalists. But you can't call the movement reactionary. There are representatives of leftist tendencies within it. These leftist tendencies have not yet consolidated themselves, but I'm sure that they will fulfill their plans.[57]

As the interviewee frankly explained, the crackdown on Uyghur Communists had indeed driven a number of activists back into Xinjiang. Qadir Akhun Shamsuddinov, who had studied in Vernyi before the revolution and then at KUTV, was not the only runaway seeking to put his Soviet training into practice during the rebellion.[58] According to the Soviet consul in Kashgar, a former Musabayev employee and a one-time editor of *Liberation* named Khudaberdi

Baqiev arrived in town in 1930 claiming to have been sent by the Comintern and advocating the formation of a Communist cell. Other dissident Uyghur Communists active in Xinjiang included KUTV alumnus Abdumumin Hasanhajiev, purged from the party in 1927, and who came to Kashgar via Ghulja in 1929.[59]

Yet any "leftist" tendencies, such as they were, had little role left to play in what was rapidly turning into a test of military strength. A few weeks after this interview, the Politburo decided to dispatch two Red Army divisions to Xinjiang to defend Sheng Shicai in Ürümchi. The Soviet divisions reached Xinjiang's capital in January 1934, just in time to repel an assault of Ma Zhongying's Dungans by strafing and dropping poison gas on his columns on the outskirts of the city. Suffering heavy losses, Ma Zhongying turned south toward Kashgar and Khoja Niyaz Haji's fragile East Turkistan Republic. At this point, Khoja Niyaz might have expected that the Soviets would intervene to halt the advancing Ma Zhongying, but they let the Dungans sack Kashgar and bring to an end the brief existence of the ETR, seizing the city in the name of the Guomindang. Then, in a bizarre turn of events, and one yet to be fully explained, Ma Zhongying went to a meeting at the Irkeshtam crossing and vanished into the Soviet Union. Khoja Niyaz Haji left for Ürümchi to take up his new role as deputy chairman of Xinjiang Province. He left his second-in-command, Mahmud Muhiti, in Kashgar's Old City, while Chinese forces loyal to Sheng took up residence in the New City.

Sheng Shicai and the Uyghur Minzu

By 1935, a tenuous alliance held throughout much of the province between regional leaders nominally loyal to Sheng Shicai and Khoja Niyaz Haji in Ürümchi. In Kashgar, Mahmud Muhiti cobbled together a new administration known as the National Assembly, which made schooling one of its top priorities. In Ghulja, the leading Muslim official was Turdi Akhun Almasbekov, the one-time *aqsaqal* in Toqmaq who had since prospered doing business with the Soviets.[60] One of the original Hami rebels of 1931, Yolbars Khan, presided in Hami. The only oasis in open defiance of Ürümchi was Khotan, occupied by the remaining Dungans of Ma Zhongying's 36th Division. Rather than dislodge them by force, Soviet negotiators hoped to persuade the 36th Division to break with the GMD and side with Sheng Shicai. Ma Zhongying, it seems, was being held hostage on the outskirts of Moscow to this end.[61]

The glue that held this coalition in place were the Soviet-trained Communists—Russians, Chinese, and locals—who supervised much of Sheng's bureaucracy and military. The first cohort, consisting of some twenty individuals, arrived in 1933 with the initial Soviet pact with Sheng. While outwardly they were assigned to local officials in an advisory capacity, there is little doubt that they were often the dominant partners in such pairings. One of these was Mansur Effendi (Mashur Ruziev) from Kazakhstan, who was assigned to Khoja Niyaz Haji. A second group accompanied the Red Army intervention, forming the Border Affairs Bureau. As Sheng consolidated his position, a new police force was set up introducing the efficient methods of the Stalinist OGPU to the towns and villages of Xinjiang. Guided initially by a Russian, Pagodin, this organization evolved from a small intelligence unit into the Xinjiang Provincial Public Security Bureau (PSB), many of whose posts were filled by returnees from the Soviet Union. When Pagodin left Xinjiang, the Comintern sent the Chinese Communist Zeng Xiufu (code name: Kalashnikov) to serve as the province's PSB chief.[62] Many of these individuals were unknown quantities, but not in Kashgar. There, the man responsible for introducing the new political policing was the Kashgari Communist Qadir Haji, who now set foot in Xinjiang again for the first time in more than fifteen years. It was, in a sense, the realization of Qadir Haji's ambition to return to Xinjiang on Soviet instructions, though he can hardly have relished doing so under a Chinese warlord in Ürümchi.

On consolidating his position in Ürümchi, Sheng Shicai eschewed Sun Yat-sen's Three People's Principles in favor of his own Eight Great Proclamations of 1934 and the Nine Tasks of 1935, which were summed up in the Six Great Policies: anti-imperialism, peace, ethnic equality, clean government, construction, and friendship with the Soviet Union. These six policies were represented as a six-pointed star on the new flag Sheng created for the province and in the name of his intelligence service, the Six Star Society. As the regime grew in confidence, the mutiny of April 1933 that had installed Sheng in Ürümchi was upgraded to the status of a "revolution," to be celebrated by annual commemorative rallies. In April 1934, however, ongoing fighting meant that the first of these celebrations was poorly attended. Another rally was held on August 1 in Ürümchi to toast the new regime, the Congress on the Anniversary of Xinjiang's Peaceful Unification. This meeting launched the Xinjiang Anti-Imperialist Union, which would serve as the coordinating body for most of Sheng's political campaigns.[63]

On the issue of ethnic equality, Sheng and his advisers were not inclined to recognize any form of territorial autonomy, opting instead for a scheme of cultural autonomy, implemented through a set of organizations representing each of the province's various nationalities. Apart from promoting Sheng's policies and anti-imperialist work, these were assigned the tasks of developing schools and libraries, publishing periodicals, and raising the province's cultural level. On August 5, 1934, under the auspices of the Anti-Imperialist Union, the Uyghur Enlightenment Association was born.[64] According to official figures, by 1936 the Uyghur Enlightenment Association had eight regional branches, forty-one county branches, and twenty-three village branches. Alongside it there gradually came into being a Hui Association, a Mongol Association (which in 1938 split into Mongol and Sibe-Solon-Manchu associations), as well as Kazakh-Kirghiz, Uzbek, and Chinese associations, and in Ghulja, Tatar and Russian associations.[65] While in some ways reminiscent of the Austro-Marxist approach to nationalities policy, the enlightenment associations also invoked the Soviet goal of fostering national culture within strictly defined political limits. Here, instead of Stalin's prescription of "national in form, socialist in content," the content of the enlightenment association national cultures was to conform to Sheng's Six Great Policies.[66] Echoing the paradox implicit in Soviet nationalities policy, the constitution of the enlightenment associations explained that the goal of promoting particular national cultures was ultimately to transcend national boundaries, that is, "to remove the barriers between nationalities and national cultures and create a common culture."[67]

The founding of the Uyghur Enlightenment Association preceded any official revision of the province's categories of nationality. While the concept of the enlightenment association came from the Soviet Union, its specifically "Uyghur" brand was the brainchild of intellectuals in Ürümchi such as Yunus Saidi from Turfan, a survivor of the ETR who was now working in Sheng's administration. Burhan Shahidi, the Tatar businessman who held a leading position in the Anti-Imperialist Union, describes discussions with Yunus on the need for Sheng's administration to replace the Chinese term "Chantou" with "Uyghur."[68] The Uyghur Enlightenment Association sent a petition to Sheng to this effect, and the proposal was approved at a meeting of the Anti-Imperialist Union.[69] In doing so, for the first time in history Ürümchi endorsed the idea of a Uyghur nation in Xinjiang.

The question now arose as to how to write "Uyghur" in Chinese, as no standard transcription existed and a variety of forms were in circulation (e.g.,

畏兀爾, 威吾兒, or 威吾爾, all representing *weiwuer*).[70] This was a potentially sensitive issue, and not simply a question for linguists. Throughout Chinese history, the transcription of ethnonyms into Chinese has been manipulated to add connotations to the name itself. At the meeting of the Anti-Imperialist Union, for example, some argued in favor of 威武爾, the first two characters of which mean "powerful." Sheng Shicai personally vetoed this transcription as connoting "an exaggerated sense of self-esteem."[71] Another Chinese participant in the meeting proposed 維吾爾, arguing that it stood for defense (*wei* 維) of the motherland, and collectivity (*wu* 吾—an archaic first-person pronoun). He suggested that the three characters expressed the meaning that "we are a big family, that all of Xinjiang's nationalities are united in harmony, they will defend and develop Xinjiang together, and drive out the imperialists and liberate China." This was a stretch of linguistic imagination, but his arguments carried the day, and the official transcription of "Uyghur" was fixed.

The adoption of the new category of nationality was first decreed in December 1934 and publicized in April 1935 at the Second Congress of People's Representatives in Ürümchi, which drew delegates from across Xinjiang.[72] Kashgar's chief qadi, Abdulghafur Damolla, spoke from the platform, citing from the Quran and hadith to legitimize collaboration with Ürümchi. As was typical of discourse during the Sheng period, the recognition, even celebration, of nationality went hand in hand with a stern warning against nationalism: "Don't go around causing trouble by saying 'so-and-so's a Uyghur,' 'so-and-so's a Mongol,' or 'so-and-so's Chinese.'" While the Soviet inspiration for the new nationalities policy was evident, Abdulghafur cautioned that Sheng would not be implementing the nativization (*korenizatsiia*) of provincial administration. "Just because you make up 90 percent of the population of Xinjiang," he told delegates, "don't think that positions will be given to you proportionally. The positions will go to those who study and serve the government."[73]

The congress declared Xinjiang to be home to fourteen nationalities, or *minzu* in Chinese—a considerable increase over the five races for the whole of China posited by the Guomindang. Small Tungusic-speaking groups of Solon and Sibe became *minzu* in their own right. The province's Mongols were combined into one group, with the exception of the Daurs of the Ili Valley. Immigrant Tatars, Uzbeks, and Russians were classified among the province's nationalities, as were Chinese. Ethnic distinctions within the "Muslims" were teased out into the Chinese-speaking Dungan (Hui), the linguistically Iranian Tajiks of the Pamirs, and the Turkic-speaking Kirghiz, Kazakh, and Uyghurs.

Left to right: Provincial Chairman Li Rong; director of the Provincial Bank Xu Lian; Sheng Shicai; and Diplomatic Office and Finance Department head Chen Deli at the Second Congress of People's Representatives, Ürümchi, April 1935. (Russian State Archive of Socio-Political History 532/4/333.)

So far this conformed to existing Soviet classifications; but there was one obvious exception: the Taranchis were also recognized as one of Xinjiang's fourteen official *minzu*.

The retention of the Taranchis shows that nationality policy in Xinjiang cannot simply be thought of as a carbon copy of Soviet classifications. By now, the notion of a distinct Taranchi nationality had been thoroughly criticized by Uyghur activists in the Soviet Union, and many have seen Sheng's decision to recognize the Taranchi as a *minzu* as evidence for his "divide-and-rule" policies. Yet there are several other factors to be taken into consideration. Officially, there was still ambiguity on this point in the Soviet Union, and it was not until the 1937 census that "Taranchi" and "Kashgari" were conclusively merged into the category of Uyghur. Ethnographic descriptions of Xinjiang available to the

Khoja Niyaz Haji at the Second Congress of People's Representatives, Ürümchi, April 1935. (Russian State Archive of Socio-Political History 532/4/333.)

Soviets tended to follow Kashgaris such as Qadir Haji in describing the Uyghurs of the south and the Taranchis of the north as two groups. A CCP report to the Comintern in 1930, for example, described the Taranchis as follows: "By nationality they belong to the Uyghurs, but while living in Ili for more than a hundred years they mixed with other peoples residing there, and since then consider themselves a distinct Taranchi nationality."[74]

The decision to recognize the Taranchis probably also reflected the prevailing mood among elites in Ghulja. In the years after the Russian Revolution, Ghulja had offered refuge to those who had rallied behind early efforts at Taranchi organizing in Semireche, most notably the Taranchi-Dungan Committee, whose leader Husayn Beg Yunusov had become a prominent publicist and politician in exile in Ghulja. Yunusov was among the Ghulja representatives at the Second Congress of People's Representatives and earned the nickname "Husayn Taran" for advocating the existence of a Taranchi nation.[75] Others representing Ghulja in Ürümchi included Hakimbeg Khoja, from the line of Qing aristocrats in Ili who had been restored to the position when the Russians withdrew in the 1880s. Men such as Hakimbeg Khoja must have been highly suspicious of the political motives behind the idea of a Uyghur nation and the Soviet regime in which it had emerged. They had little to gain, moreover, from collapsing the Taranchis into the province's Uyghur population. With the political questions raised by the 1931–1933 rebellion now settled in Ürümchi's favor, any incentive toward unity among the Muslims of Xinjiang created by the mobilization was lost. It was now determined that Xinjiang would remain in the hands of a Chinese warlord, who presided over a hierarchy of ethnic representatives through which resources would be distributed. For the Ghulja faction, therefore, maintaining their identity as Taranchis was a way to obtain an independent seat at Sheng's negotiating table in Ürümchi and preserve their ability to lobby for local interests instead of competing with Uyghurs from elsewhere in Xinjiang.

Yet although there was still a Taranchi *minzu*, there was no corresponding Taranchi enlightenment association. Xinjiang's enlightenment associations were rallying points for the province's pro-Soviet intelligentsia, and in this milieu there was little sympathy for Taranchi particularism. In December 1934 a branch of the Uyghur Enlightenment Association was established in Ghulja and took its political coloring from Uyghurist intellectuals and returnees who held to the position of a single Uyghur nation. (In Uyghur novelist Ziya Sämädiy's fictionalized account of this period, these men are referred to as "Rozibaqievists.")[76] In the 1940s, the Ghulja branch of the Uyghur Enlightenment Association was a focal point of local anti-GMD networks, and one of the organizing centers for the rebellion that founded the second East Turkistan Republic in 1944.

Uyghur Nationalism and the Red Terror

The recognition of the Uyghurs within Xinjiang's new nationalities policy was a concession to those willing to collaborate with Ürümchi and the Soviets, not a top-down imposition intended as a means of controlling the population or dividing a preexisting Turkic unity. Far from enthusiastic proponents of a Uyghur nation, many Soviet Xinjiang experts, particularly those in the OGPU and Red Army, were deeply hostile to the idea and the aspirations it represented. During his interviews with Uyghur Communists in 1933, Akhmatov took a dim view of those migrants from Xinjiang who had intersected with Soviet Uyghur organizations but was enthusiastic about prospects for political work among recent émigrés, who were untainted by such associations. "Fortunately for us," he explained, "the great majority of them have no inkling of the existence of a Uyghur newspaper and its editor in Tashkent. Some cannot even pronounce the word 'Uyghur' correctly, and indicate their nationality by their place of origin (Kashgari, Khotani, etc.)."[77] In the course of a decade, we see, the Soviet discourse on "oasis identities" had come full circle. Where once such native-place loyalties had been thought of as a sign of backwardness to be corrected by a process of national consolidation, from the OGPU point of view they were now seen as a good thing.

In Kashgar, the Uyghur Enlightenment Association was built from within the Society for the Promotion of Education, a body that had revived during the East Turkistan Republic and carried on the legacy of earlier Jadidist societies. Abdulkarim Khan Makhdum, the ETR's minister of education, continued to play a leading role in educational work in Mahmud Muhiti's Kashgar administration.[78] The Kashgar association first began work in April 1935 and took responsibility for publishing and schooling in Kashgar, greatly increasing the availability of primary schooling.[79] To fund this expansion the enlightenment association took charge of Kashgar's *zakāt* (Islamic charity) and *waqf*, redirecting the wealth of local shrines to pay for textbooks and teachers.[80] Reflecting his position as the Uyghur figurehead for the Sheng administration, the new primary school textbooks carried the portrait of Khoja Niyaz Haji, as did the walls of the classrooms. Qadir Haji, the Old City's chief of police, was among those who contributed to Mahmud Muhiti's educational push. While serving in Kashgar he raised funds and founded a school in his native village of Qaziriq on Kashgar's outskirts, which until the founding of the People's Republic of China was known as the "Qadir Haji School."[81]

Now titled *New Life* and edited by members of the Uyghur Enlightenment Association, from late 1934 onward Kashgar's only newspaper showed a shift in perspective on the question of national identity. Between 1934 and 1935 *New Life* published a series of articles explaining the significance of the Uyghur ethnonym to its readers. These articles assumed no familiarity with the category and began with the basics, starting with an article on the question "What Does Uyghur Mean?"[82] The discourse on the Uyghur nation that emerged at this time was not derived exclusively from Soviet orthodoxy but drew likewise on Ottoman and Turkish thinking on the Uyghurs as synonymous with civilized Turks. The revival of the once mighty nation of the Uyghurs was the theme of Abbas Effendi's 1934 article "What is a Uyghur?": " 'Uyghur' means a civilized people who live in cities. Our ancestors lived in a civilized fashion, but in later years, living under tyrannical rule, we forgot our national name and were completely lost from the ranks of humanity. Now that we have rediscovered our own name, let us also find the prosperity and civilization we once had. Let us bring into being the Uyghur words and stirring Uyghur songs that were lost and call to mind our former condition. As far as possible, let all of our speech be Uyghur. Especially at our newly opened schools, they should teach in our own mother tongue of Uyghur. Let our poems and songs be Uyghur—as far as possible. In this way, let us rediscover our lost Uyghur language and sounds." This was followed by a forceful editorial proclaiming that "Our National and Rightful Name is Uyghur!"[83]

The Uyghur Enlightenment Association's activities in Kashgar aroused suspicion among those up the chain of command in the Soviet Union. Although the NKID publicly encouraged the view that Xinjiang was in the grip of a pan-Islamic or pan-Turkic conspiracy, or threatened by unidentified imperialists, hardheaded military analysts were more worried by the growing strength of Uyghur nationalist sentiment, which the recognition of the Uyghurs as one of the province's nationalities had only amplified. In early December 1935 an intelligence report reached the desk of the Central Asian Military Command, noting that while Sheng had consolidated his position in Ürümchi "along with this the Uyghur national movement is strengthening. The idea of an independent Uyghuristan continues to occupy an important place in the thinking of many Uyghur leaders, even supporters of the Ürümchi regime."[84]

In Kashgar tensions were high, as Mahmud Muhiti and his circle increasingly clashed with the pro-Soviet faction, among them Qadir Haji. The preferred method of undermining Mahmud Muhiti was to summon his deputies to Tashkent or Ürümchi for military training.[85] In late 1935, Khoja Niyaz Haji's Soviet-trained shadow, Mansur Effendi, visited Kashgar and tried to seize control of the Uyghur Enlightenment Association's finances. In this he failed, but he succeeded in appointing a Chinese Communist to the editorship of *New Life*, effectively neutralizing it as an anti-Ürümchi organ. A prominent casualty in this conflict was Kashgar's chief qadi, Abdulghafur Damolla, who was seen as close to Qadir Haji and the Communists, and was assassinated in May 1936.[86] At the end of 1936, the Ürümchi consul in Apresov himself went to Kashgar for talks with Muhiti and accused him of seeking Japanese support.[87] When a summons from Sheng came for Muhiti to present himself at the Third Congress of People's Representatives in 1937, he chose to escape to India instead. With Muhiti's flight, the fragile peace between Sheng Shicai and Khoja Niyaz Haji's allies broke down, and Kashgar was the scene of a new rebellion, led by two of Mahmud Muhiti's deputies and reinforced by the Dungans of the 36th Division, who were now led by a man named Ma Hushan.

The 1937 uprising was only put down by the direct intervention of two Soviet divisions of Kirghiz and Russian troops, accompanied by tanks and bombing raids that reached as far south as Khotan. After the suppression of the uprising and the execution of hundreds of Dungan and Uyghur prisoners, the Red terror throughout Xinjiang was stepped up, and Communists in Kashgar took much greater liberties in fingering imperialist spies and reactionaries. In his memoirs, OGPU operative Vladimir Petrov describes the terror visited on the oasis of Khotan, where mass executions were a daily event.[88] Besides direct repression, the purge also served to sweep away the local elites whose collaboration Sheng had initially relied on to construct his regime. In Ürümchi, Khoja Niyaz Haji was imprisoned and forced to confess to crimes for which he was sentenced to death. In Ghulja, a similar fate befell Turdi Akhun Almasbekov. This initial purge coincided with the arrival in Ürümchi of Chinese Communists Kang Sheng and Wang Ming, who identified a handful of Chinese Trotskyists who had fled from the Soviet Union in 1933–1934.[89] Thus the imperialist threat merged with the inner-party witch hunt of Trotskyists. The consul Apresov was one of the first to be fingered as part of the international anti-Soviet conspiracy and brought back to Russia.

Whatever Qadir Haji's original aspirations for his term at Kashgar, he served Ürümchi and the Soviets loyally during the uprising. During the rebels' brief ascendancy in Kashgar, he was imprisoned and, according to the British consul, "suffered somewhat at the hands of the Tungans and Turkis." Yet he survived, and in early 1938 the consul still thought of him as "one of the most powerful persons in South Sinkiang at the present time."[90] Qadir Haji's role in suppressing the last-ditch rebellion has earned him a black name among Uyghur historians. According to one story, during the uprising he was responsible for setting fire to a prison in which the prominent nationalist poet Muhammad Ali Effendi perished. Yet despite his service to the Soviet cause, a man such as Qadir Haji, who carried with him the legacy of the 1920s, was unlikely to escape the roundup for long. Back in the Soviet Union, men like him were now being regularly denounced as agents of Japanese imperialism or German fascism, as the Great Purge entered full swing. Since 1934, the Soviets had been recruiting locals from Kashgar for political training, making Sheng Shicai's regime increasingly less reliant on intermediaries such as Qadir Haji. In 1938 they decided to purge the purgers in Xinjiang, and Qadir Haji was recalled to Soviet territory.[91] Wiping

the slate clean, Sheng and his Soviet allies now set about creating a new corps
of intellectuals and officials cut off from the Jadidist and Uyghur Communist
legacy of the 1920s.[92]

From his pilgrimage to Mecca in 1916, through his rise to leadership of the
Kashgaris of Soviet Turkistan, to his sudden recall from Kashgar in 1938, Qadir
Haji's odyssey embodies many of the contradictions and ambiguities of Uyghur
nationalist politics. Having swung behind a Uyghurist position in the mid-
1920s, Qadir Haji had been among the most active in cultivating a form of
Soviet-aligned Uyghur nationalist politics among Xinjiang Muslims. By the
time he was able to return to Xinjiang, however, the Soviets themselves were
suspicious, even hostile, toward such politics. In his own way, he probably still
harbored lingering aspirations for some kind of Uyghur sovereignty in Xinjiang,
and no doubt he viewed himself as a seasoned political actor in comparison with
naive local nationalists, but in the end he too participated in snuffing out the
aspirations for Uyghur self-determination that developed in the 1930s.[93] Qadir
Haji's fate after his return to the Soviet Union is unknown, but his name had
come up repeatedly during the Andijan crackdown of 1927 and in the OGPU
investigation into Uyghur Communists in 1933. Given his long history of cross-
border associations, interrogators in 1938 would not have found it difficult to
construct a case against him. After all, even those who had studiously avoided
such incriminating links were doomed. In September 1937, Abdullah Rozibaqiev
was accused of conspiring to overthrow the Soviet Union and sentenced to
death. And far off in Mongolia, Lavaryn Demberel met with a similar end. His
work for the Comintern in Xinjiang was reinterpreted as a Western Mongolian
separatist plot aimed at establishing a counterrevolutionary base with Japanese
support, and in May 1938 he died in prison.

Conclusion

The Great Purge of the 1930s, with its reverberations in Xinjiang and Mongolia, ended the careers of those most closely involved in the fashioning of Uyghur claims to Xinjiang in the 1920s, but of course the history of Uyghur nationalism does not end there. Sheng Shicai's adoption of a Soviet-style nationalities policy—the first instance of this in Chinese history—entailed that politics in Xinjiang would exhibit significant continuity with the struggles and debates described in this book. While the institutionalization of Uyghur nationality has provided a means for the state to direct cultural expression and political activity, it has equally provided a basis for the ongoing contestation of Chinese policy in Xinjiang. In and of itself, I emphasize, the creation of the Uyghur nation does not explain this conflict. In offering the Uyghurs various forms of cultural or political autonomy in exchange for loyalty, the Chinese state has presented them with a bargain, and the outcome of this bargain was not predetermined. It would require a different set of historical studies to determine the extent to which nationalist agitation from the 1930s onward found traction in the towns and villages of Xinjiang, or the extent to which Chinese policies successfully headed off such opposition. And as in any national conflict, issues of class and gender must be taken into consideration before we can reach any conclusions about the inherent attraction of nationalist politics. Hopefully this book has laid a foundation for such research, should conditions in Xinjiang allow it.

History Wars on the Eve of Liberation

As a coda, it is necessary to turn to the late 1940s, a point at which elements of the new nationalities policy in Xinjiang were called into question. Sheng Shicai's

Soviet satellite phase lasted only until the early 1940s, and there were further turns to come before the final incorporation of Xinjiang into the People's Republic of China in 1949. Chafing under Soviet domination, Sheng seized on the outbreak of World War II to turn toward the Guomindang (GMD). This brought with it a new round of imprisonments and executions, further depleting the province's non-Chinese political and intellectual elite. The first signs of resistance to Sheng's move came from the Altay, in an uprising among the Kazakhs. Then, in 1944, the Soviet Union fired back against its recalcitrant client by giving the green light to an uprising in the Ili Valley, leading to the formation of the second East Turkistan Republic in January 1945. Worried by the situation, Chiang Kai-shek engineered Sheng Shicai's resignation in 1944, and Wu Zhongxin stepped in as Xinjiang's first GMD-appointed provincial chairman. At the end of 1945, as fighting ceased and the two sides commenced negotiations, the Soviet-backed Ili rebels and the Chinese Nationalists entered into a cold war for control of Xinjiang. Each side presented a Turkic-speaking face to the people of the province, reigniting the symbolic contest over the history and identity of its Muslim population.

The Soviet-sponsored Ili Republic, in existence until 1949, might be thought of as the revenge of the returnees, when the Soviets finally let loose its reserve army of radicalized émigrés on Xinjiang. Yet a survey of its leadership suggests otherwise, indicating the extent to which the Soviets had dispensed with the first generation of Uyghur Communists and turned instead to cultivating a new cross-border elite. As the republic consolidated itself, a number of men with *aqsaqal* backgrounds rose to prominence: the Uyghur partisan leader Abdulkarim Abbasov, for example, was the son of Hashim Aqsaqal, who had lorded it over the Kashgari migrants in Qaraqol until 1929, when his seals of office were finally confiscated. The minister of education was Habib Yunich, son of the tsarist *aqsaqal* Faziljan, who had applied for Chinese citizenship in 1917 for fear of returning to the Soviet Union. The ETR's first chairman was Alikhan Törä, an anti-Soviet exile whose religious authority carried weight locally. He was eventually removed from office and replaced by the Soviet-educated Uyghur Ahmadjan Qasimi, but in the city of Ghulja itself, the mayor was very much a member of the old guard: Hakimbeg Khoja, heir to the line of hereditary *hakim beg*s created by the Qing.

In part because of men like Hakimbeg Khoja, early calls to arms produced by the rebels mentioned the Taranchis as one of the peoples of Xinjiang.[1] Yet the Soviet-educated leaders of the ETR, along with its official propaganda organs, espoused a militant Soviet-style Uyghur nationalism, removing the Taran-chis from view. In line with the primordialist approach to Soviet nations that was emerging in the wake of World War II, this rhetoric sidelined the Uyghurs' connection with the wider Turkic family and minimized the significance of the conversion to Islam.[2] In a speech in September 1946, Qasimi argued: "The territory of Eastern Turkistan is the land where the Uyghur tribes have been settled from time immemorial. Proof can be found for the Uyghurs' three-to-four-thousand-year occupation of Eastern Turkistan."[3]

The ETR's historical narrative placed the anti-GMD rebellion in a line of anticolonial struggles originating in the nineteenth-century khoja-led uprisings against the Qing. Some of this was expounded in local journals such as *Struggle* (*Küräsh*), in pieces that narrated the incursions of émigrés from Kokand and accused Xinjiang's rulers of genocidal intentions: "the Manchus and the Chinese intended to completely annihilate the Uyghur people, as they had the Junghars."[4] Other organs of ETR propaganda were published in Tashkent, including a journal called *Pravda of the East* (*Shärq Häqiqiti*), in which the resources of Soviet Turkology were brought to bear on the history and identity of the Turkic-speaking peoples of East Turkistan. The political climate filtered into the Tashkent and Alma-Ata academies too, as researchers lent scholarly support to the idea of a long-running national liberation struggle in Xinjiang.[5]

To the east in Ürümchi, the Uyghurs who provided the public face of the new Guomindang administration were individuals whom we have met at different points in this book, each with a different story to tell: Masud Sabri, Isa Yusuf, and Muhammad Imin Bughra, who were known collectively as the Three Effendis. Masud was the intellectual among them, a product of the first Jadidist school in Ghulja and medical training in Istanbul. He had returned to Ghulja in World War I and partnered with Turkish POWs to establish a string of short-lived schools, only to fall foul of the authorities. Isa Yusuf, by contrast, had spent his formative years in the Soviet Union, serving as translator in the Chinese consulates in Andijan and Tashkent. From there he traveled to the Chinese interior, where he headed a native-place association (*tongxianghui*) of Uyghur students studying in the capital (Nanjing until 1937, then Chongqing). Finally, Muhammad Imin Bughra was one of the leaders of the Khotan uprising in the 1930s and had fled to Afghanistan at the collapse of the first East Turkistan Republic. By different paths the three men had made their way to Chongqing and thrown in their lot with Guomindang's efforts to claim control of Xinjiang. In the mid-1940s, as the situation in Xinjiang deteriorated, the trio headed up the Gansu corridor to Lanzhou, where they waited for favorable political winds to blow them to Ürümchi.

While in exile from Xinjiang, the Three Effendis had formulated a critique of Sheng Shicai's national policies, propounding the view that the people of Xinjiang were Turks first, and Uyghurs, Kazakhs, or Kirghiz only second. To a GMD audience they pointed out that Sheng's division of Xinjiang's population into fourteen nationalities was a flagrant violation of the theory of China's five races that the Nationalists still upheld, and emphasized that Sun Yat-sen's *Three People's Principles* had referred not simply to the "Muslims" as one of these races, but specifically to the "Turks who profess Islam." For Turkic-speaking readers, meanwhile, the Three Effendis drew on the Kemalist discourse of Turkism (*Türklik*), eschewing Arabic terms for the nation such as *millat*, and instead describing the single Turk *ulus* stretching from Anatolia to Xinjiang. Culturally, too, they mimicked the Turkish Republic's promotion of Turkic names, with Isa Yusuf now styling himself Isa Yusuf Alptekin ("Heroic Prince").[6] In 1944, the Xinjiang Native-Place Association lobbied for the Chinese Republic's constitution to designate the inhabitants of Xinjiang as Turks and the province as Turkistan, a position that brought them into conflict with GMD intellectuals who were not convinced of the province's Turkic identity.[7]

Rhetorically at least, the Three Effendis were no less hostile to Chinese domination in Xinjiang than the leadership of the ETR, and the decision to send them to Xinjiang troubled GMD representatives on the ground in Ürümchi. In the face of the ETR's strident ethnonationalism, though, the Guomindang had little choice but to push such men forward. The group continued to lobby the GMD to change the name of the province and its peoples, proposing that Xinjiang should be called East Turkistan, and the various Turkic-speaking peoples should be simply called Turks.[8] By all accounts, the GMD chief in Ürümchi Zhang Zhizhong lent a sympathetic ear to such proposals but would not countenance renaming the province East Turkistan. He preferred something Chinese, but without the obvious colonial connotations of "New Frontier," such as Tianshan Province, or Kunlun Province. Ultimately Xinjiang remained Xinjiang, but in Uyghur the Three Effendis were permitted to call it "Chinese Turkistan."[9]

In 1946 the ETR and the GMD factions entered into a coalition administration headed by Zhang Zhizhong. In 1947, Masud Sabri succeeded Zhang as chairman, giving the Three Effendis an opportunity, apart from in Ili, to implement their cultural vision of a Turkic Xinjiang. A major obstacle to this program of national reengineering, as the Three Effendis saw it, was the network of nationally defined enlightenment associations stretching across the province, a legacy of Sheng Shicai's nationalities policy. It was these enlightenment associations that had given institutional reality to the official national taxonomy of the province, and in the eyes of the GMD, they were hotbeds of leftists and Soviet sympathizers. In Ürümchi, the Three Effendis took a direct approach: one night a gang of vigilantes attacked the local association's building and set it alight, forcing its members to scale the walls and flee into the night.[10] The confrontation came close to destroying the association until the Three Effendis revived it under a new name, the Turk-Uyghur Association, with a new crest bearing the designation "Chinese Turkistan." Chairman of the Turk-Uyghur Union was Chingiz Khan Damolla, an ally of the Three Effendis who had spent the previous decade in Cairo. Like-minded Tatars followed this lead and rebranded the Tatar Enlightenment Association the Turk-Tatar Association.[11]

While in Lanzhou, the Three Effendis had published a journal called *Freedom* (*Ärk*), a much more explicitly Turkist organ than the GMD's official *Xinjiang News*. After arriving in Ürümchi, *Freedom* continued to serve as their mouthpiece, printed at the newly established Altay Press. *Freedom* pursued the project of a linguistic unity among the world's Turks and introduced its readers to the principles of Turkism. It not only reprinted Republican Turkish scholarship, such as Fuad Köprülü's history of Turkic literature, but reached back to the essays of the nineteenth-century Ottoman liberal Namik Kemal. Alongside these publishing activities, in 1948 the Three Effendis established the Dernek, a cultural club harking back to the first *dernek*s established in the Ottoman Empire in 1908, when the Young Turk Revolution had restored civil freedoms to the sultan's subjects. The Ürümchi Dernek had regular meetings with a set routine of lectures, poetry, comedy, and free discussion. Lecture topics ranged from the importance of hygiene and immunization, through local history, to questions of Turkology. Chingiz Khan Damolla, for example, lectured on the significance of the word "Turkistan," while the Tatar Burhan Shahidi presented his research on the origins of the term "Siberia." The *dernekchi*s, as they were known, were obsessed with Turkological correctness.[12]

In this coalition period, Ürümchi and Ghulja kept up an exchange of publications in which the factions polemicized on questions of history and identity. For the most part the ETR tried to brand the pro-GMD Uyghurs as pan-Turkists—something akin to fascist in the Soviet Union—and as pawns of the Chinese, mocking their use of "Chinese Turkistan" as a concession to

Chinese colonialism. The GMD Uyghurs insisted on the historical accuracy of their Turkist position and highlighted the errors in the simplistic primordial view of the Uyghur nation that the ETR propounded. When the *Xinjiang News* reprinted an article by a Soviet Turkologist criticizing the idea of calling Xinjiang's inhabitants Turks, Muhammad Imin Bughra responded, arguing that while the Uyghurs were part of the province's Turkic heritage, they did not comprise the entirety of it: "It is a grave error in the scholarly field to attribute to the Uyghurs the civilization of Altishahr, where the foot of the Uyghurs never trod."[13]

One reading of these polemics is that they represent a sharp clash between two visions of the nation with very different genealogies: one presenting a Uyghur nation cultivated inside the Soviet Union and assimilated to Soviet orthodoxy; the other drawing on a distinct tradition of Turkic nationalism transmitted to the Muslims of Xinjiang by entirely different conduits. Yet the two were really not so far apart. The Three Effendis' preferred terminology of a Uyghur *tribe* belonging to a Turkish *nation* was not that different from the ETR's conception of a Uyghur *nation* belonging to a *race* of Turks (something they did not deny). As I have shown in this book, a range of actors in the Soviet Union made use of the Uyghur symbol, and it was by no means the exclusive preserve of those we would identify as "pro-Soviet." The situation in 1940s Xinjiang was in many ways a repetition of the dynamic that was witnessed in Soviet Turkistan in the 1920s, when a gulf had gradually widened between those Xinjiang Muslims who were drawn to Uyghurist interpretations of Xinjiang's Turko-Islamic past, and those who were eager to fashion an ethnicized notion of Uyghur nationality. The difference was that now the dissident Uyghurists were working with the GMD instead of seeking Soviet backing. It should not be surprising, therefore, to find points of continuity between the Kashgari Communists of the 1920s and the Three Effendis of the 1940s.

In July 1948, a meeting was held in Ürümchi to mark the second anniversary of the founding of the Altay Press. Isa Yusuf Alptekin, deputy provincial chairman, gave a speech to mark the occasion, in which he discussed his own publishing career, from his first journals in Nanjing to his arrival in Ürümchi and the work of the Altay Press. He started, though, by describing how he first came to realize the importance of the printed word to political activity.[14] It was, he said, during his time at the consulate in Andijan. As he spoke he took out an old broadsheet and held it up to the crowd. "There was a newspaper called *Liberation*," he explained. "This came into my hands in 1928, and I've kept it ever since." At this point, we read in the account of this meeting, the audience erupted into thunderous applause. "There's an article here," Isa continued, "lamenting the plight of women in our homeland. It bemoans the fact that women have been left in such a terrible state, and attacks the rich merchants." The paper Isa was proudly brandishing was, of course, a copy of Qadir Haji's *Liberation*, published in Tashkent and distributed among the Kashgari migrants. Isa Yusuf Alptekin, positioning himself as an anti-Communist champion on the eve of the Cold War, nevertheless attributed his national awakening to the activities of the Kashgari Communists in the Ferghana Valley. The irony was probably lost on the meeting, but it serves to illustrate an important point: as much as the Soviet experiment was the genesis of an orthodox construction of Uyghur identity, it was also a formative experience for many of its critics.

The Classificatory State and Its Discontents

Ultimately the outcome in the 1940s was neither a Soviet-backed Uyghuristan nor a GMD-backed Chinese Turkistan. The Chinese Communist Party's People's Liberation Army took control of Ürümchi in late 1949, and the Three Effendis were again driven into exile—first to Afghanistan, and then to Turkey. The leaders of the East Turkistan Republic, meanwhile, lost their lives in a plane crash while on their way to Beijing, an event that still arouses suspicion of a conspiracy. It seems unlikely that a Sino-Soviet deal on Xinjiang required the elimination of the ETR leadership, who had deviated little from Moscow's instructions up to this point. Nevertheless, there is evidence that sentiment in favor of a Republic of Uyghuristan did present difficulties in the early years of Communist Xinjiang, at least in Ghulja. Resisting such calls, in 1955 the Chinese Communist Party lifted the veil on the Xinjiang Uyghur Autonomous Region. The history of the ETR was rewritten to characterize it as a tributary to the mainstream of the CCP-led Chinese revolution, according to Mao Zedong's dictum that the East Turkistan Republic was "a part of the democratic revolution of the entire Chinese people." This did not immediately silence agitation for the creation of Uyghuristan, though, which became a focus of the campaign against "local nationalism" of the mid-1950s.

Discussions of minority nationhood in the Soviet Union and China usually gravitate toward one of two poles of attraction. One is the viewpoint of the state, with all its resources for classifying and defining peoples, and for inculcating its preferred sense of identity. This is how most scholars have approached

the new Soviet nations, along with many of the *minzu* of China who first received administrative recognition in China's ethnic classification project of the
1950s.[15] The other approach is the story of resistance to the state revolving
around well-established national identities built on the foundations laid by the
imperial legacy. Here we may think of the Mongols seceding from the Qing at
its downfall and the long-running Tibetan struggle for cultural and political
autonomy. Either of these two paradigms has always been a poor fit for the
Turkic-speaking peoples of Russia and China. Not only the Uyghurs, but groups
such as the Tatars, occupied an ambiguous middle ground in the imperial
period between confessional, corporate, and ethnic identities. Yet these two
poles—the gaze of the state and the sentiments of its subjects—can still guide
us in this study. We simply need to recognize an ongoing dialectic between
the two and dispense with the search for definitive moments in the "creation"
of nations.

From the fall of the Qing to the creation of the People's Republic of China,
the emergence of Uyghur nationalism was probably the most striking addition to the field of ethnonational discourses in China. At no point in this
story, though, have we encountered individuals proposing a wholesale revision
of existing repertoires of communal identification. This history takes on the
appearance of a radical invention only when we compare its starting point
with its end point. The process that eventually led to the creation of the Uyghur
nation consisted of a series of small steps, each occasioned by challenges and
opportunities presented by changing political conditions, and each entirely
logical and comprehensible in its context.

The building blocks of the Qing Empire, its constituencies as some refer to
them, have clearly played a role in this book, and the notion of the Muslims of
China was put to various uses in the early twentieth century. To be sure, divided by language and culture, and split up between various provinces, these
Muslims were not in a position to respond collectively to the fall of the Qing
in 1912. Yet talk of five races in harmony was not necessarily empty rhetoric,
and those Muslims who were oriented toward Beijing pointed to the Qing legacy
in Xinjiang as grounds for Muslim autonomy in the Chinese Republic. The fact
that Uyghurists in the Soviet Union initially presented themselves as representatives of the same constituency—the Muslims of China—obliges us to take
the Qing construction of the Hui seriously. Had the Republic not succumbed
to warlord domination and preserved a space for constitutional lobbying, who
can say that such a notion of a unified Muslim community would not have eventually found traction in Chinese politics?

When abroad, in Russia and the Ottoman Empire, we have seen that people frequently presented themselves as part of a Chinese Muslim community. What distinguished these imperial environments were the ways in which racial thinking came to be applied to such categories. In both the Ottoman and Russian empires, Uyghur history was initially treated as a part of a common Turkic history. It was as much a pan-Turkic symbol as the preserve of any particular group. In Russia, though, intellectual proponents of a unified Turk nation lost out to those seeking to construct distinct national histories for the empire's Turkic-speaking peoples, nested within a wider narrative of Turkic genealogy. It was in response to this Jadidist discourse that the Uyghur symbol was appropriated as a category situating the Muslims of China on a branch of this revised family tree. This was in many ways a continuation of traditional forms of communal identification. Nazarkhoja Abdusamadov's formula—Taranchi son of Uyghur son of Turk—conforms to the classic Turko-Mongol mode of expressing ethnogenesis in terms of tribal genealogy. Primarily this was a way of staking out a position for the Taranchis in Russian Muslim circles, but doing so emphasized a bond between the Taranchis and the rest of the Chinese Muslim community, whether Kashgaris or Dungans.

When these Taranchis were thrust into a position of community leadership in 1917, the logic of this Uyghurist position obliged them to seize the reins of political work among the Muslims of China—both in the Soviet Union and in Xinjiang. Uyghur identity remained, in the period of the Revolutionary Union, a loose category that permitted ethnic difference within it and survived the collapse of the union in this form. Having assumed for themselves the position of spokespeople for potentially millions of people in neighboring China, this was not something that the Taranchis were going to relinquish. The Uyghurist view of the three Muslim peoples of China—the Taranchis, Kashgaris, and Dungans—next found its way into party building in Soviet Turkistan. In the mid-1920s the ground shifted again, requiring activists either to transform this coalition into a more explicitly national grouping or to abandon it. Initially, the Taranchis took the first option, the Kashgaris the second; but in the course of the national delimitation process the Kashgaris, seeking to ward off a threat of assimilation, came around to the Uyghurist position. This might be seen as opportunistic, but nevertheless it was these Kashgaris who authored some of the first formulations of the Uyghurs as a nation conforming to the Stalinist orthodoxy and who introduced the terms of this discourse into politics in Xinjiang.

It was neither the state and its officials nor a well-organized national movement that created the Uyghur nation, but a small and disenfranchised body of activists, divided among themselves and seeking to obtain the best outcome from a political environment that was beyond their control. Few of those met with in this book ever exercised any real power, and only on rare occasions were proponents of Uyghur nationhood in any position to speak to the Muslims of Xinjiang. They were nevertheless able to insert this distinctive vision into official structures, ensuring that the claims of a Uyghur nation would be part of the political discourse of the People's Republic of China. If very little else could be considered a success in twentieth-century Uyghur history, the campaign that was launched in the 1920s to win over the Taranchis, Kashgaris, and eventually the Turfanis, Yarkandis, and the rest of Xinjiang's settled oasis population, to think of themselves as a single nation, achieved its goal.

By the time the Chinese Communists set about classifying the nations of the People's Republic in the 1950s, eventually coming up with a list of fifty-six, there was little work left to be done in Xinjiang. Uyghurist hegemony in the ETR in Ghulja ended talk of a Taranchi nation, and the Chinese Communists accordingly reduced the province's official tally of nationalities from fourteen to thirteen. Rather than creating them, the Chinese state, with its resources to classify and define peoples, was mobilized to legitimate a preexisting set of national categories in Xinjiang. As in the 1930s, official recognition in the 1950s was important in allowing Uyghurs to pursue the objective of fostering national identification among the province's Turkic-speaking Muslims, a goal that was that still far from realized at the inauguration of the Xinjiang Uyghur Autonomous Region.

While China's *minzu* paradigm has imposed a flat and rigid template to which categories of nationality must officially conform, my book has shown the imbricated and multivalent qualities of the Uyghur national idea. None of the transitions I have outlined here, from thinking in terms of a Muslim community of China to the fleshing-out of a Uyghur nation, eliminated earlier meanings that had been imparted to the Uyghur symbol. The Uyghur nation therefore emerged as a palimpsest of Islamic, Turkic, and Soviet notions of national history and identity and has remained a repository of these multiple discursive registers. This is a fact that China's view of its national categories finds hard to accept, preferring instead to treat its minorities as entirely self-contained units whose historical and cultural ties do not transgress the boundaries of the People's Republic of China and do not invoke wider religious or racial bonds. On this basis Chinese officials have engaged in futile efforts to police national discourse in Xinjiang, seeking to distinguish positive expressions of Uyghur identity from elements that they see as symptoms of pan-Turkist or pan-Islamic sympathies. The result has only highlighted how blurred this line is, with policies against local nationalism or illegal religious activity often spilling over into campaigns that delegitimize authorized symbols of Uyghur identity.

When I first started researching this book a decade ago, it seemed that the political implications of Uyghur nationhood were likely to remain at the heart of the ongoing conflict in Xinjiang. As I conclude it, though, it is hard to say this with any certainty. Among protagonists on both sides there are signs of people moving away from a common vocabulary of national rights. In Xinjiang itself there is a growing sense that space for promoting Uyghur interests within the system of national autonomy has vanished. In 2003, while studying in Ürümchi, I witnessed locals lining the streets to watch with respect as long-serving party official Sayfuddin Azizi's hearse drove by. With Sayfuddin's death, the cohort of Uyghur leaders linked to the ETR of the 1940s, seen as compromised but still credible spokespeople for the Uyghurs, departed the political scene. Outside China, Uyghur nationalists in exile still command a following in the diaspora and an indeterminate degree of support in Xinjiang itself, yet their activities elicit little in the way of international solidarity. Long-running national grievances toward assimilationist cultural policies, Chinese immigration, and national discrimination in Xinjiang's economy continue to fester, but much of the recent violence in Xinjiang is rooted in local conflicts, disconnected from these spheres of lobbying activity.

Many factors have contributed to what now looks to be a religious revival in Xinjiang. Some of this follows nationwide trends, as the state's withdrawal from social support has prompted a turn toward religious ethics. Much of it, of course, reflects local conditions. In an environment where many Uyghurs feel that all they have left is religious faith, repressive religious policies will inevitably create the necessary conditions to redefine the struggle in Xinjiang as a jihad. Close surveillance of the mosque, restrictions on observance of religious festivals, and the policing of Islamic dress, all have come to the fore recently as sources of resentment and sparks for public protest. As Anatolii Lunacharskii, the Soviet Union's People's commissar of education, famously put it, "Religion is like a nail: if you hit it on the head, it just goes in deeper."[16]

Xinjiang is no different from anywhere else in the world, and if Uyghurs feel that self-styled nationalist leaders have failed them, they will look elsewhere for the means to resist. Needless to say, there is no inherent contradiction between emphasizing religious grounds for opposition to Chinese rule in Xinjiang and identifying with a national cause, but in some cases this line is being drawn. Recent propaganda of Islamist Uyghurs avoids making political claims as Uyghurs, preferring instead to identify themselves as part of a common Islamic front of Turkistani Muslims. If these trends continue, we shall in some ways find ourselves back in the situation that existed a century ago, when the collapse of the Ottoman Empire and failed bids for autonomy in Russian Turkistan saw the brief coalescence of a militant coalition on a primarily Islamic basis. Should that come to pass, Chinese officials today would do well to heed the words of Yang Zengxin, a champion of Chinese national unity who steered Xinjiang through that period, when he was confronted by reports of pan-Islamic agitation on his province's doorstep: "Such trends simply reflect the national question and the religious question," he wrote to Beijing. "When we investigate their significance, they remain questions of rights. . . . The most crucial thing is to raise the standard of administration, not to exploit the Hui and the Turban-Wearing Muslims, so that the stand-in rule of the Chinese is preferred to the autonomy of the Hui and Turban-Wearing Muslims."[17] Amid the deepening counterterrorist crackdown in Xinjiang, his words have a subversive ring to them.

On the Chinese side, too, there is a growing disillusionment with the system of national autonomy. For many scholars and officials, the fall of the Soviet Union has called into question the ability of a Soviet-style national policy to resolve national tensions, and the fall itself has freed China to explore new ways of resolving such conflicts. This has set in motion a gradual conceptual shift away from a definition of China as a multinational state to China as a multiethnic nation-state, with a renewed emphasis on the existence of a single Chinese nation, the *zhonghua minzu*. As the Uyghurs now find themselves required to echo Xi Jinping's slogans on the "Great Revival of the Zhonghua Minzu," a group of scholars and officials have been debating how to "water down" (*danhua*) and depoliticize troublesome national identities such as that of the Uyghurs. These tentative proposals for what is termed a "second-generation nationalities policy" have not yet obtained approval at the highest levels of the party. It is still too early for the CCP to admit that its much-touted national policies have not resolved the national question. Yet this trend looks likely to define the terms of policy debate in this century. Instead of wrangling with Uyghur elites over the unfulfilled promise of *national* autonomy, Chinese officials may in future enjoy greater freedom to craft strategies to manage *ethnic* conflict that do not have a genealogy in Marxist theories on the right of nations to self-determination.[18]

Parallel Histories

Appropriately enough, the only public commemoration of Soviet involvement in Xinjiang in the 1930s is a monument to the "unknown Soviet soldier" erected in 2011 in an Ürümchi park. Clad in nondescript uniforms, their identification cards surrendered before entering Xinjiang, these NKVD soldiers were always intended to remain unknown.[19] The obscuring of this history allows the coming of Communist modernity to Xinjiang to be told in much the same way as the rest of the official history of Xinjiang—as a story of heroic Chinese pioneers blazing a trail into the wilds of China's northwest. A two-story building of stocky brick construction on Victory Road in Ürümchi, a bustling thoroughfare leading from Xinjiang University to the city center, bears witness to this. For a while, it housed the offices of a group of Chinese Communist Party members who were dispatched to Xinjiang from the Red Army base in Yan'an in 1938. It is now a public museum and site of patriotic education, where the exploits of these men, including Mao Zedong's brother Mao Zemin, are celebrated as a preamble to the story of Chinese Communist Party's liberation of Xinjiang in 1949.[20]

What is left unsaid is that these Chinese Communists were far from the first to consider the application of the new revolutionary ideology to Xinjiang. In coming to Xinjiang, they were following a path already well laid out by the many Uyghur, Kazakh, Mongol, Tatar, and Chinese Communists who had preceded them as members of the Communist Party of the Soviet Union. These, in turn, were but a small fraction of the hundreds of thousands of émigrés from Xinjiang in Soviet Turkistan whose lives, and identities, had been transformed by the Russian Revolution and the emerging Soviet system in ways that I have described in this book.

A two-hour flight away to the west in Almaty, a bust of Abdullah Rozibaqiev looks on as locals stroll through a leafy park in the city center, where he is remembered among a group of prominent politicians of Soviet Kazakhstan. Nearby, one of the city's major north-south boulevards bears his name, Rozybakiev Street. Shot in 1938, Rozibaqiev and his colleagues from the 1920s are conspicuously absent from the first Soviet scholarly works on the Uyghurs in Kazakhstan.[21] Rehabilitated in 1957, he is now justly recognized for the leading role he played in the history of the Uyghur community of Kazakhstan—a role that this book has confirmed.

Yet for Qadir Haji, a man who in his day had the same status among the Kashgaris of Soviet Central Asia as Rozibaqiev had among the Taranchis, there are no memorials. To the best of my knowledge, no scholars in the post-Soviet republics of Kazakhstan, Kirghizstan, or Uzbekistan have shown any interest in restoring his face to the doctored photograph that is 1920s and 1930s Soviet Uyghur history. Thus the story of Uyghur communism, as it is told in post-Soviet Central Asia, revolves around a man who never went to Xinjiang and is free from the accusation that clings to Qadir Haji, that in seeking a route to Uyghur nationhood on Soviet terms he was leading his people toward a dead end. We have to ask, though: How would these two stories be told if Rozibaqiev had been sent to Kashgar instead of Qadir Haji?

Uyghur history thus closely mirrors the fate of the Uyghurs themselves, split up between the republics of Central Asia and Xinjiang, and obliged to conform to other people's national boundaries, forcing two parallel lines that do not intersect. To the extent that this study has succeeded in elucidating some of the blind spots that this pressure has created, it will have pointed toward the possibility of a more holistic view of the history of the Uyghurs as a national community. Having gained such a vantage point, it becomes possible to see, not only what is distinctive about the Uyghur story, but also where it coincides with other stories and produces parallels of a more instructive kind. Naturally there are family resemblances here to other cases of Soviet nation building—it could not be otherwise. Yet an equally worthwhile point of comparison with the Uyghur story is that of Chinese nationalism itself. There, too, the story of men and women going abroad for work and study, coming into contact with new thinking on the nation—thinking that at times emphasized racial solidarities, at times class—plays a crucial role. Like the Uyghurs, these overseas Chinese communities were a mixture of long established émigrés who took the diaspora as the focus of their political activity and recent arrivals whose goal was to return to China and effect change there. Thus many elements of my account of Uyghur nationalism should be familiar to those versed in Chinese political history. The immediate outlook for a reconciliation of Chinese and Uyghur historical narratives is not encouraging, but such a reconciliation will be a necessary part of any lasting peace in Xinjiang. If this book has anything to offer toward this end, it may be this recognition: that in spite of differing views on the historical status of Xinjiang, the recent experiences of the Uyghurs and Chinese have much in common.

Notes

Select Bibliography

Acknowledgments

Index

Notes

Abbreviations

APRK	Arkhiv prezidenta Respubliki Kazakhstan, Almaty
AVPRI	Arkhiv vneshnei politiki Rossiiskoi Imperii, Moscow
GARF	Gosudarstvennyi arkhiv Rossiiskoi Federatsii, Moscow
IMH	Archive of the Institute of Modern History, Academia Sinica, Taibei
IOR	India Office Records, London
PFARAN	Sankt-Peterburgskii filial Arkhiva Rossiiskoi akademii nauk, Saint Petersburg
RGASPI	Rossiiskii gosudarstvennyi arkhiv sotsial'no-politicheskoi istorii, Moscow
RGVA	Rossiiskii gosudarstvennyi voennyi arkhiv, Moscow
RGVIA	Rossiiskii gosudarstvennyi voenno-istoricheskii arkhiv, Moscow
TsGARK	Tsentral'nyi gosudarstvennyi arkhiv Respubliki Kazakhstan, Almaty
TsGARU	Tsentral'nyi gosudarstvennyi arkhiv Respubliki Uzbekistan, Tashkent

Introduction

1. There is very little historical literature on this period in Uyghur in the People's Republic of China. Generally speaking, Uyghur narratives of the recent past are to be found in historical novels, particularly those of Abdurehim Ötkür and Ziya Sämädiy. The collective biography is also a popular genre, e.g., Sherip Khushtar, ed., *Shinjang Yeqinqi Zaman Tarikhidiki Mäshhur Shäkhslär* (Ürümchi: Shinjang Khälq Näshriyati, 2000). Memoir accounts in the *Shinjang Tarikh Materiyallar* series (1980–) contain valuable insights but must be used with caution.

2. Murat Khamraev, *Rastvet kul'tury uigurskogo naroda* (Almaty: Kazakhstan, 1967); Mashur Ruziev, *Yanglivashtin Tughulghan Uyghur Khälqi* (Almaty: Qazaqstan, 1968). The 1990s in Kazakhstan saw a new wave of publishing on the early Soviet period, focusing on Abdullah Rozibaqiev and his collaborators, e.g., A. Rozibaqiev, *Khälqim Üchün Köyüdu Zhüräk* (Almaty: Zhazushï, 1997); M. Rozibaqiev and N. Rozibaqieva, *Uyghur Khälqining Munävvär Pärzändi* (Almaty: Qazaqstan, 1987);

M. Rozibaqiev, *Ismayil Tayirov* (Almaty: Qazaqstan, 1990); A. Rozibaqiev, *Burhan Qasimov* (Almaty: Rauan, 1992).

3. The partial exception to this is the three-volume series *Tashkäntchilär*, ed. Abdurakhman Abdulla (Ürümchi: Shinjang Khälq Näshriyati, 2003–2006), which catalogues the Xinjiang students who studied in Tashkent in the 1930s.

4. Pamela Kyle Crossley, *A Translucent Mirror: History and Identity in Qing Imperial Ideology* (Berkeley: University of California Press, 1999); Mark Elliott, *The Manchu Way: The Eight Banners and Ethnic Identity in Late Imperial China* (Stanford, CA: Stanford University Press, 2001).

5. Peter Holquist, *Making War, Forging Revolution: Russia's Continuum of Crisis* (Cambridge, MA: Harvard University Press, 2002), 160.

6. Adeeb Khalid has does much to elucidate the crucial "Turkistan period" of 1918–1924 in *Making Uzbekistan: Nation, Empire, and Revolution in the Early USSR* (Ithaca, NY: Cornell University Press, 2015).

7. For example, Dru Gladney, "The Ethnogenesis of the Uighur," *Central Asian Survey* 9, no. 1 (1990): 1–28; Ildikó Bellér-Hann, *Community Matters in Xinjiang, 1880–1949: Towards a Historical Anthropology of the Uyghur* (Leiden: Brill, 2008); Gardner Bovingdon, *The Uyghurs: Strangers in Their Own Land* (New York: Columbia University Press, 2010).

8. Rian Thum, *The Sacred Routes of Uyghur History* (Cambridge, MA: Harvard University Press, 2014).

9. N. Ia. Bichurin, *Opisanie Chzhungarii i Vostochnogo Turkestana v drevnem i nyneshnem sostoianii* (Saint Petersburg: Karla Krai, 1829), xiii.

10. Muhämmäd Imin Bughra, *Shärqi Türkistan Tarikhi* (Ankara: Fatma Bughra, 1987), 360.

11. Peter C. Perdue, *China Marches West: The Qing Conquest of Central Eurasia* (Cambridge, MA: Belknap Press of Harvard University Press, 2005); James Millward, *Beyond the Pass: Economy, Ethnicity, and Empire in Qing Central Asia 1759–1864* (Stanford, CA: Stanford University Press, 1998); Laura Newby, *The Empire and the Khanate: A Political History of Qing Relations with Khoqand c. 1700–1860* (Leiden: Brill, 2005); Hodong Kim, *Holy War in China: The Muslim Rebellion and State in Chinese Central Asia 1864–1877* (Stanford, CA: Stanford University Press, 2004).

12. John K. Fairbank, *Trade and Diplomacy on the China Coast: The Opening of the Treaty Ports, 1842–1854* (Cambridge, MA: Harvard University Press, 1953); Pär Cassel, *Grounds of Judgment: Extraterritoriality and Imperial Power in Nineteenth-Century China and Japan* (Oxford: Oxford University Press, 2012); Joseph Esherick, *The Origins of the Boxer Uprising* (Berkeley: University of California Press, 1987).

13. Mary Backus Rankin, *Elite Activism and Political Transformation in China: Zhejiang Province, 1865–1911* (Stanford, CA: Stanford University Press, 1996).

14. "Subjecthood," although an awkward term, describes the status of Turkistan's population for much of the period covered in this book better than "citizenship" or "nationality." I refer to people consistently as "citizens" only after the introduction of the Soviet statute on citizenship and the distribution of Republican Chinese passports

among Xinjiang émigrés in Soviet Turkistan, both of which occurred in the mid-1920s. A theoretical distinction between subjects and citizens does not play a role in my discussion.

15. A good example of this approach is Carl A. Trocki, *Opium and Empire: Chinese Society in Colonial Singapore, 1800–1910* (Ithaca, NY: Cornell University Press, 1990).

16. On Yang Zengxin and the early years of Republican Xinjiang, see Andrew D. W. Forbes, *Warlords and Muslims in Chinese Central Asia: A Political History of Republican Sinkiang 1911–1949* (Cambridge: Cambridge University Press, 1986); Li Xincheng, *Yang Zengxin zai Xinjiang* (Taibei Xian Xiandian Shi: Guoshiguan, 1993); Justin M. Jacobs, *Xinjiang and the Modern Chinese State* (Seattle: University of Washington Press, 2016).

17. Adeeb Khalid, *The Politics of Muslim Cultural Reform: Jadidism in Central Asia* (Berkeley: University of California Press, 1998).

18. Michael A. Reynolds, *Shattering Empires: The Clash and Collapse of the Ottoman and Russian Empires, 1908–1918* (Cambridge: Cambridge University Press, 2011); James H. Meyer, *Turks across Empires: Marketing Muslim Identity in the Russian-Ottoman Borderlands, 1856–1914* (Oxford: Oxford University Press, 2014).

19. See, for example, Ismail Gasprinskii's writings contrasting a backward and dangerous China with the "Russo-Muslim world" in Edward Allworth, ed., *Tatars of the Crimea: Their Struggle for Survival* (Durham, NC: Duke University Press, 1988), 72–99, 202–216.

20. The most recent contribution to this debate is Danielle Ross, "The Nation That Might Not Be: The Role of Iskhaqi's Extinction after Two Hundred Years in the Popularization of Kazan Tatar National Identity among the ʻUlama Sons and Shakirds of the Volga-Ural Region, 1904–1917," *Ab Imperio* 3 (2012): 341–369. For background, see Allen Frank, *Islamic Historiography and "Bulghar" Identity among the Tatars and Bashkirs of Russia* (Leiden: Brill, 1998); Robert P. Geraci, *Window on the East: National and Imperial Identities in Late Tsarist Russia* (Ithaca, NY: Cornell University Press, 2001).

21. Mikhaėl' Friderikh, *Gabdulla Tukai kak ob"ekt ideologicheskoi bor'by* (Kazan: Tatarskoe knizhnoe izdatel'stvo, 2011), 134.

22. Terry Martin, *The Affirmative Action Empire: Nations and Nationalism in the Soviet Union, 1923–1939* (Ithaca, NY: Cornell University Press, 2001).

23. Joseph Stalin, *Marxism and the National Question* (Moscow: Foreign Languages Publishing House, 1947), 15.

24. Almost all published sources describe the congress as the point at which the "Uyghur" ethnonym was revived, so naturally this idea has featured prominently in scholarly discussions. For a recent presentation of the event that follows the conventional Uyghur historiography in Kazakhstan, see Sean Roberts, "Imagining Uyghurstan: Re-evaluating the Birth of the Modern Uyghur Nation," *Central Asian Survey* 28, no. 4 (2009): 361–381.

25. V. V. Bartol'd, *Istoriia izucheniia Vostoka v Evrope i Rossii*, 2nd ed. (Leningrad: Leningradskii institut zhivykh vostochnykh iazykov, 1925), 240; Vera Tolz, *Russia's*

Own Orient: The Politics of Identity and Oriental Studies in the Late Imperial and Early Soviet Periods (Oxford: Oxford University Press, 2011).

26. Martin, *Affirmative Action Empire*; Francine Hirsch, *Empire of Nations: Ethnographic Knowledge and the Making of the Soviet Union* (Ithaca, NY: Cornell University Press, 2005); Arne Haugen, *The Establishment of National Republics in Soviet Central Asia* (New York: Palgrave Macmillan, 2003).

27. Inner Mongolia offers the most proximate point of comparison for Xinjiang, on which see Christopher P. Atwood, *Young Mongols and Vigilantes in Inner Mongolia's Interregnum Decades, 1911–1931* (Leiden: Brill, 2002). Further afield, there are obvious commonalities in the history of Xinjiang and Iranian Azerbaijan, for which see Tadeusz Swietochowski, *Russia and Azerbaijan: A Borderland in Transition* (New York: Columbia University Press, 1995).

28. Owen Lattimore, *High Tartary* (Boston: Little, Brown, 1930), 164–165.

29. The key works in the exile tradition are Ḥamidullah bin Muḥammad Ṭurfani, *Türkistan 1331–1337 Inqilab Tarikhi* (1943; repr. Istanbul: Doğu Türkistan Dergisi, 1983); Bughra, *Shärqi Türkistan Tarikhi*; Musa Turkistani, *Ulugh Türkistan Faji'asi* (Madina: Maṭabiʿ al-Rashid, 1401/1981); İsa Yusuf Alptekin, *Esir Doğu Türkistan için* (Istanbul: Doğu Türkistan Neşriyat Merkezi, 1985).

30. Valerii Barmin was among the first to take advantage of this opening in the 1990s and remains one of the few scholars to have accessed Soviet Foreign Ministry files on Xinjiang. V. A. Barmin, *Sin'tszian v Sovetsko-Kitaiskikh otnosheniiakh 1941–1949 gg.* (Barnaul: Barnaul gosudarstvennyi pedagogicheskii universitet, 1999); V. A. Barmin, *Sovetskii soiuz i Sin'tszian 1918–1941* (Barnaul: Barnaul gosudarstvennyi pedagogicheskii universitet, 1999).

1. People and Place in Chinese Turkistan

1. Colin Mackerras, *The Uighur Empire (744–840) According to the T'ang Dynasty Histories*, Occasional Papers 8 (Canberra: Australian National University Centre of Oriental Studies, 1968); Thomas T. Allsen, "The Yüan Dynasty and the Uighurs of Turfan in the 13th Century," in *China among Equals: The Middle Kingdom and Its Neighbours, 10th–14th Centuries*, ed. Morris Rossabi (Berkeley: University of California Press, 1983); Michael R. Drompp, *Tang China and the Collapse of the Uighur Empire: A Documentary History* (Leiden: Brill, 2005).

2. Michael C. Brose, *Subjects and Masters: Uyghurs in the Mongol Empire*, Studies on East Asia 28 (Bellingham: Center for East Asian Studies, Western Washington University, 2007).

3. Huang Li, "Hunan Weiwuerzu de lishi yuanliu ji tedian," *Qinghai shehui kexue*, no. 3 (2008): 77–80.

4. M. N. Mouraviev, *Voyage en Turcomanie et à Khiva, fait en 1819 et 1820* (Paris: L. Tenré, 1823), 269. In 1926 a Russian survey found 765 Uzbeks of the Uyghur tribe living in the Kermina oasis. See *Materialy po raionirovaniiu Srednei Azii*,

vol. 1, *Territoriia i naselenie Bukhary i Khorezma* (Tashkent: Komissiia po raionirova-niiu Srednei Azii, 1926), 219.

5. İsmail Hakki Uzunçarşılı, *Anadolu Beylikleri ve Akkoyunlu, Karakoyunlu Devletleri*, 4th ed. (Ankara: Türk Tarih Kurumu, 1988), 155, citing the *Tarikh-i Uljaytu*, which records that Eretna amir was "from the Uyghur people" (*az qaum-i Üyğūr*).

6. Chen Cheng, *Xiyu fanguo zhi* (1415), Zhongguo xibei wenxian congshu, vol. 117 of Xibei minsu wenxian mulu (Lanzhou: Lanzhou guji shudian, 1990), 30.

7. Paul Pelliot, "Le Ḫoja et le Sayyid Ḥusain de l'histoire des Ming," *T'oung Pao* 38, no. 2 (1948): 130–133.

8. Muḥammad ʿIvaż, *Ẕiyaʾ al-Qulub* (Houghton Library, manuscript Persian 95), fols. 121a–121b. The name is given here in a Mongolian plural form, *Uyghud*, indicative of the strong Mongolian influence in Uyghuristan in this period. It was clearly unfamiliar to this manuscript's copyist, who wrote it as *Üy-ğūt*. A Chaghatay translation renders it as one word (*Üyğūt*): *Taẕkira-i Ḥaẕrat-i Ishān* (British Library, manuscript OR5334), fol. 154b.

9. Wang Zongzai, *Siyiguan kao* (Dongfang xuehui, 1924), juan xia, fol. 1b.

10. Liu Yingsheng, *"Huihuiguan zazi" yu "Huihuiguan yiyu" yanjiu* (Beijing: Zhongguo renmin daxue chubanshe, 2008), 90.

11. On the various senses of Moghulistan, see T. I. Sultanov, *Chingiz-khan i Chingizidy: Sud'ba i vlast'* (Moscow: AST, 2006), 169–187.

12. Following the Qing conquest, for example, Muhammad Sadiq Kashgari still took pride in Kashgar as "the most beautiful ornament of the clime of Moghulistan." Muḥammad Ṣadiq Kashghari, *Taẕkira-i ʿAzizan* (Bodleian Library, manuscript Turk D20, ca. 1785), fol. 3b.

13. Devin DeWeese, *Islamization and Native Religion in the Golden Horde: Baba Tükles and Conversion to Islam in Historical and Epic Tradition* (University Park: Pennsylvania State University Press, 1994).

14. Jeff Eden, ed. and trans., *The Life of Muhammad Sharif: A Central Asian Sufi Hagiography in Chaghatay* (Vienna: Verlag der Österreichischen Akademie der Wissenschaften, 2015).

15. Qidirkhan Yarkandi, *"Divani Qidiri"ning Muqäddimisi* (Kashgar: Qäshqär Uyghur Näshriyati, 1986).

16. B. Suleimenov, ed., *Materialy po istorii kazakhskikh khanstv XV–XVIII vekov* (Almaty: Nauka, 1969), 332.

17. Muḥammad Ṣadr Kashghari, *Athar al-Futuḥ* (Abu Rayhon Beruniy nomidagi Sharq qo'lyozmalari markazi, manuscript 753, ca. 1800).

18. Riza Quoly Khan, *Relation de l'ambassade au Kharezm (Khiva)*, trans. Charles Henri Schefer (Paris: Ernest Leroux, 1876–1879), 2:108.

19. On the name of the Uyghurs and the "fatal fascination" it has aroused among scholars, see Gerard Clauson, "The Name Uyğur," *Journal of the Royal Asiatic Society*, n.s. 95, nos. 3–4 (1963): 140–149.

20. O. F. Akimushkin, ed., *Tārīkh-i Kāshgar: Anonimnaia tiurkskaia khronika vladitelei Vostochnogo Turkestana po konets XVII veka* (Saint Petersburg: Peterburgskoe vostokovedenie, 2001).

21. Robert Shaw, *Visits to High Tartary, Yârkand and Kâshgar (Formerly Chinese Tartary), and Return Journey over the Karakorum Pass* (London: J. Murray, 1871), 209.

22. Henry Walter Bellew, *Kashmir and Kashgar: A Narrative of the Journey of the Embassy to Kashgar in 1873–4* (London: Tribner, 1875), 354.

23. Kashghari, *Athar al-Futuḥ*, fols. 147a–147b.

24. Muḥammad Kaẓim, *ʿAlam-ara-yi Nadiri* (Tehran: Kitabfurushi-i Zavvar, 1985–1986), 3:1142.

25. Nikolai Mikhailovich Przheval'skii, *Ot Kiakhty na istoki Zheltoi reki: Issledovanie severnoi okrainy Tibeta, i put' cherez Lob-Nor po basseinu Tarima* (Saint Petersburg: Tipografiia V. S. Balasheva, 1888), 420.

26. The *Shahnama* was widely read and translated in Chinese Turkistan, and the Iranian epic served to bolster local genealogies. Writing in the early twentieth century, Mulla Musa Sayrami noted that the elite of Sayram who claimed aristocratic descent traced their lineage back not only to the Qarakhanids but beyond them to mythical Iranian kings of the *Shahnama*. Mulla Musa Sayrami, *Tarikhi Hämidi*, ed. Änvär Baytur (Beijing: Millätlär Näshriyati, 1986), 592.

27. Kashghari, *Athar al-Futuḥ*, fol. 124a.

28. N. I. Veselovskii, ed., *Posol'stvo k Ziungarskomu Khun-Taichzhi Tsevan Rabtanu kapitana ot artillerii Ivana Unkovskogo i putevoi zhurnal ego za 1722–1724 gody* (Saint Petersburg: Tipografiia V. Kirshbauma, 1887).

29. Zhongguo di-yi lishi dang'anguan, ed., *Yongzhengchao Manwen zhupi zouzhe quanyi* (Hefei: Huangshan shushe, 1998), 1:711–715.

30. Christopher P. Atwood, "Titles, Appanages, Marriages, and Officials: A Comparison of Political Forms in the Zünghar and Thirteenth-Century Mongol Empires," in *Imperial Statecraft: Political Forms and Techniques of Governance in Inner Asia, Sixth-Twentieth Centuries*, ed. David Sneath (Bellingham: Center for East Asian Studies, Western Washington University, 2006).

31. See *Daqing Gaozong Chun (Qianlong) huangdi shilu* (Taibei: Huawen shuju, 1964), 10:7242 (QL 20/10/4 [November 7, 1755]), where the *Bāzārgān* are explicitly referred to as an *otog*. The *Tazkira-i Azizan* refers to them as the "court traders" (*kürä savdāgarlari*). Kashghari, *Tazkira-i ʿAzizan*, fols. 135a, 137b. Erke Beg of Aqsu was one such Muslim who held commissions for several years in the Junghar army and also served on a diplomatic mission to China. On him, see Scott C. Levi and Ron Sela, eds., *Islamic Central Asia: An Anthology of Historical Sources* (Bloomington: Indiana University Press, 2009), 237–239.

32. Muḥammad ʿAbd al-ʿAlim, *Islamnama* (Institut vostochnykh rukopisei Rossiiskoi akademii nauk, manuscript C311, 1777), fol. 58b. Kashghari, *Athar al-Futuḥ*, fol. 128b, also mentions the "elite and nobility (*aʿyān u ashrāf*) of the Taranchi and Karvaniyya."

33. I. Ia. Zlatkin, *Istoriia Dzhungarskogo khanstva (1635–1758)* (Moscow: Nauka, 1964), 179; N. F. Demidova, *Pervye Russkie diplomaty v Kitae: "Rospis" I. Petlina i stateinyi spisok F. I. Baikova* (Moscow: Nauka, 1966), 117–118.

34. M. Tatár-Fosse, "The Khotons of Western Mongolia," *Acta Orientalia Hungarica* 33, no. 1 (1979): 1–37. See also Yang Haiying, "Between Islam and Mongols: The Qotung People in Inner Mongolia, China," *Inner Asia* 6, no. 1 (2004): 5–22.

35. Veselovskii, *Posol'stvo k Ziungarskomu Khun-Taichzhi*, 186.

36. Zhao Xiangru and Reinhard F. Hahn, "The Ili Turk People and Their Language," *Central Asiatic Journal* 33, nos. 3–4 (1989): 260–289.

37. Kashghari, *Tazkira-i ʿAzizan*, fol. 89a.

38. Zhongguo di-yi lishi dang'anguan and Zhongguo bianjiang shidi yanjiu zhongxin, eds., *Qingdai Xinjiang Manwen dang'an huibian* (Guilin: Guangxi shifan daxue chubanshe, 2012), 38:160 (QL 24/5/14 [June 8, 1759]).

39. J.-B. Du Halde, *The General History of China. Containing a Geographical, Historical, Chronological, Political and Physical Description of the Empire of China, Chinese-Tartary, Corea and Tibet* (London: J. Watts, 1736), 4:181.

40. Wen Da et al., comp., *Qinzheng pingding shuomo fanglüe* (1708), in *Siku quanshu* (Shanghai: Shanghai guji chubanshe, 1987), 355:619 (KX 36/10/2 [November 15, 1697]).

41. Zhong Gengqi, *Ganzhou fuzhi* (1779), Zhongguo xibei wenxian congshu xubian, vol. 2 of Xibei xijian fangzhi wenxian juan (Lanzhou: Gansu wenhua chubanshe, 1999), 157.

42. Peter C. Perdue, *China Marches West: The Qing Conquest of Central Eurasia* (Cambridge, MA: Belknap Press of Harvard University Press, 2005), 473.

43. Kashghari, *Tazkira-i ʿAzizan*.

44. In his late-nineteenth-century verse history, for example, Mulla Bilal distinguishes the Dungans from the "Muslims" in Xinjiang and uses the word "Muslimese" (*musulmāncha*) in reference to the local Turkic dialect. Mulla Bilal bin Mulla Yusuf al-Naẓim, *Ghazat dar Mulk-i Chin* (Kazan: Universitetskaia tipografiia, 1880–1881).

45. Adeeb Khalid, *The Politics of Muslim Cultural Reform: Jadidism in Central Asia* (Berkeley: University of California Press, 1998), 191–192.

46. See, for example, the Turkic translation of the official biography of Imin Khoja in David Brophy and Onuma Takahiro, *Historical Sources on Turfan* (forthcoming, 2016).

47. W. Radloff, *Proben der Volksliteratur der türkischen Stämme*, vol. 6, *Dialect der Tarantschi* (Saint Petersburg: Tipografiia Imperatorskoi akademii nauk, 1886), 68.

48. Ch. Ch. Valikhanov, "O sostoianii Altyshara ili shesti vostochnykh gorodov Kitaiskoi provintsii Nan-Lu (Maloi Bukharii) v 1858–59 gg," in *Sobranie sochinenii v piati tomakh* (Alma-Ata: 1985), 3:157–158.

49. G. N. Potanin, *Ocherki severo-zapadnoi Mongolii* (Saint Petersburg: Tipografiia V. Kirshbauma, 1883), 2:14–15.

50. Sayrami, *Tarikhi Hämidi*, 146.

51. David Brophy, "High Asia and the High Qing: Persian Letters in the Beijing Archives," in *No Tapping around Philology: A Festschrift for Wheeler McIntosh Thackston Jr.'s 70th Birthday*, ed. Alireza Korangy and Daniel J. Sheffield (Wiesbaden: Harrassowitz, 2014), 325–367; David Brophy and Rian Thum, "The Shrine of Muḥammad Sharif and Its Qing-era Patrons," in *The Life of Muhammad Sharif*, ed. and trans. Jeff Eden (Vienna: Verlag der Österreichischen Akademie der Wissenschaften, 2015), 55–75; Valikhanov, "O sostoianii Altyshara," 186.

52. W. Radloff, *Aus Sibirien: Lose Blätter aus meinem Tagebuche* (Leipzig: T. O. Weigel, 1893), 2:335–336; Saguchi Tōru, "Taranchi jin no shakai—Iri keikoku no Uiguru buzokushi, 1760–1860," *Shigaku zasshi* 73, no. 11 (1964): 25–33.

53. Gu Yanwu, *Rizhi lu jishi* (Shanghai: Zhonghua shuju, 1927–1936), juan 29, fols. 31b–32a.

54. As Onuma Takahiro has discussed, a similar line of thinking informed an inscription to the mosque built by the Qianlong emperor for visiting Muslim dignitaries in Beijing, which played on the similarity between the words *mani* and *mulla* to connect the Manichaean Uyghurs of the steppe with the Muslims of Xinjiang. Onuma Takahiro, "The Qing Dynasty and Its Central Asian Neighbors," *Saksaha: A Journal of Manchu Studies* 12 (2014): 37–38, 42.

55. *Xiqing xujian jiabian*, Fulu (Shanghai: Hanfenlou, 1910), fol. 1a.

56. [Yong-gui?], *Xiyu zhi* (Russian State Library, Manuscript Division, fond 274, no. 287, 1762–1763), juan 1, fol. 1.

57. Tao Baolian, *Xinmao shixing ji* (Lanzhou: Gansu renmin chubanshe, 2002), 370.

58. Zhongguo shehui kexueyuan Zhongguo bianjiang shidi yanjiu zhongxin, ed., *Xinjiang xiangtu zhigao* (Beijing: Quanguo tushuguan wenxian suowei fuzhi zhongxin, 1990), 30, 470.

59. Justin Rudelson, *Oasis Identities: Uyghur Nationalism along China's Silk Road* (New York: Columbia University Press, 1997).

60. Laura Newby, "'Us and Them' in Eighteenth and Nineteenth Century Xinjiang," in *Situating the Uyghurs between China and Central Asia*, ed. Ildikó Béller-Hann, M. Cristina Cesàro, Rachel Harris, and Joanne Smith Finley (Aldershot: Ashgate, 2007), 16n2; Rian Thum, *The Sacred Routes of Uyghur History* (Cambridge, MA: Harvard University Press, 2014).

61. Sir T. D. Forsyth, *Report of a Mission to Yarkund in 1873* (Calcutta: Foreign Department Press, 1875), 498.

62. N. Katanov, "Man'chzhursko-Kitaiskii 'li' na narechii tiurkov Kitaiskogo Turkestana," *Zapiski Vostochnogo otdeleniia Imperatorskogo russkogo arkheologicheskogo obshchestva* 14 (1901): 54; Wang Shunan, ed., *Xinjiang tuzhi* (1911; repr., Taibei: Wenhai chubanshe, 1965), juan 31, fol. 9a.

63. The first documented movement of significant numbers comes from a fifteenth-century source, which describes a settlement created during Tamerlane's rule for a group of Moghuls who had left Kashgar. V. V. Bartol'd, *K istorii orosheniia Turkestana*, in *Sochineniia* (Moscow: Nauka, 1965), 3:213.

64. S. S. Gubaeva, *Ètnicheskii sostav naseleniia Fergany v kontse XIX–nachale XX v. (po dannym toponimii)* (Tashkent: Fan, 1983), 86–87.

65. B. Kh. Karmysheva, *Ocherki ètnicheskoi istorii iuzhnykh raionov Tadzhikistana i Uzbekistana* (Moscow: Nauka, 1976), 166.

66. Kawahara Yayoi, "Kōkando hānkoku ni okeru Marugiran no toratachi," *Annals of Japan Association for Middle East Studies* 20, no. 2 (2005): 269–294.

67. A. N. Boldyrev, ed., *Ta'rikh-i Badakhshan: Faksimile rukopisi, izdanie teksta, perevod s persidskogo*, Pamiatniki pis'mennosti Vostoka, vol. 98 (Moscow: Vostochnaia literatura, 1997), 46.

68. In the 1840s, Kashgar was said to be worth 10,000 gold *ṭillā*, roughly 128,000 rubles. See "Obozrenie Kokanskogo khanstva v nyneshnem ego sostoianii," *Zapiski Russkogo geograficheskogo obshchestva* 3 (1849): 196.

69. The price varied from sixteen *yambu*s for Khotan, to four for Uchturfan and Yengisar. The precise number and permitted location of *aqsaqal*s seems to have never been clarified in Qing-Kokand negotiations, but a letter from Kokand in 1848 requests that a total of fifty individuals be admitted in the party of *aqsaqal*s. Onuma Takahiro et al., "Guoli gugong bowuyuan suocang 1848 nian liangjian Haohan laiwen zaikao," *Furen lishi xuebao*, no. 26 (2011): 107–138.

70. John Mitchell and Robert Mitchell, *The Russians in Central Asia: Their Occupation of the Kirghiz Steppe and the Line of the Syr-Daria: Their Political Relations with Khiva, Bokhara, and Khokand: Also Descriptions of Chinese Turkestan and Dzungaria. By Capt. Valikhanof, M. Veniukof, and Other Russian Travellers* (London: Edward Stanford, 1865), 231. The *aqsaqal* Bay Khan (in office 1849–1852), for instance, prohibited Andijanis from dismounting before Qing officials, as was required of local Muslims. Valikhanov, "O sostoianii Altyshara," 186.

71. Laura Newby, *The Empire and the Khanate: A Political History of Qing Relations with Khoqand c. 1700–1860* (Leiden: Brill, 2005).

72. "Obozrenie Kokanskogo khanstva," 196.

73. Mirza Shams-i Bukhari, *Ta'rikh-i Bukhara, Khoqand va Kashghar* (Tehran: Ayina-i Miraṣ, 1998), 103.

74. Mitchell and Mitchell, *Russians in Central Asia*, 212. There was a Kashgari *mahalla* in Tashkent. N. G. Mallitskii, "Tashkentskie makhallia i mauza," in *V. V. Bartol'du turkestanskie druzia, ucheniki i pochitateli*, ed. A. E. Shmidt and E. K. Betger (Tashkent: Obshchestvo dlia izucheniia Tadzhikistana i iranskikh narodnostei za ego predelami, 1927), 113.

75. Valikhanov, "O sostoianii Altyshara," 149–150.

76. V. Nalivkin, *Kratkaia istoriia Kokandskogo khanstva* (Kazan: Tipografiia Imperatorskogo universiteta, 1886), 185.

77. Valikhanov, "O sostoianii Altyshara," 184.

78. S. S. Gubaeva, "Uigury i dungane Ferganskoi doliny," in *Sovremennoe razvitie ètnicheskikh grupp Srednei Azii i Kazakhstana* (Moscow: Institut ètnologii i antropologii imeni N. N. Miklukho-Maklaia, 1992), 121; Sergei Abashin, *Natsionalizmy v Srednei Azii v poiskakh identichnosti* (Saint Petersburg: Aleteiia, 2007), 65.

79. Cited in A. K. Kamalov, "Migratsiia naseleniia Kashgarii v Ferganskuiu dolinu posle padeniia Kashgarskogo èmirata v kontse XIX v," in *Uigurovedenie v Kazakhstane: Traditsiia i novatsiia*, ed. A. K. Kamalov (Almaty: Nash Mir, 2006), 93.

80. Valikhanov, "O sostoianii Altyshara," 164.

81. A. M. Reshetov mentions a Kashgari neighborhood in Khojand called "Akhun's Lane" (*guzār-i ākhūn*) in "Uigury v Tadzhikistane," in *Ètnicheskaia istoriia i traditsionnaia kul'tura narodov Srednei Azii i Kazakhstana* (Nukus: Karakalpakstan, 1989), 195. Another name by which the migrants were known was "Taghliq" (mountain men), reflecting the fact that militant followers of the *khoja*s were often drawn from communities inhabiting mountainous no-man's-lands in the Tianshan. On this term see Michael Friedrich, "'Taghlik' und 'Turkmen' bzw. 'Türk': Zu einer (einer?) wenig bekannten ethnischen Gruppe in Xinjiang," *Wiener Zeitschrift für die Kunde des Morgenlandes* 91 (2001): 105–159.

82. Mitchell and Mitchell, *Russians in Central Asia*, 197–198.

83. Omonbek Jalilov, *Xushhol G'aribiy* (Tashkent: Fan, 2005), 5.

84. Tsentral'nyi statisticheskii komitet, ed., *Pervaia vseobshchaia perepis' naseleniia Rossiiskoi imperii 1897 g.*, vol. 7 (Saint Petersburg: N. P. Nyrkin, 1905), 9.

85. Ferganskii oblastnii statisticheskii komitet, *Statisticheskii obzor Ferganskoi oblasti za 1904 god* (Novyi Margelan: Tipografiia Ferganskogo oblastnogo pravleniia, 1905); *Statisticheskii obzor Ferganskoi oblasti za 1906 god* (Skobelev: Tipografiia Ferganskogo oblastnogo pravleniia, 1908). For Chinese figures, see "Xin Yi zai E zhi huaqiao," *Shenbao*, May 5, 1912, 6.

86. J. G. A. Pocock, *Barbarism and Religion*, vol. 4, *Barbarism, Savages and Empires* (Cambridge, Cambridge University Press, 2005).

87. Barthélemy d'Herbelot, *Bibliothèque orientale* (Paris: Compagnie des Libraires, 1697), 2:316; *Histoire généalogique des Tatars Traduite du manuscrit tartare d'Abulgasi-Bayadur-Chan & enrichie d'un grand nombre de remarques authentiques & très-curieuses sur le véritable estat présent de l'Asie Septentrionale* (Leiden: Abram Kallewier, 1726).

88. Antoine Gaubil, *Histoire de Gentchiscan et de toute la dinastie des Mongous ses successeurs, conquérans de la China* (Paris: Briasson & Piget, 1739), 13; Joseph de Guignes, *Histoire générale des Huns, des Turcs, des Mogols, et des autres Tartares occidentaux* (Paris: Desaint & Saillant, 1756–1758); Claude de Visdelou, "Suite des observations," in *Bibliothèque orientale* (Maestricht: J. E. Dufour & Roux, 1776), 157.

89. Julius Klaproth, *Beleuchtung und Widerlegung der Forschungen über die Geschichte der Mittelasiatichen Völker des Herrn J.-J. Schmidt* (Paris: Dondey-Dupré, 1824), 6–7.

90. Julius Klaproth, "Über die Sprache und Schrift der Uiguren," *Fundgruben des Orients* 2 (1811): 167–195. Klaproth expanded his work and published it as a monograph in Berlin the following year: *Abhandlung über die Sprache und Schrift der Uiguren* (Berlin, 1812).

91. Abel Rémusat, *Recherches sur les langues tartares, ou Mémoires sur différents points de la grammaire et de la littérature des Mandchous, des Mongols, des Ouigours et des Tibétains* (Paris: Imprimerie Royale, 1820).

92. I. J. Schmidt, "Einwürfe gegen die Hypothesen des Herrn Hofr. Klaproth: Über Sprache und Schrift der Uiguren," *Fundgruben des Orients* 6 (1818): 321–338.

93. Julius Klaproth, *Abhandlung über die Sprache und Schrift der Uiguren. Nebst einem Wörterverzeichnisse und anderen uigurischen Sprachproben, aus dem Kaiserlichen Übersetzungshofe zu Peking* (Paris: In der Königlichen Druckerey, 1820).

94. I. J. Schmidt, *Forschungen im Gebiete der älteren religiösen, politischen und literärischen Bildungsgeschichte der Völker Mittel-Asiens, vorzüglich der Mongolen und Tibeter* (Saint Petersburg: Karl Kray, 1824), 114.

95. Klaproth, *Beleuchtung und Widerlegung*; Klaproth, "Demonstration définitive que les Ouigour étaient un peuple de race turque," *Bulletin des sciences historiques, antiquités, philologie* 2 (1824): 118–119.

96. I. J. Schmidt, *Würdigung und Abfertigung der Klaprothschen sogenannten Beleuchtung und Widerlegung seiner Forschungen im Gebiete der Geschichte der Völker Mittel-Asiens* (Leipzig: Carl Cnobloch, 1826).

97. Monakh Iakinf, *Zapiski o Mongolii* (Saint Petersburg: Karl Krai, 1828). Two essays written by non-Russian intellectuals in Kazan similarly sought Mongolian etymologies for the name of the Uyghurs: Mirza Aleksandr Kazem-Bek, "Issledovaniia ob Uigurakh," *Zhurnal Ministerstva narodnogo prosveshcheniia* 8 (1841): 1–86; Dorzhi Banzarov, "Ob Oiratakh i Uigurakh," in *Sobranie sochinenii* (Moscow: Izdatel'stvo Akademii nauk SSSR, 1955), 185.

98. The libraries of Istanbul were a rich source of such material, much of it brought to light by the Ottomanist Joseph von Purgstall Hammer. See his "Uigurisches Diplom Kutlugh Timur's vom Jahre 800 (1397)," *Fundgruben des Orients* 6 (1818): 359–362. See also M. Amédée Jaubert, "Notice d'un manuscrit turc, en caractères ouïgours, envoyé par M. de Hammer, à M. Abel-Rémusat," *Journal Asiatique* 6 (1825): 39–52.

99. Hermann Vambery, *Uigurische Sprachmonumente und das Kudatku Bilik* (Innsbruck: Druck der Wagner'schen Universitäts-Buchdruckerei, 1870), 3–12.

100. V. P. Vasil'ev, *O dvizhenii magometanstva v Kitae: Godichnyi torzhestvennyi akt v S.-Peterburgskom universitete 2 dekabria 1867 g.* (Saint Petersburg: V. Golovin, 1867); reprinted as V. P. Vasil'ev, "Magometanstvo v Kitae," in *Otkrytie Kitaia i drugie stat'i akademika V. P. Vasil'eva* (Saint Petersburg: Stolichnaia tipografiia, 1900), 106–138; translated by Rudolf Loewenthal as *Islam in China*, Central Asian Collectanea 3 (Washington, DC: 1960).

101. E. Delmar Morgan, "On Muhammadanism in China," *The Phoenix* 2 (1872): 133–134, 154–157, 176–180; P. Dabry de Thiersant, *Le Mahométisme en Chine et dans le Turkestan Oriental* (Paris: E. Leroux, 1878).

102. Radloff, *Aus Sibirien*, 1:125. See also his comments in W. Radloff, *Phonetik der nördlichen Türksprachen* (Leipzig: Weigel, 1882), xxxv–xxxvi.

103. Robert P. Geraci, *Window on the East: National and Imperial Identities in Late Tsarist Russia* (Ithaca, NY: Cornell University Press, 2001), 140–149; Mustafa Tuna, *Imperial Russia's Muslims: Islam, Empire, and European Modernity, 1788–1914* (Cambridge: Cambridge University Press, 2015).

104. A. G. Sertkaia, "Zhizn' i deiatel'nost' N. N. Pantusova. Bibliograficheskii spisok trudov," in *Nasledie N. F. Katanova: Istoriia i kul'tura tiurkskikh narodov Evrazii* (Kazan: Alma Lit, 2005).

105. Sergei Efimovich Malov, "N. F. Katanov, prof. Kazanskogo universiteta (1862–1922 gg.)," in *Nikolai Fedorovich Katanov: Materialy i soobshcheniia*, ed. N. Domozhakov (Abakan: Khakasskoe knizhnoe izdatel'stvo, 1958). After his return to Russia, Katanov gradually fell out with the Saint Petersburg intellectuals, who reproached him for not taking any interest in the ancient ruins of Turfan, which were now known to contain manuscripts (allowing the British and Germans to get the jump on them). His linguistic work was also criticized for lacking literary merit.

106. *Izvestiia Russkogo komiteta dlia izucheniia Srednei i Vostochnoi Azii* 10 (March 1910), 14.

107. PFARAN 177/2/161, ll. 5–5ob.

108. Borhan Shahid, "Uyghïrlar Arasïnda 'Ilmi Tädqiqat," *Vaqït*, October 4, 1914, 2.

109. Papers of George Ernest Morrison, State Library of New South Wales, file 312/228, p. 171.

2. The Making of a Colonial Frontier

1. Hodong Kim, *Holy War in China: The Muslim Rebellion and State in Chinese Central Asia 1864–1877* (Stanford, CA: Stanford University Press, 2004).

2. S. V. Moiseev, ed., *Russko-kashgarskie otnosheniia v 60–70-x gg. XIX v.: Dokumenty i izvlecheniia* (Barnaul: Azbuka, 2008), 36–37.

3. A. D'iakov, "Vospominaniia iliiskogo sibintsa o dungansko-taranchinskom vosstanii v 1864–1871 godakh v Iliiskom Krae," *Zapiski Vostochnogo otdeleniia Imperatorskogo russkogo arkheologicheskogo obshchestva* 18, nos. 2–3 (1908): 233–282.

4. "Pravitel' Altyshara," in *Materialy dlia statistiki Turkestanskogo kraia*, ed. N. A. Maev (Saint Petersburg: Turkestanskii statisticheskii komitet, 1872–1879), 2:200.

5. N. Borneman, "Ocherk Tarbagataiskogo kraia (Donesenie konsula v Chuguchake)," *Sbornik konsul'skikh donesenii* 3, no. 3 (1900): 209–236.

6. Şerif Mardin, *The Genesis of Young Ottoman Thought: A Study in the Modernization of Turkish Political Ideas* (Princeton, NJ: Princeton University Press, 1962), 60n110.

7. "Putevye zamechaniia lekaria Omskogo garizonnogo polka F. K. Zibbershteina (17 iulia–2 oktiabria 1825 g.)," in *Istoriia Kazakhstana v Russkikh istochnikakh*, ed. M. A. Kul-Mukhammed (Almaty: Daik-Press, 2007), 6:249.

8. N. I. Veselovskii, *Poezdka N. I. Liubimova v Chuguchak i Kul'dzhu v 1845 godu pod vidom kuptsa Khorosheva* (Saint Petersburg: Tipografiia Ministerstva putei soobsheniia, 1909), 179, 183.

9. K. E. v. Baer and Gr. v. Helmersen, eds., *Beiträge zur Kenntniss des Russischen Reiches und der angränzenden Länder Asiens*, vol. 2, *Nachrichten über Chiwa, Buchara,*

Chokand und den nordwestlichen Theil des chinesischen Staates (Saint Petersburg: Im Verlage der Kaiserlichen Akademie der Wissenschaften, 1839), 84–85.

10. *Türkistan Vilayatining Gazeti*, July 26, 1871, 1. The sultan of Ghulja was exiled to Vernyi, where he and his large family were kept on a pension from Ghulja's tax revenues. Abu'l-Ala died in 1879. See "Iz Vernogo" (1883), *Turkestanskii sbornik*, 326:132.

11. On the course of the Muslim rebellion in Ili, see Kim, *Holy War in China*. On the diplomatic resolution of the crisis, see Immanuel C. Y. Hsu, *The Ili Crisis: A Study of Sino-Russian Diplomacy, 1871–1881* (Oxford: Oxford University Press, 1965).

12. Mulla Bilal bin Mulla Yusuf al-Naẓim, *Ghazat dar Mulk-i Chin* (Kazan: Universitetskaia tipografiia, 1880–1881), 123, line 9; 44, line 12.

13. Baron A. V. Kaulbars, "Poezdka v Kul'dzhu," in *Materialy*, ed. N. A. Maev, 2:248.

14. G. L. Kolpakovskii, "G. L. Kolpakovskogo o zaniatii Kul'dzhinskogo raiona v 1871 godu," in *Russkii Turkestan: Sbornik izdannyi po povodu politechnicheskoi vystavki* (Saint Petersburg: Tipografiia tovarishchestva "obshchestvennaia pol'za," 1872), 231.

15. For further discussion of the Ili Valley under Russian administration, see Noda Jin, "Reconsidering the Ili Crisis: The Ili Region under the Russian Rule (1871–1881)," in *Reconceptualizing Cultural and Environmental Change in Central Asia: An Historical Perspective on the Future*, ed. M. Watanabe and J. Kubota (Kyoto: Research Institute for Humanity and Nature, 2010).

16. N. N. Pantusov, *Svedeniia o Kul'dzhinskom raione za 1871–1877 gody* (Kazan: Universitetskaia tipografiia, 1881), 72–75.

17. TsGARK 21/1/170, l. 122ob; TsGARK 21/1/379, l. 15.

18. Eugene Schuyler, *Turkistan: Notes of a Journey in Russian Turkistan, Khokand, Bukhara, and Kuldja* (New York: Scribner, Armstrong, 1876), 2:194–195.

19. A. P. Khoroshkhin, *Sbornik statei kasaiushchikhsia do Turkestanskogo kraia* (Saint Petersburg: Tipografiia i khromolitografiia A. Transhelia, 1876), 324. Bushri also showed the members of De Ujfalvy's French scientific mission around town. See Ch. E. de Ujfalvy de Mezö-Kovesd, *Le Kohistan, le Ferghanah et Kouldja avec un appendice sur la Kachgarie* (Paris: Ernest Leroux, 1878), 133.

20. G. N. Potanin, "O karavannoi torgovle s Dzhungarskoi Bukhariei v XVIII stoletii," *Chteniia v Imperatorskom obshchestve istorii i drevnosti rossiiskikh pri Moskovskom universitete 1868 g.* 2 (1868), 45.

21. Zhongguo di-yi lishi dang'anguan and Zhongguo bianjiang shidi yanjiu zhongxin, eds., *Qingdai Xinjiang Manwen dang'an huibian* (Guilin: Guangxi shifan daxue chubanshe, 2012), 38:160 (QL24/5/14 [June 8, 1759]); 202:41–50 (QL59/10/6 [October 29, 1794]).

22. Ch. Ch. Valikhanov, "O sostoianii Altyshara ili shesti vostochnykh gorodov Kitaiskoi provintsii Nan-Lu (Maloi Bukharii) v 1858–59 gg," in *Sobranie sochinenii v piati tomakh* (Alma-Ata, 1985), 3:162–163.

23. S. Rostovskii, "Tsarskaia Rossiia i Sin'-Tszian v XIX–XX vekakh," *Istorik-marksist*, no. 3 (1936): 26–53.

24. Sir T. D. Forsyth, *Report of a Mission to Yarkund in 1873* (Calcutta: Foreign Department Press, 1875), 500.

25. Immanuel C. Y. Hsu, "The Great Policy Debate in China, 1874: Maritime Defense vs. Frontier Defense," *Harvard Journal of Asiatic Studies* 25 (1964–1965): 212–228.

26. Zuo Zongtang, *Zuo Wenxiang gong zoushu*, Xubian (Shanghai: Tushu jicheng, 1890), juan 58, fol. 2a. For an overview of the grain problem, see Wen-djang Chu, *The Moslem Rebellion in Northwest China, 1862–1878: A Study of Government Minority Policy* (The Hague: Mouton, 1966), 181–191.

27. P. Ia. Piasetskii, *Neudachnaia ekspeditsiia v Kitai 1874–1875 gg.* (Saint Petersburg: Tipografiia M. Stasiulevicha, 1881), 88. This book was a rejoinder to reviews of Piasetskii's initial account of the journey, published in 1880. In it he accused Sosnovskii of greatly exaggerating the commercial and political results of the mission to the point of lying about where the mission had actually traveled. On the various publications resulting from the mission, see G. I. Kurnykina, "Iz istorii ucheno-torgovoi ekspeditsii 1874–1875 gg. (ili 'Nagliadnoe znakomstvo s Kitaem')," in *Tsentral'naia Aziia i Sibir': Pervye nauchnye chteniia pamiati E. M. Zalkinda*, ed. V. A. Moiseev (Barnaul: Azbuka, 2003), 149–161.

28. RGVIA 400/1/490, ll. 127, 156.

29. Wang Shunan, ed., *Xinjiang tuzhi* (1911; repr., Taibei: Wenhai chubanshe, 1965), juan 116, fol. 14b.

30. On Vali Bay's relationship with the Jalilov brothers Bushri and Jamaluddin, see G. K. Gins, "Taranchi i dungane: Ocherk iz poezdki po Semirech'iu," *Istoricheskii vestnik* 125 (1911), 706.

31. TsGARK 21/1/329.

32. P. P. Matveev, *Poezdka v zapadnyi Kitai* (Tashkent: Tipografiia Voenno-narodnogo upravleniia, 1879), 32.

33. On these migrations, see Kh. Iusurov, *Pereselenie Dungan na terretoriiu Kirgizii i Kazakhstana* (Bishkek: Kirgizgosizdat, 1961).

34. I. Mushketov, "K voprosu o Kul'dzhe" (1879), *Turkestanskii sbornik*, 245:7–14.

35. V. A. Moiseev, *Rossiia i Kitai v Tsentral'noi Azii (vtoraia polovina XIX v.–1917 g.)* (Barnaul: Azbuka, 2003), 166.

36. "Kul'dzha," (1879), *Turkestanskii sbornik*, 245:35–36.

37. RGVIA 400/1/636.

38. For obituaries, see "Nekrolog," *Otchet Imperatorskogo russkogo geograficheskogo obshchestva za 1882 god* (1883): 16–17; "Report on Russian Geography for the Year," *Proceedings of the Royal Geographical Society and Monthly Record of Geography*, n.s. 5, no. 7 (1883): 389–392.

39. Eric Lohr, *Russian Citizenship: From Empire to Soviet Union* (Cambridge, MA: Harvard University Press, 2012).

40. Dai Liangzuo, "Yili jiangjun Jin-shun shuping," *Yili shifan xueyuan xuebao*, no. 1 (2006): 37.

41. RGVIA 400/1/4897, l. 3.

42. TsGARU 1/1/1475.

43. TsGARU 1/17/977, ll. 195ob–196.

44. "Iz Kul'dzhi" (1882), *Turkestanskii sbornik*, 326:49.

45. "Iz Kul'dzhi" (1882), *Turkestanskii sbornik*, 326:60; see also *Turkestanskii sbornik*, 298:232. Judd Kinzley refers to Qing officials taking out loans from Muslim merchants in Ghulja in 1877. See "Staking Claims to China's Borderland: Oil, Ores and State-Building in Xinjiang Province, 1893–1964" (Ph.D. diss., University of California, San Diego, 2012), 51.

46. TsGARU 1/17/977, l. 196.

47. "Iz Kul'dzhi" (1882), *Turkestanskii sbornik*, 326:67.

48. Moiseev, *Rossiia i Kitai v Tsentral'noi Azii*, 206–207, suggests that the total number of Taranchis, Dungans, and Kazakhs who took up Russian subjecthood may have been more than 107,000.

49. "Iz Kul'dzhi" (1883), *Turkestanskii sbornik*, 326:20.

50. Qasim Beg, *Ghuljaning Vaqiʿatlarining Bayani* (Institut vostochnykh rukopisei Rossiiskoi akademii nauk, manuscript B4018, late 19th c.), fol. 13b.

51. Konstantin Konstantinovich Palen, *Otchet po revizii Turkestanskogo kraia, proizvedennoi po Vysochaishemu poveleniiu* (Saint Petersburg: Senatskaia tipografiia, 1910), 1:11.

52. "Ukaz ego imperatorskogo velichestva," *Semirechenskie oblastnye vedomosti*, June 29, 1899, 266–267.

53. Adeeb Khalid, "Culture and Power in Colonial Turkestan," *Cahiers d'Asie centrale*, nos. 17–18 (2009): 419n16.

54. O. Shkapskii, "Pereselentsy i agrarnyi vopros v Semirechenskoi oblasti," *Voprosy kolonizatsii* 1, no. 1 (1907): 34.

55. P. P. Rumiantsev, *Uezdy Zhetysu* (Almaty: Zhalïn Baspasï, 2000), 234.

56. Another remnant of Qing Xinjiang's decimal system of village administration can be seen in the large number of Taranchi toponyms in Semireche that end in *-yüzi* (hundred), e.g., Islam Yüzi, Khudayqul Yüzi, Tokhchi Yüzi (ibid., 245–250).

57. *Russkii Turkestan*, January 15, 1906, 5. In Ili, the Chinese officials levied approximately 10 percent, while Vali Bay's tenants paid as much as half of their harvest in rent.

58. Gins, "Taranchi i dungane," 707.

59. Ivan Ivanovich Poklevskii-Kozell, *Novyi torgovyi put' ot Irtysha v Vernyi i Kul'dzhu i issledovanie reki Ili na parakhode "Kolpakovskii"* (Saint Petersburg: Tipografiia i litografiia D. I. Shemetkina, 1885), 10. The ship was made to order at the Edward Hayes shipyards in Stony Stratford.

60. Vali Bay's mill is shown on the map of Ghulja in S. Fedorov, *Opyt voenno-statisticheskogo opisaniia Iliiskogo kraia* (Tashkent: Tipografiia shtaba Turkestanskogo voennogo okruga, 1903).

61. *Semirechenskie oblastnye vedomosti*, March 2, 1899, 90; March 5, 1899, 95.

62. Kataoka Kazutada, *Shinchō Shinkyō tōchi kenkyū* (Tokyo: Yūzankaku, 1991), 155.

63. Tao Baolian, *Xinmao shixing ji* (Lanzhou: Gansu renmin chubanshe, 2002), 55.

64. Liu Jintang, *Liu Xiangqin gong zougao* (1898), Qingdai Xinjiang xijian zoudu huibian, vol. 1 of Tongzhi, Guangxu, Xuantong chao juan (Ürümchi: Xinjiang renmin chubanshe, 1997), 105.

65. Wang, *Xinjiang tuzhi*, juan 98, fol. 2a.

66. See the documents in IMH 01-20-006-02.

67. S. Rostovskii, "Tsarskaia Rossiia i Sin'-Tszian v XIX–XX vekakh," *Istorik-marksist*, no. 3 (1936): 41.

68. TsGARU 1/29/735.

69. AVPRI 242/630/5.

70. See, for example, Philip D. Curtin, *Cross-Cultural Trade in World History* (Cambridge: Cambridge University Press, 1984).

71. Nikolai Viacheslav Bogoiavlenskii, *Zapadnyi zastennyi Kitai: Ego proshloe, nastoiashchee sostoianie i polozhenie v nem Russkikh poddannykh* (Saint Petersburg: Tipografiia A. S. Suvorina, 1906), 340.

72. Qurban 'Ali Khalidi, *Tavarikh-i Khamsa-i Sharqi* (Kazan: Ürnäk Maṭba'asï, 1910), 759.

73. Forsyth, *Report of a Mission to Yarkund*, 97. According to this account, the Badakhshani *aqsaqal* had the same privileges as the Kokandi, but Kashmiris paid regular taxes through the *aqsaqal* to the local *wang*.

74. IOR L/PS/10/825, p. 128.

75. Mirqasïm Gosmanov, *Yabïlmagan Kitab yaki Chächelgän Orlïqlar* (Kazan: Tatarstan Kitap Näshriyati, 1996), 35.

76. Bogoiavlenskii, *Zapadnyi zastennyi Kitai*, 367–368; RGVA 25895/1/832, l. 19.

77. Peter Fleming, *News from Tartary: A Journey from Peking to Kashmir* (London: Jonathan Cape, 1936), 241.

78. Khalidi, *Tavarikh-i Khamsa-i Sharqi*, 759, calls one such honor a "dragon-shaped decoration with a red cover," perhaps describing the Order of the Double Dragon, a decoration reserved for foreigners. In 1902, the Ili general Ma-liang awarded two Russian-subject Dungan *aqsaqals* in Ghulja and Suiding the "jeweled star." Ma-liang and Guang-fu, *Yili jiangjun Ma-liang, Guang-fu zougao*, Qingdai Xinjiang xijian zoudu huibian, vol. 3 of Tongzhi, Guangxu, Xuantong chao juan (Ürümchi: Xinjiang renmin chubanshe, 1997), 1,237.

79. Yang Zengxin, *Buguozhai wendu* (1921; repr., Taibei: Wenhai chubanshe, 1965), 2,404–2,405.

80. "Burazan. Donesenie Khotanskogo torgovogo agenta Abdu-s-Sattar N. F. Petrovskomu," *Zapiski Vostochnogo otdeleniia Imperatorskogo russkogo arkheologicheskogo obshchestva* 9, nos. 1–4 (1896): 267–269.

81. For a photograph of Badruddin, see Aurel Stein, *Ruins of Desert Cathay: A Personal Narrative of Explorations in Central Asia and Westernmost China* (London: Macmillan, 1912), vol. 2, facing p. 434.

82. Yang Zengxin, *Buguozhai wendu sanbian* (1934), Zhongguo xibei wenxian congshu xubian, vol. 4 of Xibei shidi wenxian juan (Lanzhou: Gansu wenhua chubanshe, 1999), 556.

83. Sälim, "Qïṭay Ḥökümätinä Tabiʿ Olan 'Gholja' Shähreneng Äḥväle," *Vaqït*, May 1, 1908, 4–5. According to a British report, the Ghulja qadi derived his income from a 10 percent levy on property transactions that he witnessed. IOR L/PS/10/825, p. 188b.

84. V. A. Moiseev, "Novye dannye o mezhdunarodnykh s"ezdakh na russko-kitaiskoi granitse v Tsentral'noi Azii v 80-x gg. XIX–nachale XX v," in *Tsentral'naia Aziia i Sibir'*, 167–171.

85. Li Sheng, *Xinjiang dui Su (E) maoyi shi, 1600–1990* (Ürümchi: Xinjiang renmin chubanshe, 1994), 206ff.

86. IOR L/PS/7/104, doc. 691.

87. Wang, *Xinjiang tuzhi*, juan 45, fols. 10a–b. The bureau had only a skeleton staff—two officials for each of the province's four circuits.

88. *Xinjiang ziyiju choubanchu diyici baogaoshu* (1910), Zhongguo bianjiang xingji diaochaji baogaoshu deng bianwu ziliao congbian, vol. 39 of Chubian (Hong Kong: Fuchi shuyuan chuban youxian gongsi, 2009), 321–322.

89. Zhang Dajun, *Xinjiang fengbao qishi nian* (Taibei: Lanxi chubanshe, 1980), 207.

90. Bogoiavlenskii, *Zapadnyi zastennyi Kitai*, 326–327.

91. Zhang Shaobo, *Xinjiang waijiao baogaoshu* (Dihua: Xinjiang jiaoshe gongshu waijiao yanjiusuo, 1913).

92. Carl Gustaf Emil Mannerheim, *Across Asia from West to East in 1906–1908* (Helsinki: Suomalai-Ugrilainen Seura, 1940), 1:219.

93. *Ningyuan xian xiangtuzhi*, in *Hayashida Kenjiro shōrai Shinkyō-shō kyōdoshi sanjisshu*, ed. Kataoka Kazutada (Kyoto: Chūgoku Bunken kenkyūkai, 1986), 102.

94. *Zhengwusi yanjiu Eyue guanyu Xinjiang renmin guoji wenti yian*, Zhongguo bianjiang xingji diaocha baogaoshu deng bianwu ziliao congbian, vol. 9 of Chubian (Hong Kong: Fuchi shuyuan chuban youxian gongsi, 2009). Noting the continuing confusion, Xinjiang's Republican authorities dealt with the issue again in 1915. This enquiry recommended a final year of amnesty in which resident Taranchis and Dungans who were still Russian subjects would be obliged to move to Russian territory or else be unilaterally classified as Chinese subjects.

95. N. A. Maev, ed., *Materialy dlia statistiki Turkestanskogo kraia* (Saint Petersburg: Tipografiia K. V. Trubnikova, 1872–1876), 1:149; Forsyth, *Report of a Mission to Yarkund*.

96. "Khiṭay Tarafidin Kelgän Khabar," *Türkistan Vilayatining Gazeti*, May 15, 1876, 3; A. N. Kuropatkin, *Kashgaria: Eastern or Chinese Turkistan: Historical and Geographical Sketch of the Country, Its Military Strength, Industries, and Trade*, trans. Walter E. Gowan (Calcutta: Thacker, Spink, 1882), 58.

97. Note that after the 1911 revolution, passports began to be labeled as "permit to exit the country" (*chuguo zhizhao*), reflecting a new sense of China as a territorially delimited state.

98. "Kashgartsy i pasportnaia sistema" (1909), *Turkestanskii sbornik*, 507:113–115.

99. IOR L/PS/7/163, doc. 760.

100. TsGARU 19/1/13505, ll. 1–1ob.

101. IOR L/PS/7/164, doc. 933, p. 2.

102. *Russkii Turkestan*, March 18, 1906, 3; March 25, 1906, 4.

103. Palen, *Otchet po revizii Turkestanskogo kraia*, 1:12.

104. Xu Jingcheng, *Xu Wensu gong yigao*, Qingdai Xinjiang xijian zoudu huibian, vol. 2 of Tongzhi, Guangxu, Xuantong chao juan (Ürümchi: Xinjiang renmin chubanshe, 1997), 863.

105. Tak, "Nepriiatnosti iz Kashgara" (1909), *Turkestanskii sbornik*, 506:82–83.

106. E. M. Mamedova, "Iz istorii vzaimootnoshenii Turkestanskogo kraia i Sintsziana v nachale XX veka," in *Vzaimootnosheniia narodov Srednei Azii i sopredel'nikh stran Vostoka v XVIII–nachale XX veka* (Tashkent: Akademiia nauk Uzbekskoi SSR, 1963), 160, 166.

107. F. Näjmeddin, "Qïṭay Möselmanlarï (Kashghardan Mäktub)," *Vaqït*, July 4, 1915, 1.

108. AVPRI 143/491/2690 l. 4. According to Kashgar consul Sergei Kolokolov, by the early twentieth century a quarter of goods imported from Russia were in transit from China. See "Ėkonomicheskii obzor Kashgarii (Donesenie konsula v Kashgare)," *Sbornik konsul'skikh donesenii* 9, no. 3 (1906): 183–257.

3. Imperial and Islamic Reform between Turkistan and Turkey

1. Yusuf Sarınay, ed., *Belgelerle Osmanlı-Türkistan İlişkileri (XVI–XX Yüzyıllar)* (Ankara: T. C. Başbakanlık Devlet Arşivleri Genel Müdürlüğü, 2004), 108.

2. Allen J. Frank and Mirkasyim A. Usmanov, *Materials for the Islamic History of Semipalatinsk: Two Manuscripts by Ahmad-Walî al-Qazânî and Qurbân 'Ali Khâlidî* (Berlin: Das Arabische Buch, 2001), 71.

3. Mulla Musa Sayrami, *Tarikhi Hämidi*, ed. Änvär Baytur (Beijing: Millätlär Näshriyati, 1986), 38.

4. On the activities of this official in the 1870s, see Kemal H. Karpat, "Yakub Bey's Relations with the Ottoman Sultans: A Reinterpretation," *Cahiers du monde russe et soviétique* 32, no. 1 (1991): 17–32.

5. Naganawa Norihiro, "The Hajj Making Geopolitics, Empire, and Local Politics: A View from the Volga-Ural Region at the Turn of the Nineteenth and Twentieth Centuries," in *Central Asian Pilgrims: Hajj Routes and Pious Visits between Central Asia and the Hijaz*, ed. Alexandre Papas, Thomas Welsford, and Thierry Zarcone (Berlin: Klaus Schwarz, 2012), 168–198.

6. AVPRI 143/491/2305, ll. 1–3.

7. Lâle Can, "Trans-Imperial Trajectories: Pilgrimage, Pan-Islam, and Ottoman-Central Asian Relations, 1865–1914" (Ph.D. diss., New York University, 2012).

8. "Pekin Möselmanlarïndan Mäktub," *Tärjeman*, June 23, 1906, 2.

9. Karçınzade Süleyman Şükrü, *Seyahatü'l-Kübra* (Istanbul: Sinan Ofset, 2005), 623.

10. Vasiliyef, "Çin'de İslamiyet," *Sebil'ür-Reşad*, Rebiyülevvel 9, 1332/February 5, 1914, 347–348; Rebiyülevvel 16, 1332/February 12, 1914, 365–367; Rebiyülevvel 30, 1332/February 26, 1914, 400–402; Rebiyülahir 21, 1332/March 19, 1914, 32–33; Rebiyülahir 28, 1332/March 26, 1914, 50–51.

11. Abdülaziz Kolcalı, *Çin'de Din-i Mübin-i İslam ve Çin Müslümanları* (Istanbul: Mahmud Bey Matbaası, 1321/1904).

12. "Çin Müslümanları ve Hükümet-i Çin," *İkdam*, January 13, 1898, 1; "Çin'de Müslümanlar," *İkdam*, January 14, 1898, 3.

13. AVPRI 188/761/1402.

14. Ali Rıza, "Hadim-i Millet Muteber Sırat-ı Müstakim İdare-i Behiyesine," *Sırat-ı Müstakim*, Muharrem 4, 1329/January 5, 1911, 298–299.

15. IMH 01-34-002-07.

16. AVPRI 143/491/517.

17. Adil Hikmet Bey, *Asya'da Beş Türk* (Istanbul: Ötüken, 1998), 361–362. His recitation style was in fact considered illicit by local Muslims, but his associations with Ottoman learning won over the locals.

18. Xie Bin, *Xinjiang youji* (Shanghai: Zhonghua shuju, 1927), 183.

19. Näüshirvan Yaushef, "Törkestan-i Chinidä Iqtisadi Eshlär," *Vaqït*, September 20, 1915, 2–3.

20. AVPRI 143/491/446, l. 392. See also Zhong Yong, *Xijiang jiaoshe zhiyao* (1914; repr., Taibei: Taiwan shangwu yinshuguan, 1963), juan 6, fol. 8a.

21. "Aldanuv!" *Vaqït*, December 21, 1910, 3. Ahmed Kemal mentions similar cases in *Çin-Türkistan Hatıraları* and *Şanghay Hatıraları* (Istanbul: Ötüken, 1997).

22. V. A. Moiseev, *Rossiia i Kitai v Tsentral'noi Azii (vtoraia polovina XIX v.–1917 g.)* (Barnaul: Azbuka, 2003), 214.

23. G. K. Gins, "Taranchi i dungane: Ocherk iz poezdki po Semirech'iu," *Istoricheskii vestnik* 125 (1911): 707.

24. I. V. Selitskii, *Kul'dzhinskie pereselentsy pogranichnoi s Kitaem polosy* (Kazan: Tipografiia Imperatorskogo universiteta, 1905), 80.

25. Nizamuddin Akhun, the most learned and respected of the Taranchi ulama, died in 1902. "Zharkänt," *Tärjeman*, August 3, 1902, 116.

26. See, for example, "Jarkänd," *Yoldiz*, June 15, 1908, 3.

27. References can be found in Rizaeddin Fäkhreddin, *Asar: 3 häm 4 Tomnar* (Kazan: Rukhiiat, 2010), 237; Muḥammad Murad al-Ramzi al-Qazani, *Talfiq al-Akhbar wa Talqih al-Athar fi Waqaʾiʿ Qazan wa Bulghar wa Muluk al-Tatar* (Orenburg: Maṭbuʿat al-Karimiyya wa-l-Ḥusayniyya, 1908), 477. In 1901, Muhammadi made a three-month journey to Kazan and Bukhara, which he described in *Öch Ayliq Säyaḥät* (Orenburg: Karimof Matbaʿası, 1905).

28. "Gholja," *Tärjeman*, March 14, 1899, 56.

29. "Chughuchaqdan," *Tärjeman*, April 11, 1900, 99.

30. S. Fedorov, *Opyt voenno-statisticheskogo opisaniia Iliiskogo kraia* (Tashkent: Tipografiia shtaba Turkestanskogo voennogo okruga, 1903), 2:59n4.

31. Galiia Shakhmukhammadkyzy Karmysheva, *K istorii Tatarskoi intelligentsii 1890–1930-i gody* (Moscow: Nauka, 2004), 80, 444–446.

32. Ḥusayn Khan Tajalli, *Barq-i Tajalli va Sabq-i Mujalli* (Kashgar: Maṭbaʿ-i Khurshid, 1900), 59.

33. Rian Thum, *The Sacred Routes of Uyghur History* (Cambridge, MA: Harvard University Press, 2014), 178–181.

34. [Mäsʿud Sabri], "Yurtimizning Täjäddüd Tarikhi," *Shingjang Gäziti*, July 21, 1948, 4.

35. "Gholjadan," *Tärjeman*, January 22, 1898, 11; "Gholja," *Tärjeman*, June 25, 1900, 172.

36. "Gholjalï Möʿallim," *Tärjeman*, August 3, 1902, 116.

37. Sarınay, *Belgelerle Osmanlı-Türkistan İlişkileri*, 104–105; Mönadi, "Qïṭay Mämläkätindä: Gholjadan," *Vaqït*, August 22, 1906, 4.

38. M., "Qïṭayda Tatar Möʿallime," *Vaqït*, November 13, 1910, 2–3.

39. ʿI. Äḥmädi, "Qïṭay Möselmanlarï," *Vaqït*, September 21, 1913, 3.

40. G. B. Nikol'skaia and A. M. Matveev, "Vliianie revoliutsii 1905–1907 gg. na sin'tszianskikh vykhodtsev v Turkestane," in *Materialy po istorii i arkheologii Srednei Azii*, Nauchnye trudy Tashkentskogo gosudarstvennogo universiteta, no. 392 (1970), 85–86.

41. "Dzharkent," *Russkii Turkestan*, November 11, 1905, 3.

42. "Oblastnyi otdel," *Russkii Turkestan*, April 14, 1906, 3; *Yarkänd Möselmanlarnïng Kitabkhanä häm Qïraʾätkhanäseneng Uṣṭafï* (Kazan: Maṭbuʿa-i Karimiyya, 1906).

43. "Jarkänd," *Yoldïz*, June 15, 1908, 3.

44. E. Fedorov, "1905 god i korennoe naselenie Turkestana," in *Ocherki revoliutsionnogo dvizheniia v Srednei Azii* (Moscow: Nauchnaia assotsiatsiia vostokovedeniia pri TsIK SSSR, 1926), 36.

45. *Vaqït*, June 29, 1906, 2; *Vaqït*, May 20, 1906, 2. On the institution of the *maḥkama-i sharʿiyya* see Paolo Sartori, "The Tashkent *'Ulamā'* and the Soviet State (1920–38): A Preliminary Research Note Based on NKVD Documents," in *Patterns of Transformation in and around Uzbekistan*, ed. Paulo Sartori and Tommaso Trevisani (Reggio Emilia: Diabasis, 2007), 161–184.

46. Taranchïlar, "Jarkäntlik Vali Baygha Achïq Mäktub," *Taraqqi*, August 12, 1906, 2–3. Ultimately the tsar dismissed the first Duma before elections in Turkistan could be held.

47. *Semirechenskie oblastnye vedomosti*, June 13, 1906, 345.

48. Taranchïlar, "Jarkäntlik Vali Baygha Achïq Mäktub," *Taraqqi*, August 12, 1906, 2–3.

49. Naẓar Khuja ʿAbdelṣamadof, "Taranchä Möselmanlar," *Vaqït*, June 9, 1910, 3.

50. Rossiiskii gosudarstvennyi istoricheskii arkhiv 1386/1/256 ll. 339–340, accessible at http://zerrspiegel.orientphil.uni-halle.de/t767.html.

51. Konstantin Konstantinovich Palen, *Mission to Turkestan: Being the Memoirs of Count K. K. Pahlen*, trans. Richard Pierce (Oxford: Oxford University Press, 1964), 208–210.

52. S. Kolokolov, "Ėkonomicheskii obzor Kashgarii (Donesenie konsula v Kashgare)," *Sbornik konsul'skikh donesenii* 9, no. 3 (1906): 230–232.

53. IOR L/PS/7/210, doc. 288, p. 15.

54. S. Kolokolov, "Russkaia torgovlia v Kashgarii (Donesenie konsula v Kashgare)," *Sbornik konsul'skikh donesenii* 11, no. 1 (1908): 120.

55. IOR L/PS/7/231, doc. 1467.

56. IOR L/PS/7/194, doc. 1869; Kolokolov, "Ėkonomicheskii obzor Kashgarii," 231.

57. IOR L/PS/7/206, doc. 1761; L/PS/7/216, doc. 1136; AVPRI 143/491/480, l. 68.

58. IOR L/PS/7/221, doc. 1775.

59. IOR L/PS/7/219, doc. 1559; L/PS/7/222, doc. 2000.

60. AVPRI 188/761/769, l. 12.

61. IOR L/PS/7/218, doc. 1344.

62. Tunji Khangdi [Tongzhi huangdi], *Qanun al-Ṣin*, trans. Saʿid al-ʿAsali al-Ṭrabulsi al-Shami (Cairo: Maṭbuʿat Madrasat Valida ʿAbbas al-Avval, 1906), iii–vi; Martin Hartmann, *Chinesisch-Turkestan: Geschichte, Verwaltung, Geistesleben, und Wirtschaft* (Halle: Gebauer-Schwetschke Druckerei und Verlag, 1908), 37, 101–102; B. M. Babadzhanov, A. K. Muminov, and A. fon Kiugel'gen, eds., *Disputy musul'manskikh religioznykh avtoritetov v Tsentral'noi Azii v XX veke* (Almaty: Daik-Press, 2007), 75.

63. Wang Shunan, ed., *Xinjiang tuzhi* (1911; repr., Taibei: Wenhai chubanshe, 1965), juan 38, 6a.

64. AVPRI 188/761/769, l. 12ob.

65. Ibid., ll. 56–57ob.

66. IOR L/PS/7/217, doc. 1234; IOR L/PS/7/229, doc. 1045, p. 1.

67. IOR L/PS/7/233, doc. 1645, p. 5.

68. IOR L/PS/7/234, doc. 1741.

69. IOR L/PS/7/248, doc. 770; L/PS/249, doc. 1015.

70. IOR L/PS/246, doc. 252; L/PS/7/247, doc. 410; L/PS/7/251, doc. 1380.

71. In a process repeated elsewhere in the Islamic world, locals in Tuyuq had come to associate a nearby cave with that mentioned in sura 18 of the Quran, itself a reflection of the Christian legend of a group of youths who escaped religious persecution by sleeping in a cave for hundreds of years. See Shinmen Yasushi, "The History of the Mausoleum Aṣḥāb al-Kahf in Turfan," *Memoirs of the Research Department of the Toyo Bunko*, no. 61 (2003): 83–104.

72. Sayrami, *Tarikhi Hämidi*, 669–702.

73. Qurban ʿAli Khalidi, *An Islamic Biographical Dictionary of the Eastern Kazakh Steppe, 1770–1912*, ed. Allen J. Frank and Mirkasym A. Gosmanov (Leiden: Brill, 2005), 70.

74. Ashirbek Muminov, "Shami-damulla i ego rol' v formirovanii 'sovetskogo islama,'" *Kazanskii federalist*, no. 1 (2005): 231–247.

75. "Misafir-i Fazılemizin Nutku," *Beyan'ül-Hak*, Recep 25, 1328/August 2, 1910, 1393–1396; Hüseyin Hazım, "Said Efendi Hazretlerinin Nutku Beliğlerinin Tercümesi," *Beyan'ül-Hak*, Şaban 2, 1328/August 9, 1910, 1409–1412.

76. Michael A. Reynolds, *Shattering Empires: The Clash and Collapse of the Ottoman and Russian Empires, 1908–1918* (Cambridge: Cambridge University Press, 2011), 93; "Kaşgar Şeyhü'l-İslam Mı, Baba Tahir'in Refik-i Sabıkı Mı?" *Tearüf-i Müslimin* 1, no. 8 (1328/1910): 136–137.

77. IMH 03-32-103-02-001.

78. IMH 03-36-044-03-043.

79. Başbakanlık Osmanlı Arşivi, Bab-ı Ali Evrak Odası, doc. 4204/315286, p. 5.

80. ʿAbd al-Qadir Damulla, *Miftah al-Adab* (1910; repr., Ürümchi: Shinjang Khälq Näshriyati, 2002); Damella ʿAbdelqadir, "Ädäbi ber Moṣaḥäbä," *Shura*, no. 12 (1916): 302–303.

81. Shakir äl-Mokhtari, "Damella ʿAbdelqadir Ḥäżrät Ḥaqqïnda," *Shura*, no. 1 (1917), 24.

82. S. Fedorov, "Russkaia torgovlia v Iliiskoi oblasti (Donesenie general'nogo konsula v Kul'dzhe)," *Sbornik konsul'skikh donesenii* 12, no. 4 (1909): 276–277. Other accounts give the capital as only 150,000 taels.

83. Chang-geng, "Chouban Yili yaozheng liutiao xianglu," in *Qing Guangxu jingying Xinjiang huiyi zhezou* (Beijing: Quanguo tushuguan wenxian suowei fuzhi zhongxin, 2010), 765–768.

84. IOR L/PS/7/230, doc. 1103.

85. Ismaʿïl Mulla Akhundof, "Gholjadan," *Vaqït*, December 21, 1910, 3.

86. Kazanlı Carullah Hafdi, "Sırat-ı Müstakim Heyet-i Tahririyesine," *Sırat-ı Müstakim*, Kanunievvel 9, 1326/December 22, 1910, 268–269; Munir Erzin, *Stanovlenie i razvitie uigurskoi sovetskoi pechati* (Almaty: Nauka, 1988), 28–32.

87. Uyghïr Balası N[aẓar Khuja] ʿA[bdelṣamadof], "Taranchï Törkläre," *Shura*, no. 15 (1914): 456.

88. See "Chindä Törk Ghazetasï," *Tärjeman*, May 13, 1911, 1; "Qïṭayda Möselman Ghazetasï," *Vaqït*, October 12, 1910, 2; "Qïṭayda Möselman Ghazetasï," *Vaqït*, September 4, 1910, 2–3. "Çin'de Müslüman Gazetesi," *Sırat-ı Müstakim*, Şevval 9, 1328/October 14, 1910, 102.

89. "Gholjadan Yazalar," *Vaqït*, July 15, 1911, 4.

90. Damulla ʿAbd al-Qadir b. ʿAbd al-Varis al-Kashghari, *ʿAqayid-i Żaruriya* (Orenburg: Vaqït Maṭbaʿasï, 1911); *Mukhtaṣar-i ʿIbadat-i Islamiyya* (Kazan: Maṭbaʿa-i Karimiyya, 1911); *ʿAqaʾid-i Żaruriyat* (Kazan: Maṭbaʿa-i Karimiyya, 1911); *Tajvid-i Turki* (Kazan: Millät Maṭbaʿasï, 1912); *Tashil al-Ḥisab* (Kazan: Millät Maṭbaʿasï, 1912).

91. Although cast as a reactionary in Uyghur historiography, Umar Akhunbayev is credited with supporting an accounting school in a madrasa that he funded. Sherip

Khushtar, ed., *Shinjang Yeqinqi Zaman Tarikhidiki Mäshhur Shäkhslär* (Ürümchi: Shinjang Khälq Näshriyati, 2000), 273.

92. Mönadi, "Qïṭay Mämläkätindä: Gholjadan," *Vaqït*, August 22, 1906, 4.

4. The End of Empire and the Racial Turn

1. "Xinjiang zhi shishi feifei," *Shenbao*, April 4, 1912, 6–7; M. Tärjemani, "Elä Vilayatï Khäbärläre," *Vaqït*, April 27, 1912, 2; M. Tärjemanof, "Elä Vilayatï Vaqiʻalarï," *Vaqït*, March 16, 1912, 2–3.

2. IOR L/PS/10, doc. 1529, p. 77b.

3. "Chin Derelde!" *Tärjeman*, May 4, 1912, 1.

4. M[anṣur] Sh[äekhof], "Elä Vilayatï Vaqiʻalarï," *Vaqït*, March 6, 1912, 2; Münir Abdurreşid, "Çin Müslümanları'nın Hataları ve Hükümet-i Osmaniye'nin Çin'deki Vezaifi," *Sebil'ür-Reşad*, Mayıs 7, 1328/May 20, 1912, 307.

5. "Chindä Jömhüriyat vä Möselmanlar," *Tärjeman*, May 25, 1912, 1.

6. IOR L/PS/10/241, doc. 1654, p. 170; L/PS/10/241, doc. 4498, p. 11.

7. RGVIA 400/1/4074, l. 287ob; RGVIA 400/1/4111.

8. IOR L/PS/10/241, doc. 1392, p. 173b.

9. "Qïṭay Möselmanlarïnïng Ṭäläbe," *Vaqït*, May 25, 1912, 1.

10. "Tulufan laidian," *Canyiyuan gongbao*, no. 4 (June 1913): 12. On Jin Yunlun, see Anthony Garnaut, "The Shaykh of the Great Northwest: The Religious and Political Life of Ma Yuanzhang (1853–1920)" (Ph.D. diss., Australian National University, 2011), 244–245.

11. IOR L/PS/10/825, doc. 2729, p. 199; "Mengzangyuan cheng heni Gansu Xinjiang diaochayuan Huibu Yusupu Boke qingxi gongjue cha gaijue bing wu shijue wangdi ziyang, weibian zhaozhun, zhi qingshi qi," *Xinjiang gongbao*, no. 27 (November 1914): 3b–4a.

12. I. G. Polinov, "Revoliutsionnye sobytiia v severnoi chasti Sin'tsziana v 1911–1913 gg," *Trudy instituta vostokovedeniia akademiia nauk Uzbekskoi SSR* 4 (1956): 54.

13. On Yang's relationship with Hui military leaders, see Anthony Garnaut, "From Yunnan to Xinjiang: Governor Yang Zengxin and His Dungan Generals," *Etudes Orientales*, no. 25 (2008): 93–125.

14. "Mengzang shiwuju cheng da zongtong ju Xinjiang yiyuan Hadeer lichen Chanmin lilai kunku qingxing ni ken chiling Xinjiang dudu jiayi zhengdun ge xiang jiaoyu shiye qing pishi zhizunwen bing pi," *Zhengfu gongbao*, July 26, 1913, 24–25. The Russian Muslim press praised Abdulqadir for raising the subject of Xinjiang's Muslims in the nation's capital. See "Chindä Möselmanlïq," *Tärjeman*, September 5, 1913, 1.

15. "Huizu wanliu Yang Dudu," *Shenbao*, March 29, 1914, 6.

16. Pang Shiqian, *Aiji jiunian* (Beijing: Yuehua wenhua fuwushe, 1951), 62.

17. Li Qian, *Huibu gongdu* (Shanghai: Zhonghua yinshuachang, 1924), 506.

18. "Hami Sha Qinwang fu Mengzangyuan zongcai dian," *Zhengfu gongbao*, September 4, 1916, 17–18.

19. IOR L/PS/10/297, doc. 414, p. 249b.

20. "Kashgartsy i pasportnaia sistema" (1909), *Turkestanskii sbornik*, 507:113–115.

21. "Ṭoqmaq Uyäzindä," *Dala Vilayatining Gazeti*, July 27, 1890, 3.

22. IMH 03-32-384-03-004.

23. AVPRI 143/491/437, l. 1; Zhang Shaobo, *Xinjiang waijiao baogaoshu* (Dihua: Xinjiang jiaoshe gongshu waijiao yanjiusuo, 1913), 21b.

24. IOR L/PS/7/252, doc. 1726, p. 3.

25. IOR L/PS/7/249, doc. 1015, p. 3.

26. C. P. Skrine and Pamela Nightingale, *Macartney at Kashgar: New Light on British, Chinese and Russian Activities in Sinkiang, 1890–1918* (London: Methuen, 1973), 233.

27. To cite one such case, upon his arrest in 1918 Muhammad Ali, a shaykh who led an uprising in Kucha, was found to be in possession of a "little receipt" from the local British *aqsaqal*. Zhongyang yanjiuyuan jindaishi yanjiu suo, ed., *Zhong-E guanxi shiliao: E zhengbian yu yiban jiaoshe 1917–1919* (Nangang: Zhongyang yanjiuyuan jindaishi yanjiu suo, 1960), 2:23.

28. Joseph Esherick, *The Origins of the Boxer Uprising* (Berkeley: University of California Press, 1987).

29. A history of Republican Xinjiang refers to the Chira riot as the "patriotic struggle of the Uyghur people of Chira against Russian imperialism." Chen Chao and Chen Huisheng, *Minguo Xinjiang shi* (Ürümchi: Xinjiang renmin chubanshe, 1999), 131.

30. Skrine and Nightingale, *Macartney at Kashgar*, 205.

31. Zhang, *Xinjiang waijiao baogaoshu*, 22b.

32. IMH 03-32-027-01-013, p. 2.

33. TsGARU 2/1/345, ll. 2–2ob.

34. Ibid., ll. 7–7ob.

35. Maya Karin Peterson, "Technologies of Rule: Empire, Water and the Modernization of Central Asia, 1867–1941" (Ph.D. diss., Harvard University, 2011), 310.

36. In Andijan, Abdurahman Qari Haji Tairov, who held the title of chief *aqsaqal*, was an Akhunbayev employee. Sadiq Akhun, the *aqsaqal* in Kokand, was the son of Turdi Haji, who according to the British consul was the "head of Kerim Bay Bacha's [i.e., Karim Akhunbayev's] house." IOR L/PS/7/227, doc. 593.

37. IMH 03-18-028-01-016; TsGARU 2/1/345, l. 49.

38. TsGARU 2/1/345, ll. 41–48.

39. "Kashghar vä Gholja Iʻanäse," *Tärjeman*, May 4, 1912, 4. This is probably the same donation as that mentioned in Fatih Kerimi, *İstanbul Mektupları* (Istanbul: Çağrı Yayınları, 2001), 90.

40. Gholjalï, "Qïṭay Möselmanlarï," *Vaqït*, September 10, 1913, 3.

41. Quṭlugh Ḥaji and Yaʻqub Akhund, "Kashghardan Mäktub," *Tärjeman*, February 17, 1913, 2. According to tsarist intelligence reports, which were sensitive to cross-border connections among Russian Muslims, Shawqi and his co-thinkers invited Ismail Gasprinskii to personally pay a visit to Kashgar. TsGARU 461/1/1319, l. 304.

42. Damella ʿAbdelqadir, "Ädäbi ber Moṣaḥäbä," *Shura*, no. 12 (1916): 303.

43. Ayşe Fersahoğlu Eroğlu, "Habibzâde Ahmet Kemal'in Kahramanlık Temalı Ninni Şiirleri," *Atatürk Üniversitesi Türkiyat Araştırmaları Enstitüsü Dergisi* 17, no. 44 (2010): 157–181. For similar work, see Ahmed Kemal, *Öç Duyguları* (Istanbul: Mahmud Bey Matbaası, 1915). On his life, see the introduction by Yusuf Gedikli to Ahmet Kemal İlkul, *Çin-Türkistan Hatıraları* and *Şanghay Hatıraları* (Istanbul: Ötüken, 1997), 9–23.

44. Hamada Masami, "La transmission du mouvement nationaliste au Turkestan oriental (Xinjiang)," *Central Asian Survey* 9, no. 1 (1990): 35.

45. Adil Hikmet Bey, *Asya'da Beş Türk* (Istanbul: Ötüken, 1998), 118–119.

46. Ḥaji Muḥammad ʿAli Nauruz Ḥaji Oghlï, "Kashghar Aḥvalï," *Ṣada-yi Farghana*, November 30, 1914, 3–4.

47. al-Kashghari, *ʾAqaʾid-i Żaruriyat*, 10.

48. Aḥmed Kemal Ḥabibzade, *Alifba-yi Turki* (Orenburg: Vaqït Maṭbuʿasï, 1915), 21–25.

49. Nauruz Ḥaji Oghlï, "Kashghar Aḥvalï."

50. İlkul, *Çin-Türkistan Hatıraları*, 118; Näüshirvan Yaushef, "Kashghar Näshr-i Mäʿarif Jämʿïyate," *Vaqït*, May 25, 1916, 3.

51. IMH 03-36-033-01.

52. IOR L/PS/10/825, doc. 2646 (1916), p. 169b.

53. R[iżaeddin] F[äkhreddin], "Qïṭay (Chin)," *Shura*, no. 1 (1917): 6.

54. Dardli, "Gholjadan," *Il*, March 8, 1914, 4.

55. ʿAbdelʿaziz Monasibzadä, "Gholja," *Vaqït*, July 24, 1907, 3.

56. ʿAbdelʿaziz Monasib, *Taranchï Qïzï, yaki Ḥälimneng Berenche Mäḥäbbäte* (Kazan: Ümet Maṭbaʿasï, 1918). A Cyrillic version was published in *Ädäbi Miras* 2 (1992): 125–202.

57. Galiia Karmysheva gives the impression that she read the novel as an autobiographical work. *K istorii Tatarskoi intelligentsii 1890–1930-i gody* (Moscow: Nauka, 2004), 289.

58. S. Fedorov, "Russkaia torgovlia v Kul'dzhe (Donesenie konsula v Kul'dzhe)," *Sbornik konsul'skikh donesenii* 9, no. 5 (1906): 377, gives 4,800 households of "Kashgari Sarts," compared to only 3,250 households of Taranchis.

59. Näüshirvan Yaushef, "Felyeton: Mädäniyat vä Khïtay," *Ṣada-yi Turkistan*, January 15, 1915, 2.

60. Näüshirvan Yaushef, "Säyaḥät Parchalarï: Ṭurfan," *Ṣada-yi Turkistan*, February 6, 1915, 2.

61. N[äüshirvan] Y[aushef], "Qïṭay Möselmanlar ichün Idarä-i Shärʿiya," *Vaqït*, April 11, 1915, 1.

62. Näüshirvan Yaushef, "Törkestan-i Chinidä Iqtisadi Eshlär," *Vaqït*, September 20, 1915, 2–3.

63. Näüshirvan Yaushef, "Törkestan Tarikhï," *Shura*, no. 15 (1915): 455–457.

64. Näüshirvan Yaushef, "Altï Shähär Tarikhïndan ber Parcha," *Shura*, no. 4 (1916): 479–481; "Säyaḥät Parchalarï: Gholja," *Ṣada-yi Turkistan*, September 2, 1914, 2–3.

65. Shah Maḥmud Churas, *Khronika. Kriticheskii tekst, perevod, kommentarii, issledovanie i ukaziteli O. F. Akimushkin*, 2nd ed. (Saint Petersburg: Peterburgskoe lingvisticheskoe obshchestvo, 2010), 11–12.

66. Näüshirvan Yaushef, "Milliyat vä Islamiyat," *Shura*, no. 13 (1917): 292–293; "Törkestan-i Chinidä Säyaḥät (Kuchadan Kashghargha)," *Shura*, no. 11 (1915): 332–336; "Säyaḥät Parchalarï: Gholja."

67. Näüshirvan Yaushef, "Artush Tä'siratï," *Shura*, no. 17 (1915): 518–520.

68. İsmail Gaspıralı, "Mükaleme-i Selatin," in *Seçmiş Eserleri*, vol. 1, *Roman ve Hikayeleri*, ed. Yavuz Akpınar, Bayram Orak, and Nazim Muradov (Istanbul: Ötüken, 2003), 491–503.

69. Yaushef, "Artush Tä'siratï."

70. On this paranoia, see Mustafa Tuna, *Imperial Russia's Muslims: Islam, Empire, and European Modernity, 1788–1914* (Cambridge: Cambridge University Press, 2015), 208–209.

71. TsGARU 461/1/1172, l. 217ob.

72. N[aẓar Khuja] 'A[bdelṣamadof] Ṭoghru, "Törkestan-i Chini Törkläre," *Shura*, no. 13 (1912): 395; TsGARU 461/1/1172, ll. 226–226ob.

73. Uyghur Balisi [Näzärghoja Abdusemätov], *Taranchi Türklärning Tarikhi* (Almaty: Uyghur Kommunistlirining Vilayät Byurasi, 1922), 38.

74. Naẓar Khuja 'Abdelṣamad Ulï, "Törkestan-i Chini Sartlarïnïng Milli Tarikhï Ḥaqqïnda ber Rija'," *Shura*, no. 20 (1911): 617–618.

75. Naẓar Khuja, "Taranchïlar," *Shura*, no. 6 (1912): 177.

76. Uyghïr Balasï N[aẓar Khuja] 'A[bdelṣamadof], "Taranchï Törkläre," *Shura*, no. 15 (1914): 455–457.

77. Zarif Bäshiri, "Mäzhit Gafuri Turahïnda Ithtäleklär," *Ädhäbi Bashqortostan*, no. 6 (1958): 85–89.

78. Ẓarif äl-Bäshiri, *Chuvashlar* (Orenburg: Karimof, Ḥösäynof, 1909); *Chuvash Qïzï Änisä* (Kazan: Karimiyya, 1910).

79. Naẓar Khuja 'Abdelṣamad Ulï, "Kashghar Törkläreneng Islam Qabul Itüvläre vä Iske Kitablar," *Shura*, no. 11 (1913): 332–333; "Ghaljat," *Shura*, no. 10 (1914): 312.

80. Naẓar Khuja 'Abdelṣamadof, "Taranchä Möselmanlar," *Vaqït*, June 9, 1910, 3.

81. Uyghïr Balasï [Naẓar Khuja 'Abdelṣamadof], "Taranchï Törkläre Qandaq Ṭoralar?" *Shura*, no. 10 (1915): 293–296.

82. Mulla Ämir, "'Taranchï Törkläre Qandaq Toralar' Digän Mäqaläni Intiqad," *Shura*, no. 18 (1915), 558–559; Uyghïr Balasï [Naẓar Khuja 'Abdelṣamadof], "Taranchï Törklär Qandaq Ṭoralar?" *Shura*, no. 23 (1915): 709–711. See also Tuna's discussion of the "alienation" of the Muslim intelligentsia in *Imperial Russia's Muslims*.

83. Naẓar Khuja 'Abdelṣamad [Ulï], "Yul Khatïrïmdan," *Shura*, no. 8 (1914): 233–237.

84. Şemseddin Sami, *Qamus-i Türki* (Istanbul: İkdam, 1318/1899–1900), 227–228.

85. Ahmet Ferit Tek, *Turan* (Istanbul: Turan Kültür Vakfı, 1999), 153.

86. Ḥasanʿata ʿAbashi, *Mufaṣṣal Taʾrikh-i Qaum-i Turki* (Ufa: Sharq Maṭbuʿasï, 1909), 201–209. For a similar account, see Ähmäd Zäki Välidi, *Törk vä Tatar Tarikhï* (Kazan: Millät, 1912), 1:57–64.

87. Geoffrey Lewis, *The Turkish Language Reform: A Catastrophic Success* (Oxford: Oxford University Press, 1999), 122.

88. The most thorough recent discussion of this question is Danielle M. Ross, "From the Minbar to the Barricades: The Transformation of the Volga-Ural ʿUlama into a Revolutionary Intelligentsia, 1860–1918" (Ph.D. diss., University of Wisconsin, 2011).

89. Uyghïr, "Miḥnätkäsh Taranchïlagha," *Kümäk*, November 24, 1919, 3. Reprinted in Näzärghoja Abdusemätov, *Yoruq Sahillar* (Almaty: Zhazushï, 1991), 157–159.

5. Rebellion, Revolution, and Civil War

1. N. P., "Pamiat' V. A. Yuldasheva," *Semirechenskie oblastnye vedomosti*, March 23, 1916, 2; March 24, 1916, 2; March 25, 1916, 2.

2. Marko Buttino, *Revoliutsiia naoborot: Sredniaia Aziia mezhdu padeniem tsarskoi imperii i obrazovaniem SSSR* (Moscow: Zven'ia, 2007).

3. A report by the circuit commandant of Zharkent, who was responsible for communicating the decree to the Taranchis, can be found in A. V. Piaskovskii, ed., *Vosstanie 1916 goda v Srednei Azii i Kazakhstane: Sbornik dokumentov* (Moscow: Akademiia nauk SSSR, 1960), 327–329.

4. See reports in *Semirechenskie oblastnye vedomosti*, November 19, 1916, 2; February 23, 1917, 2. According to Nazarkhoja Abdusamadov, a total of one thousand Taranchi laborers were sent to Ekaterinoslav (Dnipropetrovsk) in Ukraine. Abdusemätov, *Yoruq Sahillar* (Almaty: Zhazushï, 1991), 59.

5. RGASPI 62/2/405, l. 35.

6. The only incident involving Taranchis in a long summary of events in Semireche is the killing of the Qoram canton head. See M. K. Kozybaev, ed., *Qaharlï 1916 zhïl / Groznyi 1916-i god* (Almaty: Qazaqstan, 1998), 1:139.

7. AVPRI 143/491/498.

8. TsGARK 77/2/130, ll. 6–7b.

9. A. Rozybakiev, "Alma-Ata v 1917–1918 (vospominaniia)," *Tughan Ölkä / Rodnoi Krai*, nos. 1–2 (2003): 44–58; "Oktiabr'skii perevorot v Alma-Ate (vospominaniia)," *Tughan Ölkä / Rodnoi Krai*, no. 3 (2004): 30–44.

10. Sabirjan Ḥaji ʿArabshah Ulï, "Alma-Ata," *Olugh Törkestan*, July 2, 1918, 4.

11. Like many Turkistan Bolsheviks, Muraev was a railway worker. He became politically active in the Kushka Soviet in 1917–1918, took part in the disarmament of Cossacks returning from Iran, then fought on the Bukharan front. See RGVA 110/3/1290, l. 1. He died in Russia in 1921.

12. GARF 200/1/470, l. 18ob.

13. I. N. Shendrikov, "Nuzhdy semirechenskogo kazach'ego voiska," *Belaia gvardiia*, no. 8 (2005): 240–241. Shendrikov refers to Muraev's troops as

"Hungarian-Bolshevik bands," suggesting that they were drawn from Hungarian POWs in Turkistan.

14. GARF 200/1/470, l. 19ob; APRK 3/1/299, l. 9.

15. Mashur Ruziev, *Yanglivashtin Tughulghan Uyghur Khälqi* (Almaty: Qazaqstan, 1968), 95–97; Mashur Ruziev, *Vozrozhdennyi uigurskii narod*, 2nd ed. (Almaty: Kazakhstan, 1982), 132–133.

16. V. A. Moiseev, *Rossiia i Kitai v Tsentral'noi Azii (vtoraia polovina XIX v.–1917 g.)* (Barnaul: Azbuka, 2003), 310.

17. Zhongyang yanjiuyuan jindaishi yanjiu suo, ed., *Zhong-E guanxi shiliao: Xinjiang bianfang 1917–1919* (Nangang: Zhongyang yanjiuyuan jindaishi yanjiu suo, 1960), 358–360. The familiarity the text shows with the Ili Valley's ethnic composition indicates that it was written locally, though the party affiliations of the leaflet's authors cannot be determined from the content.

18. Komissiia po izdaniiu diplomaticheskikh dokumentov pri MID SSSR, ed., *Dokumenty vneshnei politiki SSSR* (Moscow: Izdatel'stvo politicheskoi literatury, 1957), 1:234.

19. Zhang Dajun, *Xinjiang fengbao qishi nian* (Taibei: Lanxi chubanshe, 1980), 472–473.

20. In 1918, on intelligence provided by the tsarist consul, three suspected Bolsheviks were expelled from Ghulja for attempting to establish an "enlightenment society" (*kaizhihui*); *Zhong-E guanxi shiliao: Xinjiang bianfang*, 153. I cannot accept Michael Share's interpretation, which sees Russian Muslim sentiment as anti-Bolshevik and local opinion as revolutionary; Michael Share, "The Russian Civil War in Chinese Turkestan (Xinjiang), 1918–1921: A Little Known and Explored Front," *Europe-Asia Studies* 62, no. 3 (2010): 398.

21. Zhang, *Xinjiang fengbao qishi nian*, 441; *Zhong-E guanxi shiliao: Xinjiang bianfang*, 49. A White account written in 1919 claims that Yang Feixia offered to assist the Cossacks militarily as long as they were able to take control of Zharkent, thereby stabilizing the border region and reducing any threat of Bolshevik attack on Ili. When they achieved this, Yang reneged. GARF 200/1/470, l. 19.

22. AVPRI 491/143/3070, l. 22.

23. Niccolò Pianciola, *Stalinismo di frontiera: Colonizzazione agricola, sterminio dei nomadi e costruzione statale in Asia centrale (1905–1936)* (Vicenza: Viella, 2009), 195.

24. In November, Spanish flu claimed up to a thousand lives. "Qolja Ähväle," *Jide Şu Eshche Khäliq Mökhkbire*, September 25, 1918, 4.

25. RGVA 110/3/1091, l. 72ob.

26. Ibid., l. 73.

27. B. P. Gurevich, "Vzaimootnosheniia sovetskikh respublikh i provintsiei Sin'tszian v 1918–1920 gg," *Sovetskoe kitaevedenie* 2 (1958): 98.

28. V. A. Moiseev, "Grazhdanskaia voina v Turkestane i pozitsiia kitaiskikh vlastei Sin'tsziana," in *Sovremennoe istoricheskoe sibirevedenie XVII–nachala XX vv. Sbornik nauchnikh trudov* (Barnaul: Azbuka, 2005), 318.

29. IMH 03-32-112-02-012.

30. IMH 03-32-108-01-037.

31. GARF 200/1/459, l. 39.

32. Zhang, *Xinjiang fengbao qishi nian*, 473–474.

33. GARF 200/1/470, ll. 39ob–40.

34. RGASPI 122/1/29, l. 109; APRK 3/1/299, l. 11.

35. Yang Zengxin, *Buguozhai wendu* (1921; repr., Taibei: Wenhai chubanshe, 1965), 3416.

36. GARF 200/1/456, ll. 4–5ob; GARF 200/1/451, l. 33.

37. For the Russian text of the agreement, see *Dokumenty vneshnei politiki SSSR*, 3:546–549, and for the Chinese text, Yuan Tung-li, ed., *Zhong-E xibei tiaoyue ji*, Xinjiang yanjiu congkan, vol. 4 (Hong Kong, 1963), 89–90.

38. TsGARU 702/1/35, ll. 67–67ob; TsGARU 702/1/95, ll. 142–43.

39. On Awlani and the Turan group, see Adeeb Khalid, *The Politics of Muslim Cultural Reform: Jadidism in Central Asia* (Berkeley: University of California Press, 1998), 258.

40. I., "Uyghur Inqilabchilarining Yätti Yillik Bäyrämidä," *Qizil Özbäkistan*, February 26, 1925, 2; Aḥmad Ayyubof, "Uyghur Özgärishchilarining 8-inchi Yili," *Qizil Özbäkistan*, February 9, 1926, 2.

41. TsGARU 461/1/1319, l. 199.

42. "Alma Ata," *Vaqït*, February 25, 1915, 4; TsGARU 461/1/1477, ll. 29ob, 31.

43. "Buradär Rozibaqining Märkäzgä Ketishi Münasibäti Bilän," *Kämbäghällär Awazi*, December 16, 1924, 3.

44. Munir Erzin, *Stanovlenie i razvitie Uigurskoi Sovetskoi pechati* (Almaty: Nauka, 1988), 35. I have been unable to locate any extant copies of this newspaper, but brief excerpts can be found in *Olugh Törkestan*, e.g., April 23, 1918, 4.

45. G. I. Trofimov, "Iz proshlogo kompartii v Dzhetysu," in *V revoliutsii: Vospominaniia uchastnikov Velikoi Oktiabrskoi revoliutsii i grazhdanskoi voiny v Kazakhstane*, ed. P. M. Pakhmurnyi and T. E. Eleuov (Almaty: Kazakhskoe gosudarstvennoe izdatel'stvo, 1957), 225.

46. Rozybakiev, "Alma-Ata v 1917–1918"; "Oktiabr'skii perevorot v Alma-Ate."

47. "Taranchï Törkläri Shiväsindä Teyatro," *Kümäk*, June 28, 1919, 4.

48. "'Oṣmanlï Törk Afitsärläre," *Kümäk*, September 25, 1919, 4.

49. Chänto, "Jide Ṣu Faji'alarï," *Jide Ṣu Eshche Khäliq Mökhkbire*, July 5, 1918, 2–3.

50. On the Muslim Bureau, see Adeeb Khalid, "Turkestan v 1917–1922 godakh: bor'ba za vlast' na okraine Rossii," in *Tragediia velikoi derzhavy: Natsional'nyi vopros i raspad Sovetskogo Soiuza* (Moscow: Sotsial'no-politicheskaia mysl', 2005), 211–215.

51. Buttino, *Revoliutsiia naoborot*, chap. 5.

52. APRK 3/1/299, ll. 19, 21.

53. Terry Martin, *The Affirmative Action Empire: Nations and Nationalism in the Soviet Union, 1923–1939* (Ithaca, NY: Cornell University Press, 2001), 61.

54. On the Sovinterprop, see A. M. Matveev, "Deiatel'nost' 'Soveta internatsional'noi propagandy na Vostoke' v Srednei Azii (1919–1920 gg.)," *Narody Azii i Afriki* 5 (1978): 45–52; Oliver Bast, "The Council for International Propaganda and the Establishment

of the Iranian Communist Party," in *Iran and the First World War: Battleground of the Great Powers*, ed. Touraj Atabaki (London: I. B. Tauris, 2006); Kirill S. Kudukhov, "Deiatel'nost' Soveta internatsional'noi propagandy na Vostoke v 1920 g. Itogovyi doklad," *Vostochnyi arkhiv*, no. 23 (2011): 61–67.

55. RGASPI 514/1/181, l. 21ob.

56. Zhang, *Xinjiang fengbao qishi nian*, 1192.

57. Buttino, *Revoliutsiia naoborot*, 234.

58. RGVA 25898/1/89, l. 13; IOR L/PS/10/721, p. 189.

59. *Zhong-E guanxi shiliao: Xinjiang bianfang*, 18.

60. "Tashkänddä Qïtay Ilchese," *Kümäk*, August 21, 1919, 2.

61. Yang, *Buguozhai wendu*, 3602–3606.

62. A. G. Larin, *Kitaiskie migranty v Rossii: Istoriia i sovremennost'* (Moscow: Vostochnaia kniga, 2009), 26.

63. On the Red Beards see Mark Mancall and Georges Jidkoff, "Les Honghuzi de la Chine du Nord-Est (1860–1910)," in *Mouvements populaires et sociétés secrètes en Chine aux XIX et XX siècles*, ed. Jean Chesneaux (Paris, 1970), 297–315.

64. Liu Zerong, "Shiyue geming qianhou wo zai Sulian de yiduan jingli," in *Wenshi ziliao xuanji*, Hedingben, vol. 21 (Beijing: Zhongguo wenshi chubanshe, 2000), 168.

65. For this and other documents, see the appendix to Li Yongchang, *Lü E Huagong yu shiyue geming* (Zhengzhou: Hebei jiaoyu chubanshe, 1988).

66. RGASPI 495/154/10, ll. 1–3.

67. IMH 03-32-108-04-019. This may be the envoy mentioned in Larin, *Kitaiskie migranty v Rossii*, 77.

68. RGASPI 122/1/29, ll. 267ob–268.

69. Accounts vary as to the origins of these groups, with some attributing the initiative to Chinese Communists returning to China, others to local Kashgaris. Yang, *Buguozhai wendu*, 3,760–3,761; *Buguozhai wendu xubian* (Beijing: Xinjiang zhujing gongyu, 1926), juan 9xia, fol. 1a.

70. Ibid., juan 9xia, fol. 9b; IOR L/PS/10/976, p. 315. Yang Zengxin's source was probably a copy of the newspaper *Haqiqat* dated December 29, 1920, which was brought to the attention of officials in Kashgar because of an inflammatory article quoting "Speeches by Chinese laborers and peasants in Andijan." IOR L/PS/10/976, doc. 2196, p. 315.

71. IMH 03-32-424-03-021, p. 118, records his name as Abdulqadir son of Hashim (*A-xi-mu zhi zi A-bu-duo-ka-di-er*). The average loss was 7,213 rubles, which indicates that Qadir Haji was not a particularly wealthy merchant.

72. APRK 666/1/116; APRK 666/1/117.

73. APRK 666/1/116, l. 1ob.

74. This must have been close to the entire Kashgari population of the city. In 1917, the number of Kashgaris resident in Vernyi was only 376 (242 men and 134 women). TsGARK 48/1/873, ll. 81ob–82. My thanks to Niccolò Pianciola for this reference.

75. APRK 666/1/116, l. 1ob.

76. RGASPI 544/4/36, l. 71.

77. Li Sheng, *Xinjiang dui Su (E) maoyi shi, 1600–1990* (Ürümchi: Xinjiang renmin chubanshe, 1994), 257.

78. RGASPI 62/2/43, ll. 12–13.

79. RGASPI 514/1/181, l. 21; RGASPI 62/2/405, l. 3. See also A. S. Takenov, "K voprosu uchastiia Uigurskikh trudiashchikhsia v revoliutsionnom dvizhenii v Semirech'e," in *Aktual'nye problemy sovetskogo uigurovedeniia: Materialy 1 respublikan-skoi uigurovedcheskoi konferentsii 29–31 maia 1979 g.*, ed. G. S. Sadvakasov (Almaty: Nauka, 1983), 224–227.

80. Lars-Erik Nyman, *Great Britain and Chinese, Russian and Japanese Interests in Sinkiang, 1918–1934* (Stockholm: Esselte Studium, 1977), 71.

81. Allen Suess Whiting, *Soviet Policies in China, 1917–1924* (New York: Columbia University Press, 1954), 150.

82. GARF 200/1/459, ll. 39–40.

83. RGASPI 544/4/36, l. 13. The Turkistan Front command also assigned Dungans and Kashgaris for work in Xinjiang. See RGASPI 62/2/405, l. 26.

84. Leon Trotsky, *The Trotsky Papers 1917–1922* (The Hague: Mouton, 1964), 1:625.

85. RGASPI 61/2/18, l. 117.

86. Iu. N. Tikhonov, "Dokumenty o revizii raboty Turkestanskogo Biuro Kominterna v kontse 1921 g," *Vostochnyi arkhiv*, no. 21 (2010): 49–55; RGASPI 544/4/36, ll. 69, 72.

87. A. Mumämmädi, "Yaqub Eliyop," *Kämbäghällär Awazi*, December 3, 1927, 3.

88. RGASPI 544/4/36, ll. 194–194ob.

89. Masayuki Yamauchi, *Hoşnut Olamamış Adam—Enver Paşa Türkiye'den Türkistan'a* (Istanbul: Bağlam, 1995), 315.

90. RGASPI 514/1/995, l. 22. In his memoirs, Ahmed Kemal refers to Ali Haji as his "soul-companion" (*enis-i ruhum*). Ahmet Kemal İlkul, *Çin-Türkistan Hatıraları* and *Şanghay Hatıraları* (Istanbul: Ötüken, 1997), 184.

91. For one such account, see Ziya Yergök, *Sarıkamış'tan Esarete (1915–1920): Tuğgeneral Ziya Yergök'ün Anıları*, ed. Sami Önal (Istanbul: Remzi, 2005), 185–211. The author was accompanied by Shami Damolla for much of his journey from Xinjiang to Soviet Turkistan.

92. [Mäs'ud Sabri], "Yurtimizning Täjäddüd Tarikhi," *Shingjang Gäziti*, July 22, 1948, 4.

93. See the detailed studies by A. V. Ganin: *Chernogorets na russkoi sluzhbe: General Bakich* (Moscow: Russkii put', 2004); *Ataman A. I. Dutov* (Moscow: Tsentrpoligraf, 2006). On Yang Zengxin's policy toward these White holdouts, see Justin Jacobs, "Empire Besieged: The Preservation of Chinese Rule in Xinjiang, 1884–1971" (Ph.D. diss., University of California, San Diego, 2011).

94. RGASPI 544/4/36, l. 196ob.

95. On Xinjiang as a front in the Civil War, see Share, "Russian Civil War in Chinese Turkestan." The Red Army's sweep through Xinjiang is usually considered the end of the civil war along the Russia-China frontier, but recent research in White sources

has shown that Colonel Sidorov in Ghulja continued to plan for the possibility of an anti-Soviet uprising in Semireche well into 1922. See M. N. Ivlev, "Antibol'shevitskoe dvizhenie v semirechenskom kazach'em voiske," *Belaia gvardiia*, no. 8 (2005): 225–235.

96. RGASPI 17/3/174, l. 18; A. N. Kheifets, *Sovetskaia diplomatiia i narody Vostoka, 1921–1927* (Moscow: Nauka, 1968), 129.

97. V. A. Barmin, *Sovetskii soiuz i Sin'tszian 1918–1941* (Barnaul: Barnaul gosu-darstvennyi pedagogicheskii universitet, 1999), 86–87.

6. From Party to Nation

1. Joseph Stalin, *Marxism and the National Question* (Moscow: Foreign Languages Publishing House, 1947), 15.

2. RGASPI 544/4/35, l. 2.

3. This information on Mahmudov is derived from RGASPI 514/1/181, l. 22; RGASPI 62/2/407, l. 23.

4. RGASPI 544/4/35, ll. 15ob–16.

5. Ibid., l. 13.

6. Ibid., l. 18.

7. Ibid., ll. 6, 21ob, 25ob.

8. Ibid., ll. 15, 19.

9. Ibid., ll. 15, 23.

10. Iu. N. Tikhonov, "Dokumenty o revizii raboty Turkestanskogo biuro Kominterna v kontse 1921 g," *Vostochnyi arkhiv*, no. 21 (2010): 49–55.

11. RGASPI 514/1/181, ll. 22–22ob.

12. Tikhonov, "Dokumenty o revizii raboty," 54.

13. According to Zeki Velidi Togan, "Sabir Bey" was with him in Samarkand in early 1921. In late 1922 he was killed in the vicinity of Namangan while fighting alongside the Basmachi leader Rahman Qul. See A. Zeki Velidi Togan, *Bugünkü Türkili (Türkistan) ve Yakin Tarihi* (Istanbul: Arkadaş, İbrahim Horoz ve Güven Basimevleri, 1942–1947), 463. Abdullah Rozibaqiev says that Polatkhojaev was killed in battle, and Mahmudov was captured and imprisoned in Ferghana. RGASPI 514/1/181, l. 23.

14. RGASPI 514/1/181, l. 23.

15. Ibid., l. 22.

16. Ibid., l. 24.

17. In Qaraqol, the Uyghur Union continued to exist illegally until 1924. APRK 666/1/1150, l. 25b.

18. RGASPI 62/2/405, l. 4.

19. RGASPI 514/1/181, l. 24.

20. APRK 666/1/879.

21. APRK 666/1/1150, l. 44b.

22. "Qashqarliq Mäktipi," *Kämbäghällär Awazi*, October 26, 1923, 2.

23. Uyghur Balisi [Näzärghoja Abdusemätov], *Taranchi Türklärning Tarikhi* (Almaty: Uyghur Kommunistlirining Vilayät Byurasi, 1922). In 1925 a newly formed Uyghur drama troupe staged a performance of *Nazugum* in the Uyghur Club, drawing an audience of five hundred. Ghojash Oghli, "Uyghur Troppasi Tüzülüp Ishqa Bashlidi," *Kämbäghällär Awazi*, March 27, 1925, 4.

24. APRK 666/1/637, l. 41. Sabirjan Shakirjanov was born in 1880 in the Ufa region and received a madrasa education before being called up by the army. Wounded in the Russo-Japanese War, he took up work as a teacher, coming in 1907 to Vernyi, where he taught in a Russo-native school and a Tatar school. The Tatar school was shut in 1913 for refusing to display the portrait of the tsar. After fighting in the civil war in the 1st Siberian Division (which went over to the Red Army), he became the editor of the first pro-Soviet Tatar newspapers in Vernyi. See TsGARK 1261/1/2.

25. APRK 666/1/1150, l. 38. "Tärräqipärvär Mollilar Siyäzi," *Kämbäghällär Awazi*, September 14, 1924, 4.

26. G. B. Nikol'skaia and A. M. Matveev, "Vliianie revoliutsii 1905–1907 gg. na sin'tszianskikh vykhodtsev v Turkestane," *Nauchnye trudy Tashkentskogo gosudarstvennogo universiteta*, no. 392 (1970): 78–88.

27. APRK 3/1/286, ll. 2, 5, 12.

28. APRK 666/1/1150, l. 37; APRK 666/1/1152, l. 80; "Mäshräplär Bashlanmaqda," *Kämbäghällär Awazi*, December 4, 1923, 2; Shiripay Oghli, "Mäshäp Yashliri," *Kämbäghällär Awazi*, January 1, 1925, 4.

29. APRK 666/1/637, l. 2.

30. Sabirjan Shakirjan, "Dungän Türkläri Bayankhu," *Kämbäghällär Awazi*, November 7, 1922, 3.

31. "Qashqaristanda Angliz Misiyonerlar Nä Eshläylär!" *Ochqïn*, May 31, 1920, 4.

32. Muhämmädi, "Yash Yürigim," *Kämbäghällär Awazi*, August 17, 1922, 3. See also 'Abdulghafur Rozibaqi, "Uyghurstan Ölkisi," *Kämbäghällär Awazi*, July 21, 1923, 2.

33. Adeeb Khalid, *Making Uzbekistan: Nation, Empire, and Revolution in the Early USSR* (Ithaca: Cornell University Press, 2015).

34. Alixonto'ra Sog'uniy, *Turkiston Qayg'usi* (Tashkent: Sharq, 2003), 214.

35. APRK 666/1/637, l. 1.

36. APRK 666/1/638, ll. 8–8ob.

37. Galindeviin Myagmarsambuu, *Lavaryn Demberel (1891–1938): Namtar, büteel* (Ulaanbaatar: Selengepress, 2008), 56–58; Aoki Masahiro, *Mongoru kindaishi kenkyū 1921–1924 nen* (Tokyo: Waseda Daigaku Shuppanbu, 2011), 359–372.

38. RGASPI 514/1/20, l. 195ob.

39. RGASPI 514/1/27, ll. 3–4. For further discussion of the Mongolia-Tibet axis in Soviet thinking, see Alexandre Andreyev, *Soviet Russia and Tibet: The Debacle of Secret Diplomacy, 1918–1930s* (Leiden: Brill, 2003).

40. John Riddell, ed., *Toward the United Front: Proceedings of the Fourth Congress of the Communist International, 1922* (Leiden: Brill, 2012), 441.

41. RGASPI 62/2/64, l. 27.

42. RGASPI 514/1/181, l. 25.

43. RGASPI 544/4/36, l. 197.

44. RGASPI 533/4/16, l. 36.

45. Z. Bashir, "Türkistan-i Chinida Inqilab Ḥarakati," *Türkistan*, February 17, 1923, 1.

46. RGASPI 514/1/56, l. 4.

47. RGASPI 514/1/56, l. 2; RGASPI 62/2/405, l. 27; RGASPI 62/2/64, l. 4.

48. RGVA 25895/1/832, ll. 267–68.

49. Aoki, *Mongoru kindaishi kenkyū*, 368.

50. B. V. Bazarov, B. D. Tsibikov, and S. B. Ochirov, eds., *Ėlbek-Dorzhi Rinchino o Mongolii* (Ulan-Ude: Institut Mongolovedeniia, buddologii i tibetologii Sibirskogo otdeleniia Rossiiskoi akademiia nauk, 1998), 126.

51. APRK 666/1/1150, l. 25.

52. A list of members from the town of Qaraqol in 1922, for example, shows not only Kashgaris and Taranchis, but also Uzbeks, Kirghiz from the Cherik clan (who traditionally nomadized in the mountains bordering Xinjiang), and a few who registered themselves as hailing from the oasis of Turfan. RGASPI 666/1/639, ll. 12–13b. Dungans are conspicuously absent from the list.

53. RGASPI 544/4/36, l. 73.

54. APRK 666/1/640, l. 28.

55. TsGARU 25/1/1440, ll. 9–10ob.

56. APRK 666/1/1152, l. 74.

57. APRK 6661/1/1151, l. 37.

58. APRK 666/1/1152, l. 76.

59. RGASPI 62/2/405, ll. 5–9.

60. RGASPI 62/2/405, l. 20.

61. See APRK 666/1/1150, ll. 44b–45, for a report by Masanchi on work among the Dungans of Pishpek and Qaraqonguz.

62. Z. Bäshir, "*Birinchi Chamdam* Mäjmuʿasi," *Kämbäghällär Awazi*, September 14, 1924, 3–4.

63. Sean Roberts, "Imagining Uyghurstan: Re-evaluating the Birth of the Modern Uyghur Nation," *Central Asian Survey* 28, no. 4 (2009): 377n17.

64. Tsentral'noe statisticheskoe upravlenie Turkestanskoi respubliki, *Materialy vserossiiskikh perepisei: Perepis naseleniia v Turkestanskoi Respublike*, vol. 4, *Sel'skoe naselenie Ferganskoi oblasti po materialam perepisi 1917 g.* (Tashkent: TsSU Turkrespubliki, 1924), 44.

65. Mäʿsum, "Qäshqär Qishlaqda," *Kämbäghällär Awazi*, March 27, 1925, 3.

66. RGASPI 62/2/104, l. 106.

67. RGASPI 62/2/109, l. 183.

68. RGASPI 62/2/405, ll. 3–5.

69. Ibid., l. 9.

70. Burhan Qasim, "Orta Aziyaning Milli Jumhuriyätlärgä Bölünishi häm Uyghur Khälqläri," *Kämbäghällär Awazi*, September 25, 1924, 2.

71. Arne Haugen, *The Establishment of National Republics in Soviet Central Asia* (New York: Palgrave Macmillan, 2003), 144–145.

72. APRK 3/1/299, ll. 17–18; RGASPI 17/67/93, l. 40.

73. Reports describe landless Taranchi peasants drifting south from Zharkent into what was soon to become Kirghizstan. Zayit Isma'il Oghli, "Qaraqoldäki Uyghurlar," *Kämbäghällär Awazi*, May 22, 1925, 3.

74. RGASPI 25/67/93, ll. 66–67.

75. GARF 1235/122/293, l. 6.

76. "Ikki Rayon Bolmaqchi," *Kämbäghällär Awazi*, December 14, 1927, 1; Badraq, "Milli Bolus Yasaldi," *Kämbäghällär Awazi*, October 22, 1927, 3. On rayonization in Kazakhstan, see Niccolò Pianciola, *Stalinismo di frontiera: Colonizzazione agricola, sterminio dei nomadi e costruzione statale in Asia centrale (1905–1936)* (Vicenza: Viella, 2009), 332–337.

77. APRK 666/1/1153, l. 33.

78. I. I. Zarubin, *Spisok narodnostei Turkestanskogo kraia*, Trudy komissii po izucheniiu plemennogo sostava naseleniia Rossii i sopredel'nykh stran, vol. 9 (Leningrad: Rossiiskaia akademiia nauk, 1925), 18–19.

79. Francine Hirsch, *Empire of Nations: Ethnographic Knowledge and the Making of the Soviet Union* (Ithaca, NY: Cornell University Press, 2005), 126.

80. Tsentral'noe statisticheskoe upravlenie SSSR, *Vsesoiuznaia perepis' naseleniia 1926 goda*, vol. 8, *Kazakhskaia SSR, Kirgizskaia SSR*, vol. 15, *Uzbekskaia SSR* (Moscow: Izdanie TsSU Souiza SSR, 1928).

81. S. S. Gubaeva, "Uigury i dungane Ferganskoi doliny," in *Sovremennoe razvitie ètnicheskikh grupp Srednei Azii i Kazakhstana* (Moscow: Institut ètnologii i antropologii imeni N. N. Miklukho-Maklaia, 1992), 122.

82. RGASPI 62/2/484, l. 7.

83. "Uyghur-Özbäk Birligi," *Türkistan*, January 3, 1924, 4.

84. RGASPI 62/2/742, ll. 48–49.

85. L. S. Gatagova, L. P. Kosheleva, and L. A. Rogovaia, eds., *TsK RKP(b)-VKP(b) i natsional'nyi vopros*, vol. 1, *1918–1933 gg.* (Moscow: Rosspen, 2005), 581.

86. *Vsesoiuznaia perepis' naseleniia 1926 goda*, 15:9.

87. RGASPI 514/1/181, l. 20.

7. Between the Chinese Revolution and the Stalin Revolution

1. "Khitay Urushlari va Qashqarlar," *Türkistan*, November 28, 1924, 4.

2. Khodosov, "Iliiskaia oblast'," *Zhizn' natsional'nostei*, July 17, 1922, 5.

3. TsGARU 702/1/95, ll. 67–67ob, 142–143.

4. O. Bukshtein, "Torgovlia SSSR s Sin'tszianskoi provintsiei," *Novyi Vostok*, nos. 20–21 (1928): 202.

5. A. Afanas'ev-Kazanskii, "Ėkonomicheskoe polozhenie Zapadnogo Kitaia," *Novyi Vostok*, no. 3 (1923): 119.

6. Zhang was thought of as an enemy of Yang Zengxin by the Soviets (RGASPI 62/2/530, ll. 1–2), an opinion that is confirmed in Isa Yüsüf Alptekin's account of these appointments, 'Isa Yusuf Beg, "Türkistan vä Rusiya," *Chini Türkistan Awazi* 9 (February 1934): 23–26.

7. V. N. Ksandrov, K. Kh. Danishevskii, M. I. Kalmanovich, A. V. Ozerskii, V. N. Voskresenskii, and M. A. Granat, eds., *Torgovlia SSSR s Vostokom (sbornik statei i materialov)* (Moscow: Promizdat, 1927), 263; Naganawa Norihiro, "The Hajj Making Geopolitics, Empire, and Local Politics: A View from the Volga-Ural Region at the Turn of the Nineteenth and Twentieth Centuries," in *Central Asian Pilgrims: Hajj Routes and Pious Visits between Central Asia and the Hijaz*, ed. Alexandre Papas, Thomas Welsford, and Thierry Zarcone (Berlin: Klaus Schwarz, 2012), 168–198.

8. On such cases, see *Zhong-E guanxi shiliao: Yiban jiaoshe 1920* (Nangang: Zhongyang yanjiuyuan jindaishi yanjiu suo, 1968), 212, 222, 237, 243. While reluctant to allow such requests, Governor Yang reasoned that with their wealth they would be able to acquire British subjecthood, and hence reluctantly acceded.

9. Bukshtein, "Torgovlia SSSR s Sin'tszianskoi provintsiei," 211.

10. O. Bukshtein, "Vostok na sovetskikh iarmarkakh," *Novyi Vostok*, nos. 13–14 (1926): 217.

11. Bukshtein, "Torgovlia SSSR s Sin'tszianskoi provintsiei," 217. The handbook for the 1926 Nizhnyi-Novgorod fair lists Bahauddin Musabayev as an agent for cotton, leather, and wool. "Dopolnitel'nyi spisok," in *Vsesoiuznaia Nizhegorodskaia iarmarka: Katalog i putevoditel'* (Kanavino: Krasnii pechatnik, 1926), 17.

12. P. P. Ivanov, "Iarmarochnaia torgovlia v Kazakstane," *Novyi Vostok*, nos. 13–14 (1926): 230.

13. Ksandrov et al., *Torgovlia SSSR s Vostokom*, 264.

14. RGVA 25895/1/832, ll. 49–51.

15. Judd Kinzley, "Staking Claims to China's Borderland: Oil, Ores and State-Building in Xinjiang Province, 1893–1964" (Ph.D. diss., University of California, San Diego, 2012), 140–141.

16. 'Isa Yusuf Beg, "Türkistan vä Rusiya," *Chini Türkistan Awazi* 1, no. 3 (December 1934): 26.

17. IOR L/PS/10/976, doc. 7709, p. 37b.

18. Justin Jacobs, "Empire Besieged: The Preservation of Chinese Rule in Xinjiang, 1884–1971" (Ph.D. diss., University of California, San Diego, 2011), 206.

19. "Qizil Chaykhanä Echildi," *Kämbäghällär Awazi*, March 27, 1925, 3.

20. RGASPI 62/2/2331, l. 121.

21. RGASPI 62/2/742, l. 49.

22. RGASPI 62/2/3038, ll. 15, 42.

23. G. K. Sadvakasov, *Iazyk Uigurov Ferganskoi doliny* (Almaty: Nauka, 1970), 1:116. I have modified Sadvaqasov's transcription.

24. "Xinjiang yiyuan fandui Xibei bianfang duban," *Shenbao*, April 20, 1924, 7; "Xibei bianfang duban guanzhi zhi fanxiang," *Shenbao*, November 11, 1923, 7.

25. On the redivision plan, see An Han, *Xibei kenzhi lun* (1932), Zhongguo xibei wenxian congshu xubian, vol. 7 of Xibei shidi wenxian juan (Lanzhou: Gansu wenhua chubanshe, 1999), 314–317.

26. One such rumor held that Ma Fuxing's brother now stood at the head of Dungan forces on Xinjiang's eastern front. RGASPI 62/2/530, l. 8.

27. Henning Haslund, *Men and Gods in Mongolia* (New York: E. P. Dutton, 1935), 243.

28. "Mäskavdiki 'Uyghur' Oqughuchiliri Uyushmisi," *Kämbäghällär Awazi*, June 21, 1925.

29. RGASPI 532/2/158.

30. RGASPI 514/1/181, ll. 104–106.

31. RGASPI 62/2/530, l. 10.

32. RGASPI 514/1/181, ll. 5–7.

33. RGASPI 62/2/880, ll. 35–36.

34. Andrew D. W. Forbes, *Warlords and Muslims in Chinese Central Asia: A Political History of Republican Sinkiang 1911–1949* (Cambridge: Cambridge University Press, 1986), 119.

35. To this day, scholars debate whether or not there was any reality to this coup plot. See Alex McKay, "Tibet 1924: A Very British Coup Attempt?" *Journal of the Royal Asiatic Society*, 3rd ser. 7, no. 3 (1997): 411–424.

36. RGASPI 514/1/181, l. 112.

37. Ibid., ll. 14–18.

38. RGASPI 62/2/405, l. 28.

39. Masayuki Yamauchi, *Hoşnut Olamamış Adam: Enver Paşa Türkiye'den Türkistan'a* (Istanbul: Bağlam, 1995), 275.

40. RGASPI 62/2/405, l. 27; RGASPI 62/2/1150, ll. 56b–58.

41. RGASPI 62/2/530, l. 91.

42. *Kämbäghällär Awazi*, January 1, 1925, 2.

43. RGASPI 62/2/245, l. 6; RGASPI 62/2/742, ll. 23, 49.

44. RGASPI 62/2/875, l. 22.

45. *Kämbäghällär Awazi*, November 29, 1925, 2.

46. RGASPI 514/1/1022, ll. 138–139.

47. İsa Yusuf Alptekin, *Esir Doğu Türkistan için* (Istanbul: Doğu Türkistan Neşriyat Merkezi, 1985), 110.

48. RGASPI 62/2/874, ll. 77–78.

49. Benjamin H. Loring, "Building Socialism in Kyrgyzstan: Nation-Making, Rural Development, and Social Change, 1921–1932" (Ph.D. diss., Brandeis University, 2008), 255.

50. RGASPI 514/1/995, l. 9.

51. RGASPI 62/2/879, l. 112.

52. Islamov managed to survive, and in 1933, when he again came to the attention of the OGPU, he was in possession of a party card. These 1933 reports claim that in 1926 Islamov created an underground Uyghur organization called "Sharp Sword" (Ötkür Qilich), which organized the illicit distribution of arms and secret crossings into Kashgar. RGASPI 514/1/1022, ll. 24, 38.

53. RGASPI 495/154/457, l. 52.

54. Alptekin, *Esir Doğu Türkistan için*, 113.

55. W. Radloff, *Proben der Volksliteratur der türkischen Stämme*, vol. 6, *Dialect der Tarantschi* (Saint Petersburg: Tipografiia Imperatorskoi akademii nauk, 1886); A. G. Sertkaia, "Zhizn' i deiatel'nost' N. N. Pantusova. Bibliograficheskii spisok trudov," in *Nasledie N. F. Katanova: Istoriia i kul'tura tiurkskikh narodov Evrazii* (Kazan: Alma Lit, 2005).

56. APRK 666/1/637, l. 58.

57. APRK 666/1/1150, l. 41.

58. Z. Bashir, "Matbu'at va Adabiyat: Uyghur Alifbasi," *Qizil Özbäkistan*, December 5, 1924, 4; "Matbu'at va Adabiyat: Uyghur Alifbasi Toghrisida," *Qizil Özbäkistan*, January 11, 1925, 5.

59. L. Änsari, Z. Bäshir, B. Khudayqul, and S. Ibrahimi, eds., *Uyghur Äl Ädäbiyati* (Moscow: Tsentral'noe izdatel'stvo narodov SSSR, 1925), 4–5.

60. Sabirjan Shakirjanov, "Uyghur Äl Ädäbiyati," *Kämbäghällär Awazi*, January 13, 1925, 3.

61. Abdughupur Rozibaqi, "Tilimiz Toghrisidiki Chataqla," *Kämbäghällär Awazi*, February 23, 1926, 2–3.

62. RGASPI 62/2/215, l. 42.

63. Khäwärchi, "Dinchilär Ädäb Ketti," *Kämbäghällär Awazi*, February 15, 1926, 4.

64. Häqiqätchi, "Dini Soyuz," *Kämbäghällär Awazi*, January 13, 1926, 4. The article's author scoffed at the suggestion that these imams would be able to contest the elections, knowing that as clergy they would be prohibited from standing by Soviet electoral law.

65. Bazghan, "Yarkäntdima Dinchila Täräqqi Tapmaqda," *Kämbäghällär Awazi*, March 11, 1927, 4.

66. Yash Ishchi, "Dinchilani Qarang," *Kämbäghällär Awazi*, January 15, 1927, 4.

67. "Dögiläk yasaldi," *Kämbäghällär Awazi*, July 8, 1927, 4; Kütküchi, "Dini Khurapatla Bilän Chelishish Dögiligi Yasaldi," *Kämbäghällär Awazi*, July 8, 1927, 4.

68. Khäwärchi, "Tegishlik Jazasi Berildi," *Kämbäghällär Awazi*, December 10, 1926, 4.

69. "'Din' Khizmitidin Kächkänlä," *Kämbäghällär Awazi*, March 31, 1928, 3.

70. Khäwärchi, "Mäshräblä Bolup Yatidu," *Kämbäghällär Awazi*, February 13, 1928, 3.

71. Adeeb Khalid, *Islam after Communism: Religion and Politics in Central Asia* (Berkeley: University of California Press, 2007), 68.

72. T. Qutluq, "Bizdä Til, Ädäbiyat Mätbuʿat Mäs'ililiri," *Kämbäghällär Awazi,* July 18, 1927, 2–3. These critical comments were left out of the edited version of Rozibaqiev's articles, A. Rozibaqiev, *Khälqim Üchün Köyüdu Zhüräk* (Almaty: Zhazushï, 1997), 106.

73. Näzärghoja Abdusemätov, *Yoruq Sahillar* (Almaty: Zhazushï, 1991), 172.

74. Uyghur Balisi [Näzärghoja Abdusemätov], "Tänqidgä Javab," *Kämbäghällär Awazi,* January 30, 1928, 2–3.

75. Little is known about Abdusamadov's life in Xinjiang other than that he died in 1951. See Mahmud Zä'idi, "Uyghur Balisi—Näzärghoja," *Shinjang Täzkirisi* 31, no. 2 (1994): 49–52.

76. Abdulhäy Muhämmädi, *Uyghurchä Yeziq Yolliri* (Moscow: Tsentral'noe izdatel'stvo narodov SSSR, 1926), 10.

77. Hashim Ḥajiyef, "Altishähär-Junghariyä Uyghurlirining Oktäbr Inqilabining 10 Yilliq Dävridä Qilghan Ishliri," *Qutulush,* November 7, 1927, 3. This article is the only public discussion I have seen of the reasons behind the dissolution of the Revolutionary Union in 1921.

78. Uchqun, "Uyghurlar Arasida Til häm Maʿarip," *Qutulush,* February 16, 1928, 2–3.

79. Terry Martin, *The Affirmative Action Empire: Nations and Nationalism in the Soviet Union, 1923–1939* (Ithaca, NY: Cornell University Press, 2001), 185–203.

80. Mukhbir, "Uyghurlardin Väkil," *Kämbäghällär Awazi,* December 15, 1925, 3.

81. "Latinchiliq Yolidiki Birinchi Kengäshmäjlisi Nätijiliri," *Kämbäghällär Awazi,* May 26, 1928, 2–3.

82. Änsari, "Latinchiliq Yolida," *Kämbäghällär Awazi,* August 15, 1928, 1; "Ilmi Kengäshmädä Qaralghan Mäsililä Toghruluq," *Kämbäghällär Awazi,* September 3, 1928, 2.

83. Abdulhəj Muhəmmədij, "Til, Imla Məsililiri," *Inqilabchi Shärq,* no. 2 (1929): 21.

84. Sergei Efimovich Malov, "Izuchenie zhivykh turetskikh narechii Zapadnogo Kitaia," *Vostochnye zapiski* 1 (1927): 168–172.

85. *Pervyi vsesoiuznyi tiurkologicheskii s"ezd 26 fevralia–5 marta 1926 g. (Stenograficheskii otchet)* (Baku: Nagïl Evi, 2011), 189.

86. Sergei Efimovich Malov, "Materialy po uigurskim narechiiam Sin'tsziana," in *Sergeiu Fedorovichu Ol'denburgu: K piatidesiatiletiiu nauchno-obshchestvennoi deiatel'nosti* (Leningrad: 1934), 307. Malov also cited Raquette, who in one publication referred to the Kashgar-Yarkand vernacular as the "Uigur-Uzbek" dialect.

87. *2-Uyghur Til-Imla Känpirinsiyining Tokhtamliri 13–18/V 30 y.* (Kyzyl Orda: Kazizdat, 1932), 8–9, 28.

88. Ibid., 21.

89. Ibid., 10, 28.

90. Ibid., 30.

91. Sergei Efimovich Malov, *Uigurskii iazyk, Khamiiskoe narechie: Teksty, perevody, i slovar'* (Moscow: Akademiia nauk, 1954).

92. PFARAN 1079/3/270, l. 3.

93. PFARAN 1079/2/12.

94. Laura Newby, "The Rise of Nationalism in Eastern Turkestan, 1930–1950" (Ph.D. diss., Oxford University, 1990), 99.

8. The Battle for Xinjiang and the Uyghur Nation

1. Andrew D. W. Forbes, *Warlords and Muslims in Chinese Central Asia: A Political History of Republican Sinkiang 1911–1949* (Cambridge: Cambridge University Press, 1986); Laura Newby, "The Rise of Nationalism in Eastern Turkestan, 1930–1950" (Ph.D. diss., Oxford University, 1990); Shinmen Yasushi, "The Eastern Turkistan Republic (1933–1934) in Historical Perspective," in *Islam in Politics in Russia and Central Asia (Early Eighteenth to Late Twentieth Centuries)*, ed. Stéphane A. Dudoignon and Komatsu Hisao (London: Kegan Paul, 2001), 133–164.

2. "Xinjiang Huiwang daibiao zhi qingyuan," *Shenbao*, December 22, 1927, 13.

3. "Huizu daibiao xiang guofu qingyuan: Kuoda Mengzang weihui zuzhi jiaru Huibu," *Shenbao*, April 10, 1928, 9.

4. "Lüjing Huiwang daibiao zhi xuanyan: Qing guoren yuanzhu jiechu Huimin tongku," *Shenbao*, February 21, 1928, 7.

5. "Xinjiang shengfu yeyi chengli: Yang Zengxin jiu Xinjiang zongsiling," *Shenbao*, July 5, 1928, 4. Soviet sources confirm the suggestion of appointing Ma Fuxiang to Xinjiang. See RGASPI 62/2/1344, l. 33.

6. For a reading of events that places Feng at the center of the conspiracy, see Luo Shaowen, "Yang Zengxin, Feng Yuxiang zhijian de maodun he Xinjiang 'sanqi' zhengbian," *Xibei shidi*, no. 4 (1995): 67–84.

7. "Jin Shuren ji Yang jiuzhi: Xinsheng dangbu qing guofu renming," *Shenbao*, July 21, 1928, 4.

8. "Shoudu jiwen," *Shenbao*, November 29, 1928, 6.

9. "Huibu tongdian tao Feng," *Shenbao*, June 1, 1929, 9.

10. RGASPI 62/2/2209, ll. 2, 16.

11. Ibid., ll. 9–11.

12. Nicholas Roerich, *Altai-Himalaya: A Travel Diary* (New York: Frederick A. Stokes, 1929), 282.

13. RGASPI 62/2/879, ll. 241–242.

14. Owen Lattimore, *The Desert Road to Turkestan* (New York: Kodansha International, 1995), 299.

15. RGASPI 62/2/879, ll. 261–262.

16. "Xinjiang xianzhuang zhi yiban," *Shenbao*, July 19, 1928, 9–10.

17. IOR L/PS/12/2336, pp. 95–96; Reginald C. F. Schomberg, "A Fourth Journey in the Tien Shan," *The Geographical Journal* 79, no. 5 (1932): 368–378.

18. Soviet observers applauded these early moves, suspecting that Xinjiang's Mongol aristocrats were in league with counterrevolutionaries who had escaped from Communist Mongolia to Xinjiang, and with the British. RGASPI 495/154/457, ll. 3–4.

19. On Qasim, see Sherip Khushtar, ed., *Shinjang Yeqinqi Zaman Tarikhidiki Mäshhur Shäkhslär* (Ürümchi: Shinjang Khälq Näshriyati, 2000), 101–108; "Qasim Äfändining Khizmäti Khälqimiz Yadidin Mängü Chiqmaydu," *Inqilabi Shärqi Türkistan,* September 7, 1948, 1.

20. Galindeviin Myagmarsambuu, *Lavaryn Demberel (1891–1938): Namtar, büteel* (Ulaanbaatar: Selengepress, 2008), 78–91.

21. Myagmarsambuu, *Lavaryn Demberel,* 81–83; David Brophy, "The Qumul Rebels' Appeal to Outer Mongolia," *Turcica* 42 (2010): 329–341.

22. While in Xinjiang, some of Demberel's companions invited representatives of the Torghud khan for talks. Although the Torghud never joined in the uprising, these contacts may have influenced the regent's decision to adopt a position of neutrality toward it. When Jin Shuren ordered the Mongols to mobilize against the Muslims, the regent ignored his instructions.

23. Guang Lu, consul in Tashkent in the 1930s, was in no doubt that the Mongolian emissaries to Hami were sent directly by Moscow. According to his analysis, the Soviet objective was not to arm the rebels for victory, but rather to force Jin Shuren to move closer to Moscow. See Guang Lu, *Guang Lu huiyilu* (Taibei: Wenxing shudian, 1964), 149–153.

24. In desperation, Ma is said to have tried sending a local Uzbek to Andijan to try and recruit new troops, but he too followed Osman in joining the rebels. Polat Qadiri, *Ölkä Tarikhi* (Ürümchi: Altay Näshriyati, 1948), 68–69.

25. Musa Turkistani, *Ulugh Türkistan Faji'asi* (Madina: Maṭabi' al-Rashid, 1401/1981), 2:53.

26. Umar Akhunbayev eventually left Kashgar on the hajj in 1933, returning in 1936 in the company of Mosul Bay, Mahmud Muhiti's brother. IOR L/PS/12/2332, doc. 6815, p. 61.

27. Yunus Saidi was formerly employed in the Ürümchi telegraph office, where he supplied rebels with information on the deployment of Jin Shuren's troops. Fearing arrest, he fled to Hami, where he supported the uprising before marching on Kashgar with Temür.

28. Zhongguo di-er lishi dang'anguan, ed., *Zhonghua minguoshi dang'an ziliao huibian* (Nanjing: Jiangsu renmin chubanshe), 25:554–555.

29. Ḥamidullah bin Muḥammad Ṭurfani, *Türkistan 1331–1337 Inqilab Tarikhi* (Mecca: Muḥammad Qasim Amin, 1943; repr., Istanbul: Doğu Türkistan Dergisi, 1983), 123–124.

30. Imin Bäg Wahidi, *Äslätmä* (manuscript, 1939), 33–35; Ṭurfani, *Türkistan 1331–1337,* 122.

31. Wahidi, *Äslätmä,* 41.

32. RGASPI 62/2/3037 contains descriptions of detentions at the border and intelligence reports on large numbers of "bay" and "kulak" elements intending to emigrate to Kashgar, allegedly to join Basmachi forces led by Qur Shirmat.

33. A list of members of this society is provided in Turkistani, *Ulugh Türkistan Faji'asi,* 2:44.

34. Shinmen, "Eastern Turkistan Republic."

35. Näüshirvan Yaushef, "Kashghar Näshr-i Mä'arif Jäm'ïyate," *Vaqït*, May 25, 1916, 3. For a speculative biography based on PRC sources, see Michael Dillon, *Xinjiang and the Expansion of Chinese Communist Power: Kashgar in the Twentieth Century* (Abingdon: Routledge, 2014), 182–189. Musa Turkistani records that Abdulkarim Khan was imprisoned in Aqsu for seven years before the outbreak of the revolt. Turkistani, *Ulugh Türkistan Faji'asi*, 2:66–67.

36. Ṭurfani, *Türkistan 1331–1337*, 185–186.

37. Zarif Bäshir, *Uyghïr Ädäbiyate* (Kazan: Yangalif, 1931), 45.

38. RGASPI 514/1/995, l. 22.

39. Abdurusul Ömär, ed., *Abdukhaliq Uyghur She'irliri* (Ürümchi: Shinjang Khälq Näshriyati, 1995), 8.

40. Ibid., 3, 13.

41. *Istiqlal*, nos. 1–2 (1933), 14.

42. Ibid., 67.

43. Du Jianyi and Gu Peiyu, *Xinjiang tongyuan tushuo* (Ürümchi: Xinjiang renmin chubanshe, 1998), 143–155.

44. Ibrahim Alip Tekin, ed., *Mämtili Äpändi She'irliri* (Ürümchi: Shinjang Khälq Näshriyati, 2000), 12.

45. One result of this study was M. Kazanin, "Natsional'nyi sostav Kitaia," *Problemy Kitaia*, no. 11 (1933): 98–154.

46. One article from 1929 noted that, in Qaraqol, Hashim Aqsaqal's seals had finally been confiscated, but that he remained an influential figure: "he takes advantage of the situation in Manchuria and spreads all sorts of rumors to bring the people to his breast." Dätmän, "Qaraqoldäki Uyghur," *Kämbäghällär Awazi*, September 7, 1929, 4.

47. RGASPI 514/1/588, ll. 80–81.

48. M. Nemchenko, "Kolonial'nyi rezhim i agrarnye otnosheniia v Sin'tsziane," *Problemy Kitaia* 8–9, nos. 3–4 (1931): 190.

49. RGASPI 17/162/11, l. 10.

50. V. A. Barmin, *Sovetskii soiuz i Sin'tszian 1918–1941* (Barnaul: Izdatel'stvo Barnaulskogo gosudarstvennogo pedagogicheskogo universiteta, 1999), 124.

51. RGASPI 62/2/3038, l. 34.

52. Ibid., l. 17.

53. This is corroborated by stories told elsewhere by Kashgaris of making the trip intending to "earn some money and free my father from the *bay*." RGASPI 495/226/64, l. 5.

54. RGASPI 62/2/3038, ll. 12–13.

55. "1931-nchi Yil April–1932-nchi Yil Mart Künchiqish Türkistan-Qumul (Khamida) Dikhanlar Qozghulangi," *Kämbäghällär Awazi*, March 22, 1932, 2–3.

56. RGASPI 514/1/1022, l. 77.

57. Ibid., ll. 21–22.

58. Ibid., l. 138.

59. RGASPI 514/1/955, ll. 26–27, 31.

60. Alixonto'ra Sog'uniy, *Turkiston Qayg'usi* (Tashkent: Sharq, 2003), 187.

61. For what little is known of Ma Zhongying's fate in the Soviet Union, see V. A. Barmin, "Neraskrytie tainy dunganskogo 'Bonaparta' (o roli sovetskogo faktora v sud'be rukovoditelia povstancheskogo dvizheniia korennykh narodov Sin'tsziana 1931–1934 gg. Ma Chzhun"ina," *Izvestiia Altaiskogo gosudarstvennogo universiteta*, no. 76 (2012): 27–35.

62. Zhang Dajun, *Xinjiang fengbao qishi nian* (Taibei: Lanxi chubanshe, 1980), 3450–3451; "Ürümchi Khäbärläri," *Chini Türkistan Awazi*, no. 9 (1934): 67–68.

63. Baoerhan, *Xinjiang wushi nian* (Beijing: Wenshi ziliao chubanshe, 1984), 193. The creation of the Anti-Imperialist Union in Xinjiang was an initiative of the Soviet consul-general, Garegin Apresov, whose proposal was discussed and approved by the Bolshevik Central Committee in July 1934. RGASPI 17/162/16, l. 140.

64. The enlightenment associations blended Soviet, Turkic, and Chinese models of cultural progress. "Enlightenment association" was the Uyghur name for these associations (*mädäni-aqartish uyshmisi*). Some sources replace the Uyghur *aqartish* with the Tatar *agartuv*, which confirms that the associations drew heavily on Tatar notions of cultural progress. The word itself derives from the Russian *prosveshchenie*, connoting both the concrete institution of education and the abstract notion of enlightenment. In Chinese they were known as "cultural progress associations" (*wenhua cujinhui*), a designation that linked them to Republican institutions elsewhere, such as Qinghai warlord Ma Bufang's Muslim Cultural Progress Association and the Mongol-Tibet Cultural Progress Association (founded in 1932 and 1933 respectively).

65. Du Zhongyuan, *Sheng Shicai yu xin Xinjiang* (Guangzhou: Shenghuo shudian, 1938), 83; Tahir Mämteli and Mämät Häsän, "Qäshqär Vilayätlik Qazaq-Qirghiz Mädäniy Aqartish Uyushmisi Toghrisida Äslimä," *Shinjang Tarikh Materiyalliri*, no. 27 (1989): 289–293; Änwär Khanbaba, "Ölkilik Özbäk Mädäni Aqartish Uyushmisi Häqqidä Äslimä," *Shinjang Tarikh Materiyalliri*, no. 30 (1991): 173; Zuo Hongwei, "Xinjiang Menggu wenhua cujinhui de zuzhi jiegou he jingfei laiyuan," *Xinjiang daxue xuebao* 36, no. 5 (2008): 72–76.

66. Li Wending, "Tantan yi minzu wei xingshi yi fandi wei neirong zhi minzu wenhua," *Xinjiang ribao*, December 3, 1935, 4.

67. Zuo Hongwei, "Xinjiang Weiwuer wenhua cujinhui zuzhi goucheng kao," *Xinjiang shifan daxue xuebao (zhexue shehui kexue ban)* 28, no. 2 (2007): 25.

68. Baoerhan, *Xinjiang wushi nian*, 269.

69. He Yuzhu and Kang Binglin, "Guanyu Xinjiang 'Minzhong fandi lianhehui' ji qita," in *Xinjiang minzhong fandi lianhehui ziliao huibian*, ed. Li Qingjian (Ürümchi: Xinjiang qingshaonian chubanshe, 1986), 452–453.

70. Baoerhan, *Xinjiang wushi nian*, 244.

71. Du, *Sheng Shicai yu xin Xinjiang*, 57.

72. "Xinjiang sheng zhengfu linggai Chanhui mingcheng wei Weiwuer bugao," *Tianshan yuekan* 1, no. 5 (1935): 53.

73. "Qurultay Khäbärläri," *Bizning Tavush*, May 10, 1935, 2.

74. RGASPI 532/4/327, l. 115ob. See also Kazanin, "Natsional'nyi sostav Kitaia."

75. Baoerhan, *Xinjiang wushi nian*, 241. I owe this insight about Yunusov's nickname to a personal communication from the late Imin Tursun.

76. Ziya Sämädiy, *Zhillar Siri* (Almaty: Zhazushï, 1985), 2:410. Sämädiy blames Hakimbeg Khoja for the survival of the Taranchi ethnonym, depicting it as a scheme devised in collaboration with Sheng Shicai to split the Uyghur nation.

77. RGASPI 514/1/1022, l. 116.

78. "Millät Mäjlisid[ä] Muhim Qararlar," *Yengi Ḥayat*, September 20, 1934, 2.

79. "Aqartu Uyushmisi," *Yengi Ḥayat*, April 29, 1935, 1.

80. Details on the growth of schools in this period can be found in Shimizu Yuriko, "Kashugaru ni okeru Uiguru jin no kyōiku undō (1934–37 nen)," *Nairiku Ajiashi kenkyū* 22 (2007): 61–82.

81. Osman Qasim, Yaqutkhan Yünüs, and Ghäyrätjan Osman, "Qaziriqta Ma'arip vä Sän'ät," in *Qäshqär Tarikh Materiyalliri*, vol. 4 (Kashgar: Qäshqär Geziti, 1999), 227.

82. "Uyghur Nä Demäkdur?" *Yengi Ḥayat*, September 13, 1934, 2.

83. 'Abbas Äfändi, "Uyghur Nädur?" *Yengi Ḥayat*, December 17, 1934, 1–2; "Bizning Milli vä Ḥäqiqi Atimiz Uyghurdur!" *Yengi Ḥayat*, February 7, 1935, 1. For a similar article from the north of Xinjiang, see Abdurahman Turdi, "Uyghur Sözi," *Bizning Tavush*, August 2, 1935, 2.

84. Pavel Aptekar', "Ot Zheltorosii Do Vostochno-Turkestanskoi Respubliki," http://www.rkka.ru/oper/sinc/sinc.htm.

85. Qadiri, *Ölkä Tarikhi*, 105.

86. IOR L/PS/12/2332, doc. 5038 (1936), p. 65. A year later Qadir Haji presided over a commemorative service for Abdulghafur. See "5-inchi Ayning 4-inchi Küni 'Abd Ghafur Damollam Marḥumning Vafatigha bir Yil Bolghan Toghridin Bolghan Murasimda," *Yengi Ḥayat*, May 27, 1937, 1.

87. Ṭurfani, *Türkistan 1331–1337*, 226–227. Although Muhiti did eventually join up with Muslims in Tokyo, according to Lin Hsiao-ting he only reluctantly went to Japan when collaboration with the Guomindang fell through. See Hsiao-ting Lin, *Modern China's Ethnic Frontiers: A Journey to the West* (Abingdon: Routledge, 2011), 86–87.

88. Vladimir Petrov and Evdokia Petrov, *Empire of Fear* (London: A. Deutsch, 1956), 61–66.

89. This is according to the research of Alexander Pantsov; Pantsov, *The Bolsheviks and the Chinese Revolution 1919–1927* (Honolulu: University of Hawai'i Press, 2000), 256.

90. IOR L/PS/12/2332, doc. 2542 (1938), p. 24.

91. IOR L/PS/12/2392, p. 29.

92. In 1939 a new police force arrived in Kashgar made up of Russians and locals who had been sent to the Soviet Union for training. IOR L/PS/12/2383, doc. 1793 (1939), p. 268.

93. Not surprisingly, Qadir Haji preferred people to think that had been forced to leave Kashgar for engaging in revolutionary activities. This, at least, was his story as the British consul heard it. IOR, L/PS/12/2392, p. 29.

Conclusion

1. See, for example, the rebel pamphlet translated in Linda Benson, *The Ili Rebellion: The Muslim Challenge to Chinese Authority in Xinjiang, 1944–49* (Armonk, NY: M. E. Sharpe, 1990), 200.

2. On this shift, see Lowell Tillet, *The Great Friendship: Soviet Historians on the Non-Russian Nationalities* (Chapel Hill: University of North Carolina Press, 1969).

3. Ähmätjan Qasimi, *Maqalä vä Nutuqlar* (Almaty: Qazaqstan, 1992), 29.

4. "Shärqi Türkistan Toghrisida," *Küräsh*, nos. 4–5 (1946): 15–26.

5. For example, Khamid Ziiaev, "Vosstanie 1826 goda v Vostochnom Turkestane," Avtoreferat dissertatsii (Institut istorii i arkheologii Akademiia nauk UzSSR, 1949). For administrative reasons, Ziiaev's work was not approved, and he submitted a new version in Moscow in 1952. By then, the official line on Xinjiang had shifted considerably, and Ziiaev rewrote his conclusions to reflect this. Khamid Ziiaev, "Vosstanie 1826 goda v Vostochnom Turkestane," Avtoreferat dissertatsii (Institut vostokovedeniia Akademii nauk SSSR, 1952).

6. For an analysis of Masud Sabri's 1940s publications, see K. Talipov, "Pantiurkizm v Vostochnom Turkestane v 30–40-e gody XX veka," in *Issledovaniia po uigurovedeniiu*, ed. A. Tiliwaldi and A. Kamalov (Almaty: Tsentr uigurovedeniia Instituta vostokovedeniia, 2000).

7. Gardner Bovingdon, "The History of the History of Xinjiang," *Twentieth-Century China* 26, no. 2 (2001): 104–111. The correspondence between the Native Place Association and Li Dongfang was republished in Uyghur by the Altay Press in 1948. See Muḥämmäd Imin Bughra, *Qalam Küräshi* (Ürümchi: Altay, 1948). The most recent analysis of this debate is to be found in Ondřej Klimeš, *Struggle by the Pen: Uyghur Discourse of Nation and National Interest, c. 1940–1949* (Leiden: Brill, 2015).

8. Polat Qadiri, *Ölkä Tarikhi* (Ürümchi: Altay Näshriyati, 1948), 165–166.

9. "Ölkümizning Ismi Ḥäqqidä Bir-Ikki Eghiz Söz," *Inqilabi Shärqi Türkistan*, July 3, 1948, 1.

10. İsa Yusuf Alptekin, *Esir Doğu Türkistan için* (Istanbul: Doğu Türkistan Neşriyat Merkezi, 1985), 492.

11. 'A. Hashimi, "Türk-Uyghur Uyushmasi Öz Yolida Ishläydur," *Ärk*, September 8, 1947, 2–3.

12. Quchqach, "13-inchi Nävbätlik Därnäk," *Ärk*, November 10, 1948, 1–2; "13-nchi Sanliq Därnäk vä 'Sibirya' Sözi üstidä Konfirans," *Shingjang Gäziti*, October 26, 1948, 3.

13. Muḥämmäd Imin Bughra, "Bä'zi Qarashlarning Khaṭaliqini Körsätish," *Shingjang Gäziti*, December 12, 1948, 4.

14. "Altayning 2-Yilliq Khaṭirä Akhshami 'Isa Bäg Äfändi Ṭäräfidin Berilgän Daklad," *Shingjang Gäziti*, July 8, 1948, 1.

15. Thomas S. Mullaney, *Coming to Terms with the Nation: Ethnic Classification in Modern China* (Berkeley: University of California Press, 2011).

16. A. A. Lunacharskii, "Politika i religiia," *Izvestiia*, June 8, 1929, 2.

17. Yang Zengxin, *Buguozhai wendu xubian* (Beijing: Xinjiang zhujing gongyu, 1926), juan 2, fol. 53a.

18. For further discussion, see James Leibold, *Ethnic Policy in China: Is Reform Inevitable?* (Honolulu: East-West Center, 2013).

19. Ia. Gritsenko, "Chto èto bylo? K sobytiiam v Sin'tsziane v 1933–34 gg," *Problemy Dal'nego Vostoka*, no. 5 (1990): 79–84.

20. For a synthesis of this hagiographical literature, see Michael Dillon, *Xinjiang and the Expansion of Chinese Communist Power: Kashgar in the Twentieth Century* (Abingdon: Routledge, 2014).

21. These men, along with their organ *Voice of the Poor*, could not be mentioned in the chapter on the Soviet Uyghurs in M. N. Kabirov, *Ocherki istorii Uigurov Sovetskogo Kazakhstana* (Almaty: Nauka, 1975), 124–125. Instead, Kabirov chose the figure of a *kolkhoznik*, Sadiq Gaitov, through which to tell the story of Soviet construction among the Uyghurs of Kazakhstan.

Select Bibliography

ʿAbashi, Ḥasanʿata. *Mufaṣṣal Taʾrikh-i Qaum-i Turki*. Ufa: Sharq Maṭbuʿasï, 1909.

ʿAbd al-ʿAlim, Muḥammad. *Islamnama*. Institut vostochnykh rukopisei Rossiiskoi akademii nauk, manuscript C311, 1777.

Abdusemätov, Näzärghoja [Uyghur Balisi, pseud.]. *Taranchi Türklärning Tarikhi*. Almaty: Uyghur Kommunistlirining Vilayät Byurasi, 1922.

———. *Yoruq Sahillar*. Almaty: Zhazushï, 1991.

Afanas'ev-Kazanskii, A. "Ėkonomicheskoe polozhenie Zapadnogo Kitaia." *Novyi Vostok*, no. 3 (1923): 114–121.

Akimushkin, O. F., ed. *Tārīkh-i Kāshgar: Anonimnaia tiurkskaia khronika vladitelei Vostochnogo Turkestana po konets XVII veka*. Saint Petersburg: Peterburgskoe vostokovedenie, 2001.

Alip Tekin, Ibrahim, ed. *Mämtili Äpändi She'irliri*. Ürümchi: Shinjang Khälq Näshriyati, 2000.

Alptekin, İsa Yusuf. *Esir Doğu Türkistan için*. Istanbul: Doğu Türkistan Neşriyat Merkezi, 1985.

An Han 安漢. *Xibei kenzhi lun* 西北墾殖論 (1932). Zhongguo xibei wenxian congshu xubian, vol. 7 of Xibei shidi wenxian juan. Lanzhou: Gansu wenhua chubanshe, 1999.

Änsari, L., Z. Bäshir, B. Khudayqul, and S. Ibrahimi, eds. *Uyghur Äl Ädäbiyati*. Moscow: Tsentral'noe izdatel'stvo narodov SSSR, 1925.

Babadzhanov, B. M., A. K. Muminov, and A. fon Kiugel'gen, eds. *Disputy musul'manskikh religioznykh avtoritetov v Tsentral'noi Azii v XX veke*. Almaty: Daik-Press, 2007.

Baer, K. E. v., and Gr. v. Helmersen, eds. *Beiträge zur Kenntniss des Russischen Reiches und der angränzenden Länder Asiens*. Vol. 2, *Nachrichten über Chiwa, Buchara, Chokand und den nordwestlichen Theil des chinesischen Staates*. Saint Petersburg: Im verlage der Kaiserlichen Akademie der Wissenschaften, 1839.

Banzarov, Dorzhi. "Ob Oiratakh i Uigurakh." In *Sobranie sochinenii*, 180–186. Moscow: Izdatel'stvo Akademii nauk SSSR, 1955.

Baoerhan 包尔汉. *Xinjiang wushi nian* 新疆五十年. Beijing: Wenshi ziliao chubanshe, 1984.

Bartol'd, V. V. *Istoriia izucheniia Vostoka v Evrope i Rossii.* 2nd ed. Leningrad: Leningradskii institut zhivykh vostochnykh iazykov, 1925.

Bäshiri, Zarif. *Chuvashlar.* Orenburg: Karimof, Ḥösäynof, 1909.

———. *Chuvash Qïzï Änisä.* Kazan: Karimiyya, 1910.

———. "Mäzhit Gafuri Turahïnda Ithtäleklär." *Ädhäbi Bashqortostan,* no. 6 (1958): 85–89.

———. *Uyghïr Ädäbiyate.* Kazan: Yangalif, 1931.

Bazarov, B. V., B. D. Tsibikov, and S. B. Ochirov, eds. *Élbek-Dorzhi Rinchino o Mongolii.* Ulan-Ude: Institut Mongolovedeniia, buddologii i tibetologii Sibirskogo otdeleniia Rossiiskoi akademiia nauk, 1998.

Bellew, Henry Walter. *Kashmir and Kashgar: A Narrative of the Journey of the Embassy to Kashgar in 1873–4.* London: Tribner, 1875.

Bichurin, N. Ia. *Opisanie Chzhungarii i Vostochnogo Turkestana v drevnem i nyneshnem sostoianii.* Saint Petersburg: Karl Krai, 1829.

Bogoiavlenskii, Nikolai Viacheslav. *Zapadnyi zastennyi Kitai: Ego proshloe, nastoiashchee sostoianie i polozhenie v nem Russkikh poddannykh.* Saint Petersburg: A. S. Suvorin, 1906.

Boldyrev, A. N., ed. *Ta'rikh-i Badakhshan: Faksimile rukopisi, izdanie teksta, perevod s persidskogo.* Pamiatniki pis'mennosti Vostoka, vol. 98. Moscow: Vostochnaia literatura, 1997.

Borneman, N. "Ocherk Tarbagataiskogo kraia (Donesenie konsula v Chuguchake)." *Sbornik konsul'skikh donesenii* 3, no. 3 (1900): 209–236.

Bughra, Muhämmäd Imin. *Shärqi Türkistan Tarikhi.* Ankara: Fatma Bughra, 1987.

Bukshtein, O. "Torgovlia SSSR s Sin'tszianskoi provintsiei." *Novyi Vostok,* nos. 20–21 (1928): 201–217.

———. "Vostok na sovetskikh iarmarkakh." *Novyi Vostok,* nos. 13–14 (1926): 209–222.

"Burazan. Donesenie Khotanskogo torgovogo agenta Abdu-s-Sattar N. F. Petrovskomu." *Zapiski Vostochnogo otdeleniia Imperatorskogo russkogo arkheologicheskogo obshchestva* 9, nos. 1–4 (1896): 267–269.

Chang-geng 長庚. "Chouban Yili yaozheng liutiao xianglu 籌辦伊犁要政六條詳錄." In *Qing Guangxu jingying Xinjiang huiyi zhezou* 清光緒經營新疆會議摺奏, 703–834. Beijing: Quanguo tushuguan wenxian suowei fuzhi zhongxin, 2010.

Chen Cheng 陳誠. *Xiyu fanguo zhi* 西域藩國志 (1415). Zhongguo xibei wenxian congshu, vol. 117 of Xibei minsu wenxian mulu. Lanzhou: Lanzhou guji shudian, 1990.

Churas, Shah Maḥmud. *Khronika. Kriticheskii tekst, perevod, kommentarii, issledovanie i ukaziteli O. F. Akimushkin.* 2nd ed. Saint Petersburg: Peterburgskoe lingvisticheskoe obshchestvo, 2010.

Dabry de Thiersant, P. *Le Mahométisme en Chine et dans le Turkestan Oriental.* Paris: E. Leroux, 1878.

Daqing Gaozong Chun (Qianlong) huangdi shilu 大清高宗純(乾隆)皇帝實錄. 30 vols. Taibei: Huawen shuju, 1964.

Demidova, N. F. *Pervye Russkie diplomaty v Kitae: "Rospis" I. Petlina i stateinyi spisok F. I. Baikova.* Moscow: Nauka, 1966.

D'iakov, A. "Vospominaniia iliiskogo sibintsa o dungansko-taranchinskom vosstanii v 1864–1871 godakh v Iliiskom Krae." *Zapiski Vostochnogo otdeleniia Imperatorskogo russkogo arkheologicheskogo obshchestva* 18, nos. 2–3 (1908): 233–282.

Du Halde, J.-B. *The General History of China. Containing a Geographical, Historical, Chronological, Political and Physical Description of the Empire of China, Chinese-Tartary, Corea and Tibet.* Vol. 4. London: J. Watts, 1736.

Du Zhongyuan 杜重遠. *Sheng Shicai yu xin Xinjiang* 盛世才與新新疆. Guangzhou: Shenghuo shudian, 1938.

Eden, Jeff, ed. and trans. *The Life of Muhammad Sharif: A Central Asian Sufi Hagiography in Chaghatay.* Vienna: Verlag der Österreichischen Akademie der Wissenschaften, 2015.

Fäkhreddin, Rizaeddin. *Asar: 3 häm 4 Tomnar.* Kazan: Rukhiiat, 2010.

Fedorov, E. "1905 god i korennoe naselenie Turkestana." In *Ocherki revoliutsionnogo dvizheniia v Srednei Azii*, 15–44. Moscow: Nauchnaia assotsiatsiia vostokovedeniia pri TsIK SSSR, 1926.

Fedorov, S. *Opyt voenno-statisticheskogo opisaniia Iliiskogo kraia.* 2 vols. Tashkent: Tipografiia shtaba Turkestanskogo voennogo okruga, 1903.

———. "Russkaia torgovlia v Iliiskoi oblasti (Donesenie general'nogo konsula v Kul'dzhe)." *Sbornik konsul'skikh donesenii* 12, no. 4 (1909): 271–285.

———. "Russkaia torgovlia v Kul'dzhe (Donesenie konsula v Kul'dzhe)." *Sbornik konsul'skikh donesenii* 9, no. 5 (1906): 359–378.

Ferganskii oblastnii statisticheskii komitet. *Statisticheskii obzor Ferganskoi oblasti za 1904 god.* Novyi Margelan: Tipografiia Ferganskogo oblastnogo pravleniia, 1905.

———. *Statisticheskii obzor Ferganskoi oblasti za 1906 god.* Skobelev: Tipografiia Ferganskogo oblastnogo pravleniia, 1908.

Fleming, Peter. *News from Tartary: A Journey from Peking to Kashmir.* London: Jonathan Cape, 1936.

Forsyth, Sir T. D. *Report of a Mission to Yarkund in 1873.* Calcutta: Foreign Department Press, 1875.

Frank, Allen J., and Mirkasyim A. Usmanov. *Materials for the Islamic History of Semipalatinsk: Two Manuscripts by Ahmad-Walî al-Qazânî and Qurbân 'Ali Khâlidî.* Berlin: Das Arabische Buch, 2001.

Gaspıralı, İsmail. "Mükaleme-i Selatin." In *Seçmiş Eserleri.* Vol. 1, *Roman ve Hikayeleri*, edited by Yavuz Akpınar, Bayram Orak, and Nazim Muradov, 491–503. Istanbul: Ötüken, 2003.

Gatagova, L. S., L. P. Kosheleva, and L. A. Rogovaia, eds. *TsK RKP(b)-VKP(b) i natsional'nyi vopros.* Vol. 1, *1918–1933 gg.* Moscow: Rosspen, 2005.

Gaubil, Antoine. *Histoire de Gentchiscan et de toute la dinastie des Mongous ses successeurs, conquérans de la China.* Paris: Briasson & Piget, 1739.

Gins, G. K. "Taranchi i dungane: Ocherk iz poezdki po Semirech'iu." *Istoricheskii vestnik* 125 (1911): 672–708.

Gritsenko, Ia. "Chto èto bylo? K sobytiiam v Sin'tsziane v 1933–34 gg." *Problemy Dal'nego Vostoka*, no. 5 (1990): 79–84.

Guang Lu 廣祿. *Guang Lu huiyilu* 廣祿回憶錄. Taibei: Wenxing shudian, 1964.

Guignes, Joseph de. *Histoire générale des Huns, des Turcs, des Mogols, et des autres Tartares occidentaux.* Paris: Desaint & Saillant, 1756–1758.

Gu Yanwu 顧炎武. *Rizhi lu jishi* 日知錄集釋. Edited by Huang Rucheng 黃汝成. Shanghai: Zhonghua shuju, 1927–1936.

Ḥabibzade, Aḥmed Kemal. *Alifba-yi Turki.* Orenburg: Vaqït Maṭbuʿasï, 1915.

Hartmann, Martin. *Chinesisch-Turkestan: Geschichte, Verwaltung, Geistesleben, und Wirtschaft.* Halle: Gebauer-Schwetschke Druckerei und Verlag, 1908.

Haslund, Henning. *Men and Gods in Mongolia.* New York: E. P. Dutton, 1935.

Herbelot, Barthélemy d'. *Bibliothèque orientale.* Paris: Compagnie des Libraires, 1697.

He Yuzhu 何语竹 and Kang Binglin 康炳麟. "Guanyu Xinjiang 'Minzhong fandi lianhehui' ji qita 关于新疆《民众反帝联合会》及其它." In *Xinjiang minzhong fandi lianhehui ziliao huibian* 新疆民众反帝联合会资料汇编, edited by Li Qingjian 李青建, 447–453. Ürümchi: Xinjiang qingshaonian chubanshe, 1986.

Hikmet Bey, Adil. *Asya'da Beş Türk.* Edited by Yusuf Gedikli. Istanbul: Ötüken, 1998.

Histoire généalogique des Tatars Traduite du manuscrit tartare d'Abulgasi-Bayadur-Chan & enrichie d'un grand nombre de remarques authentiques & très-curieuses sur le véritable estat présent de l'Asie Septentrionale. Leiden: Abram Kallewier, 1726.

Iakinf, Monakh. *Zapiski o Mongolii.* Saint Petersburg: Karl Krai, 1828.

2-Uyghur Til-Imla Känpirinsiyining Tokhtamliri 13–18/V 30 y. Kyzyl Orda: Kazizdat, 1932.

Ivanov, P. P. "Iarmarochnaia torgovlia v Kazakstane." *Novyi Vostok*, nos. 13–14 (1926): 223–233.

Jalilov, Omonbek. *Xushhol G'aribiy.* Tashkent: Fan, 2005.

Jaubert, M. Amédée. "Notice d'un manuscrit turc, en caractères ouïgours, envoyé par M. de Hammer, à M. Abel-Rémusat." *Journal Asiatique* 6 (1825): 39–52.

Karmysheva, Galiia Shakhmukhammadkyzy. *K istorii Tatarskoi intelligentsii 1890–1930-i gody.* Moscow: Nauka, 2004.

al-Kashghari, Damulla ʿAbd al-Qadir b. ʿAbd al-Variṣ. *ʿAqayid-i Żaruriya.* Orenburg: Vaqït Maṭbaʿasï, 1911.

———. *Miftaḥ al-Adab* (1910). Ürümchi: Shinjang Khälq Näshriyati, 2002.

———. *ʿAqaʾid-i Żaruriyat.* Kazan: Maṭbaʿa-i Karimiyya, 1911.

———. *Mukhtaṣar-i ʿIbadat-i Islamiyya.* Kazan: Maṭbaʿa-i Karimiyya, 1911.

———. *Tajvid-i Turki.* Kazan: Millät Maṭbaʿasï, 1912.

———. *Tashil al-Ḥisab.* Kazan: Millät Maṭbaʿasï, 1912.

Kashghari, Muḥammad Ṣadiq, *Tazkira-i ʿAzizan.* Bodleian Library, manuscript Turk D20, ca. 1785.

Kashghari, Muḥammad Ṣadr, *Athar al-Futuḥ.* Abu Rayhon Beruniy nomidagi Sharq qo'lyozmalari markazi, manuscript 753, ca. 1800.

Katanov, N. "Man'chzhursko-Kitaiskii 'li' na narechii tiurkov Kitaiskogo Turkestana." *Zapiski Vostochnogo otdeleniia Imperatorskogo russkogo arkheologicheskogo obshchestva* 14 (1901): 31–75.

Kataoka Kazutada 片岡一忠, ed. *Hayashida Kenjiro shōrai Shinkyō-shō kyōdoshi sanjisshu* 林田賢次郎将来新疆省郷土志三十種. Kyoto: Chūgoku Bunken kenkyūkai, 1986.

Kazanin, M. "Natsional'nyi sostav Kitaia." *Problemy Kitaia* 11 (1933): 98–154.

Kazem-Bek, Mirza Aleksandr. "Issledovaniia ob Uigurakh." *Zhurnal Ministerstva narodnogo prosveshcheniia* 8 (1841): 1–86.

Kazim, Muḥammad. *ʿAlam-ara-yi Nadiri*. Tehran: Kitabfurushi-i Zavvar, 1985–1986.

Kemal, Ahmed. *Öç Duyguları*. Istanbul: Mahmud Bey Matbaası, 1915.

Kemal İlkul, Ahmet. *Çin-Türkistan Hatıraları* and *Şanghay Hatıraları*. Edited by Yusuf Gedikli. Istanbul: Ötüken, 1997.

Kerimi, Fatih. *İstanbul Mektupları*. Edited by Fazil Gökçek. Istanbul: Çağrı Yayınları, 2001.

Khalidi, Qurban ʿAli. *An Islamic Biographical Dictionary of the Eastern Kazakh Steppe, 1770–1912*. Edited by Allen J. Frank and Mirkasym A. Gosmanov. Leiden: Brill, 2005.

———. *Tavarikh-i Khamsa-i Sharqi*. Kazan: Ürnäk Maṭbaʿasï, 1910.

Khan, Riza Quoly. *Relation de l'ambassade au Kharezm (Khiva)*. Translated by Charles Henri Schefer. Paris: Ernest Leroux, 1876–1879.

Khoroshkhin, A. P. *Sbornik statei kasaiushchikhsia do Turkestanskogo kraia*. Saint Petersburg: Tipografiia i khromolitografiia A. Transhelia, 1876.

Klaproth, Julius. *Abhandlung über die Sprache und Schrift der Uiguren*. Berlin, 1812.

———. *Abhandlung über die Sprache und Schrift der Uiguren. Nebst einem Wörterverzeichnisse und anderen uigurischen Sprachproben, aus dem Kaiserlichen Übersetzungshofe zu Peking*. Paris: In der Königlichen Druckerey, 1820.

———. *Beleuchtung und Widerlegung der Forschungen über die Geschichte der Mittelasiatichen Völker des Herrn J.-J. Schmidt*. Paris: Dondey-Dupré, 1824.

———. "Demonstration definitive que les Ouigour étaient un peuple de race turque." *Bulletin des sciences historiques, antiquités, philologie* 2 (1824): 118–119.

———. "Über die Sprache und Schrift der Uiguren." *Fundgruben des Orients* 2 (1811): 167–195.

Kolcalı, Abdülaziz. *Çin'de Din-i Mübin-i İslam ve Çin Müslümanları*. Istanbul: Mahmud Bey Matbaası, 1321/1904.

Kolokolov, S. "Ėkonomicheskii obzor Kashgarii (Donesenie konsula v Kashgare)." *Sbornik konsul'skikh donesenii* 9, no. 3 (1906): 183–257.

———. "Russkaia torgovlia v Kashgarii (Donesenie konsula v Kashgare)." *Sbornik konsul'skikh donesenii* 11, no. 1 (1908): 115–157.

Kolpakovskii, G. L. "G. L. Kolpakovskogo o zaniatii Kul'dzhinskogo raiona v 1871 godu." In *Russkii Turkestan: Sbornik izdannyi po povodu politechnicheskoi vystavki*, 217–232. Saint Petersburg: Tipografiia tovarishchestva "obshchestvennaia pol'za," 1872.

Komissiia po izdaniiu diplomaticheskikh dokumentov pri MID SSSR, ed. *Dokumenty vneshnei politiki SSSR*. Moscow: Izdatel'stvo politicheskoi literatury, 1957–1977.

Kozybaev, M. K., ed. *Qaharlï 1916 zhïl / Groznyi 1916-i god*. Almaty: Qazaqstan, 1998.

Ksandrov, V. N., K. Kh. Danishevskii, M. I. Kalmanovich, A. V. Ozerskii, V. N. Voskresenskii, and M. A. Granat, eds. *Torgovlia SSSR s Vostokom*. Moscow: Promizdat, 1927.

Kudukhov, Kirill S. "Deiatel'nost' Soveta internatsional'noi propagandy na Vostoke v 1920 g. Itogovyi doklad." *Vostochnyi arkhiv*, no. 23 (2011): 61–67.

Kuropatkin, A. N. *Kashgaria: Eastern or Chinese Turkistan: Historical and Geographical Sketch of the Country, Its Military Strength, Industries, and Trade*. Translated by Walter E. Gowan. Calcutta: Thacker, Spink, 1882.

Lattimore, Owen. *High Tartary*. Boston: Little, Brown, 1930.

Li Qian 李謙. *Huibu gongdu* 回部公牘. Shanghai: Zhonghua yinshuachang, 1924.

Liu Jintang 劉錦堂. *Liu Xiangqin gong zougao* 劉襄勤公奏稿 (1898). Qingdai Xinjiang xijian zoudu huibian, vol. 1 of Tongzhi, Guangxu, Xuantong chao juan. Ürümchi: Xinjiang renmin chubanshe, 1997.

Liu Yingsheng 刘迎胜. *"Huihuiguan zazi" yu "Huihuiguan yiyu" yanjiu* 《回回馆杂字》与《回回馆译语》研究. Beijing: Zhongguo renmin daxue chubanshe, 2008.

Maev, N. A., ed. *Materialy dlia statistiki Turkestanskogo kraia*. 5 vols. Saint Petersburg: Tipografiia K. V. Trubnikova, 1872–1879

Ma-liang 馬亮 and Guang-fu 廣福. *Yili jiangjun Ma-liang, Guang-fu zougao* 伊犁將軍馬亮廣福奏稿. Qingdai Xinjiang xijian zoudu huibian, vol. 3 of Tongzhi, Guangxu, Xuantong chao juan. Ürümchi: Xinjiang renmin chubanshe, 1997.

Mallitskii, N. G. "Tashkentskie makhallia i mauza." In *V. V. Bartol'du turkestanskie druzia, ucheniki i pochitateli*, edited by A. E. Shmidt and E. K. Betger, 108–121. Tashkent: Obshchestvo dlia izucheniia Tadzhikistana i iranskikh narodnostei za ego predelami, 1927.

Malov, Sergei Efimovich. "Izuchenie zhivykh turetskikh narechii Zapadnogo Kitaia." *Vostochnye zapiski* 1 (1927): 168–172.

———. "Materialy po uigurskim narechiiam Sin'tsziana." In *Sergeiu Fedorovichu Ol'denburgu: K piatidesiatiletiiu nauchno-obshchestvennoi deiatel'nosti*, 307–332. Leningrad: Akademiia nauk SSSR, 1934.

———. "N. F. Katanov, prof. Kazanskogo Universiteta (1862–1922 gg.)." In *Nikolai Fedorovich Katanov: Materialy i soobshcheniia*, edited by N. Domozhakov, 33–51. Abakan: Khakasskoe knizhnoe izdatel'stvo, 1958.

———. *Uigurskii iazyk, Khamiiskoe narechie: Teksty, perevody, i slovar'*. Moscow: Akademiia nauk, 1954.

Mannerheim, Carl Gustaf Emil. *Across Asia from West to East in 1906–1908*. Helsinki: Suomalai-Ugrilainen Seura, 1940.

Materialy po raionirovaniiu Srednei Azii. Vol. 1, *Territoriia i naselenie Bukhary i Khorezma*. Tashkent: Komissiia po raionirovaniiu Srednei Azii, 1926.

Matveev, P. P. *Poezdka v zapadnyi Kitai*. Tashkent: Tipografiia Voenno-narodnogo upravleniia, 1879.

Mezö-Kovesd, Ch. E. de Ujfalvy de. *Le Kohistan, le Ferghanah et Kouldja avec un appendice sur la Kachgarie*. Paris: Ernest Leroux, 1878.

Mirza Shams-i Bukhari. *Ta'rikh-i Bukhara, Khoqand va Kashghar*. Tehran: Ayina-i Miraṣ, 1998.

Mitchell, John, and Robert Mitchell. *The Russians in Central Asia: Their Occupation of the Kirghiz Steppe and the Line of the Syr-Daria: Their Political Relations with Khiva, Bokhara, and Khokand: Also Descriptions of Chinese Turkestan and Dzungaria. By Capt. Valikhanof, M. Veniukof, and Other Russian Travellers*. London: Edward Stanford, 1865.

Monasib, ʿAbdelʿaziz. *Taranchï Qïzï, yaki Ḥälimneng Berenche Mähäbbäte*. Kazan: Ümet Maṭbaʿasï, 1918.

———. "Taranchï Qïzï Yaki Khälimneng Berenche Mäkhäbbäte." *Ädäbi Miras* 2 (1992): 125–202.

Morgan, E. Delmar. "On Muhammadanism in China." *The Phoenix* 2 (1872): 133–134, 154–157, 176–180.

Mouraviev, M. N. *Voyage en Turcomanie et à Khiva, fait en 1819 et 1820*. Paris: L. Tenré, 1823.

Muḥämmäd Imin Bughra. *Qalam Küräshi*. Ürümchi: Altay, 1948.

Muḥammad ʿIvaż. *Żiya' al-Qulub*. Houghton Library, manuscript Persian 95.

Muḥämmädi, Abdulhäy. *Uyghurchä Yeziq Yolliri*. Moscow: Tsentral'noe izdatel'stvo narodov SSSR, 1926.

Mulla Bilal bin Mulla Yusuf al-Naẓim. *Ghazat dar Mulk-i Chin*. Edited by Nikolai Nikolaevich Pantusov. Kazan: Universitetskaia tipografiia, 1880–1881.

Nalivkin, V. *Kratkaia istoriia Kokandskogo khanstva*. Kazan: Tipografiia Imperatorskogo Universiteta, 1886.

"Nekrolog." *Otchet Imperatorskogo Russkogo geograficheskogo obshchestva za 1882 god* (1883): 16–17.

Nemchenko, M. "Kolonial'nyi rezhim i agrarnye otnosheniia v Sin'tsziane." *Problemy Kitaia* 8–9, nos. 3–4 (1931): 181–190.

"Obozrenie Kokanskogo khanstva v nyneshnem ego sostoianii." *Zapiski Russkogo geograficheskogo obshchestva* 3 (1849): 176–216.

Ömär, Abdurusul, ed. *Abdukhaliq Uyghur She'irliri*. Ürümchi: Shinjang Khälq Näshriyati, 1995.

Onuma Takahiro 小沼孝博, Shinmen Yasushi 新免康, and Kawahara Yayoi 河原弥生. "Guoli gugong bowuyuan suocang 1848 nian liangjian Haohan laiwen zaikao 国立故宮博物院所蔵1848年両件浩罕来文再考." *Furen lishi xuebao* 輔仁歴史學報 26 (2011): 107–138.

Palen, Konstantin Konstantinovich. *Mission to Turkestan: Being the Memoirs of Count K. K. Pahlen*. Translated by Richard Pierce. Oxford: Oxford University Press, 1964.

———. *Otchet po revizii Turkestanskogo kraia, proizvedennoi po Vysochaishemu poveleniiu*. Saint Petersburg: Senatskaia tipografiia, 1910.

Pang Shiqian 龐士謙. *Aiji jiunian* 埃及九年. Beijing: Yuehua wenhua fuwushe, 1951.

Pantusov, N. N. *Svedeniia o Kul'dzhinskom raione za 1871–1877 gody*. Kazan: Universitetskaia tipografiia, 1881.

Pervyi vsesoiuznyi tiurkologicheskii s"ezd 26 fevralia–5 marta 1926 g. (Stenograficheskii otchet). Baku: Nagïl Evi, 2011.

Petrov, Vladimir, and Evdokia Petrov. *Empire of Fear*. London: A. Deutsch, 1956.

Piasetskii, P. Ia. *Neudachnaia ėkspeditsiia v Kitai 1874–1875 gg*. Saint Petersburg: Tipografiia M. Stasiulevicha, 1881.

Piaskovskii, A. V., ed. *Vosstanie 1916 goda v Srednei Azii i Kazakhstane: Sbornik dokumentov*. Moscow: Akademiia nauk SSSR, 1960.

Poklevskii-Kozell, Ivan Ivanovich. *Novyi torgovyi put' ot Irtysha v Vernyi i Kul'dzhu i issledovanie reki Ili na parakhode "Kolpakovskii"*. Saint Petersburg: Tipografiia i litografiia D. I. Shemetkina, 1885.

Potanin, G. N. *Ocherki severo-zapadnoi Mongolii*. Saint Petersburg: Tipografiia V. Kirshbauma, 1883.

———. "O karavannoi torgovle s Dzhungarskoi Bukhariei v XVIII stoletii." *Chteniia v Imperatorskom obshchestve istorii i drevnosti rossiiskikh pri Moskovskom universitete 1868 g*. 2 (1868): 21–113.

Przheval'skii, Nikolai Mikhailovich. *Ot Kiakhty na istoki Zheltoi reki: Issledovanie severnoi okrainy Tibeta, i put' cherez Lob-Nor po basseinu Tarima*. Saint Petersburg: Tipografiia V. S. Balasheva, 1888.

Purgstall Hammer, Joseph von. "Uigurisches Diplom Kutlugh Timur's vom Jahre 800 (1397)." *Fundgruben des Orients* 6 (1818): 359–362.

"Putevye zamechaniia lekaria Omskogo garizonnogo polka F. K. Zibbershteina (17 iulia–2 oktiabria 1825 g.)." In *Istoriia Kazakhstana v Russkikh istochnikakh*, vol. 6, edited by M. A. Kul-Mukhammed, 222–253. Almaty: Daik-Press, 2007.

Qadiri, Polat. *Ölkä Tarikhi*. Ürümchi: Altay Näshriyati, 1948.

Qasim Beg, *Ghuljaning Vaqi'atlarining Bayani*. Institut vostochnykh rukopisei Rossiiskoi akademii nauk, manuscript B4018, late 19th c.

Qasimi, Ähmätjan. *Maqalä vä Nutuqlar*. Almaty: Qazaqstan, 1992.

äl-Qazani, 'Abderraḥman bine 'Ata'ullah. *Öch Ayliq Säyaḥät*. Orenburg: Karimof Matba'asï, 1905.

Radloff, W. *Aus Sibirien: Lose Blätter aus meinem Tagebuche*. Leipzig: T. O. Weigel, 1893.

———. *Phonetik der nördlichen Türksprachen*. Leipzig: Weigel, 1882.

———. *Proben der Volksliteratur der türkischen Stämme*. Vol. 6, *Dialect der Tarantschi*. Saint Petersburg: Tipografiia Imperatorskoi akademii nauk, 1886.

al-Ramzi al-Qazani, Muḥammad Murad. *Talfiq al-Akhbar wa Talqiḥ al-Athar fi Waqa'i' Qazan wa Bulghar wa Muluk al-Tatar*. Orenburg: Maṭbu'at al-Karimiyya wa-l-Ḥusayniyya, 1908.

Rémusat, Abel. *Recherches sur les langues tartares, ou Mémoires sur différents points de la grammaire et de la littérature des Mandchous, des Mongols, des Ouigours et des Tibétains*. Paris: Imprimerie Royale, 1820.

"Report on Russian Geography for the Year." *Proceedings of the Royal Geographical Society and Monthly Record of Geography*, n.s. 5, no. 7 (1883): 389–392.

Riddell, John, ed. *Toward the United Front: Proceedings of the Fourth Congress of the Communist International, 1922*. Leiden: Brill, 2012.

Roerich, Nicholas. *Altai-Himalaya: A Travel Diary*. New York: Frederick A. Stokes, 1929.

Rostovskii, S. "Tsarskaia Rossiia i Sin'-Tszian v XIX–XX vekakh." *Istorik-marksist*, no. 3 (1936): 26–53.

Rozibaqiev, A. "Alma-Ata v 1917–1918 (vospominaniia)." *Tughan Ölkä / Rodnoi Krai*, nos. 1–2 (2003): 44–58.

———. *Khälqim Üchün Köyüdu Zhüräk*. Almaty: Zhazushï, 1997.

———. "Oktiabr'skii perevorot v Alma-Ate (vospominaniia)." *Tughan Ölkä / Rodnoi Krai*, no. 3 (2004): 30–44.

Rozibaqiev, M. *Ismayil Tayirov*. Almaty: Qazaqstan, 1990.

Rozibaqiev, M., and N. Rozibaqieva. *Uyghur Khälqining Munävvär Pärzändi*. Almaty: Qazaqstan, 1987.

Rumiantsev, P. P. *Uezdy Zhetysu*. Almaty: Zhalïn Baspasï, 2000.

Sami, Şemseddin. *Qamus-i Türki*. Istanbul: İkdam, 1318/1899–1900.

Sarınay, Yusuf, ed. *Belgelerle Osmanlı-Türkistan İlişkileri (XVI–XX Yüzyıllar)*. Ankara: T. C. Başbakanlık Devlet Arşivleri Genel Müdürlüğü, 2004.

Sayrami, Mulla Musa. *Tarikhi Hämidi*. Edited by Änvär Baytur. Beijing: Millätlär Näshriyati, 1986.

Schmidt, I. J. "Einwürfe gegen die Hypothesen des Herrn Hofr. Klaproth: Über Sprache und Schrift der Uiguren." *Fundgruben des Orients* 6 (1818): 321–338.

———. *Forschungen im Gebiete der älteren religiösen, politischen und literärischen Bildungsgeschichte der Völker Mittel-Asiens, vorzüglich der Mongolen und Tibeter*. Saint Petersburg: Karl Kray, 1824.

———. *Würdigung und Abfertigung der Klaprothschen sogenannten Beleuchtung und Widerlegung seiner Forschungen im Gebiete der Geschichte der Völker Mittel-Asiens*. Leipzig: Carl Cnobloch, 1826.

Schomberg, Reginald C. F. "A Fourth Journey in the Tien Shan." *The Geographical Journal* 79, no. 5 (1932): 368–378.

Schuyler, Eugene. *Turkistan: Notes of a Journey in Russian Turkistan, Khokand, Bukhara, and Kuldja*. 2 vols. New York: Scribner, Armstrong, 1876.

Selitskii, I. V. *Kul'dzhinskie pereselentsy pogranichnoi s Kitaem polosy*. Kazan: Tipografiia Imperatorskogo Universiteta, 1905.

Shaw, Robert. *Visits to High Tartary, Yârkand and Kâshgar (Formerly Chinese Tartary), and Return Journey over the Karakorum Pass*. London: J. Murray, 1871.

Shendrikov, I. N. "Nuzhdy semirechenskogo kazach'ego voiska." *Belaia gvardiia*, no. 8 (2005): 240–241.

Shkapskii, O. "Pereselentsy i agrarnyi vopros v Semirechenskoi oblasti." *Voprosy kolonizatsii* 1, no. 1 (1907): 19–52.

Skrine, C. P., and Pamela Nightingale. *Macartney at Kashgar: New Light on British, Chinese and Russian Activities in Sinkiang, 1890–1918*. London: Methuen, 1973.

Sog'uniy, Alixonto'ra. *Turkiston Qayg'usi.* Tashkent: Sharq, 2003.

Stalin, Joseph. *Marxism and the National Question.* Moscow: Foreign Languages Publishing House, 1947.

Stein, Aurel. *Ruins of Desert Cathay: A Personal Narrative of Explorations in Central Asia and Westernmost China.* 2 vols. London: Macmillan, 1912.

Şükrü, Karçınzade Süleyman. *Seyahatü'l-Kübra.* Istanbul: Sinan Ofset, 2005.

Tajalli, Ḥusayn Khan. *Barq-i Tajalli va Sabq-i Mujalli.* Kashgar: Maṭbaʿ-i Khurshid, 1900.

Tao Baolian 陶保廉. *Xinmao shixing ji* 辛卯侍行记. Edited by Liu Man 刘满. Lanzhou: Gansu renmin chubanshe, 2002.

Tek, Ahmet Ferit. *Turan.* Edited by Necati Gültepe. Istanbul: Turan Kültür Vakfı, 1999.

Tikhonov, Iu. N. "Dokumenty o revizii raboty Turkestanskogo biuro Kominterna v kontse 1921 g." *Vostochnyi arkhiv,* no. 21 (2010): 49–55.

Togan, A. Zeki Velidi. *Bugünkü Türkili (Türkistan) ve Yakin Tarihi.* Istanbul: Arkadaş, İbrahim Horoz ve Güven Basimevleri, 1942–1947.

Trofimov, G. I. "Iz proshlogo kompartii v Dzhetysu." In *V ogne revoliutsii: Vospominaniia uchastnikov Velikoi Oktiabrskoi revoliutsii i grazhdanskoi voiny v Kazakhstane,* edited by P. M. Pakhmurnyi and T. E. Eleuov, 224–229. Almaty: Kazakhskoe gosudarstvennoe izdatel'stvo, 1957.

Tsentral'noe statisticheskoe upravlenie SSSR. *Vsesoiuznaia perepis' naseleniia 1926 goda.* Vol. 8, *Kazakhskaia SSR, Kirgizskaia SSR.* Vol. 15, *Uzbekskaia SSR.* Moscow: Izdanie TsSU Souiza SSR, 1928.

Tsentral'noe statisticheskoe upravlenie Turkestanskoi respubliki. *Materialy vserossiiskikh perepisei: Perepis naseleniia v Turkestanskoi Respublike.* Vol. 4, *Sel'skoe naselenie Ferganskoi oblasti po materialam perepisi 1917 g.* Tashkent: TsSU Turkrespubliki, 1924.

Tsentral'nyi statisticheskii komitet, ed. *Pervaia vseobshchaia perepis' naseleniia Rossiiskoi imperii 1897 g.* Vol. 7. Saint Petersburg: N. P. Nyrkin, 1905.

Tunji Khangdi [Tongzhi huangdi 同治皇帝]. *Qanun al-Ṣin.* Translated by Saʿid al-ʿAsali al-Ṭrabulsi al-Shami. Cairo: Maṭbuʿat Madrasat Valida ʿAbbas al-Avval, 1906.

Ṭurfani, Ḥamidullah bin Muḥammad. *Türkistan 1331–1337 Inqilab Tarikhi* (1943). Istanbul: Doğu Türkistan Dergisi, 1983.

Turkestanskii sbornik. Sobranie statei o stranakh Srednei Azii voobshche i Turkestanskoi oblasti v osobennosti. Compiled by V. N. Mezhov. 594 vols. National Library of Uzbekistan, Tashkent, 1878–1917.

Turkistani, Musa. *Ulugh Türkistan Fajiʿasi.* 2 vols. Madina: Maṭabiʿ al-Rashid, 1401/1981.

Välidi, Ähmäd Zäki. *Törk vä Tatar Tarikhï.* Kazan: Millät, 1912.

Valikhanov, Ch. Ch. "O sostoianii Altyshara ili shesti vostochnykh gorodov Kitaiskoi provintsii Nan-Lu (Maloi Bukharii) v 1858–59 gg." In *Sobranie sochinenii v piati tomakh,* 3:97–218. Alma-Ata, 1985.

Vambery, Hermann. *Uigurische Sprachmonumente und das Kudatku Bilik.* Innsbruck: Druck der Wagner'schen Universitäts-Buchdruckerei, 1870.

Vasil'ev, V. P. "Magometanstvo v Kitae." In *Otkrytie Kitaia i drugie stat'i akademika V. P. Vasil'eva*, 106–138. Saint Petersburg: Stolichnaia tipografiia, 1900. Translated by Rudolf Loewenthal as *Islam in China*. Central Asian Collectanea 3 (Washington, DC: n.p., 1960).

———. *O dvizhenii magometanstva v Kitae: Godichnyi torzhestvennyi akt v S.-Peterburgskom Universitete 2 dekabria 1867 g.* Saint Petersburg: V. Golovin, 1867.

Veselovskii, N. I., ed. *Poezdka N. I. Liubimova v Chuguchak i Kul'dzhu v 1845 godu pod vidom kuptsa Khorosheva*. Saint Petersburg: Tipografiia Ministerstva putei soobsheniia, 1909.

———. *Posol'stvo k Ziungarskomu Khun-Taichzhi Tsevan Rabtanu kapitana ot artillerii Ivana Unkovskogo i putevoi zhurnal ego za 1722–1724 gody*. Saint Petersburg: Tipografiia V. Kirshbauma, 1887.

Visdelou, Claude de. "Suite des observations." In Barthélemy d'Herbelot, *Bibliothèque orientale*. Maestricht: J. E. Dufour & Roux, 1776.

Vsesoiuznaia Nizhegorodskaia iarmarka: Katalog i putevoditel'. Kanavino: Krasnii pechatnik, 1926.

Wahidi, Imin Bäg. *Äslätmä*. Manuscript, 1939.

Wang Shunan 王樹楠, ed. *Xinjiang tuzhi* 新疆圖志 (1911). Taibei: Wenhai chubanshe, 1965.

Wang Zongzai 王宗載. *Siyiguan kao* 四夷館考. Dongfang xuehui, 1924.

Wen Da 溫達 et al., comp. *Qinzheng pingding shuomo fanglüe* 親征平定朔漠方略 (1708). In *Siku quanshu*, vols. 354–355. Shanghai: Shanghai guji chubanshe, 1987.

Xie Bin 謝彬. *Xinjiang youji* 新疆遊記. Shanghai: Zhonghua shuju, 1927.

Xinjiang ziyiju choubanchu diyici baogaoshu 新疆咨議局籌辦處第一次報告書 (1910). Zhongguo bianjiang xingji diaochaji baogaoshu deng bianwu ziliao congbian, vol. 39 of chubian. Hong Kong: Fuchi shuyuan chuban youxian gongsi, 2009.

Xiqing xujian jiabian 西清續鑑甲編. Shanghai: Hanfenlou, 1910.

Xu Jingcheng 許景澄. *Xu Wensu gong yigao* 許文肅公遺稿. Qingdai Xinjiang xijian zoudu huibian, vol. 2 of Tongzhi, Guangxu, Xuantong chao juan. Ürümchi: Xinjiang renmin chubanshe, 1997.

Yamauchi, Masayuki. *Hoşnut Olamamış Adam: Enver Paşa Türkiye'den Türkistan'a*. Istanbul: Bağlam, 1995.

Yang Zengxin 楊增新. *Buguozhai wendu* 補過齋文牘 (1921). Taibei: Wenhai chubanshe, 1965.

———. *Buguozhai wendu sanbian* 補過齋文牘三編 (1934). Zhongguo xibei wenxian congshu xubian, vol. 4 of Xibei shidi wenxian juan, pp. 411–587. Lanzhou: Gansu wenhua chubanshe, 1999.

———. *Buguozhai wendu xubian* 補過齋文牘續編. Beijing: Xinjiang zhujing gongyu, 1926.

Yarkandi, Qidirkhan. *"Divani Qidiri"ning Muqäddimisi*. Edited by Mämtimin Yüsüp and Tokhti Abikhan. Kashgar: Qäshqär Uyghur Näshriyati, 1986.

Yarkänd Möselmanlarnïng Kitabkhanä häm Qïra'ätkhanäseneng Uṣṭafi. Kazan: Maṭbuʿa-i Karimiyya, 1906.

Yergök, Ziya. *Sarıkamış'tan Esarete (1915–1920): Tuğgeneral Ziya Yergök'ün Anıları.* Edited by Sami Önal. Istanbul: Remzi, 2005.

[Yong-gui 永貴 ?]. *Xiyu zhi* 西域誌. Russian State Library, Manuscript Division, fond 274, no. 287, 1762–1763.

Yuan Tung-li 袁同禮, ed. *Zhong-E xibei tiaoyue ji* 中俄西北條約集. Xinjiang yanjiu congkan, vol. 4. Hong Kong, 1963.

Zarubin, I. I. *Spisok narodnostei Turkestanskogo kraia.* Trudy komissii po izucheniiu plemennogo sostava naseleniia Rossii i sopredel'nykh stran, vol. 9. Leningrad: Rossiiskaia akademiia nauk, 1925.

Zhang Dajun 張大軍. *Xinjiang fengbao qishi nian* 新疆風暴七十年. Taibei: Lanxi chubanshe, 1980.

Zhang Shaobo 張紹伯. *Xinjiang waijiao baogaoshu* 新疆外交報告書. Dihua: Xinjiang jiaoshe gongshu waijiao yanjiusuo, 1913.

Zhengwusi yanjiu Eyue guanyu Xinjiang renmin guoji wenti yian 政務司研究俄約關於新疆人民國籍問題議案. Zhongguo bianjiang xingji diaocha baogaoshu deng bianwu ziliao congbian, vol. 9 of Chubian. Hong Kong: Fuchi shuyuan chuban youxian gongsi, 2009.

Zhong Gengqi 鍾賡起. *Ganzhou fuzhi* 甘州府志 (1779). Zhongguo xibei wenxian congshu xubian, vol. 2 of Xibei xijian fangzhi wenxian juan. Lanzhou: Gansu wenhua chubanshe, 1999.

Zhongguo di-er lishi dang'anguan 中国第二历史档案馆, ed. *Zhonghua minguoshi dang'an ziliao huibian* 中华民国史档案资料汇编. Nanjing: Jiangsu renmin chubanshe, 1979–2000.

Zhongguo di-yi lishi dang'anguan 中国第一历史档案馆, ed. *Yongzhengchao Manwen zhupi zouzhe quanyi* 雍正朝满文朱批奏折全译. 2 vols. Hefei: Huangshan shushe, 1998.

Zhongguo di-yi lishi dang'anguan 中国第一历史档案馆 and Zhongguo bianjiang shidi yanjiu zhongxin 中国边疆史地研究中心, eds. *Qingdai Xinjiang Manwen dang'an huibian* 清代新疆满文档案汇编. 283 vols. Guilin: Guangxi shifan daxue chubanshe, 2012.

Zhongguo shehui kexueyuan Zhongguo bianjiang shidi yanjiu zhongxin 中国社会科学院中国边疆史地研究中心, ed. *Xinjiang xiangtu zhigao* 新疆乡土志稿. Beijing: Quanguo tushuguan wenxian suowei fuzhi zhongxin, 1990.

Zhongyang yanjiuyuan jindaishi yanjiu suo, ed. *Zhong-E guanxi shiliao 1917–1919.* 8 vols. *1920.* 3 vols. Nangang: Zhongyang yanjiuyuan jindaishi yanjiu suo, 1959–1969.

Zhong Yong 鍾鏞. *Xijiang jiaoshe zhiyao* 西疆交涉志要 (1914). Taibei: Taiwan shangwu yinshuguan, 1963.

Zuo Zongtang 左宗棠. *Zuo Wenxiang gong zoushu* 左文襄公奏疏. Shanghai: Tushu jicheng, 1890.

Acknowledgments

I have incurred numerous debts in writing this book, only some of which can be properly acknowledged here. The project initially came into being under the expert guidance of Mark Elliott, and he remains for me an example of scholarly rigor and professionalism. Terry Martin, James Millward, and Adeeb Khalid have also been sources of advice and inspiration throughout my research. In Cambridge, I benefited greatly from time spent with Wheeler Thackston, Beatrice Manz, and Cemal Kafadar. My compatriot Margaret Lindsey helped me immensely in the course of my studies and never tired in her commitment to Harvard's Inner Asian and Altaic Studies program. I was also lucky enough to receive the support of research grants from Harvard's Asia Center, a Kennedy Fellowship for archival research in 2008–2009, and a fellowship at the Harvard Academy for International and Area Studies.

From 2011 to 2013, the newly established Australian Centre on China in the World at the Australian National University provided an ideal environment for me to continue to work on the book. The center's director, Geremie Barmé, along with Linda Jaivin both contributed their great scholarly and literary expertise at crucial points in bringing it to completion. Since 2013, the University of Sydney has become my research and teaching home, and I thank colleagues in the Department of History for giving me such a warm welcome, and the School of Philosophical and Historical Inquiry for providing support for my research.

Among those who assisted me elsewhere, I must begin by paying my respects to my teachers and friends during a memorable year at Xinjiang University in 2003–2004. Following that period of study, Murod and Roziya generously opened their house in Samarkand to me for three months and have done so several times since then. In Kazakhstan I was very glad to make contact with Ablet Kamalov, Rähmätjan, and the rest of the Uyghur scholars at the Institute of Oriental Studies in Almaty. In accessing the state archive in Uzbekistan I drew on the help of the staff of the Institut français d'études sur l'Asie centrale. All along, I have relied heavily on the expertise of archivists and librarians, most recently at the Menzies Library at ANU and the National Library of Australia, where staff were willing to acquire new resources on Xinjiang at my request.

Among a number of Uyghur friends inside and outside China, discussions with Ablet Semet were particularly valuable in orienting myself toward this period of Xinjiang's history. Colleagues in Australia have also given me much support for my work, beginning with Lewis Mayo at the University of Melbourne, who first encouraged me in the study of Central Asia, along with Anthony Garnaut and Ayxem Eli. In Japan, I owe Onuma Takahiro a particular debt for a very enjoyable and productive stay at the Gakushūin in Tokyo in the spring of 2010, and Sugawara Jun and Naganawa Norihiro have also been generous in sharing materials with me. For help with locating sources, exchanging ideas, reading drafts, and providing scholarly solidarity at various points along the way, I would like to express my gratitude to Helga Anetshofer, Christopher Atwood, Ildikó Bellér-Hann, Jeff Eden, Allen Frank, Josh Freeman, Philippa Hetherington, Justin Jacobs, Astrid Menz, Niccolò Pianciola, Paolo Sartori, Eric Schluessel, Gulchehra Sultonova, and Rian Thum.

I thank Kathleen McDermott at Harvard University Press for having confidence in the book and guiding it through to publication. Three anonymous reviewers contributed very helpful comments and corrections on the draft, and Philip Schwartzberg did an excellent job with the three maps. Barbara Folsom was of invaluable assistance in polishing the manuscript, and Pamela Nelson showed great patience in responding to my editing queries.

Ying Qian has been a constant source of encouragement and intellectual companionship. She has given much to the book with her thoughtful readings.

Above all I wish to thank my parents, Mary and Brian, for their love and support throughout my lengthy studies and as I pursued my interests into ever more remote realms. Having long fended off their questions as to whether the book was finished or not, I'm happy to finally tell them that it is. I dedicate it to them.

Index